Clive Oxenden
Christina Latham-Koenig

with **Jane Hudson**
David Jay
Gill Hamilton

D1080816

New
ENGLISH FILE

Beginner
Teacher's Book

OXFORD
UNIVERSITY PRESS

Paul Seligson and Clive Oxenden are the original co-authors of
English File 1 (pub. 1996) and *English File 2* (pub. 1997).

187182   428.24 OXE
Teaching materials
EFL Zone.

(includes CD)

OXFORD
UNIVERSITY PRESS

Great Clarendon Street, Oxford OX2 6DP

Oxford University Press is a department of the University of Oxford.
It furthers the University's objective of excellence in research, scholarship,
and education by publishing worldwide in

Oxford New York

Auckland Cape Town Dar es Salaam Hong Kong Karachi
Kuala Lumpur Madrid Melbourne Mexico City Nairobi
New Delhi Shanghai Taipei Toronto

With offices in

Argentina Austria Brazil Chile Czech Republic France Greece
Guatemala Hungary Italy Japan Poland Portugal Singapore
South Korea Switzerland Thailand Turkey Ukraine Vietnam

OXFORD and OXFORD ENGLISH are registered trade marks of
Oxford University Press in the UK and in certain other countries

© Oxford University Press 2009

The moral rights of the author have been asserted

Database right Oxford University Press (maker)

First published 2009

2013
10 9 8 7

Photocopying

Any websites referred to in this publication are in the public domain and
their addresses are provided by Oxford University Press for information only.
Oxford University Press disclaims any responsibility for the content

ISBN: 978 0 19 451875 8   TEACHER'S BOOK
ISBN: 978 0 19 451877 2   TEACHER'S BOOK WITH CD-ROM PACK

Printed in China

ACKNOWLEDGEMENTS

*The authors would like to thank all the teachers and students round the world whose
feedback has helped to shape New English File, and also all those at Oxford University
Press (both in Oxford and around the world) who have contributed their skills and ideas
to producing this course.*

*Very special thanks from Clive to Maria Angeles, Lucia, and Eric, and from Christina
to Cristina, for all their help and encouragement. Christina would also like to thank her
children Joaquin, Marco, and Krysia for their constant inspiration.*

*The publisher would like to thank the following for their permission to reproduce
extracts and adaptations of copyright material:* p.202 'D.I.S.C.O' Words and Music
by Jean Joseph Kluger/Daniel Vangarde © Chelsea Music Publishing, used by
permission. p.203 'You're Beautiful' Words and music by James Blunt, Sacha
Skarbek and Amanda Ghost © 2002 EMI Music Publishing Ltd and Bucks Music
Group Ltd. Reproduced by permission of International Music Publications
Ltd (a trading name of Faber Music Ltd). All Rights Reserved. p.204 'Friday
I'm In Love' Words by Robert Smith © Copyright 1992 Fiction Songs Limited.
All Rights Reserved. International Copyright Secured. p.205 'Money Money
Money' Words and Music by B Andersson/B Ulvaues © Bocu Music Ltd., used by
permission. p.206 'Perfect Day' Words and Music by Lou Reed © 1972 Oakfield
Avenue Music Ltd. Screen Gems-EMI Music Inc, USA. Screen Gems-EMI Music
Ltd, London WC2H 0QY. Reproduced by permission of International Music
Publications Ltd. All Rights Reserved. p.207 'I'm a Believer' © Copyright
1966 (Renewed) Stonebridge Music and Foray Music. All rights on behalf of
Stonebridge Music administered by Sony/ATV Music Publishing (75%). Used
by permission of IMP and Music Sales Limited. EMI Music Ltd (25%). All rights
reserved. International Copyright Secured. p.208 'Three Little Birds' Words
and Music by Bob Marley © Copyright 1977 Blue Mountain Music Limited.
Used by permission of Music Sales Limited. All Rights Reserved. International
Copyright Secured.

*The publisher would like to thank the following for their permission to reproduce
photographs:* Alamy pp.163 (Allstar Picture Library/Zhang Ziyi/Christina
Aguilera/Ken Watanabe/Javier Bardem/Helen Mirren/Gilberto Gil, Vario
Images GmbH & Co. KG/Orhan Pamuk), 181 (DEK C/Kanye West, Redferns/
Beyoncé, Ukraft/Robbie Williams), 187 (Steve Bloom Images/Safari, Picture
Contact/Trans-Siberian Express), Allstar and Sportsphoto p.207 (Dreamworks),
Getty Images pp.163 (Sean Gallup/Roman Polanski, Scott Gries/Giorgio
Armani, WireImage/Eamonn McCormack/Gael García Bernal, AFP/Jakub
Sukup/Agnes Kovacs), Oxford University Press p.187 (Carlos, Gemma, Kate,
Inca Trail), PA Photos pp.163 (Abaca/Gregorio Binuya/Maria Sharapova), 181
(AP/Manu Fernandez/Christian Bale, AP/Hermann J Knippertz/Penelope Cruz,
Empics/Doug Peters/JK Rowling, AP/Ricardo Del Luca/Cate Blanchett, Landov/
Otto/Robert De Niro, AP/Pier Paolo Cito/Roberto Benigni, AP/Joerg Sarbach/
Denzel Washington, Landov/Anthony J Causi/Mariah Carey, Abaca/Hahn-
Nebinder-Orban/Leonardo DiCaprio)

Illustrations by: Cartoonstock/Ian Baker pp.123, 133, 139, 150, 197, Cartoonstock/
Clive Goddard pp.131, 141, 143, Paul Dickinson pp.203, 205, Phil Disley p.144,
Mark Duffin p.166, Martina Farrow pp.134, 142, 167, Hand Made Maps pp.148,
189, Marie-Helene Jeeves pp.135, 204, Joanna Kerr pp.127, 165, 171, 177,
Meiklejohn Illustration/Peter Ellis p.129, Ellis Nadler pp.124, 151, 172, Gavin
Reece pp.140, 145, 147, 183, 202, 206, Colin Shelbourn pp.128, 130, 136, 138,
168, 174, 178, 188, Kath Walker Illustration pp.125, 126, 132, 137, 146, 149,
152, 161, 175, 186, 193, 199, Annabel Wright p.208

Picture research and illustrations commissioned by: Catherine Blackie

Photocopiable material designed by: Stewart Grieve

- **What do Beginner students need?**
- **Study Link**
- **Course components**
  Student's Book Files 1–7
  Back of the Student's Book
- **For students**
  Workbook
  MultiROM
  Student's website
- **For teachers**
  Teacher's Book
  Video / DVD
  Class audio CDs
  Test and Assessment CD-ROM
  Teacher's website

Contents
Grammar activity answers
Grammar activity masters
Communicative activity instructions
Communicative activity masters
Vocabulary activity instructions
Vocabulary activity masters
Song activity instructions
Song activity masters

Syllabus checklist

Pronunciation	Speaking	Listening	Reading
word stress; /h/, /əʊ/, and /ɒ/	introducing yourself	people introducing themselves	
sentence stress; /ɪ/ and /aɪ/	*Where are you from? Where is he from? Where is she from? Where is it from?*	Can you hear the difference?	
word stress; /e/, /iː/, and /ʃ/	talking about nationalities	understanding a dialogue	
		song: *D-I-S-C-O*; People in the street: *What's your name? How do you spell it? Where are you from?*	
/z/ and /s/; plural endings	What's in your bag?	understanding short conversations	
/ð/, /ʌ/, and /ə/	talking about family and friends	understanding dialogues	
/æ/, /eɪ/, /ɑː/, and /ɔː/	talking about cars	song: *You're beautiful*	What car? – Men and women are different
		People in the street: *Do you have brothers and sisters? How old are they?*	
/uː/, /w/, and /v/; linking	talking about your lifestyle	understanding a longer conversation	
word stress; /tʃ/, /dʒ/, and /g/	food questionnaire	a radio programme: *You are what you eat*	Breakfast in Japan and Hungary
3rd person *s*; word and sentence stress	talking about people who work	understanding a dialogue	English at work
silent consonants		song: *Friday I'm in love*; People in the street: *What do you do? Do you like it? What time do you start and finish?*	
sentence stress	questionnaire: *Do you like mornings?*	an interview	A day in the life of James Blunt
/eə/, /ɒ/, /aʊ/, and /j/	your free time	an interview	Hammerfest in winter
sentence rhythm	*Can you...?*	understanding dialogues	
/ʊə/, /s/, and /k/	saying prices	understanding prices; song: *Money, money, money* People in the street: *Where do you usually have lunch? What do you have? How much is it?*	

Pronunciation	Speaking	Listening	Reading
/ɜː/ and *was / were*	Where were they?		
sentence stress	What did you do yesterday?	a phone conversation song: *Perfect day*	One day in history
regular past simple endings	What did you do this morning / yesterday?, etc.		I lived, I loved, I cried…
		People in the street: *When's your birthday?* *What did you do on your last birthday?*	
/eə/ and /ɪə/	Is there a TV? Where is it?	dialogue: asking about hotel facilities	Hotels with a difference
the letters *ea*	Good or bad holiday?	Jeff and Kelly's holiday	One man's dream
sentence stress	answering questions about a story	Strangers on a train; song: *I'm a believer*	Strangers on a train
strong stress		People in the street: *What's the last film you saw?* *What did you think of it?*	
/ʊ/, /uː/, and /ŋ/	What do you like doing?		Free time
sentence stress	future plans: a dream trip	Liz's trip to South America	
revision of sounds	What's going to happen?	weather forecast; song: *Three little birds*	
polite intonation		understanding directions People in the street: *Is there a / an … near here?*	

New English File Beginner is for real beginners, or for false beginners who need a slower, more supportive approach. It gives you and your students the complete *New English File* package, with all the in-class and out-of-class components your students need to learn successfully, and with all the teacher support that accompanies other levels of the series.

The aim of every level of *New English File* is to get students talking and Beginner is no exception. To achieve this, beginners need two things above all else: motivation and support. Beginners' language level is low, but they need interesting topics and texts just as much as Intermediate or Advanced students. Support is also vital – beginners need clear aims, clear material, and clear reference. We've also incorporated new Student's Book features, including 'listen and repeat' in the Grammar Banks and Vocabulary Banks so that students get plenty of opportunity to pronounce new language.

Students who complete *New English File Beginner* could go on to study *New English File Elementary* with real confidence, knowing that they have a solid grounding in the basics of English. We very much hope that you enjoy using it.

What do Beginner students need?

Grammar, Vocabulary, and Pronunciation

If we want students to speak English with confidence, we need to give them the tools they need – Grammar, Vocabulary, and Pronunciation (G, V, P). We believe that 'G + V + P = confident speaking', and in *New English File Beginner* all three elements are given equal importance. Each lesson has clearly stated grammar, vocabulary, and pronunciation aims. This keeps lessons focused and gives students concrete learning objectives and a sense of progress.

Grammar

Beginner students need
- clear and memorable presentations of basic structures.
- plenty of regular and varied practice.
- student-friendly reference material.

We have tried to provide memorable contexts for new language that will engage students, using real-life stories and situations, humour, and suspense.

The **Grammar Bank** gives students a single, easy-to-access grammar reference section, with clear rules, example sentences, and common errors. The example sentences are all on the class audio CDs so that students can listen and repeat, and practise the pronunciation of the new structures. There are then two practice exercises for each grammar point.
◐ Student's Book *p.88*.

The **photocopiable Grammar activities** in the Teacher's Book can be used for practice in class or for self-study, especially with slower classes.
◐ Teacher's Book *p.123*.

When explaining grammar rules to students, and sometimes when setting up complicated activities, teachers who know their students' mother tongue may wish to use it. Although you should try to keep these occasions to a minimum we believe that very judicious use of students' L1 can save time and help build good teacher–class rapport. Contrasting how English grammar works with the rules in students' L1 can also help students to assimilate the rules more easily.

Vocabulary

Beginner students need
- to expand their knowledge of high-frequency words and phrases rapidly.
- to use new vocabulary in personalized contexts.
- accessible reference material to help them review and consolidate their vocabulary.

Every lesson in *New English File Beginner* focuses on high-frequency vocabulary and common lexical areas, but keeps the language load realistic. Many lessons are linked to the **Vocabulary Banks**, which contain pictures to help present and practise the vocabulary in class, and provide a clear reference bank to enable students to revise and test themselves in their own time. As students are beginners they are not asked to match words and pictures (as in higher levels of *New English File*) but simply to listen and repeat the words and phrases. All the lexis in the Vocabulary Banks is on the class audio CD to make it easier to drill the pronunciation. Where we think the pronunciation of a word may be especially tricky, we have provided the phonemic script.
◐ Student's Book *p.102*.

Students can practise the pronunciation of all the words from the **Vocabulary Banks** using the **MultiROM**.

Photocopiable Vocabulary activities can be found in the Teacher's Book.
◐ Teacher's Book *p.191*.

Pronunciation

Beginner students need
- to learn the English vowel and consonant sounds and practise them intensively.
- to see where there are rules and patterns in sound–spelling relationships.
- systematic practice of other aspects of pronunciation, e.g. stress and sentence rhythm.

New English File has its own unique system of teaching the sounds of English, through simple memorable pictures of key words which illustrate the sound and also incorporate the phonetic symbol. Students visualize and remember the words and sounds together, and the word is then used as a reference point when learning the pronunciation of other words with the same sound. It is up to you to decide whether you wish your students to use phonetic symbols actively, or simply to become familiar with the symbols through the pictures.

New English File Beginner has a pronunciation focus in every lesson, which focuses on either sounds, word stress, or sentence stress.
◐ Student's Book *p.5*.

In the Revise & Check sections, students are sent to the **Sound Bank**, a reference section where they can see common sound–spelling patterns for the sounds which they have practised in the File.
◐ Student's Book *p.117*.

Speaking

Beginner students need
- regular opportunities to use new language orally.
- topics that will arouse their interest and prompt them to express their own experiences and ideas in English.
- realistic and achievable tasks.

The ultimate aim of most students is to be able to communicate in English. Every lesson in *New English File Beginner* has a carefully controlled speaking activity which activates new grammar, vocabulary, and pronunciation, giving students the chance to 'personalize' the target language.
◗ Student's Book *p.5*.

The **Communication** section of the Student's Book provides 'information gap' activities to give students a reason to communicate.
◗ Student's Book *p.76*.

Photocopiable Communicative activities can be found in the Teacher's Book. These include pairwork activities, mingles, and games.
◗ Teacher's Book *p.161*.

Listening

Beginner students need
- to be exposed to as much aural English as possible.
- to build their confidence by listening to short and simple utterances.
- to learn to get the gist of what is being said by focusing on the key words in an utterance.

Most students at beginner level need to start by listening with the script in front of them and progress to listening to simple exchanges from which they can extract the key information. Most lessons have a listening comprehension task, and these become increasingly challenging as the course progresses. After students have listened two or three times without a script, they are sometimes asked to have a final listen with the listening script at the back of the Student's Book. This helps build students' confidence and shows them that they do not need to understand every word to get 'the message' of what was said.

Each File also contains an authentic listening task in the **Practical English** lesson where students listen to mini-interviews with members of the public. This task is carefully staged so that students know exactly what information they have to listen for.
◗ Student's Book *p.11*.

New English File Beginner also contains seven **songs** which we hope students will find enjoyable and motivating. For copyright reasons, these are mainly cover versions.

Reading

Beginner students need
- engaging topics and stimulating texts which will motivate them to read in English.
- manageable tasks that help them to read.
- to learn how to deal with unknown words in a text.

Many students need to read in English for their work or studies, and reading is also important in helping students to build vocabulary and to consolidate grammar. The key to encouraging students to read is to give them motivating but accessible material and manageable tasks. *New English File Beginner* reading texts are staged so that they progress from one-line sentences to short articles adapted from a variety of real sources (the British press, magazines, and news websites). These articles have been chosen for their intrinsic interest. Students are frequently encouraged to guess the meaning of new words from their context.
◗ Student's Book *p.29*.

The Revise & Check sections also include a short text where students develop their reading skills and measure their progress in this area.
◗ Student's Book *p.33*.

Practical English

Beginner students need
- to learn high-frequency functional phrases.
- to know what to say in common situations, e.g. buying a coffee.

The Practical English lessons introduce students to areas like spelling their names, asking and answering personal questions, telling the time and saying dates, asking about prices, asking and giving opinions, and understanding simple directions. The lessons build up to a speaking activity where students practise the language learnt in the lesson and listen to authentic mini-interviews in the **People in the street** section.

These short interviews are also on the *New English File Beginner* **DVD** which teachers can use instead of the class audio. Using the DVD will make the lessons more enjoyable and will help students to understand faster speech with the help of paralinguistic features. On the **MultiROM** students have the opportunity to watch and listen to more street interviews.

Revision

Beginner students need
- regular recycling of grammar, vocabulary, and pronunciation.
- motivating reference and practice material.
- a sense of progress.

However clearly structures or vocabulary are presented, students will usually only assimilate and *remember* new language if they have the chance to see it and use it several times. Grammar, Vocabulary, and Pronunciation are recycled throughout *New English File Beginner*.

At the end of each File there is a **Revise & Check** section. **What do you remember?** revises the Grammar, Vocabulary, and Pronunciation of each File. **What can you do?** provides a series of skills-based challenges, including **Writing** tasks, and helps students to measure their increasing competence. These pages are designed to be used flexibly according to the needs of your students.
◗ Student's Book *p.12*.

The photocopiable Grammar, Communicative, and Vocabulary activities also provide many opportunities for recycling.
◗ Teacher's Book *p.123*, *p.161*, and *p.191*.

(Study Link)

The Study Link feature in *New English File Beginner* is designed to help you and your students use the course more effectively. It shows **what** resources are available, **where** they can be found, and **when** to use them.

The Student's Book has these Study Link references:
- from the Grammar Bank ◗ MultiROM and website.
- from the Vocabulary Bank ◗ MultiROM and website.
- from the Sound Bank ◗ MultiROM and website.

These references lead students to extra activities and exercises that link in with what they have just studied.

The Workbook has these Study Link references:
◗ the Student's Book Grammar and Vocabulary Banks.
◗ the MultiROM.
◗ the student's website.

The Teacher's Book has Study Link references to remind you where there is extra material available to your students.

Student's Book organization

The Student's Book has seven Files. Each File is organized like this:

A, B, and C lessons Three two-page lessons which form the core material of the book. Each lesson presents and practises **Grammar** and **Vocabulary** and has a **Pronunciation** focus. There is a balance of reading and listening activities, and lots of opportunities for spoken practice. These lessons have clear references ➡ to the Grammar Bank and Vocabulary Bank at the back of the book.

Practical English Two-page lessons which teach functional language and vocabulary (aspects like telling the time or asking directions). The lessons feature interviews with people in the street, and link with the *New English File Beginner* DVD.

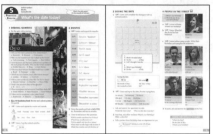

Revise & Check A two-page section – the left and right-hand pages have different functions. The **What do you remember?** page revises the **Grammar**, **Vocabulary**, and **Pronunciation** of each File. The **What can you do?** page provides **Reading**, **Writing**, **Listening**, and **Speaking** 'Can you…?' challenges to show students what they can achieve.

! After File 7 a two-page board game provides revision of the language covered in the book. This gives students a chance to review what they have learned and assess what they can now do in English.

The back of the Student's Book

In the back of the Student's Book you'll find these three Banks of material:

Grammar Bank (*pp.88–101*)
Two pages for each File, divided into A–C to reflect the three main lessons. The left-hand page has the grammar rules and the right-hand page has two exercises for each lesson. Students are referred ➡ to the Grammar Bank when they do the grammar in each main A, B, and C lesson.

Vocabulary Bank (*pp.102–116*)
An active picture dictionary to help students learn, practise, and revise key words. Students are referred ➡ to the Vocabulary Bank from the main lessons. The Vocabulary Bank includes an irregular verb list (*p.116*).

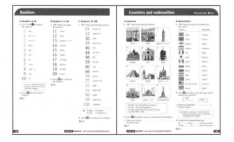

Sound Bank (*pp.117–119*) A three-page section with the *English File* sounds chart and typical spellings for all sounds. Students are referred ➡ to the Sound Bank from the Revise & Check lessons.

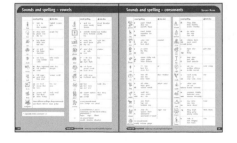

You'll also find:
- **Communication activities** (*pp.76–81*)
  Information gap activities and roleplays.
- **Listening scripts** (*pp.82–87*)
  Scripts of key listenings.

More for students

New English File Beginner gives your students everything they need for successful learning and motivating home study.

Workbook Each A–C lesson in the Student's Book has a two-page section in the Workbook. This provides all the grammar, vocabulary, and pronunciation practice and revision students need. Each section also has:

- **Words and phrases to learn**, which revises vocabulary from the lesson which is not in the Vocabulary Bank.
- **Listen and repeat**, where students listen and repeat dialogues which incorporate key language from the lesson. (The audio for these is on the MultiROM.)

Each Practical English lesson also has a two-page section in the Workbook, and includes full practice of the functional language students have learnt.

The Workbook is available with and without key.

MultiROM

The MultiROM works in two ways:

- It's a CD-ROM, containing revision of **Grammar**, **Vocabulary**, **Pronunciation**, **Words and phrases to learn**, and **Practical English** (with more video interviews).
- It's an audio CD for students to use in a CD player. It has the audio material for the Workbook 'Listen and repeat' activities.

Student's website

www.oup.com/elt/englishfile/beginner
Extra learning resources including:

- grammar exercises
- vocabulary activities
- pronunciation practice
- Practical English activities
- a vocabulary calendar
- the Study Link learning record

More for teachers

New English File Beginner gives you everything you need to teach motivating, enjoyable lessons, to save you time, and to make your life easier.

Teacher's Book The Teacher's Book has detailed lesson plans for all the lessons. These include:

- an optional 'books-closed' lead-in for every lesson.
- **Extra idea** suggestions for optional extra activities.
- **Extra challenge** suggestions for ways of exploiting the Student's Book material in a more challenging way if you have a stronger class.
- **Extra support** suggestions for ways of adapting activities or exercises to make them more accessible for slower learners.

All lesson plans include keys and complete listening scripts. Extra activities are colour coded in purple so you can see extra material at a glance when you're planning your classes.

You'll also find over 70 pages of photocopiable materials in the Teacher's Book:

Photocopiable Grammar activities see *pp.121–152*
There is a photocopiable Grammar activity for each A, B, and C lesson and a revision activity for each File. These provide extra grammar practice, and can be used either in class or for self-study.

Photocopiable Communicative activities see *pp.153–190*
There is a photocopiable Communicative activity for each A, B, C, and Practical English lesson. These give students extra speaking practice.

Photocopiable Vocabulary activities see *pp.191–199*
There is a photocopiable Vocabulary activity for each File. These provide extra practice using new vocabulary, and can be used either in class or for self-study.

Photocopiable Song activities see *pp.200–208*
New English File Beginner has a song for every File in the Teacher's Book.

All the photocopiable material is accompanied by clear instructions and keys.

Photocopiable Test and Assessment activities see CD-ROM in the back of this book
Complete tests as PDFs and Word documents, new listening material, and CEF assessment material.

DVD The DVD contains short interviews with members of the public answering questions from the **Practical English** section of each File. All the interviews are unscripted and provide an opportunity for students to practise listening to English spoken at a natural speed. Each episode can be used with the tasks in the Student's Book **People in the street** sections of the **Practical English** lessons as an alternative to the Class CD.

The *New English File Beginner* package also includes:

- **Three class audio CDs**
  These contain all the listening materials for the Student's Book.
- **Teacher's website**
  www.oup.com/elt/teacher/englishfile
  This gives you extra teaching resources, including
  – a guide to *New English File* and the Common European Framework
  – Common European Framework mapping and Portfolios
  – wordlists
  – the Study Link learning record
  – listening scripts
  – extra teaching ideas and material

CEF mapping documents and Portfolios are available for download on the
English File Teacher's site, www.oup.com/elt/teacher/englishfile.

What is the CEF? What are its aims?

The CEF, developed by the Council of Europe, encourages
us to learn languages and develop our ability to
communicate with people from other countries and
cultures. It consists of a carefully developed descriptive
framework. It has educational and social aims – these are
very often closely linked, and include the following:

- to encourage the development of language skills, so that
  we can work together more effectively.
- to encourage the development of inter-cultural
  awareness and 'plurilingualism'.
- to examine and define *what we can do* with a language.
- to help us compare the language levels of individuals in
  an accurate and impartial way, across different countries,
  education systems, ages, and cultures.
- to encourage learner autonomy and lifelong learning.
- to promote a coherent approach to language teaching
  – not by imposing a system, but by encouraging the
  sharing of ideas.

What are the CEF levels?

There are six global levels in the CEF. Behind these levels
are a very large number of competences which make up a
person's language ability – these are defined by 'descriptors'.
The levels are intended to be common reference points.
It's important to remember that they are *purely descriptive*
– they don't necessarily correspond to a year of study, or
to 100 hours of study. Everyone has different aims and
learns at different speeds, in different environments, and
in different ways. The CEF is careful to point out that the
levels are not 'linear' – that is, the time needed to move
from A1 to A2 may not be the same as that needed to move
from B1 to B2 or C1 to C2, and progress from level to level
slows down as we move up the levels.

A real strength of the CEF for students is that it focuses on
the positive – on what students can do, not on what they
can't do. All levels of performance from A1 upwards are
valued, and students should feel positive about the growing
list of things that they know they can do.

proficient	C2		This level doesn't equal 'native speaker' mastery – though a student at this level would be a very successful learner who can use a language with real precision and fluency.
	C1		At this level students command a wide range of language.
independent	B2		This level is where language use begins to become more 'abstract', for example giving opinions, summarizing a short story or plot, or giving detailed instructions.
	B1		At this level students can maintain a conversation and express ideas. They can also begin to deal with problems and situations where they meet unpredictable language.
basic	A2		This level has lots of descriptors for social functions, for example greeting people, asking about work and free time, and making invitations.
	A1	*New English File Beginner*	This is the lowest level of 'generative language use' – students can interact in a simple way and ask and answer simple questions.

The CEF recognizes a level of ability below **A1**, which includes descriptors like 'can say *yes, no, please, thank you*', 'can use some basic greetings', 'can fill in uncomplicated forms'.	For a breakdown of the six global levels above, see chapter 3 of the CEF.
The CEF also recognizes that there can be levels between these six global levels, like **A1+, A2+, B1+,** and **B2+**.	For detailed scales for each area of competence, see chapter 4 of the CEF.

What is a Portfolio?

The European Language Portfolio is a document for learners. It has three parts:

- the Passport
- the Biography
- the Dossier

The main aim of the Portfolio is to facilitate mobility in Europe by presenting an individual's language qualifications in a clear and comparable way. It allows all language and language-learning experiences (whether in the classroom or not) to be recorded, and it should be regularly updated. In a teaching situation where a coursebook is used over a year of study, we'd recommend updating the Portfolio several times a year, perhaps at the end of each term.

■ The Passport

This is a summary of language-learning experience, including time spent abroad, courses attended, books used, an assessment grid for each language skill area (graded from **A1–C2**), and any certificates or diplomas. It also outlines future plans for language learning.

The Passport shows at a glance the user's current level of language proficiency in different languages.

■ The Biography

This summarizes the learner's language-learning history, including languages they've grown up with, their language-learning experience at school and university, and how they use their languages now. It helps learners plan their learning by asking them to reflect on how and where they learn languages, and how they can develop autonomous learning.

The Biography also contains the CEF checklists for self-assessment.

■ The Dossier

This is a collection of pieces of personal work of different kinds which illustrate what the learner has achieved in different languages. This work could include written work from a course (for example from the Writing sections of *New English File Beginner*), self-assessment sheets, and audio and video recordings – anything that can 'prove' the learner's language history and level.

Is New English File CEF-compatible?

Yes, definitely. The CEF focuses on using language for a communicative purpose, and so does *New English File*. The CEF encourages the development of the ability to 'do things' in a foreign language, not just to 'know about' that language – though you also need to 'know about' a language in order to function successfully in that language. As the CEF says, '…a language learner has to acquire both form and meaning'. For example, take the A1 descriptor 'I can produce simple phrases about places'. In order to do this, students need to have a range of vocabulary to name places (*restaurant, school*, etc.) and to describe them (*cheap, good*, etc.), together with simple grammatical tools to make these words into phrases (*There's a very good restaurant near our school*), and accurate pronunciation. *New English File* teaches the language and skills that students will need in order to develop their range of communicative competences.

Here are some examples of how *New English File* fits with the aims of the CEF:

- The **Study Link** feature, which helps students find extra help and extra practice. The CEF states that learners need to take responsibility for planning and carrying out their own learning, and that they need to 'learn to learn'. One of the main obstacles to autonomous learning is that students don't know what to do, and Study Link helps to make it clear. There are regular Study Link references to the Grammar Bank, the Vocabulary Bank, the MultiROM, and the student's website.

- A **Grammar**, **Vocabulary**, and **Pronunciation** syllabus that gives students the linguistic competences they need to be able to communicate successfully.

- Regular **receptive and productive work** in the four skills – every lesson has speaking activities, and every File has listening, reading, and writing – the emphasis is on what students *do* with English.

- Clear **lesson aims** for each lesson, so learners know what the lesson objectives are.

- The **Practical English** lessons teach students language for performing essential everyday functions such as asking for directions, asking opinions, and saying the date. The lessons include real interviews in which people in the street answer questions connected with the topic of the lesson. This controlled introduction to authentic English (native-speaker and non-native speaker) builds students' receptive skills at the same time as building their confidence.

- The **What can you do?** pages at the end of every File, which ask students to see what they can achieve with the language they've studied.

- The *English File* **pronunciation pictures** – these help students to work on pronunciation autonomously, and to use dictionaries more effectively.

- A **Workbook**, **MultiROM**, and **Student's website** which all give students extra practice and learning resources.

- A **Teacher's Book** which gives you all the support you need, including extra photocopiable material and ideas so you can respond to your students' needs.

Remember – you can find full CEF mapping and Portfolio documents at www.oup.com/elt/teacher/englishfile.

G verb *be*: *I* and *you*
V numbers 0–10
P word stress; /h/, /əʊ/, and /ɒ/

1A Hello!

File 1 overview

In this first File (**1A-1C**) SS are gradually introduced to all forms of the verb *be*. In **1A** the *I* and *you* forms are presented, in **1B** SS learn the *he*, *she*, and *it* form, and in **1C** they learn the plural forms (*we*, *you*, and *they*) and practise the negative forms for all persons. In **Practical English** 1 SS learn to use the alphabet and to understand simple instructions in the classroom.

Lesson plan

The first lesson introduces SS to basic greetings, and the *I* and *you* forms of the verb *be* in positive sentences, questions, and short answers. The context is a British student arriving late to class on the first day of a course. The activities here also help your SS to get to know each other's names. In Vocabulary, SS learn numbers 0 to 10. In Pronunciation, they are introduced to the concept of word stress through 'international' two-syllable words, e.g. *taxi*, *hotel*, and also to the *New English File* system of teaching the sounds of English.

Optional lead-in (books closed)

- Introduce yourself to the class. Say *Hello. I'm (…)* twice. Repeat your name and write it on the board. Then look at one student and say *Hello. I'm (…)*. Wait for him/her to respond. At this stage do not correct anything they say. If the student fails to respond, move onto another student until you get the right response. Praise SS when they respond. Say *Good* or *Very good* as often as is necessary. Repeat this process with other SS round the class. This activity will break the ice with your class on the first day.
- You may wish now, or at some stage in this lesson, to do the photocopiable activity **Classroom language** on *p.161* (instructions on *p.153*). This teaches essential phrases that SS can use in every lesson, such as *Excuse me, What's … in English?*, *I don't understand*, etc.

1 LISTENING & SPEAKING

a ● **1.1** Books open. Demonstrate this by opening your own book and saying *Open your books*. Say the page number and write it on the board. Focus on the four photos and the speech bubbles by pointing at your book and saying *Look at the photos*. Then tell SS to listen and repeat. Demonstrate *listen* by putting your hand to your ear, pointing to the CD player, and saying *Listen*.

- Play the CD once for SS just to listen. Then play the recording again for SS to repeat in chorus, allowing time for them to repeat.

⚠ If you find the repeat pauses aren't long enough, use the pause button on your CD player. Encourage SS to try to copy the rhythm. Getting the rhythm right is one of the most important aspects of good pronunciation.

> **1.1** CD1 Track 02
>
> **Molly** Hi, I'm Molly.
> **Harry** Hi, I'm Harry.
> **Ann** Hello, I'm Ann Potter.
> **Rob** Hello, I'm Rob Jones.

- Depending on the size of your class get all or some SS to repeat individually.
- Point out that *hi* and *hello* mean the same, but that *hi* is more informal.

b ● Focus on the speech bubble. Demonstrate by saying *Hello, I'm* (name + surname). Then elicit *Hello, I'm (…)* from all the SS. If they are having problems, stop to drill the pronunciation of *hello* and *I'm* with the whole class before continuing.

⚠ *Hello* is also sometimes written *hallo* or (less frequently) *hullo* but the pronunciation is normally /həˈləʊ/.

c ● **1.2** Focus on the pictures and the two dialogues. Play the CD once for SS to listen and read. Go through the dialogue making sure the meaning is clear to SS. Some TT may want to do this in L1. (See **Introduction** on *p.8* for comments on use of mother tongue.)

- Focus on *Excuse me/Sorry/Sorry?* Write the three phrases on the board. Elicit the meaning and use of *Excuse me* (for politely attracting someone's attention) by giving an example with one student. Say *Excuse me. Are you (wrong name)?* Then elicit the meaning and use of *Sorry* (to apologize) by knocking a student's pencil on the floor. Finally, elicit the meaning and use of *Sorry?* (to ask for repetition). Say *Are you (name)?* to one student and pretend not to hear by putting your hand to your ear.

⚠ You can also say *Pardon?* when you want someone to repeat something. If you personally as a T tend to say *Pardon?*, it might be worth teaching it here as well. If so, model and drill the pronunciation /ˈpɑːdən/.

> **1.2** CD1 Track 03
>
> **1 Receptionist** Hello. What's your name?
> **Tom** Tom.
> **Receptionist** Are you Tom Banks?
> **Tom** No, I'm not. I'm Tom King.
> **Receptionist** You're in room 2.
> **Tom** Sorry?
> **Receptionist** You are in room 2.
> **Tom** OK. Thank you.
>
> **2 Tom** Excuse me.
> **Teacher** Hello. Are you Tom?
> **Tom** Yes. Nice to meet you.
> **Teacher** Nice to meet you.
> **Tom** Am I late?
> **Teacher** Yes, you are.
> **Tom** Sorry!

d ● **1.3** Play dialogue 1 on the CD and get SS to repeat each phrase in chorus. Encourage SS to copy the rhythm. Model the phrase yourself if SS are not copying the rhythm correctly.

- Put SS in pairs, **A** and **B**. Demonstrate that they are going to practise the dialogue. Give each student a role. Demonstrate the activity with a good pair. Now ask SS to practise the dialogue. When they finish, tell them to change roles. Listen for pronunciation mistakes and write them on the board, then model and drill them with choral and individual repetition.

1.3		CD1 Track 04

1

Receptionist	Hello. What's your name?
Tom	Tom.
Receptionist	Are you Tom Banks?
Tom	No, I'm not. I'm Tom King.
Receptionist	You're in room 2.
Tom	Sorry?
Receptionist	You are in room 2.
Tom	OK. Thank you.

e ● **1.4** Repeat for dialogue 2.

1.4		CD1 Track 05

2

Tom	Excuse me.
Teacher	Hello. Are you Tom?
Tom	Yes. Nice to meet you.
Teacher	Nice to meet you.
Tom	Am I late?
Teacher	Yes, you are.
Tom	Sorry!

Extra challenge

Ask one student in each pair to close their book and respond to their partner from memory. **A** reads his/her lines and **B** responds from memory. Then SS swap roles.

2 GRAMMAR verb *be*: *I* and *you*

a ● Focus on the chart. Highlight that *I'm* is the contraction of two words. Write *I'm = I am* on the board. Focus on the second example. Explain that *you're* is the contraction of two words. Elicit that the missing word is *are*. Write *You're = You are* on the board. Establish a gesture to remind SS to contract verb forms, e.g. a scissor or concertina gesture.
- Highlight and drill the pronunciation of *I'm* /aɪm/ and *you're* /jɔː/.

b ● Before SS go to the **Grammar Bank** you could teach them the words *positive*, *negative*, and *question*. This can be done in English by writing symbols on the board:
  + = positive
  − = negative
  ? = question
  You could explain this in L1 if you prefer.
- Tell SS to go to **Grammar Bank 1A** on *p.88*. You may need to write the page number on the board. Show SS that all the grammar rules and exercises are in this section of the book.
- ● **1.5** SS will be repeating all the sentences which are highlighted in the chart on *p.88*. Play the CD and ask SS to listen and repeat the example sentences. Use the pause button as necessary.

1.5		CD1 Track 06

I'm Rob.
You're in room 2.

Am I late?	Yes, you are.	No, you aren't.
Are you Holly?	Yes, I am.	No, I'm not.

- Go through the rules with the class using the expanded information in the **Grammar notes** below to help you. You may want to use L1 here if you know it.

Grammar notes

- In English we always use a name or pronoun with the verb.
- *I* is always written with a capital letter.
- There is only **one** form of *you*. There is no formal and informal form, unlike in many other languages.
- Native and fluent speakers of English nearly always use contractions in conversation.
- The subject usually changes position in questions in English.
- You can answer a question with a short answer in English instead of answering just *yes* or *no*. Emphasize that *you are* in the positive short answer is not contracted.
- ⚠ The *you* form of the verb *be* has two possible negations: *you aren't* and *you're not*. Both forms are common, but we recommend you teach only *you aren't* so as not to confuse SS.

- Focus on the exercises for **1A** on *p.89*. You may want to get SS to do these in pairs or individually and then compare with a partner.
- Check answers.

a	1 I'm	2 You're	3 I'm	4 You're	
b	1 B 'm			4 A Are	B am
	2 A Am	B aren't		5 A Am	B are
	3 A Are	B not			

Study Link SS can find more practice of this grammar on the MultiROM and on the *New English File Beginner* website.
- Tell SS to go back to the main lesson on *p.5*.

3 VOCABULARY numbers 0–10

a ● **1.6** Some SS may already know some numbers in English, but real beginners are unlikely to know the correct pronunciation or spelling. Write the numbers (in numerals not words) from 0 to 10 on the board and focus on the photo.
- Play the CD once and ask SS the question *What are the numbers?* Circle the numbers (1, 2, 3) on the board as SS say them.

1.6		CD1 Track 07

Man	One two three, one two three, one two three.
Woman	Ow!
Man	Sorry!

- Try to elicit the numbers 4 to 10 and 0 by pointing to the numbers you have written on the board. For 0 teach *zero* /ˈzɪərəʊ/.

b ● Tell SS to go to **Vocabulary Bank** *Numbers* on *p.102*. Write the page number on the board. Highlight that these pages (**Vocabulary Banks**) are their vocabulary section where they will first do all the exercises as required by the Student's Book, and will then have the pages for reference to help them remember the words.

● Focus on part **A Numbers 0–10**.

● **1.7** Focus on the instructions for **a**. Play the CD and get SS to repeat the numbers in chorus. Use the pause button as necessary. Then drill with individual SS.

● In the **Vocabulary Bank** the phonetic transcription is given for words whose sound–spelling relationship is irregular. Explain this to SS, and tell them that they will be learning the phonetic symbols gradually throughout the course, but not to worry about them for the time being. Word stress is also marked (by underlining) on multi-syllable words.

● Focus on the instructions for **b**. Ask SS to cover the words and say the numbers. They could do this with a partner.

● Monitor and help. Make a note of any pronunciation problems they are having. Point to the numbers on the board and model and drill the ones that SS find difficult.

1.7	CD1 Track 08
zero one two three four five six seven eight nine ten	

Study Link SS can find more practice of these numbers on the MultiROM and on the *New English File Beginner* website.

● Tell SS to go back to the main lesson on *p.5*.

c ● Count round the class from zero to ten. Point to SS at random and encourage them to count a little bit faster each time you start from zero. Then count backwards from ten to zero.

Extra challenge

Get SS to count up and down in twos, i.e. *2, 4, 6,* etc.

d ● **1.8** Focus on the instructions and demonstrate by saying two numbers yourself and eliciting the next one from the class. Then play the CD and pause after the next pair of numbers. Ask SS what the next number is. Make sure SS are clear what they have to do before continuing.

● Play the rest of the CD and give SS time to say the next number.

● Repeat the activity, this time getting individual SS to respond.

1.8		CD1 Track 09
1, 2, ... 3	3, 2, ... 1	3, 4, ... 5
7, 8, ... 9	9, 8, ... 7	2, 1, ... zero
6, 5, ... 4	4, 3, ... 2	
6, 7, ... 8	8, 9, ... 10	

Extra idea

Give SS more practice by doing simple sums with them on the board.

4 PRONUNCIATION word stress; /h/, /əʊ/, and /ɒ/

a ● Focus on the information box (or write the words on the board) and demonstrate how one of the syllables in these words is pronounced more strongly than the other. Say each word both ways (LIsten and liSTEN, REpeat and rePEAT) and ask SS which way is right (LIsten and rePEAT).

● Highlight the points in the **Pronunciation notes** below. You may want to use L1 here if you know it. The information in these notes is primarily for TT's reference. Decide how much of it you think would be useful for your SS at this stage of the course.

Pronunciation notes

● In all multi-syllable English words one syllable is stressed more than the other syllable(s). There aren't any firm rules governing this, although the majority of two-syllable words are stressed on the first syllable.

● The number of syllables a word has is determined by the way it is pronounced, not by how it is written, e.g. *nice* = one syllable, not two, because the *e* is not pronounced.

● There are no written accents in English. A dictionary shows which syllable in a word is stressed, e.g. *sorry* /ˈsɒri/. The syllable after the apostrophe is the stressed one.

● SS need to be careful with the pronunciation of words which are the same or similar to ones in their language as the stress pattern may be different.

● **1.9** Focus on the international words. SS will probably recognize them and know what they mean. Give SS a minute to match the words and the photos in pairs. Play the CD for SS to check their answers (see listening script 1.9).

1.9	CD1 Track 10
1 email 2 taxi 3 coffee 4 hotel 5 photo	

b ● Now focus on the international words again. Play the CD and ask SS to listen and repeat.

● Explain that you are going to play the CD again and you want SS to underline the stressed syllable in each word. Demonstrate this by underlining LI- and -PEAT in *listen* and *repeat* on the board. Teach SS 'syllable one' and 'syllable two' for them to use when they feed back their answers.

● Write the words on the board. Play the CD, pausing and replaying as necessary as SS underline the stressed syllable. Get SS to compare their answers with a partner. Then play the CD again and elicit answers ('syllable one' or 'syllable two'), and underline the correct syllable on the board.

- Encourage SS to mark the stress on new words by underlining the stressed syllable.

<u>co</u>ffee   <u>pho</u>to   <u>e</u>mail   ho<u>tel</u>   <u>ta</u>xi

Pronunciation notes

- (See **Introduction** *p.8* for a full explanation of the *New English File* approach to teaching sounds and phonetic symbols through the use of 'sound pictures'.)
- The majority of consonants (e.g. *b, c, d,* etc.) in English have only one pronunciation.
- All vowels (*a, e, i, o, u*) can be pronounced in more than one way, e.g. *o* is commonly /əʊ/ or /ɒ/, but can also be /ʌ/ or /ə/.
- You may want to highlight to SS the following sound–spelling patterns:

  /h/   *h* at the beginning of a word is pronounced /h/, e.g. *hello*. (There are a few exceptions, but apart from *hour* these are not relevant for SS at this level.)

  /əʊ/ /ɒ/   single *o* (not double *o*) is most commonly pronounced /əʊ/ or /ɒ/, e.g. *no, not.*

  /əʊ/   *o* + consonant + *e* is usually /əʊ/, e.g. *phone.*

- Double consonants e.g. *hello, sorry, coffee,* are pronounced the same as single consonants.

c ● **1.10** Focus on the three sound pictures *house, phone,* and *clock.* Write the words on the board. Tell SS that they are example words to help them to remember English sounds.
- Explain that the phonetic symbol in the picture represents the sound. Phonetic symbols are used in dictionaries to help learners pronounce words correctly.
- Focus on the sound picture for *house* and model and drill the word and the sound /h/.
- Repeat for the other two sounds and words (*phone* and *clock*).
- Now focus on the example words after each sound picture. Explain that the pink letters are the same sound as the picture word.
- Play the CD for SS to listen. Then play it again pausing after each word for SS to repeat.

1.10		CD1 Track 11
house	/h/	hello, hi, Harry, hotel
phone	/əʊ/	no, OK, hello, hotel
clock	/ɒ/	not, sorry, coffee, Molly

Study Link SS can find more practice of these sounds on the MultiROM and on the *New English File Beginner* website.

d ● **1.11** Focus on the sentences and play the CD just for SS to listen. Then play the CD for SS to listen and repeat.
- Tell SS to practise the sentences in pairs. Monitor and help with any pronunciation problems.

1.11	CD1 Track 12
Hello. Harry's Hotel.	
Oh no! The phone!	
Are you Molly? No, sorry, I'm not.	

5 SPEAKING

- Focus on the flow chart. Model and drill the dialogue on the left side with a student whose name you remember. Repeat with two other SS.
- Model the right side of the dialogue with a student whose name you pretend to have forgotten. Repeat with two other SS. Ask a different student to model the dialogue with a student sitting on the other side of the class. Repeat with two more pairs.
- Ask SS to practise the dialogues with the people sitting next to them following the flow chart.
- Get SS to get up and roleplay the dialogue from memory with other SS.
- Monitor and help, dealing with any general pronunciation problems at the end.

Extra support

Tell SS to close their books. Elicit the two dialogues onto the board. They can refer to this during the activity if they can't remember the phrases.

Extra idea

Before they start you could put music on. Tell SS to move around the room. When the music stops, the SS should do their roleplay with the person nearest them.

WORDS AND PHRASES TO LEARN

Focus on the words and phrases to learn. Make sure SS understand the meaning of each phrase. If necessary, remind SS of the context in which they came up in the lesson. If you speak your SS' L1, you might like to elicit a translation for the words/phrases for the SS to write next to them.

Study Link SS can find more practice of these words and phrases on the MultiROM and on the *New English File Beginner* website.

Extra photocopiable activities

Classroom language
p.161 (instructions *p.153*)
Grammar
be: *I* and *you p.123*
Communicative
Nice to meet you *p.162* (instructions *p.153*)

Homework

Study Link Workbook *pp.4–5*

G verb *be*: *he, she, it*
V countries
P sentence stress; /ɪ/ and /aɪ/

Where are you from?

Lesson plan

In this lesson SS continue with the verb *be* and here they learn the *he*, *she*, and *it* form. In the first part of the lesson SS learn twelve country words. *He is, She is,* and *It is* are presented through a dialogue about where two actors are from. Pronunciation introduces SS to the concept of sentence stress, and practises the /ɪ/ and /aɪ/ sounds. Finally, in the speaking activity SS guess the nationality of actors who are very famous in their country, but probably less famous internationally.

Note that because SS are beginners we have restricted the number of countries taught in the Vocabulary Bank to twelve, and these same countries are then recycled and revised in subsequent lessons. Teachers may also want to teach SS their own and neighbouring countries if these do not appear in the Vocabulary Bank.

Optional lead-in (books closed)

- Pin a world map to the wall. Point to SS' country/countries and elicit the name(s). Write it/them on the board.
- Point to Italy, Japan, Turkey, and Poland and elicit their names. Write them on the board.

1 VOCABULARY countries

a ● Books open. Focus on the four countries and the photos and ask SS to match them.

⚠ If the words for these countries are very different in your SS' L1, you may need to first establish where/what they are.

> **1** Turkey **2** Poland **3** Japan **4** Italy

b ● ⟨1.12⟩ Play the CD for SS to check their answers. Elicit the meaning of *Where is it?* and write the question on the board.

⟨1.12⟩	CD1 Track 13
1 Where is it? Turkey.	
2 Where is it? Poland.	
3 Where is it? Japan.	
4 Where is it? Italy.	

c ● Tell SS to go to **Vocabulary Bank** *Countries and nationalities* on *p.103*. Write the page number on the board.

● ⟨1.13⟩ Focus on the instructions for **a** in part **A Countries**. Play the CD and get SS to repeat the countries in chorus. Use the pause button as necessary. Highlight the word stress and the pronunciation of the more difficult words, whose pronunciation is written in phonetics.

⟨1.13⟩	CD1 Track 14
Brazil China England Hungary Italy Japan Mexico Poland Russia Spain Turkey the United States	

- Drill the countries again with individual SS, either with the CD or modelling yourself.
- Focus on the information box and go through it with the class. You may want to explain that the United Kingdom = England, Scotland, Wales, and Northern Ireland.
- Focus on the instructions for **b**. Show SS how to cover the words (three by three) with a piece of paper.
- Monitor and help. Listen for any general pronunciation mistakes. Write the words on the board, and model and drill them with choral and individual repetition.
- Focus on **c**. Teach SS the name of their country if it is not in the list. Write it on the board and model and drill the word. Tell SS to write it in the space.

Study Link SS can find more practice of these words on the MultiROM and on the *New English File Beginner* website.

- Tell SS to go back to the main lesson on *p.6*.

d ● ⟨1.14⟩ Focus on the dialogue. Play the CD once. Then play it again, pausing after each line for SS to repeat. Encourage them to get the rhythm right, stressing *from* in the question but not in the answer. SS will focus on sentence stress in more detail in **Pronunciation**.

⟨1.14⟩	CD1 Track 15
A Where are you from?	
B I'm from England.	
A Where in England?	
B I'm from London.	

- Elicit/explain the meaning of each phrase.

e ● Put SS in pairs, **A** and **B**. Demonstrate that they are going to practise the dialogue. Give each student a role. Demonstrate the activity with a good pair.

- Now ask SS to get up and practise the dialogue with the other SS using their own countries and cities.

Extra idea

If your SS all come from the same place, ask them to choose a different country and city.

2 GRAMMAR verb *be*: *he, she, it*

a ● ⟨1.15⟩ Focus on the photo and the dialogue. You could ask SS in their L1 if they've seen the film. Elicit the meaning of *a good film* and *fantastic*. Then tell SS to listen to and read the dialogue and complete the spaces with a country.

- Play the CD once for SS to complete the dialogue.
- Play the CD again, pausing after each space for SS to check their answers.

> **1** Mexico **2** Mexico **3** Spain

<table>
<tr><td>

1.15 / **1.16** CD1 Tracks 16/17

A Where's he from?
B He's from Mexico.
A Is she from Mexico too?
B No, she isn't. She's from Spain.
A Is it a good film?
B Yes, it is. It's fantastic.

</td><td>

a 1 It's 2 She's 3 He's 4 It's 5 He's 6 She's
    7 It's 8 She's
b 1 **B** isn't, 's
    2 **A** 's, Is **B** is
    3 **A** Is **B** 's
    4 **A** 's **B** 's
    5 **A** Is **B** isn't, 's

</td></tr>
</table>

b ● **1.16** Play the CD again, pausing for SS to listen and repeat. Elicit/explain the meaning of *too*.

c ● Put SS in pairs, **A** and **B**. Demonstrate that they are going to practise the dialogue. Give each student a role. Demonstrate the activity with a good pair. Now ask SS to practise the dialogue. When they finish tell them to change roles. Monitor and help. Write and correct any pronunciation mistakes on the board.

d ● Focus on the pictures. Ask *he, she, or it?* for each picture. Tell SS to complete the spaces.

> 1 he 2 she 3 it

e ● Tell SS to go to **Grammar Bank 1B** on *p.88*.
 ● **1.17** Play the CD and ask SS to listen and repeat the example sentences. Use the pause button as necessary.

<table>
<tr><td colspan="3">

1.17 CD1 Track 18

He's from Italy.
She's from Spain.
It's from China.

</td></tr>
<tr><td>Is he late?</td><td>Yes, he is.</td><td>No, he isn't.</td></tr>
<tr><td>Is she from Turkey?</td><td>Yes, she is.</td><td>No, she isn't.</td></tr>
<tr><td>Is it good?</td><td>Yes, it is.</td><td>No, it isn't.</td></tr>
<tr><td colspan="3">

What's your name?
Where are you from?
Where's he from?

</td></tr>
</table>

● Go through the rules with the class using the expanded information in the **Grammar notes** below to help you. You may want to use L1 here if you know it.

Grammar notes

● In English *he* is used for a man and *she* for a woman. *It* is used for everything which is not a man or a woman, e.g. things, countries, places, buildings, etc. Animals are often *it* but can also be *he* or *she* if they are yours and you know the sex.

● Remind SS that in conversation it is more common to use contractions.

● Point out that *is* is contracted in conversation after question words, e.g. *What's your name? Where's he from?* but *are* isn't contracted in *Where are you from?*

⚠ The *he/she/it* form of the verb *be* has two possible negations: *he/she/it isn't* and *he/she/it's not*. Both forms are common, but we recommend you teach only *he/she/it isn't* so as not to confuse SS. Only point this out if SS ask about it.

● Focus on the exercises for **1B** on *p.89* and get SS to do the exercises individually or in pairs. If they do them individually, get them to compare answers with a partner. Check answers, getting SS to read out the full sentences.

Study Link SS can find more practice of this grammar on the MultiROM and on the *New English File Beginner* website.

● Tell SS to go back to the main lesson on *p.7*.

3 PRONUNCIATION sentence stress; /ɪ/ and /aɪ/

a ● Focus on the questions and answers in the speech bubbles, and model the sentences, exaggerating the stressed words a bit so that SS can hear the rhythm clearly. Highlight the points in the **Pronunciation notes** below. You may want to use L1 here if you know it.

Pronunciation notes

● In English the words that carry the important information are said more strongly than others, e.g. in *Where are you from? where* and *from* are pronounced more strongly than *are* and *you*. *Where* and *from* are important to understand the question. In the answer *I'm from England*, *I'm* and *England* are stressed because they are important to understand the answer.

● To understand English you need to listen out for the important, stressed words. To pronounce well with a good rhythm SS need to stress these words themselves. Obviously the ability to do this will improve with time and is not something SS can pick up immediately.

● Drill the questions and answers in the sentence stress box with choral and individual repetition.

● Focus on the exercise and give SS a few minutes to write the sentences.

b ● **1.18** Play the CD for SS to listen and check their answers (see listening script below).

<table>
<tr><td>

1.18 / **1.19** CD1 Tracks 19/20

1 Is she from Brazil? No, she isn't.
2 It's from China.
3 She's from Japan.
4 Is he from Turkey? Yes, he is.
5 He's from Spain.
6 Is she from Poland? No, she isn't.
7 She's from England.
8 Where's he from? He's from Hungary.

</td></tr>
</table>

c ● **1.19** Play the CD again, pausing for SS to listen and repeat each phrase in chorus. Encourage SS to try and copy the rhythm. You may need to stop and model the phrase yourself if you notice that SS are not copying it correctly.

Pronunciation notes

- You may want to highlight the following sound–spelling rules:

  /ɪ/ the letter *i* between two consonants is usually pronounced /ɪ/, e.g. *fish*.

  /aɪ/ in the combination *i* + consonant + *e*, *i* is usually pronounced /aɪ/, e.g. *bike*.

d ● **1.20** Focus on the sound picture *fish* and write the word on the board. Play the CD to model and drill the word and sound (pause after the sound).

- Now focus on the words after *fish*. Remind SS that the pink letters are the /ɪ/ sound. Play the CD pausing after each word for SS to repeat.

⚠ Highlight that *England* has the /ɪ/ sound even though it is spelt with an *e*. This is not a common sound–spelling combination, though it does occur sometimes with words like *remember, repeat*, etc.

- Repeat the above process for *bike*.
- If either or both of these sounds are difficult for your SS, you may want to model them yourself so that SS can see your mouth position.
- Play the CD for SS to listen. Then play it again pausing for SS to repeat.

1.20		CD1 Track 21
fish	/ɪ/	it, Italy, six, Mexico, England
bike	/aɪ/	China, I, five, nine, hi, nice

Study Link SS can find more practice of these sounds on the MultiROM and on the *New English File Beginner* website.

e ● **1.21** Focus on the sentences and play the CD just for SS to listen. Then play the CD for SS to repeat.

- Tell SS to practise the sentences in pairs. Monitor and help with any pronunciation problems.

1.21	CD1 Track 22
It's from Italy.	
Liverpool is in England.	
Hi. I'm from China. Nice to meet you.	

4 LISTENING & SPEAKING

a ● **1.22** This section gives SS practice in distinguishing aurally between *he* and *she* and then trying to make the distinction themselves. Depending on your SS' nationality many SS will find this quite tricky.

- Focus on the sentences. Play the CD for SS to hear the difference between the sentences.

1.22		CD1 Track 23
1 **a** Is he from Italy?	**b** Is she from Italy?	
2 **a** She's from Russia.	**b** He's from Russia.	
3 **a** Where's he from?	**b** Where's she from?	
4 **a** It's from Spain.	**b** He's from Spain.	
5 **a** She's late.	**b** He's late.	
6 **a** Where is he?	**b** Where is she?	

b ● **1.23** Focus on the sentences in **a** again. Explain that SS are going to hear only <u>one</u> of the sentences and they have to tick the one they hear.

- Play the CD, pausing for SS to tick the sentences.
- Play the CD again for SS to check their answers.

1 b	2 b	3 a	4 a	5 a	6 a

1.23	CD1 Track 24
1 Is she from Italy?	4 It's from Spain.
2 He's from Russia.	5 She's late.
3 Where's he from?	6 Where is he?

c ● Focus on the sentences in **a** again. Get SS to practise saying them in pairs.

Extra challenge

Put SS in pairs, **A** and **B**. **A** reads a sentence and **B** says *a* or *b*. Then they swap roles.

d ● Focus on the photos, and the example speech bubble. Explain that they are actors who are very famous in their own countries, but not internationally (the actors are Oksana Akinshina, from Russia, and Rodrigo Santoro, from Brazil).

- Tell SS to first try to guess where the woman is from, and elicit questions (*Is she from Italy?* etc.) Answer *No, she isn't* until SS guess the right country. Then repeat for the man.

e ● Put SS in pairs, **A** and **B**. Tell them to go to **Communication** *Guess the countries*, **A** on *p.76*, **B** on *p.78*.

- Go through the instructions and make sure SS understand what they have to do. Stress that they must continue asking *Is he/she from…?* until they have guessed the right country.
- Tell SS to go back to the main lesson on *p.7*.

WORDS AND PHRASES TO LEARN

Focus on the words and phrases to learn. Make sure SS understand the meaning of each phrase. If necessary, remind SS of the context in which they came up in the lesson. If you speak your SS' L1, you might like to elicit a translation for the words/phrases for the SS to write next to them.

Study Link SS can find more practice of these words and phrases on the MultiROM and on the *New English File Beginner* website.

Extra photocopiable activities

Grammar
be: he, she, it p.124
Communicative
Where are they from? p.163 (instructions *p.153*)

Homework

Study Link Workbook *pp.6–7*

G verb *be*: *we, you, they*; negatives (all persons)
V nationalities; numbers 11–20
P word stress; /e/, /iː/, and /ʃ/

We're from the USA. We're American.

Lesson plan

In this lesson SS complete their knowledge of the verb *be*. Here they study the positive forms and question forms for *we*, *you*, and *they* and the negative forms of all parts of the verb. (In the two previous lessons, although they have seen *aren't, isn't*, etc. in short answers, they haven't focused on full negative sentences.) SS begin by learning the nationality adjectives for the countries they learnt in **1B**. The grammar is then presented through the context of a British family checking into a hotel and meeting an American couple. The pronunciation focus is on word stress in country and nationality words.

In Speaking SS practise talking about what nationality different people and things are, and finally learn numbers 11–20.

Optional lead-in (books closed)

● Give SS a quick quiz on capital cities to revise the countries they already know. Tell SS that you are going to say a capital city, and they have to say the country. You could make this a team game by dividing the class down the middle.

1	Warsaw	7	Mexico City
2	Madrid	8	London
3	Beijing	9	Brasilia
4	Budapest	10	Rome
5	Moscow	11	Ankara
6	Tokyo	12	Washington DC

1	Poland	7	Mexico
2	Spain	8	England
3	China	9	Brazil
4	Hungary	10	Italy
5	Russia	11	Turkey
6	Japan	12	the USA (the United States)

1 VOCABULARY nationalities

a ● Focus on photo number 1 and the speech bubble. Ask the class *Where is she from?* and elicit *Poland*. Give SS time to complete the other sentences. Check answers.

1 Poland	2 the United States	3 Mexico	4 Italy

● Highlight the difference between country and nationality, e.g. *Poland–Polish* and the change in stress between *Italy* and *Italian*.

b ● Tell SS to go to **Vocabulary Bank *Countries and nationalities*** on *p.103*.
● Focus on part **B Nationalities**.
● **1.24** Focus on the instructions for **a**. Play the CD and get SS to repeat the countries and nationalities. Use the pause button as necessary.

1.24   CD1 Track 25

Brazil… Brazilian	Poland… Polish
China… Chinese	Russia… Russian
England… English	Spain… Spanish
Hungary… Hungarian	Turkey… Turkish
Italy… Italian	the United States… American
Japan… Japanese	the UK… British
Mexico… Mexican	

● Focus on *the UK/British*. Remind SS that the UK (the United Kingdom) = England, Scotland, Wales, and Northern Ireland. The official nationality for people from these countries is *British*. If somebody is *English* it means that they are both British and from England, not Scotland, etc.

⚠ *Great Britain* is also often used but technically refers to the island including England, Scotland, and Wales, but not Northern Ireland.

● Focus on the instructions for **b**, and get SS to cover the flags and to remember and say the countries and nationalities. They could do this with a partner.

● Monitor and help. Make a note of any pronunciation problems they are having. Write the words on the board and model and drill the ones that SS find difficult.

● Focus on the instructions for **c**. Teach SS how to say their nationality if it is not in the list. Give SS time to complete the space.

● Focus on the information box. Point out that the word for nationality and language is usually the same but not always, e.g. for *the United States* the nationality is *American* but the language is *English*, or for *Brazil* the nationality is *Brazilian* but the language is *Portuguese*.

● Write the following sentence on the board and ask SS to correct it: *She's spanish.* (She's Spanish) to highlight that these words must begin with a capital letter.

● Focus on the instructions for **d**. Give SS time to complete the sentences. Ask individual SS to say their sentences.

Study Link SS can find more practice of these words on the MultiROM and on the *New English File Beginner* website.

● Tell SS to go back to the main lesson on *p.8*.

c ● **1.25** Focus on the instructions and the speech bubble. Explain to SS that they are going to hear a man or a woman saying *I'm from* + a country, and they have to say the nationality using *he's* if it's a man and *she's* if it's a woman.

● Play the first example, pausing for SS to say *He's Spanish* in chorus. Continue with the other people on the CD. Make a note of any mistakes in pronunciation and correct them later on the board.

● Repeat the activity getting individual SS to respond.

1 I'm from Spain… He's Spanish.
2 I'm from Brazil… She's Brazilian.
3 I'm from Russia… She's Russian.
4 I'm from the United States… He's American.
5 I'm from Mexico… He's Mexican.
6 I'm from Italy… She's Italian.
7 I'm from Poland… He's Polish.
8 I'm from Japan… She's Japanese.
9 I'm from England… He's English.
10 I'm from China… He's Chinese.
11 I'm from Hungary… She's Hungarian.
12 I'm from Turkey… He's Turkish.

2 LISTENING & READING

a • **1.26** Focus on the three pictures and get SS to cover the conversations. Ask *Where are they?* to elicit (*at a*) *hotel*.

• Play the CD once for SS to number the pictures. Play again if necessary and then check answers.

1 C   2 A   3 B

1.26 / **1.27**   CD1 Tracks 27/28

J = John, R = receptionist, S = Sally,
A = Anna, M = Mike, L = Liz, T = Travis
1 J   Hello. We're John and Sally Clarke.
  R   Hello. You're in room 211 and they're in room 212.
  S   Thank you.

2 S   Hurry up. We're late.
  A   We aren't late. Breakfast is from seven to ten. And Mike isn't ready.

3 L   Hi. Are you American?
  M   No, we aren't. We're English.
  L   Are you on holiday?
  A   Yes, we are.
  L   We're on holiday too. We're Liz and Travis, from Texas.
  T   Bye. Have a nice day!
  A   Goodbye.

b • Play the dialogues again while SS read.

• Now focus on sentences 1–6 and give SS time to read them. Elicit the meaning of *on holiday*. Then give SS a few minutes to read the dialogues again and mark the sentences right or wrong. Get them to compare their answers with a partner's and then check answers.

1 ✗   2 ✗   3 ✓   4 ✗   5 ✓   6 ✗

c • Focus on the example and the wrong answers in **b**. Give SS a few minutes to correct the wrong sentences. Check answers by getting SS to read out complete sentences.

⚠ Write the numbers of the wrong sentences on the board so SS know which ones to change.

1 John and Sally are in room 211.
2 Breakfast is from seven to ten.
4 Liz and Travis are American.
6 Liz and Travis are on holiday.

d • **1.27** Play the CD again pausing after each dialogue to elicit/explain any words or phrases that SS don't understand, e.g. *hurry up, breakfast, ready, too, goodbye, bye, have a nice day.*

• Highlight that *bye* is more informal than *goodbye*.

• Finally, play the CD pausing after each line for SS to listen and repeat. Encourage SS to copy the rhythm of the sentences.

3 GRAMMAR verb *be*: *we, you, they*; negatives (all persons)

a • Focus on the grammar chart and highlight that the first column is for positive forms and the second column is for negative forms. Tell SS to look at the dialogues and give them two minutes to try and complete the chart.

• Check answers, writing the missing words on the board.

⊞	⊟	⊞	⊟
Singular		**Plural**	
I'm	*I'm not*	We're	*We aren't*
You're	You aren't	*You're*	You aren't
He's	*He isn't*	*They're*	They aren't

b • Tell SS to go to **Grammar Bank 1C** on *p.88*.

• **1.28** Play the CD and ask SS to listen and repeat the example sentences. Use the pause button as necessary.

1.28   CD1 Track 29

We're American.
You're Japanese.
They're Hungarian.

Are we late?	Yes, you are.	No, you aren't.
Are you from Russia?	Yes, we are.	No, we aren't.
Are they Mexican?	Yes, they are.	No, they aren't.

I'm not English.
You aren't late.
He isn't Brazilian.
She isn't from Hungary.
It isn't good.
We aren't on holiday.
You aren't in room 10.
They aren't from London.

• Go through the rules with the class using the expanded information in the **Grammar notes** below to help you. You may want to use L1 here if you know it.

Grammar notes

• *we, you,* and *they* are plural pronouns.

• *we* and *you* can be used for men or women or both.

• The pronoun *you* and the verb form after it is the same in the singular and the plural.

• *they* can be used for people or things.

• Remind SS that people normally use contractions in conversation.

• Contractions are <u>not</u> used in positive short answers, e.g. *Yes, they are* NOT ~~*Yes, they're*~~.

⚠ For *we/you/they* there are two possible negations – *we/you/they aren't* and *we/you/they're not* – but we recommend you teach only *we/you/they aren't* so as not to confuse SS.

- Focus on the exercises for **1C** on *p.89* and get SS to do the exercises individually or in pairs. If they do them individually, get them to compare answers with a partner.
- Check answers.

a	1 We 2 It 3 they 4 she 5 They
	6 He 7 You 8 We
b	1 A Are B aren't, 're 5 A Is B isn't, 's
	2 A Are B are, 're 6 A Are B are, 's
	3 isn't 7 'm not
	4 aren't 8 aren't

Study Link SS can find more practice of this grammar on the MultiROM and on the *New English File Beginner* website.

- Tell SS to go back to the main lesson on *p.9*.

c • **1.29** Focus on the instructions and the example. Then play the CD and pause after the first sentence. Elicit the negative sentence from SS.
- Play the rest of the CD pausing if necessary after each sentence to give SS time to say the negative in chorus.
- Repeat the activity, this time getting individual SS to respond.

1.29	CD1 Track 30
1 I'm Hungarian.	I'm not Hungarian.
2 They're Japanese.	They aren't Japanese.
3 She's Brazilian.	She isn't Brazilian.
4 We're English.	We aren't English.
5 It's Italian.	It isn't Italian.
6 You're American.	You aren't American.
7 He's Russian.	He isn't Russian.

Extra support

You could play the CD once and ask SS to write the negative. Then play the CD again and ask them to say it.

Study Link SS can find more practice of this grammar on the MultiROM and on the *New English File Beginner* website.

4 PRONUNCIATION word stress; /e/, /iː/, and /ʃ/

a • **1.30** Write *Brazil* and *Brazilian* on the board. Ask SS to tell you which syllable is stressed in each word (the second). Teach/elicit the words *the same* and write *S* next to the words on the board.
- Repeat for *China* and *Chinese* (first/second). Teach/elicit the word *different* and write *D* next to the words on the board.
- Focus on the instructions for the exercise. Play the CD once, pausing after each pair for SS to underline the stress and write *S* or *D* in the space.
- Get SS to compare answers with a partner and play the CD again, pausing to check answers.

3 S 4 D 5 S 6 D 7 D 8 S	

1.30		CD1 Track 31
1 Bra<u>zil</u> Bra<u>zil</u>ian	5 <u>Russ</u>ia <u>Russ</u>ian
2 <u>Chi</u>na Chi<u>nese</u>	6 <u>Hung</u>ary Hun<u>gar</u>ian
3 <u>Eng</u>land <u>Eng</u>lish	7 <u>Jap</u>an Jap<u>an</u>ese
4 <u>It</u>aly <u>It</u>alian	8 <u>Tur</u>key <u>Tur</u>kish

Extra challenge

You could get SS to try to mark the stress first and then listen and check.

b • Play the CD again and ask SS to listen and repeat.

Pronunciation notes

- Tell SS that the two dots in the symbol /iː/ mean that it's a long sound.
- You may want to highlight the following sound–spelling patterns:

/e/	a single letter *e* is <u>usually</u> pronounced /e/, e.g. *ten*. Sometimes the vowels *ea* also have this sound, e.g. *breakfast*.
/iː/	a single *e* is sometimes pronounced /iː/ at the end of a word, e.g. *he, me.* The vowels *ee* are always pronounced /iː/, e.g. *three*.
/ʃ/	the consonants *sh* are always pronounced /ʃ/, e.g. *she.* The letters *tion* also produce this sound, e.g. *nationality*.

⚠ Make sure SS make a /ʃ/ sound and not a /s/ sound for /ʃ/. If necessary, tell SS that /ʃ/ is the sound of silence by putting your finger to your mouth and saying *shhhhhh*.

c • **1.31** Focus on the sound picture *egg* and write the word on the board. Play the CD to model and drill the word and sound (pause after the sound).
- Now focus on the words after *egg*. Remind SS that the pink letters are the /e/ sound. Play the CD pausing after each word for SS to repeat.
- Repeat for the other two sounds and words (*tree* and *shower*).
- Focus especially on sounds that are difficult for your SS and model them so that SS can see your mouth position. Get SS to repeat these sounds a few times.

1.31		CD1 Track 32
egg	/e/	Mexico, ten, seven, breakfast
tree	/iː/	we, he, she, meet, three
shower	/ʃ/	she, Spanish, English, Russian, nationality

Study Link SS can find more practice of these sounds on the MultiROM and on the *New English File Beginner* website.

d • **1.32** Focus on the sentences and play the CD just for SS to listen. Then play the CD for SS to listen and repeat.
- Tell SS to practise the sentences in pairs. Monitor and help with any pronunciation problems.

1.32	CD1 Track 33
Breakfast is from seven to ten.	
He's Chinese.	
She isn't Russian, she's Spanish.	

5 SPEAKING

- Focus on the photo of dim sum and the prompt, and also on the speech bubble. Elicit the right sentence from the class (Dim sum isn't Polish. It's Chinese.).
- Now focus on the other photos and the prompts and explain to SS that some are right and some are wrong.
- Put SS in pairs and give them a few minutes to make similar sentences about the other pictures.
- Monitor and help, encouraging SS to guess if they don't know the right answer.
- You could get pairs of SS to say their sentences to other pairs.
- Check answers by getting SS to say the two complete sentences.

> Dim sum isn't Polish. It's Chinese.
> Gisele Bündchen isn't Hungarian. She's Brazilian.
> The Rolling Stones aren't American. They're English.
> Andrea Bocelli isn't Brazilian. He's Italian.
> Seat cars aren't Italian. They're Spanish.
> Casio is Japanese.
> Burritos aren't Spanish. They're Mexican.
> Keira Knightley is British.

6 VOCABULARY numbers 11–20

a • **1.33** Focus on the photos and the instructions. Put SS in pairs to decide if they are English or American.
- Play the CD for SS to listen and check their answers. Check answers. For each picture say *Is he English or American?*

> **1.33**   CD1 Track 34
> **A** He's English. He's number eleven.
> **B** He's American. He's number twelve.

- Focus on the numbers on the players' shirts and ask SS *Can you remember? What are the numbers?* and elicit that A is eleven and B is twelve. Play the recording again if necessary. Write the numbers on the board and ask SS to say which syllable is stressed in *eleven* and underline it.

b • Tell SS to go to **Vocabulary Bank Numbers** on *p.102*. Write the page number on the board.
- Focus on part **B Numbers 11–20**.
- **1.34** Focus on the instructions for **a**. Play the CD and get SS to repeat the numbers in chorus. Use the pause button as necessary. Emphasize that the stress on *thirteen, fourteen*, etc. is on the second syllable.
- Focus on the instructions for **b**. Ask SS to cover the words and say the numbers. They could do this with a partner.
- Monitor and help. Make a note of any pronunciation problems they are having. Write the words on the board and model and drill the ones that SS find difficult.

> **1.34**   CD1 Track 35
> eleven   twelve   thir<u>teen</u>   four<u>teen</u>   fif<u>teen</u>   six<u>teen</u>
> seven<u>teen</u>   eigh<u>teen</u>   nine<u>teen</u>   <u>twenty</u>

- **Study Link** SS can find more practice of these numbers on the MultiROM and on the *New English File Beginner* website.
- Tell SS to go back to the main lesson on *p.9*.

c • Focus on the instructions. Start counting slowly *1, 3, 5…* and elicit the rest of the numbers.
- Repeat for 2, 4, 6…
- Correct any mistakes on the board. Model and drill these chorally and individually.

d • Explain to SS they are going to play Bingo and focus attention on the card. Tell SS to write any six numbers from 1–20 in the bingo card in pencil (you could do this individually or in pairs with SS sharing a card).
- Demonstrate the activity by drawing a card on the board and writing six numbers in.
- Explain/demonstrate that SS have to cross out the numbers on their card if they are called. When all their numbers have been crossed out they call *Bingo!* Give SS practice in saying *Bingo!* before you start.
- Get SS to complete their card <u>in pencil</u> (if you would like to play more than once).
- When they have completed their bingo cards, read out the numbers below slowly and <u>in random order</u>, repeating each number once and circling or underlining it so that you remember which numbers you have called.
  1 2 3 4 5 6 7 8 9 10 11 12 13 14 15 16 17 18 19 20
- Continue until a student/a pair has crossed off all their numbers and shouted *Bingo!*
- Check that the winning card is correct by getting SS to say the numbers on their card, comparing it with the numbers you have called out. If the SS have made a mistake, then continue calling out numbers until there is a genuine winner.
- Now get SS to rub out the numbers and play the game again. If SS have written in pen, they can draw a new card on a piece of paper.

Extra ideas

You could write some simple additions and subtractions on the board for SS to call out the answer, e.g.

$7 + 5 = (12)$, $16 - 3 = (13)$.

You could call out two numbers for the class to say the next one, e.g. *11, 12… (13); 19, 18… (17)*.

WORDS AND PHRASES TO LEARN

Focus on the words and phrases to learn. Make sure SS understand the meaning of each phrase. If necessary, remind SS of the context in which they came up in the lesson. If you speak your SS' L1, you might like to elicit a translation for the words/phrases for the SS to write next to them.

Study Link SS can find more practice of these words and phrases on the MultiROM and on the *New English File Beginner* website.

Extra photocopiable activities

Grammar
be: we, you, they; negatives *p.125*
Communicative
Match the sentences *p.164* (instructions *p.153*)

Homework

Study Link Workbook *pp.8–9*

The alphabet
Spelling your name
Classroom language

Lesson plan

This is the first in a series of seven **Practical English** lessons (one per File), which teach SS basic functional language to help them survive in English in an English-speaking environment. Here SS learn the alphabet and how to spell their names. The context used to show the importance of learning the alphabet is a Spanish businessman flying from Amsterdam to Manchester. SS hear his flight being called and gate number given. On arrival he checks into a hotel and spells his name. SS are given a pronunciation chart to help them learn and remember how the alphabet is pronounced.

SS then come to a section called **People in the street**, which appears in all the **Practical English** lessons. In this section SS listen to people in the street – not actors – who are stopped and asked simple questions. In this lesson they are asked what their names are and how they are spelt, and where they are from. For this section TT have the option of using the class audio CD or the *New English File Beginner* DVD (see **Introduction** *p.11*). Although SS will find these listening exercises more challenging, they should find them motivating too.

In **Vocabulary** they learn the words for things in the classroom, and how to understand simple instructions the teacher uses in class. The lesson ends with the song *D-I-S-C-O*.

Optional lead-in (books closed)

- Write *OK* and *USA* on the board and ask SS if they know how to say them in English.
- Now get SS to say them slowly and elicit the individual letters, i.e. *O, K, U, S*, and *A*.

1 LISTENING

a ● **1.35** Books open. Demonstrate that you want SS to cover the sentences under the pictures in situation 1. They can do this with a piece of paper. Focus on the pictures and ask *Where is he?* and elicit that the man is at an airport. You may want to teach the phrase *He's asleep.*

- Play the CD once for SS to listen to the three airport announcements.
- Now tell SS to uncover the sentences and explain that they are going to hear the announcements again and have to number them in the right order.
- Play the CD again for SS to number the sentences. Check answers, playing the CD again and pausing after each flight call.
- Elicit/explain the meaning of any new words, e.g. *final call, passengers, flight, urgently, gate*. Model and drill pronunciation.
- Finally, see if SS can remember how the flight and gate numbers were said (KLM 1258, B14).
- Now get SS to cover the dialogue in situation 2. Focus on the picture and ask *Where is he?* and elicit that he is at a hotel.
- Play the CD once for SS to listen to the man checking

into the hotel.

- Now tell SS to uncover the sentences and explain that they are going to hear the conversation again and have to number the sentences in the right order.
- Play the CD again for SS to number the sentences. Check answers, playing the CD again and pausing after each line.
- Elicit/explain the meaning of any new words, e.g. *Good morning, reservation, How do you spell...?* and model and drill pronunciation.
- Focus on the information box to explain the difference between (*first*) *name* and *surname*, and *double* for a repeated letter. You may also want to teach *last name* as an alternative to *surname*.

1	2	3	1				
2	4/6	2	5	3	7	1	4/6

1.35 / **1.36**   CD1 Track 36

1 Passengers on Flight KLM 1258 to Manchester, please go to gate B14.
This is the final call for passengers on Flight KLM 1258 to Manchester. Please go urgently to gate B14.
Mr Pablo Torres on flight KLM 1258 to Manchester, please go urgently to gate B14.

CD1 Track 37

2 R = receptionist, P = Pablo
R   Good morning.
P   Hello. I'm Pablo Torres. I have a reservation.
R   How do you spell your surname?
P   T-O-double R-E-S.
R   Sorry?
P   T-O-double R-E-S.
R   Thank you.

Extra support

To make the distinction clear between *name* and *surname*, write your first name and your surname on the board. Elicit which is your first name and which is your surname.

Highlight that you can say *name* or *first name*, and *surname* or *last name*. When asked *What's your name?* you usually reply with your first name in an informal situation or your surname or full name in a formal situation, e.g. checking into a hotel.

You may want to point out that when we give our full name we always say first name then surname, and that some people have one or more middle names.

Ask a few SS *What's your first name?* and *What's your surname?* to practise the difference between the two. Then get SS to ask each other.

Extra idea

You could bring in photos of famous people and show them to the class and ask *What's his/her first name? What's his/her surname?*

b ● **1.36** Go through each line of dialogue 2, getting SS to listen and repeat after the CD. You could get SS to practise the dialogue in pairs.
Finally, write the name *Torres* on the board and ask SS if they can remember how the letters were pronounced.

2 THE ALPHABET

a ● **1.37** Choose a student and ask *What's your surname?* Show that you want to write the surname on the board and pretend that you don't know how to spell it. Ask *How do you spell it?* Let SS try and tell you the letters in English (they may remember some from the previous activity). Explain that it's important to learn the English alphabet because you often need to spell names, town names, etc. (especially when you're talking on the phone). Letters of the alphabet are also important for flight numbers, car number plates, email addresses, etc.

● Explain that all the letters in the English alphabet have one of seven sounds. Tell SS that they're going to learn the sounds before they learn the letters.

● Play the CD once, pausing for SS to repeat the words and sounds. You may need to stop and model the sound yourself so that they can see the position of your mouth if you notice that SS are not copying the sound correctly. Remind SS that the two dots in *tree* /triː/, *boot* /buːt/, and *car* /kɑː/ mean that these are long sounds. *Train* /treɪn/, *bike* /baɪk/, and *phone* /fəʊn/ are **diphthongs**, i.e. sounds made up of two vowel sounds.

1.37			CD1 Track 38
train	/eɪ/	phone	/əʊ/
tree	/iː/	boot	/uː/
egg	/e/	car	/ɑː/
bike	/aɪ/		

b ● **1.38** Tell SS that now they are going to learn the letters of the alphabet according to their pronunciation.

● Play the CD, pausing for SS to listen and repeat each letter. Model the sounds yourself if necessary showing SS what position their mouths should be in.

● Now write letters at random on the board for SS to try and pronounce them using the chart to help them.

1.38	CD1 Track 39
AHJK BCDEGPTV FLMNSXZ IY O QUW R	

c ● **1.39** This activity is to help SS distinguish between letters that are sometimes confused. Depending on your SS' L1 some of these pairs will be more difficult than others.

● Play the CD once for SS to hear the difference between the letters. Ask *Can you hear the difference?* If SS answer 'no', model the letters yourself to help them hear the difference between the sounds. Play the CD again if necessary.

1.39						CD1 Track 40
1 M	N	4 E	I	7 B	V	
2 K	Q	5 Y	I	8 E	A	
3 G	J	6 U	W			

d ● **1.40** Now tell SS they're only going to hear one of the letters from each pair. Explain that they have to circle the letter they think they hear.

● Play the CD once for SS to circle the letter.

● Get SS to compare their answers with a partner. Play the CD again if necessary.

● Check answers (see listening script 1.40) by playing the CD again and pausing after each letter and writing it on the board.

1.40							CD1 Track 41
1 N	3 J		5 Y		7 B		
2 Q	4 E		6 W		8 A		

e ● **1.41** Focus on the pictures. Explain that the words for these things are abbreviations.

● Play the CD once for SS to number the pictures. Replay as necessary.

● Get SS to compare with a partner and check answers (see listening script 1.41).

1.41					CD1 Track 42
1 DJ	3 TV		5 CD		
2 BMW	4 PC		6 DVD		

f ● Play the CD again for SS to write the letters. Replay as necessary.

● Check answers by asking SS to read out the letters and writing them on the board.

● Give SS practice saying the letters. Then call out numbers between 1–6 for SS to say the abbreviation e.g. 6...*DVD*.

g ● **1.42** Now SS listen and repeat the whole alphabet. Play the CD and pause after each letter for SS to repeat.

● Get SS to practise saying the alphabet in pairs. Then elicit the whole alphabet round the class, writing the letters on the board to help SS remember. Highlight that if they can't remember how to pronounce a letter, they can use the alphabet chart on *p.10* to help them.

1.42	CD1 Track 43
A B C D E F G H I J K L M N O P Q R S T U V W X Y Z	

h ● Focus on the names and elicit from the class how you pronounce them. Get individual SS to spell them to you and write them on the board. Remind SS that they can use *double L* when they spell *Sally*.

⚠ Although people often use *double* when there are two of the same consecutive letters in a name (e.g. *double P*), it is also acceptable to say both letters separately, e.g. *PP*. You may want to point this out to SS.

● Model and drill the question *How do you spell 'John'?*

● Repeat for the other names.

● Get SS to ask each other how to spell the names in pairs. Demonstrate with a good student.

● Monitor and help. Correct any mistakes with pronunciation on the board.

● In later classes try to recycle the alphabet whenever possible, e.g. play hangman (see **Extra idea** below) as a warmer, get SS to spell words in vocabulary exercises, have spelling quizzes, etc.

Extra idea

● Play hangman to practise the alphabet. Think of a word SS know, preferably of at least eight letters, e.g. *JAPANESE*. Write a dash on the board for each letter of the word: _ _ _ _ _ _ _ _

● SS call out letters one at a time. Encourage them to start with the five vowels and then move onto consonants. If the letter is in the word (e.g. *A*), fill it in each time it occurs, e.g. _A_A_ _ _. Only accept correctly pronounced letters. If the letter is not in the word, draw the first line of this picture on the board:

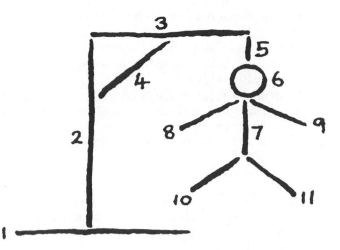

- Write any wrongly-guessed letters under the picture so SS don't repeat them. The object of the game is to guess the word before the man is 'hanged'. SS can make guesses at any time, but each wrong guess is 'punished' by another line being drawn.
- The student who correctly guesses the word comes to the board and chooses a new word.
- SS can also play on paper in pairs/groups.

3 PEOPLE IN THE STREET

Study Link This exercise is also on the *New English File Beginner* DVD, which can be used instead of the class audio (see **Introduction** *p.11*). SS can get more practice on the MultiROM, which contains more of the short street interviews with a listening task and scripts. Note that the answers to the **People in the street** listening exercises are in **bold** in the listening scripts.

a • Highlight that SS are going to listen to real people (not actors) so SS will find the recordings faster and more difficult than previous exercises.

• **1.43** Focus on the three questions in the box. Then focus on the photo of the man and explain that SS are going to hear the man being asked these questions. Ask *What's his name?* Point out that ***his** name* is used for a man, and ***her** name* for a woman. This will be presented and practised fully in lesson **2B**. Play the CD once for SS to hear the man's name. Check answers (see listening script 1.43) but <u>don't write the name on the board</u>.

1.43	CD1 Track 44
Interviewer	What's your name?
Man	My name is **Craig**.

b • **1.44** Play the CD for SS to hear the man spell his name. They listen and try to write down his name. Replay as necessary and use the pause button if SS are finding it hard. Check answers (see listening script 1.44).

1.44	CD1 Track 45
Interviewer	What's your name?
Man	My name is Craig.
Interviewer	How do you spell it?
Man	**C-R-A-I-G**.

c • **1.45** SS will hear the man say where he is from. Play the CD for SS to complete the sentence. Check answers (see listening script 1.45).

1.45	CD1 Track 46
Interviewer	What's your name?
Man	My name is Craig.
Interviewer	How do you spell it?
Man	C-R-A-I-G.
Interviewer	Where are you from?
Man	I'm from **Oxford**.

d • Explain that SS are going to listen to the six people in the photos answering the same questions.

• **1.46** Play the CD for SS to complete the information for the first person. Replay as necessary and use the pause button if SS are finding it hard. Check answers (see listening script 1.46).

• Repeat this process for the other five speakers.

1.46	CD1 Track 47
Interviewer	What's your name?
Speaker 1	My name's **Sarah**.
Interviewer	How do you spell it?
Speaker 1	**S-A-R-A-H**.
Interviewer	Where are you from?
Speaker 1	I'm from Reading, in **England**.
Interviewer	What's your name?
Speaker 2	My name's **Joshua**.
Interviewer	How do you spell it?
Speaker 2	**J-O-S-H-U-A**.
Interviewer	Where are you from?
Speaker 2	I'm from **Chicago**, in the United States of America.
Interviewer	What's your name?
Speaker 3	**Elena**.
Interviewer	How do you spell it?
Speaker 3	**E-L-E-N-A**.
Interviewer	Where are you from?
Speaker 3	**Brazil**.
Interviewer	What's your name?
Speaker 4	**Padma**.
Interviewer	How do you spell it?
Speaker 4	**P-A-D-M-A**.
Interviewer	Where are you from?
Speaker 4	I'm from Bangalore, **India**.
Interviewer	What's your name?
Speaker 5	My name's **Tom**.
Interviewer	How do you spell it?
Speaker 5	**T-O-M**.
Interviewer	Where are you from?
Speaker 5	I'm from Vancouver, in **Canada**.
Interviewer	What's your name?
Speaker 6	My name is **Dax**.
Interviewer	How do you spell it?
Speaker 6	**D-A-X**.
Interviewer	Where are you from?
Speaker 6	I'm from San Diego, **California**.

e • Explain to SS that they are going to interview each other using the questions from the interview.

• Model and drill the three questions. Highlight that in the question *How do you spell it?* 'it' refers to the name.

• Demonstrate with a good student. Get SS to ask and answer the questions in pairs.

4 SPEAKING

a • Books closed. Elicit dialogue 2 from exercise **1** onto the board prompting SS' memory if necessary by giving the first letter of a word or phrase.

 • Underline *Good morning* on the board and focus on the information box. Explain the rules to SS and highlight that these times are very approximate. Write the greetings on the board and elicit the stress. Model and drill the different greetings.

 ⚠ *Good morning*, *Good afternoon*, and *Good evening* are quite formal in English. People normally just say *Hello* when they greet each other. You may also want to teach *Goodnight*, which is usually only used when saying goodbye at night.

 • Put SS in pairs, **A** and **B**. Give each student a role and ask them to focus on the instruction for the first roleplay. Elicit that they should use *Good afternoon* instead of *Good morning*.

 • Rub the dialogue off the board and get SS to do the roleplay. Monitor and help as necessary.

Extra support

You could leave some words in the dialogue on the board to prompt weaker SS in the roleplay.

b • Focus on the instructions for the second roleplay and elicit that SS should use *Good evening* here.

 • Get SS to swap roles and do the roleplay again.

 • Monitor and help as necessary, correcting any pronunciation errors.

c • Put SS in pairs, **A** and **B**. Tell them to go to **Communication Game: *Hit the ships*, A** on *p.76* and **B** on *p.79*.

 • This game is an adapted version of *battleships*. If the game exists in your SS' country, they will not have any problems seeing how this activity works. However, if they are not familiar with the original, you may need to use L1 to make it clear. The object of the game is to guess where the other person's ships are and to 'hit' them by correctly identifying a square where part of the ship is located. When all parts of the ship have been hit then it is 'sunk'. The winner is the first person to 'sink' all the other person's ships.

 • Go through the instructions and make sure SS understand what they have to do. Demonstrate the activity on the board by drawing two small grids and taking the part of **A** and **B**. Make sure SS know what *ship*, *hit*, and *nothing* mean. Use gesture to show a ship sinking after being completely hit. Say *It's sunk!* and get SS to repeat. Write it on the board and model and drill pronunciation.

5 VOCABULARY classroom language

a • Tell SS to go to **Vocabulary Bank *Things*** on *p.104*. Write the page number on the board.

 • Focus on part **A Things in the classroom**. Focus on the instructions for **a**.

 • **1.47** Play the CD and get SS to repeat the words in chorus. Use the pause button as necessary. Remind SS that the stressed syllable is underlined.

 • Highlight the pronunciation of the words SS find most difficult, e.g. *board*, *window*, *coat*. Model and drill the pronunciation yourself if necessary.

 • Focus on the instructions for **b**. Ask SS to cover the words and look at the main picture. Tell them to say the words. They could do this with a partner.

 • Monitor and help as necessary, correcting any pronunciation errors.

 • Focus on the picture of the chairs and the door. Explain that we say **a** *chair* because it is one of many, but we say **the** *door* because there is usually one door in a room. The same is true of **the** *board*. This difference is focused on in more detail in lesson **2A**.

1.47		CD1 Track 48
the board	a chair	a book
the door	a coat	a dictionary
a window	a laptop	a piece of paper
a table		

Study Link SS can find more practice of these words on the MultiROM and on the *New English File Beginner* website.

 • Tell SS to go back to the main lesson on *p.11*.

Extra idea

Give SS extra practice by pointing to things in your classroom and asking *What's that?*

b • The focus here is on helping SS to understand simple classroom instructions.

 • Focus on the pictures and the phrases. Elicit/explain the meaning of any words SS don't understand.

 • Give SS time to match the phrases and the pictures.

c • **1.48** Play the CD and check answers (see listening script 1.48).

1.48		CD1 Track 49
1 Look at the board, please.		4 Stand up.
2 Open your books.		5 Sit down, please.
3 Go to page 14.		6 Close the door.

 • Play the CD again, pausing to allow SS to repeat the phrases. Encourage SS to copy the rhythm.

 ⚠ There may be other classroom instructions you use frequently yourself. You could teach them here too.

d • **1.49** Tell SS they are going to hear the instructions they have just learnt and they have to do the actions.

 • Play the CD and pause after each instruction and wait for all the SS to do each action. If necessary repeat the phrase yourself.

1.49		CD1 Track 50
Stand up.		Look at exercise 1b.
Sit down, please.		Look at the board.
Open your books.		Close your books.
Go to page 12.		

 • From now on, make sure you always give these instructions in English.

6 **1.50** SONG 🎵 *D-I-S-C-O*

 • This song was recorded by the group Ottawan in 1980. For SS of this level all song lyrics will include language that they don't know. Nevertheless SS are usually motivated to try to understand song lyrics. The song will help SS remember these letters of the alphabet.

- If you want to do this song in class, use the photocopiable activity on *p.202*.

> **1.50** CD1 Track 51
>
> *D-I-S-C-O*
>
> **Chorus**
> D-I-S-C-O (x4)
> She is disco / D-I-S-C-O (x4)
>
> She is D delirious
> She is I incredible
> She is S superficial
> She is C complicated
> She is O oh, oh
>
> She is D desirable
> She is I irresistible
> She is S super sexy
> She is C such a cutie
> She is O oh, oh
>
> **Chorus**
>
> She is D disastrous
> She is I impossible
> She is S super special
> She is C crazy, crazy
> She is O oh, oh
>
> She is D delightful
> She is I incredible
> She is S sensational
> She is C sweet as candy
> She is O oh, oh
>
> **Chorus**

WORDS AND PHRASES TO LEARN

Focus on the words and phrases to learn. Make sure SS understand the meaning of each phrase. If necessary, remind SS of the context in which they came up in the lesson. If you speak your SS' L1, you might like to elicit a translation for the words/phrases for the SS to write next to them.

Study Link SS can find more practice of these words and phrases on the MultiROM and on the *New English File Beginner* website.

Extra photocopiable activities

Communicative
How do you spell it? *p.165* (instructions *p.154*)
Song
D-I-S-C-O p.202 (instructions *p.200*)

Homework

Study Link Workbook *pp.10–11*

Each File finishes with two pages of revision and consolidation. The first page, **What do you remember?**, revises the grammar, vocabulary, and pronunciation. These exercises can be done individually or in pairs, in class or at home, depending on the needs of your SS and the class time available. The second page, **What can you do?**, presents SS with a series of skills-based challenges. First, there is a reading text which revises grammar and vocabulary SS have already learnt. In the early Files the texts are very simple, but later they are of a slightly higher level than those in the File. Then there is a listening exercise which focuses on small differences which can cause confusion. Finally, there is a speaking activity which measures SS' ability to use the language of the File orally. We suggest that you use some or all of these activities according to the needs of your class.

What do you remember?

GRAMMAR

1 a	2 b	3 b	4 a	5 b	6 a	7 b	8 b
9 b	10 b				

VOCABULARY

a	1	Chinese	c	1	me
	2	Italy		2	meet
	3	English		3	Good
	4	Brazilian		4	have
	5	the USA (the United States)		5	spell
b	1	eight	d	1	a coat
	2	zero		2	a laptop
	3	twelve		3	a dictionary
	4	thirteen		4	a window
	5	twenty		5	a chair

PRONUNCIATION

a	vowels:	clock, phone, fish, bike, tree, egg
	consonants:	house
c	Japan Japanese hotel sorry surname	

What can you do?

1 CAN YOU UNDERSTAND THIS TEXT?

First name	Surname	Nationality
Marta	*Ramírez*	*Spanish*
Viktor	*Petrov*	*Russian*
Kelly	*Doyle*	*American*

3   CAN YOU UNDERSTAND THESE PEOPLE?

1 a   2 b   3 a   4 a   5 b   6 a   7 b   8 a
9 b   10 b

1.51   CD1 Track 52

1   **A** Where's Danny from? Is he English?
    B No, he's from California.
2   **A** Hello. I have a reservation. I'm Bella Johnson.
    B Ah yes. You're in room 19.
3   **A** How do you spell your name, Kathy?
    B K-A-T-H-Y.
4   **A** What number bus is it?
    B 14. No, no sorry, 13.
5   **A** Is Andrzej Russian?
    B No, he's Polish.
6   Flight BA472 to Amsterdam now boarding at gate C16.
7   **A** What's your name?
    B John Reid.
    A Sorry, how do you spell your surname?
    B R-E-I-D.
8   **A** Where's Chris?
    B She's in room 11.
9   OK, now sit down and open your books. Go to page 12 and look at exercise 2c.
10 Good evening. Welcome to Hotel Cipriani.

Extra photocopiable activities

Grammar
1 revision *p.126*
Vocabulary
Hidden phrase *p.193* (instructions *p.191*)

Test and Assessment CD-ROM

File 1 Quicktest
File 1 Test

G singular and plural nouns; *a/an, the*
V small things
P /z/ and /s/, plural endings

What's in your bag?

File 2 overview

In lesson **2A** SS practise singular and plural nouns, and in lesson **2B** they are introduced to possessive adjectives and the possessive *s* through the context of family. Lesson **2C** introduces basic adjectives in the context of describing cars. Finally, in the **Practical English** lesson SS learn to ask for and give basic personal information.

Lesson plan

In Vocabulary SS revise classroom objects and go on to learn the words for common small objects. Then, real information about objects most commonly left on trains provides the context for learning plural nouns. They also learn the difference between *a/an* and *the*, although the articles have been introduced already in Vocabulary Bank *Things* in Practical English 1. The pronunciation focus is on plural endings, and in the speaking activity SS try to identify mystery objects photographed from a strange angle.

Optional lead-in (books closed)

- Play hangman with a word from **Vocabulary Bank *Things* part A** on *p.104*, e.g. *dictionary* (See *p.26* for how to play hangman).

1 VOCABULARY small things

a • Books open. Give SS time to write down the five things in the classroom.
- Check answers by getting SS to spell the words.

1	the board	4	a laptop
2	the door	5	a window
3	a chair		

b • Tell SS to go to part **B** of **Vocabulary Bank *Things*** on *p.104*.
- **2.1** Focus on the instructions for **a**. Play the CD and get SS to repeat the words in chorus. Use the pause button as necessary.
- Focus on the ⚠ box. Elicit/explain that we use *an* in front of a noun when it starts with a vowel sound, e.g. ***an** umbrella*, ***an** identity card*.

⚠ Point out that we only use *a* or *an* with singular nouns. *Glasses* is a plural noun (although it is one object), and this is true in English of things that have two parts, e.g. *trousers*. For this reason we <u>don't</u> say *a glasses*.

2.1		CD1 Track 53
a mobile	an umbrella	glasses
a pen	a credit card	an identity card
a bag	a photo	
a key	a watch	

- Focus on the instructions for **b**. Ask SS to cover the words and look at the photo. Give them time to remember the words with a partner. Remind SS to use *a* and *an* with all the nouns except *glasses*.

- Monitor and help, and correct any pronunciation mistakes.
- **Study Link** SS can find more practice of these words on the MultiROM and on the *New English File Beginner* website.

2 GRAMMAR singular and plural nouns; *a/an, the*

a • Focus on the photo and establish the context by asking *Where are the people?* (on a train).
- Focus on the text and elicit/explain the title.
- Read the first line of the text with SS and make sure they understand it. You could use L1 or a simple mime to elicit the meaning of *leave something on a train*. Make it clear that the five things are not in order.
- Focus on the instructions and give SS time to number the things 1–5 with a partner.

b • **2.2** Write numbers 1–5 in descending order on the board with 5 at the top.
- Tell SS they are going to hear the answers starting with number 5. Play the CD, pausing after each number to give SS time to write it in the correct box. Replay as necessary.
- Check answers starting with number 5 (see listening script 2.2). Ask *What's number 5?* and write the answer on the board next to number 5. Find out if any SS guessed all five right.

2.2	CD1 Track 54
Number 5 mobile phones **Number 4** glasses	
Number 3 umbrellas **Number 2** bags **Number 1** coats	

c • Demonstrate the concept of singular and plural by showing SS a pen and saying *pen*. Then show the class three pens and say *pens*. Write on the board: *singular = pen   plural = pens*
- Give SS time to write the plurals, then check answers.

2 chairs	3 books	4 laptops

d • Tell SS to go to **Grammar Bank 2A** on *p.90*.
- **2.3** Play the CD and ask SS to listen and repeat the example sentences. Use the pause button as necessary.

2.3		CD1 Track 55
What is it?	It's a book.	
What are they?	They're books.	
1 a book	books	
an umbrella	umbrellas	
a holiday	holidays	
2 a watch	watches	
3 a dictionary	dictionaries	

- Go through the rules with the class using the expanded information in the **Grammar notes** to help you. You may want to use SS' L1 here if you know it.

31

Grammar notes

Singular and plural nouns

- Regular nouns form the plural by simply adding an *s*. The only problem is the pronunciation, as the final *s* is sometimes pronounced /z/, e.g. *keys*, and sometimes /s/, e.g. *books*. This will be dealt with in **Pronunciation**.
- *es* is added to nouns ending in *-ch*, *-sh*, *-s*, *-ss*, and *-x*. This is because it would be impossible to pronounce the word by just adding an *s*, e.g. *watches*.
- With words ending in consonant + *y*, the *y* changes to *i* and *es* is added. This rule and the rule for adding *es* is important because it is also true for verbs in the third person in the present simple.

a/an, the

- Irregular plurals are dealt with in **2B**.
- Remind SS that we use *a/an* for **singular** things only, and we use *an* in front of a noun starting with a vowel sound.
- Explain that we use *the* to refer to something specific, e.g. *look at the board*, *open the door*, *close the windows*. We can use *the* with singular and plural nouns.
- Articles are easy for some nationalities and more difficult for others depending on their L1. If articles are a problem for your SS, give more examples to highlight the difference between *a/an* and *the*, e.g. *What is it? It's **a** door* (explaining what it is) and *Open **the** door* (talking about a specific door, e.g. the door of the classroom).

- Focus on the exercises for **2A** on *p.91*, and get SS to do them individually or in pairs. If they do them individually, get them to compare answers with a partner.
- Check answers.

a	2 It's a photo.	7	They're cities.
	3 They're watches.	8	It's an email.
	4 It's a chair.	9	They're buses.
	5 They're dictionaries.	10	It's an identity card.
	6 They're credit cards.		

b	1 What are they? They're laptops.
	2 What is it? It's a mobile (phone).
	3 What are they? They're keys.

> **Study Link** SS can find more practice of this grammar on the MultiROM and on the *New English File Beginner* website.

- **e** • Tell SS to go to **Communication** *Memory game* on *p.81*.
- Go through the instructions and make sure SS understand what they have to do.
- Check answers. See if any pair remembered all the things.

> The objects are two dictionaries, an umbrella, glasses, three keys, a mobile phone, two watches, a laptop, a clock, and three credit cards.

- Tell SS to go back to the main lesson on *p.14*.

3 PRONUNCIATION /z/ and /s/, plural endings

- Read the **Pronunciation notes** and decide how much of the information you want to give your SS.

Pronunciation notes

- For these sounds the phonetic symbols are the same as the alphabet letters. However, there is not an exact equivalence as the letter *s* can sometimes be /s/ or /z/.
- You may want to highlight the following sound–spelling patterns:
  - /z/   the letter *z* is always pronounced /z/, e.g. *zero*. The letter *s* at the end of a word is usually pronounced /z/, e.g. *keys*, *doors*.
  - /s/   the letter *s* at the beginning of a word is nearly always pronounced /s/, e.g. *sit*, *stand*. The letter *s* at the end of a word is pronounced /s/ at the end of a word after the 'unvoiced'* sounds /k/, /p/, /t/, and /f/, e.g. *books*, *laptops*, *coats*.
  - /ɪz/   *-es* is pronounced /ɪz/ when it is added after *ch*, *sh*, *s*, and *x*, e.g. *watches*, *buses*. Show SS that after these sounds it is very difficult to just add the /s/ sound, which is why the extra syllable is added. *-ies* is always pronounced /ɪz/, e.g. *countries*.

  *an **unvoiced** sound is one where the vocal chords in the throat do not vibrate; a **voiced** sound is one where the vocal chords vibrate. Tell SS that they can feel this by putting their hand on their throat and saying (unvoiced) *k-k-k-k*, followed by (voiced) *g-g-g-g*.

- ⚠ The difference between /s/ and /z/ is not easy for SS to notice or produce. We think it is useful to make SS aware that *s* can be /s/ or /z/ and to point out which sound it is on new words which have an *s* in them. However, don't expect perfect production at this early stage.

Extra support

You could tell SS that /s/ is the sound made by a snake ('sssss') and /z/ is the sound made by a mosquito ('zzzzz').

- **a** • **2.4** Focus on the exercise and play the CD once for SS to just listen.
- Focus on the sound picture *zebra* and write the word on the board. Play the CD to model and drill the word and sound (pause after the sound).
- Now focus on the words after *zebra*. Remind SS that the pink letters are the /z/ sound. Play the CD pausing after each word for SS to repeat.
- Repeat for *snake*.
- ⚠ As well as using the CD it may help if you model and drill the sounds yourself so that SS can see your mouth position.

2.4			CD1 Track 56
zebra	/z/	Brazil, zero, is, he's	
snake	/s/	six, seven, Spain, house	

> **Study Link** SS can find more practice of these sounds on the MultiROM and on the *New English File Beginner* website.

- **b** • **2.5** Now focus on the plurals. Explain to SS that in some cases the plural *s* is pronounced /z/, e.g. *chairs* and in others /s/, e.g. *books*. (See **Pronunciation notes**.)
- Highlight that the *-es* ending is pronounced /ɪz/, e.g. *watches*. Point out that it is two sounds (*fish* and *zebra*) so it does not have a picture.
- Play the CD for SS to listen. Then play it again pausing for SS to repeat.

2.5		CD1 Track 57
zebra	/z/	chairs, photos, keys, bags
snake	/s/	books, coats, laptops, clocks
	/ɪz/	watches, glasses, pieces, classes

c • **2.6** Focus on the instructions and demonstrate by saying a sentence and eliciting the plural from the class, e.g. *It's a bag* (They're bags). Then play the CD and pause after the first sentence. Ask SS what the plural is.

• Play the rest of the CD and give SS time to say the plural in chorus. Correct pronunciation as necessary.

• Repeat the activity, getting individual SS to respond.

2.6		CD1 Track 58
It's a photo…	They're photos.	
It's a class…	They're classes.	
It's a key…	They're keys.	
It's a door…	They're doors.	
It's a phone…	They're phones.	
It's a watch…	They're watches.	
It's a dictionary…	They're dictionaries.	
It's a table…	They're tables.	
It's a book…	They're books.	
It's a pen…	They're pens.	

4 SPEAKING & WRITING

a • Focus on the photos and the two questions. Model and drill pronunciation. Demonstrate by focusing on photo 1. Elicit from the class the question *What are they?* and the answer *They're books*.

• Give SS time to ask and answer questions about the photos.

• Monitor and correct any pronunciation mistakes.

• Check answers by asking the questions to individual SS.

1	They're books.	7	They're pieces of paper.
2	They're credit cards.	8	It's an ID card.
3	It's a watch.	9	They're pens.
4	They're keys.	10	It's a chair.
5	It's an umbrella.	11	They're glasses.
6	It's a mobile.	12	It's a laptop.

b • Focus on the instructions. Demonstrate the activity by showing SS what's in your bag/pocket and saying *In my bag I have…* and taking out any of the things mentioned that you have.

• Give SS time to see what they have in their bag/pocket.

• Ask them to tick (✓) or cross (✗) the things.

c • Tell SS they are going to write a sentence about what they have in their bag/pocket. Focus on the example and write *I have…* on the board. Elicit/explain the meaning.

• Give SS time to write their sentence. Remind them that they may have more than one of the things (e.g. pens, credit cards) in which case they should write the words in the plural without *a/an*. Monitor and help.

d • Tell SS to read their sentence to a partner.

• Monitor and correct any pronunciation mistakes.

Extra challenge

SS may want to name other things they have in their bag/pocket. If so, teach *How do you say … in English?* and write any new words on the board.

5 LISTENING

• **2.7** Focus on the instructions. Stress that each conversation mentions a small thing or things that they have just learnt in the **Vocabulary Bank**. They just have to listen for the thing/things mentioned.

• Play the first conversation twice and elicit the answer (bag). Then play the other four conversations.

• Check answers by playing the CD again and stopping after the relevant word in each conversation. For conversations 2 and 5 you could elicit that the people are in a hotel and a shop.

1	bag	3	mobile	5	credit card
2	keys	4	dictionary		

2.7		CD1 Track 59
1	A	Is this your bag?
	B	Oh! Yes, it is! Thank you.
2	A	Good afternoon.
	B	Hello. We're Paul Jones and Martin Smith. We have reservations.
	A	Let's see… Yes. Rooms 625 and 626. Here are your keys.
	A	Thank you.
	C	Thanks.
3	A	What's that music?
	B	Sorry, it's my mobile. Oh, hi Andy.
4	A	Excuse me, what's this word?
	B	Look in the dictionary.
5	A	How much is it?
	B	20 pounds.
	A	Is a credit card OK?
	B	Yes, of course.

WORDS AND PHRASES TO LEARN

Focus on the words and phrases to learn. Make sure SS understand the meaning of each phrase. If necessary, remind SS of the context in which they came up in the lesson. If you speak your SS' L1, you might like to elicit a translation for the words/phrases for the SS to write next to them.

Study Link SS can find more practice of these words and phrases on the MultiROM and on the *New English File Beginner* website.

Extra photocopiable activities

Grammar
singular and plural nouns; *a / an p.127*
Communicative
The same or different? *p.166* (instructions *p.154*)

HOMEWORK

Study Link Workbook *pp.12–13*

2B

G possessive adjectives; possessive *s*
V people and family
P /ð/, /ʌ/, and /ə/

Family and friends

Lesson plan

In this lesson SS first learn the possessive adjectives through some short dialogues, and then learn the words for people and family members in the Vocabulary Bank, and also some irregular plurals. The new vocabulary is supported by the pronunciation section, which highlights common sounds in the new words. In the second half of the lesson famous film pairs provide the context for a second grammar focus (the possessive *s*). The lesson ends with SS talking and writing about their family.

⚠ This lesson will probably take you longer than previous ones as there are two grammar focuses and SS go to the Grammar Bank twice.

Optional lead-in (books closed)

- Show SS an object which is yours, e.g. a board pen, and ask SS *What is it?* (It's a pen).
- Agree, a little unenthusiastically, with SS and then say, e.g. *It's **my** pen.*
- Model and drill with normal intonation.
- Point to different objects belonging to SS, e.g. a bag, a coat, a chair, a table, a book, a dictionary, a pen, a watch, and ask *What is it?* to elicit from the student *It's my bag, It's my coat*, etc.

1 GRAMMAR possessive adjectives

a ● **2.8** Books open. Focus on the pictures and get SS to cover the dialogues with their hand or a piece of paper. Explain that they're going to hear three dialogues and they have to number the pictures in the right order.

- Play the CD once for SS to listen and number the pictures. Check answers.

A 3 **B** 1 **C** 2

2.8	CD1 Track 60

1 A Hey! That's my bag.
  B No, it isn't. It's my bag. Your bag's there.

2 A And here are our children.
  B What are their names?
  A Her name's Lucy and his name's Eric.
  B Hello. And who's this?
  C It's my parrot.
  B What's its name?
  C Polly.
  B Hello Polly.

3 A Excuse me, where are our coats?
  B Sorry?
  A Where are our coats?
  B Your coats – they're over there on the chair.
  A Thank you. Goodnight.
  B Bye.

---

b ● Play the CD again and go through the dialogues with SS line by line. Elicit/explain/demonstrate any new words or phrases, e.g. *here are our children, parrot, over there*. Contrast *over there* with *there* (*over there* suggests a greater distance from the speaker).

⚠ Remind SS that animals are usually *it*. However, if you know whether an animal is male or female, for example, because it is your pet, you can say *he* or *she*.

- Focus on the instructions and give SS a few minutes to complete the chart.
- Check answers, writing the missing words on the board. You could also ask SS to spell the words to revise spelling.

I	*my*	we	*our*
you	*your*	you	*your*
he	*his*	they	*their*
she	*her*		
it	*its*		

c ● Tell SS to go to **Grammar Bank 2B** on *p.90*.
- **2.9** Focus on **possessive adjectives**. Play the CD and ask SS to listen and repeat the example sentences. Use the pause button as necessary.

2.9	CD1 Track 61

My name is Ana.
Your name is Ben.
His name is Marco.
Her name is Maki.
Its name is Polly.
Our names are Selma and Luis.
Your names are Marek and Ania.
Their names are Pedro and Maria.

- Go through the rules for possessive adjectives with the class using the expanded information in the **Grammar notes** below to help you. You may want to use L1 here if you know it.

Grammar notes

- Some languages use the same possessive adjective for *he*, *she*, and *it*. Highlight that in English we use three different possessive adjectives, i.e. *his* for *he*, *her* for *she*, and *its* for *it*.
- In some languages the possessive adjective agrees with the following noun, i.e. it can be masculine, feminine, plural, etc. depending on the gender, number, etc. of the noun that comes after it. In English nouns don't have gender, so adjectives don't change, and the use of *his/her* simply depends on whether we are talking about something belonging to a man or to a woman.
- Remind SS that *your* is used for singular and plural, formal and informal.
- If SS don't know the difference between an adjective and a pronoun, explain (in their L1 if you prefer) that we use a pronoun **in place of** a name or noun, e.g. *James = he*, but an adjective goes **with** a noun, e.g. *his name, French food*, etc.

⚠ Point out that the possessive adjective *its* has no apostrophe. SS may confuse this with *it's = it is*.

- Focus on exercise **a** in **2B** on *p.91*, and get SS to do it in pairs or individually. If they do it individually, get them to compare answers with a partner.
- Check answers.

a	**1** Their	**4** Our	**7** your
	2 your	**5** Its	**8** my
	3 His	**6** Her	

Study Link SS can find more practice of this grammar on the MultiROM and on the *New English File Beginner* website.

- Tell SS to go back to the main lesson on *p.16*.
- Now get SS to practise the dialogues in **a** in pairs. Rehearse dialogue 1 with the class before they read it, either getting SS to repeat it after you or the CD. SS read the dialogue and then swap roles.
- Now do the same for the other two dialogues. For dialogue 2, the person who is reading **A** also reads **C**.

d • Focus on the instructions and demonstrate the activity. Point to one student and ask another student *What's his/her name?* Elicit *His/her name is ….* Repeat with a different student.
- Tell one student to ask you about another *What's his/her name?* Pretend that you can't remember the name. Model and drill *I can't remember.*
- Put SS in pairs and give them a few minutes to ask and answer questions about the other SS' names.
- Monitor and help with any pronunciation problems.

2 VOCABULARY people and family

a • Focus on the instructions and give SS time to match the items and the pictures.
- Check answers and elicit the meaning of *man, woman, children, boys*.

a man, a woman, and two children	C
men and women	A
two boys	B

b • Tell SS to go to **Vocabulary Bank** *People and family* on *p.105*. Focus on the first part **People**.
- **2.10** Focus on the instructions for **a**. Play the CD and get SS to repeat the words in chorus. Use the pause button as necessary. Model and drill any words which are difficult for your SS and give extra practice. Remind SS that the underlined syllables are stressed more strongly.

2.10		CD1 Track 62
a boy	a man	children
a girl	a woman	friends

- Focus on the instructions for **b**. Ask SS to cover the words and look at the photos. Tell them to say the words. They could do this with a partner.
- Focus on the instructions for **c**. Go through the information in the box with SS. Explain that these four words have irregular plurals.
- **2.11** Play the CD and get SS to repeat the plural words in chorus and individually. Highlight how the pronunciation changes in *woman/women* and *child/children*. Replay as necessary. Model and drill any words which are difficult for your SS and give extra practice.

2.11	CD1 Track 63
a child – children	
a man – men	
a woman – women	
a person – people	

- Focus on the instructions for **d**. Ask SS to cover the plural words and say them. They could do this with a partner.
- Monitor and help. Make a note of any pronunciation problems SS are having. Write these words on the board, and model and drill them.
- Focus on the second part **Family**.
- **2.12** Focus on the instructions for **a**. Play the CD and get SS to repeat the words in chorus and individually.

2.12		CD1 Track 64
husband	daughter	
wife	sister	
mother	brother	
father	boyfriend	
son	girlfriend	

- Focus on the instructions for **b**. Ask SS to cover the words and look at the photos. Tell them to say the words. They could do this with a partner.
- Focus on the instructions for **c**. Put SS in pairs, **A** and **B**. Tell **B** to close their book. Tell **A** to ask **B** to spell five words. Demonstrate with a good pair.
- When SS have finished, tell them to swap.

Study Link SS can find more practice of these words on the MultiROM and on the *New English File Beginner* website.

- Tell SS to go back to the main lesson on *p.16*.

3 PRONUNCIATION /ð/, /ʌ/, and /ə/

- Read the **Pronunciation notes** and decide how much of the information you want to give your SS.

Pronunciation notes

- SS may have problems with these sounds as they may not exist in their language. The phonetic symbols are not as easily recognizable as some others.
- If SS have problems with the /ð/ sound, show them the correct mouth position, i.e. with the tongue behind the teeth.
- You may want to highlight the following sound–spelling patterns:
  - /ð/ The letters *th* are often pronounced /ð/, e.g. *father*. However, they can also be /θ/ as in *thanks, three*.
  - /ʌ/ The letter *u* is often pronounced /ʌ/, especially between consonants, e.g. *husband, Russia*. The letter *o* is sometimes pronounced /ʌ/, e.g. *mother*.
  - /ə/ This is the most common vowel sound in English. Many unstressed syllables have this sound, e.g. the **bold** syllables in Br**a**zil, **A**merica, p**a**per, dicti**o**nary.

⚠ These three sounds are **voiced** sounds. For an explanation of voiced and unvoiced sounds see **Pronunciation notes 2A** on *p.32*.

a • **2.13** Focus on the sound picture *mother* and write the word on the board. Play the CD to model and drill the word and sound (pause after the sound).

- Now focus on the words after *mother*. Remind SS that the pink letters are the /ð/ sound. Play the CD pausing after each word for SS to repeat.
- Repeat for the other two sounds and words (*up* and *computer*).
- Focus especially on sounds that are difficult for your SS and model them so that SS can see your mouth position. Get SS to repeat these sounds a few more times.

2.13		CD1 Track 65
mother	/ð/	father, they, their, the
up	/ʌ/	brother, husband, son, mother
computer	/ə/	sister, person, woman, children

Study Link SS can find more practice of these sounds on the MultiROM and on the *New English File Beginner* website.

b ● **2.14** Focus on the sentences and play the CD just for SS to listen. Then play the CD for SS to listen and repeat.

2.14	CD1 Track 66
The woman over there is my mother.	
I have one brother and three sons.	
My husband and my father are teachers.	

- Tell SS to practise the sentences in pairs. Monitor and help with any pronunciation problems.

4 GRAMMAR possessive *s*

a ● Focus on the two rows of pictures and the instructions. Elicit from the class the names of the films (in English or your SS' own language) and write them on the board: *Sex and the City*, *Pirates of the Caribbean*, *Sense and Sensibility*, *Mamma Mia!*, *The Queen*
- Go through characters A–E, and model and drill the pronunciation of names. Then do the same for characters 1–5. Point to a photo and model and drill the question *What's his/her name?*
- Demonstrate the activity by focusing on picture A (Miranda) and eliciting from the class the person from 1–5 who is paired with her (picture 3 Carrie).
- Give SS, in pairs, time to match the film characters. Check answers by asking SS to read out the numbers and letters or the two names. Write the answers on the board.

A 3	B 4	C 5	D 1	E 2

b ● Focus on the instructions. Elicit the answer to the first sentence. Although SS may not have seen the possessive *s* before, they should have no problem understanding *Carrie's friend*.
- Give SS time, in pairs, to complete the other sentences with a name.

c ● **2.15** Play the CD for SS to check. Check answers.

Extra support

Play the CD and get SS to listen and repeat sentences 1–5, chorally and individually.

1	Miranda
2	Donna
3	Captain Teague
4	Elinor
5	Prince Philip

2.15	CD1 Track 67
1 Miranda is Carrie's friend.	
2 Donna is Sophie's mother.	
3 Captain Teague is Jack Sparrow's father.	
4 Elinor is Marianne's sister.	
5 Prince Philip is the Queen's husband.	

d ● Tell SS to go to **Grammar Bank 2B** on *p.90*.
- **2.16** Focus on **possessive** *s*. Play the CD and ask SS to listen and repeat the example sentences. Use the pause button as necessary.

2.16	CD1 Track 68
Miranda is Carrie's friend.	
This is Jack's car.	
Ella is Ben's wife.	
My sister's name is Molly.	

- Go through the rules for possessive *s* with the class using the expanded information in the **Grammar notes** below to help you. You may want to use L1 here if you know it.

Grammar notes

- Many languages use a word equivalent to *of* to indicate possession. In English, instead of saying, e.g. *the brother of Jack,* we say *Jack's brother*.
- Highlight that we use the possessive *s* to talk about what people have, e.g. family members, possessions, etc., e.g. *Jack's brother/Jack's car*.
- The pronunciation of possessive *s* can be /z/, e.g. *Harry's*, or /s/, e.g. *Jack's*. This depends on whether the last sound of the name is voiced or unvoiced (see **Pronunciation notes 2A** on *p.32* for an explanation of voiced and unvoiced sounds). This is a small difference, which you may not want to focus on at this level.
- Point out that if a name already ends in *s*, you can add the possessive *s* in the same way, and it is pronounced /ɪz/, e.g. *James's* /ˈdʒeɪmzɪz/.
- **⚠** Highlight that SS need to be careful when they see an apostrophe *'s* after a name as it may be a contracted form of *is* (e.g. *Jack's from the United States*) or it may be the possessive *s* (e.g. *Jack's car is Japanese*).

- Focus on exercise **b** in **2B** on *p.91* and get SS to do it individually or in pairs. If they do it individually, get them to compare answers with a partner.
- Check answers.

1	David is Angela's brother.
2	This is Antonio's book.
3	Ann is Mark's mother.
4	They're Sara's children.
5	My brother's car is a Fiat.
6	Jim is Sally's boyfriend.
7	This is Tim's pen.
8	They're my sister's keys.

- Focus on the instructions for **c**. Give SS time to say sentences 1–8. You could ask them to do this with a partner.

Study Link SS can find more practice of this grammar on the MultiROM and on the *New English File Beginner* website.

- Tell SS to go back to the main lesson on *p.17*.

e ● Focus on the photos A–E. Tell SS to cover the sentences in **b**. Point to Miranda and ask *Who's Miranda?* (She's Carrie's friend).

● Model and drill the question *Who's Miranda?* Elicit questions for the other photos (*Who's Captain Teague? Who's Elinor?* etc.).

● Give SS time to ask and answer questions about the photos A–E.

Extra challenge

You could get SS to ask questions about photos 1–5, e.g. *Who's Jack Sparrow?* (He's Captain Teague's son).

f ● Tell SS they are now going to talk about their own friends and family.

● Demonstrate the activity: write the names of six people you know on the board. Try to include at least one person who is, e.g. your *sister's son,* to give SS practice in hearing the possessive *s*.

● Get SS to ask you *Who's …?* about the people, and tell them who they are.

● Finally, test their memory. Say *Can you remember? Who's …?* to elicit *He/She's your…*

● Now focus on the instructions and get SS to write the names of six people, family or friends, on a piece of paper.

● Put SS in pairs, **A** and **B**, and ask them to exchange papers.

● Give SS time to ask each other about the people on the piece of paper.

● Monitor and help. Correct any problems on the board.

Extra challenge

Get **A** to test **B**'s memory using his/her piece of paper and asking **B** *Can you remember? Who's …?*

5 WRITING & SPEAKING

a ● Focus on the instructions. Give SS time to read the text and write the names on the photo. Check answers.

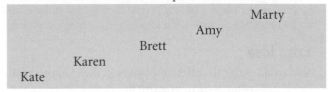

Marty
Amy
Brett
Karen
Kate

b ● Tell SS they are now going to write about their families. Explain that they should follow the model in **a**.

● Give SS time to write their text. Monitor and help with grammar, spelling, and vocabulary.

c ● Tell SS to read out their text to a partner.

Extra challenge

You could get SS to draw a family tree and tell their partner about their family from memory.

WORDS AND PHRASES TO LEARN

Focus on the words and phrases to learn. Make sure SS understand the meaning of each phrase. If necessary, remind SS of the context in which they came up in the lesson. If you speak your SS' L1, you might like to elicit a translation for the words/phrases for the SS to write next to them.

Study Link SS can find more practice of these words and phrases on the MultiROM and on the *New English File Beginner* website.

Extra photocopiable activities

Grammar
possessive adjectives *p.128*
possessive *s p.129*
Communicative
Happy families *p.167* (instructions *p.154*)

HOMEWORK

Study Link **Workbook** *pp.14–15*

2C

G adjectives
V colours and common adjectives
P /æ/, /eɪ/, /ɑː/, and /ɔː/

A man's car or a woman's car?

Lesson plan

This lesson uses the context of cars for SS to learn some common adjectives and how to use them. Although the grammar of adjectives is very simple, the vocabulary load is quite high in this lesson as it includes both colours and common adjectives. After the grammar SS read their first 'real' text, an article adapted from a US magazine about men's cars and women's cars. Pronunciation focuses on four different sounds of the letter *a*. The lesson ends with SS speaking and writing about their car and their dream car, and finally with the song *You're beautiful*.

Optional lead-in (books closed)

● Write the lesson title on the board. Then ask SS *Is a* (e.g. *Ford Ka*) *a man's car or a woman's car?* You may then also want to teach *both*.

● Elicit more makes and models of cars that SS think are men's or women's cars.

● Alternatively, you could bring in pictures of different models of cars and ask SS for each *Is it a man's car or a woman's car?*

1 VOCABULARY & SPEAKING colours and common adjectives

a ● **2.17** Books open. Focus on the photos and the instructions. Elicit the meaning of *French* and *German*.

● Give SS time to match the nationalities to the cars. Play the CD for SS to listen and check their answers.

American = 1	German = 5
British = 3	Italian = 6
French = 2	Japanese = 4

2.17	CD1 Track 69
1 It's American.	4 It's Japanese.
2 It's French.	5 It's German.
3 It's British.	6 It's Italian.

● Now elicit what cars they are. Ask *What car is it?* then write the cars on the board (1 = a Ford Mustang, 2 = a 2CV, 3 = a Mini, 4 = a Mazda Miata, 5 = a VW Beetle, 6 = a Ferrari).

b ● **2.18** Focus on the photos and on the dialogue. Play the CD for SS to listen and read.

2.18 / **2.19**	CD1 Tracks 70/71
Tim	Wow! Look at that car. It's fantastic!
Sue	It's a man's car.
Tim	A man's car?
Sue	Yes. It's fast and red. And it's very expensive. Wow! Look at that yellow car. It's fantastic!
Tim	It's a woman's car.

● Then ask SS *What are the two cars?* and elicit the answers.

| The man's car is the Ferrari. |
| The woman's car is the VW Beetle. |

Extra challenge

You could get SS to cover the dialogue with a piece of paper and just listen to the CD to answer the question.

c ● Focus on the highlighted words in the dialogue. Get SS to guess what they mean with a partner. Check answers by asking individual pairs for their ideas.

d ● **2.19** Play the CD again pausing after each phrase for SS to listen and repeat. Encourage SS to copy the rhythm and intonation. Elicit/explain/demonstrate that *Wow!* = an expression which shows great surprise or admiration.

● Put SS in pairs, **A** and **B**. Assign roles and get them to practise the dialogue.

● Monitor and help, encouraging SS to use the intonation from the CD, e.g. *Wow!* and *fantastic!*

e ● Tell SS to go to **Vocabulary Bank** *Adjectives* on *p.106*. Focus on the first part **Colours**.

● **2.20** Focus on the instructions for **a**. Play the CD and get SS to repeat the colours. Replay as necessary. Model and drill any problem words.

2.20			CD1 Track 72
red	yellow	orange	black
green	blue	brown	white

● Focus on the instructions for **b**. Ask SS to cover the words and say the colours. They could do this with a partner.

● Monitor and help. Make a note of any pronunciation problems they are having. Write the words on the board and model and drill difficult ones, e.g. *orange* and *yellow*.

Extra idea

You could point to different objects in the classroom and say *What colour is it?* to practise the eight colours in the Vocabulary Bank.

● Focus on the second part **Common adjectives**.

● **2.21** Focus on the instructions for **a**. Play the CD and get SS to repeat the adjectives in chorus and individually. Replay as necessary. Model and drill any words which are difficult for your SS and give extra practice.

2.21	CD1 Track 73
big – small   old – new   fast – slow   good – bad
cheap – expensive   long – short   tall – short

● Focus on the instructions for **b**. Ask SS to cover the words and say the adjectives. They could do this with a partner.

● Focus on the instructions for **c**. Model and drill the question *What's the opposite of 'new'?* and elicit/explain the meaning of *the opposite*.

- Give SS a few minutes to test each other on the adjectives.
- Monitor and correct any pronunciation mistakes on the board.
- **2.22** Focus on the box in **d**. Play the CD for SS to listen and repeat. Explain that we normally use *good-looking* for a man, but *beautiful* for a woman, and that *very* can be used with many adjectives, e.g. *very big*, *very expensive*, etc.

2.22	CD1 Track 74
good – very good – fantastic! bad – very bad – terrible! good-looking beautiful	

Study Link SS can find more practice of these words on the MultiROM and on the *New English File Beginner* website.

- Tell SS to go back to the main lesson on *p.18*.

f
- Focus on the photos of the cars and the instructions for **1**. Model and drill the question *What colour is it?*
- Give SS a few minutes to ask and answer questions about the cars in pairs.
- Monitor and correct any mistakes with pronunciation.
- Focus on the instructions for **2**. Give SS a few minutes to think of two adjectives for each car.

Extra support

SS could write a sentence with two adjectives about each car, e.g. *The 2CV is small and cheap.*

- Focus on the instructions for **3**. Demonstrate the activity by choosing a car and inviting SS to ask you questions, e.g. *Is it French? Is it expensive?*
- Give SS a few minutes to play the guessing game in pairs.

2 GRAMMAR adjectives

a
- Focus on the sentences and give SS time to circle the right one. Check answers.

1 a   2 b

b
- Tell SS to go to **Grammar Bank 2C** on *p.90*.
- **2.23** Play the CD and ask SS to listen and repeat the example sentences. Use the pause button as necessary.

2.23	CD1 Track 75
A Ferrari is expensive. It's a fast car. My glasses are new. They're old men.	

- Go through the rules with the class using the expanded information in the **Grammar notes** below to help you. You may want to use SS' L1 here if you know it.

Grammar notes

- In English an adjective can go after the verb *be*, but when it is with a noun it always goes BEFORE the noun, e.g. *My car is fast. It's a fast car.*
- Adjectives are the same for singular and plural nouns, unlike in many other languages, so you never add an *s* to an adjective.
- Adjectives have no masculine or feminine form.

- Focus on the exercises for **2C** on *p.91* and get SS to do them individually or in pairs. If they do them individually, get them to compare answers with a partner.
- Check answers.

a	2	It's an expensive car.
	3	They're orange umbrellas.
	4	It's a slow train.
	5	They're new glasses.
	6	It's a good book.
b	1	It's a fast car.
	2	They're very big dogs.
	3	It's a terrible photo.
	4	Maria is a very beautiful girl.
	5	This isn't a very good hotel.
	6	Their house is very small.
	7	Mark's mobile is new.
	8	Italian bags are very expensive.

c
- Now tell SS to go to **Vocabulary Bank** *Adjectives* on *p.106*.
- Focus on the picture of the mobile and elicit *It's a red mobile*. Do the same with *It's a big house*.
- Get SS to make ten sentences about the pictures in pairs.
- Monitor and help with pronunciation. Correct any grammar mistakes on the board.

Study Link SS can find more practice of this grammar on the MultiROM and on the *New English File Beginner* website.

- Tell SS to go back to the main lesson on *p.18*.

3 READING

a
- Focus on the photos and the title. Point to the Mercedes and ask *Is it a man's car or a woman's car?* (a man's car). Ask SS *Why?* (It's big, it's fast, etc.). Repeat for the VW Beetle convertible.
- Focus on the task and the questions. Elicit the meaning of *easy to park*, *luxurious* /lʌgˈzʊərɪəs/, *macho*, and *safe*.
- Then ask SS *Is question 1 (Is it a nice colour?) important for men or for women?* Elicit that it's probably more important for women, and show them how number 1 has been filled in in the first part of the article.
- Give SS, in pairs, time to write the other numbers for the questions into the article.

b
- Now focus on the article. Show SS that it is adapted from *Forbes*, an American magazine. This is the first real reading text that SS have been faced with, so emphasize that when they read they should try to focus on the words they know, and try to guess the meaning of new words.
- Give SS time to read the article on their own and check they have written in the right questions.
- Now read the first paragraph aloud slowly and deal with any problems with vocabulary, e.g. *popular*, *drivers*, *top speed*. Then check answers to what the four important questions for men are.

2, 3, 6, and 7

- Repeat with the second paragraph and elicit/explain the meaning of *convertible* and *prefer*. Then check what the four important questions for women are.

1, 4, 5, and 8

- Ask SS if they agree with the information in the article, e.g. say *Do you think this is true?*

4 PRONUNCIATION /æ/, /eɪ/, /ɑː/, and /ɔː/

- Read the **Pronunciation notes** and decide how much of the information you want to give your SS.

Pronunciation notes

- The letter *a* can be pronounced in several different ways, e.g. /æ/ *black*, /eɪ/ *day*, /ɑː/ *fast*, and /ɔː/ *tall*.
- You may want to highlight the following sound–spelling patterns:

  /æ/   *a* between consonants is often pronounced /æ/, e.g. *black*, *cat*.

  /eɪ/   The letters *ai* and *ay* are usually pronounced /eɪ/, e.g. *train*, *day*.

  /ɑː/   The letters *ar* are usually pronounced /ɑː/, e.g. *car*, *are*.

  /ɔː/   The letters *all* and *au* usually have an /ɔː/ sound, e.g. *call*, *daughter*.

- You could also point out that /eɪ/ is a diphthong (i.e. two sounds) if you think this will help SS.

⚠ In US English and many varieties of British English words like *fast* and *glasses* are pronounced /fæst/ and /ˈglæsɪz/. If this is the way you pronounce them, you may want to explain this to SS, and teach them your pronunciation rather than the pronunciation on the CD.

a ● **2.24** Focus on the sound picture *cat* and write the word on the board. Play the CD to model and drill the word and sound (pause after the sound). Replay the CD as necessary.

- Now focus on the words after *cat*. Remind SS that the pink letters are the /æ/ sound. Play the CD pausing after each word for SS to repeat.

- Repeat for the other three sounds and words (*train*, *car*, and *horse*). Remind SS that the two dots in the symbols /ɑː/ and /ɔː/ mean that they are long sounds.

- Focus especially on sounds that are difficult for your SS and model them so that SS can see your mouth position. Get SS to repeat these sounds a few more times.

2.24		CD1 Track 76
cat	/æ/	black, fantastic, bad, family, man
train	/eɪ/	same, day, say, table
car	/ɑː/	fast, glasses, card, father
horse	/ɔː/	tall, small, short, daughter board, door

Study Link SS can find more practice of these sounds on the MultiROM and on the *New English File Beginner* website.

b ● **2.25** Focus on the sentences and play the CD just for SS to listen. Then play the CD for SS to listen and repeat.

2.25		CD1 Track 77
a black cat	fast cars	
a fantastic family	a small ball	
the same day		

- Tell SS to practise the phrases in pairs. Monitor and help with any pronunciation problems.

5 SPEAKING & WRITING

a ● Demonstrate the activity by telling SS about your car, if you have one.

- Focus on the instructions and get SS to talk about their car(s) or their family's car(s) in small groups. Give SS a few moments to think about what they are going to say.
- Monitor and help with vocabulary. Correct any mistakes with pronunciation or grammar on the board.
- Get feedback from one or two SS.

b ● Focus on the instructions. Demonstrate by using the model text to tell SS what your dream car is.

- Then give SS time to complete the spaces. Monitor and help with vocabulary and spelling.

c ● Get SS to tell each other about their dream cars.

- Get feedback to find out what some SS' dream cars are.

6 ● 2.26 SONG ♫ *You're beautiful*

- This song was a Number One hit for the singer James Blunt in 2005. It is about seeing an ex-girlfriend on the London Underground with her new boyfriend. For copyright reasons this is a cover version.
- As with any authentic pop song there will be quite a lot of new vocabulary and grammar. The activity for this song revises personal pronouns and possessive adjectives, which they know.
- If you want to do this song in class, use the photocopiable activity on *p.203*.

2.26	CD1 Track 78

You're beautiful

My life is brilliant (x2)
My love is pure
I saw an angel
Of that I'm sure
She smiled at me on the subway
She was with another man
But I won't lose no sleep on that
'cause I've got a plan

Chorus
You're beautiful,
You're beautiful
You're beautiful, it's true
I saw your face in a crowded place
But I don't know what to do
'cause I'll never be with you

Yes she caught my eye
As we walked on by
She could see from my face that I was
Flying high
And I don't think that I'll see her again
But we shared a moment that will last till the end

Chorus

La la la la la la la la la

You're beautiful,
You're beautiful
You're beautiful, it's true
There was an angel with a smile on her face
When she thought that I should be with you
But it's time to face the truth
I will never be with you

WORDS AND PHRASES TO LEARN

Focus on the words and phrases to learn. Make sure SS understand the meaning of each phrase. If necessary, remind SS of the context in which they came up in the lesson. If you speak your SS' L1, you might like to elicit a translation for the words/phrases for the SS to write next to them.

Study Link SS can find more practice of these words and phrases on the MultiROM and on the *New English File Beginner* website.

Extra photocopiable activities

Grammar
adjectives *p.130*
Communicative
What is it? *p.168* (instructions *p.154*)
Song
You're beautiful p.203 (instructions *p.200*)

HOMEWORK

Study Link **Workbook** *pp.16–17*

Introducing people
Phone numbers
Numbers 21–100
Personal information: age, address, etc.

Lesson plan

In this lesson two dialogues provide the context for SS to learn how to introduce other people, and to ask how people are. The vocabulary focus is on numbers from 21–100 and words related to personal information, e.g. *address, postcode, married*, etc. In **People in the street** SS hear people talking about their brothers and sisters and how old they are. SS practise giving their own personal information by filling in a form. We have avoided forcing SS to ask what may be sensitive questions, e.g. *How old are you? Are you married?* and these questions are practised using invented information.

Optional lead-in (books closed)

- Bring in photos of members of your family (or draw funny drawings of them on the board).
- Explain to the class who the people are, saying, e.g. *This is my mother*. Elicit *What's her name?* and answer the question. Continue with the other people in the photos.
- Model and drill the phrase *This is my mother/brother/girlfriend/husband*, etc. in chorus and individually.

1 INTRODUCING PEOPLE

a ● **2.27** Books open. Focus on the instructions and get SS to cover the dialogues.
- Play the CD for SS to listen and mark the sentences T or F. Replay as necessary. Check answers.

1 F **2** F

Extra idea

Write the two questions on the board and get SS to listen the first time with their books closed to avoid the temptation to read and listen.

Extra challenge

Ask SS why the sentences are false (**1** Helen is Mike's friend, **2** The girl's brother is 26).

2.27 / **2.28**	CD1 Tracks 79/80

1 **A** Hello Mike.
 B **Hi** Sam. How are you?
 A Fine, thanks. And **you**?
 B I'm OK, thanks. This is Helen. She's a **friend** from work.
 A **Nice** to meet you.
 C Hi.
 B **Sorry**, we're in a hurry. See you soon. Bye.
 A **Bye**.

2 A Look. This is my **brother**.
B Wow. He's **very** good-looking. What's his **name**?
A Adam.
B **Is** he married?
A No, he isn't.
B How old is he?
A **He's** twenty-six.
B What's his **mobile** number?

b • Focus on dialogue 1 and play the CD again for SS to listen and complete it. Replay as necessary. Check answers (see listening script 2.27).

• Now do the same for dialogue 2.

c • **2.28** Go through dialogue 1 with SS line by line and elicit/explain/demonstrate the meaning of the new words and phrases, e.g. *How are you? Fine, thanks. This is (Helen), we're in a hurry, See you soon.*

• Highlight that *(I'm) fine/OK* are common replies to the question *How are you?*

• Highlight the use of *This is...* to introduce someone (SS saw this phrase in lesson **1C**). To SS of some languages this use of *this* (as opposed to *he* or *she*) may sound strange.

• Now go through the second dialogue, which introduces new questions, e.g. *How old is he? Is he married?* You may want to teach the opposite, *single*.

• Play the CD again for SS to listen and repeat the two dialogues. Encourage SS to copy the rhythm and intonation. Replay as necessary. Highlight the difference between <u>How</u> are you? and How <u>old</u> are you? by writing them on the board and drilling the pronunciation. Getting SS to underline the stressed syllable will help them say the phrases correctly.

d • Get SS to practise the dialogue in pairs. In the first dialogue, whoever reads **B** should also read **C**.

• Monitor and help. Make a note of any pronunciation problems they are having. Write the words or phrases on the board and model and drill them.

2 VOCABULARY phone numbers, 21–100

a • **2.29** Focus on the information in the box. Highlight that we usually say *oh* for *zero* in phone numbers and that we often say *double* for two numbers which are the same.

⚠ Many native speakers use *double*. However, it is also acceptable to just say the number twice, so don't over-correct your SS if they don't always remember to use *double*.

• Focus on the instructions. Play the CD as many times as you think SS need to write the phone number.

• Check the answer (see listening script 2.29) by asking one student to read out the number. Write it on the board.

• Explain that when we give phone numbers we give the individual digits, (usually in blocks of three or four), so that 3074128 is said as *three oh seven, four one two eight*. We <u>don't</u> say *thirty, seventy four, a hundred and twenty eight* as some nationalities might do.

2.29	CD1 Track 81

A What's your phone number?
B 0207 946 8522 (oh-two-oh-seven, nine four six, eight five double-two).
A Sorry?
B 0207 946 8522.

b • Focus on the first number. Ask an individual student to say it, and write what he/she says on the board for the class to check. Repeat with the other two numbers.

• **2.30** Play the CD for SS to listen and check. Pause the CD after each phone number and get SS to repeat it.

2.30	CD1 Track 82

1 6885713 (six double eight, five seven one three)
2 844 79029 (eight double-four, seven nine oh two nine)
3 0131 496 0261 (oh one three one, four nine six, oh two six one)

• Finally, get SS to practise saying them with a partner.

c • Focus on the dialogue in **a**. Get SS to practise the dialogue in pairs using their own number. Tell them to practise until they can say it fluently.

⚠ If SS aren't happy about using their own phone number, tell them to invent a number but with a normal number of digits from the area where they live.

• Monitor and help, encouraging SS to break the phone number up into blocks so it sounds more natural.

Extra support

You could ask SS to write their phone number on a piece of paper to read out in the dialogue.

Extra idea

You could get SS to mingle as a whole class to ask each other's phone number.

d • Tell SS to go to **Vocabulary Bank** *Numbers* on *p.102*. Focus on part **C Numbers 21–100**.

• **2.31** Focus on the instructions for **a**. Play the CD and get SS to repeat the numbers in chorus. Use the pause button as necessary. Remind SS that the underlined syllables are stressed more strongly. This is very important in the case of, e.g. *thirty, forty*, etc. (see below). Replay as necessary.

2.31			CD1 Track 83
21	twenty-one	66	sixty-six
22	twenty-two	70	seventy
30	thirty	77	seventy-seven
33	thirty-three	80	eighty
40	forty	88	eighty-eight
44	forty-four	90	ninety
50	fifty	99	ninety-nine
55	fifty-five	100	a hundred
60	sixty		

• Go through the information in the box and highlight that the stress on *thirty, forty*, etc. is on the **first** syllable whereas the stress on *thirteen, fourteen*, etc. is on the **second** syllable.

• Focus on the instructions for **b**. Ask SS to cover the words and say the numbers. They could do this with a partner.

• Monitor and help. Model and drill any problem numbers.

- Finally, write a variety of two-digit numbers up on the board for SS to practise saying them.

  Study Link SS can find more practice of these words on the MultiROM and on the *New English File Beginner* website.
- Tell SS to go back to the main lesson on *p.20*.

e ● **2.32** Remind SS of the rule about stress on numbers like *thirteen* and *thirty*.
- Focus on the activity and play the CD for SS to listen to the difference between the two numbers. Replay as necessary.

2.32							CD1 Track 84
1 a 13	**b** 30			**5 a** 17	**b** 70		
2 a 14	**b** 40			**6 a** 18	**b** 80		
3 a 15	**b** 50			**7 a** 19	**b** 90		
4 a 16	**b** 60						

f ● **2.33** Focus on the instructions and play the CD once for SS to circle the numbers.
- Play the CD again to check the answers.

1 a	**2** b	**3** b	**4** a	**5** b	**6** a	**7** a

2.33							CD1 Track 85
1 13	**2** 40	**3** 50	**4** 16	**5** 70	**6** 18	**7** 19	

- Get SS to practise saying the numbers in pairs. Monitor and help. Make a note of any pronunciation problems they are having. Write the words on the board and model and drill the ones that SS find difficult.

g ● Focus on the question. Remind SS of the meaning and pronunciation of *How old is he?*
- Go through the information in the box. Highlight that the usual way in conversation to say your or someone else's age is to just say the number, e.g. *I'm 20*. The full form *I'm twenty years old* is seen more in written English.
  ⚠ Watch out for the typical errors *I'm 20 years* or *I have 20 years*.
- Focus on the example and get SS to talk about the ages of the different members of their family.
- Monitor and help. Correct any mistakes on the board.

Extra support

You could brainstorm the family words from **Vocabulary Bank** *People and family* on *p.105* onto the board for SS to refer to while they're speaking.

Extra idea

Two number games you may like to play now or when you want to practise numbers with your SS:

1 Buzz

Get SS to sit or stand in a circle and count out loud. When they come to a number that contains 3 (e.g. 13) or a multiple of 3 (3, 6, 9, 12, etc.) they have to say *buzz* instead of the number.

If a student makes a mistake, either saying the number instead of *buzz* or simply saying the wrong number, he/she is out, and the next player continues with the correct number.

Carry on until there is only one student left, or until the group have got to 30 without making a mistake.

Note: You can use any number between 3 and 9 as the 'buzz' number.

2 Two-digit number chains

Write three two-digit numbers on the board, e.g. *27 71 13*. Show SS that the second number begins with 7, because the previous one ended with 7, and the third number begins with 1 because the second number ended with 1. Ask SS what the fourth number could be and elicit a number, e.g. 32, and then another, e.g 26, and write the numbers up on the board. Tell SS not to use 'zero numbers', e.g. 20, 30, etc.

Now make a chain round the class. You say the first number, then elicit the second from the first student on your left, and carry on round the class.

Finally, get SS to make chains in pairs, where **A** says one number, **B** says another, **A** says a third, etc.

3 PEOPLE IN THE STREET

Study Link This exercise is also on the *New English File Beginner* DVD, which can be used instead of the class audio (see **Introduction** *p.11*). SS can get more practice on the MultiROM, which contains more of the short street interviews with a listening task and scripts.

a ● Focus on the questions in the box. Highlight that in English we use the words *brothers and sisters* whereas SS' L1 may have one word for this.
  ⚠ You can also say *Do you have **any** brothers and sisters?* but at this level we think it is easier to ask the question without *any*. *Some* and *any* are taught in lesson **6A**.
- **2.34** Focus on the photo of Matthew. Ask *Does he have brothers and sisters?* Play the CD once for SS to answer the question.
- Play the CD again to check the answer (see listening script 2.34).

2.34	CD1 Track 86
Interviewer	Do you have brothers and sisters?
Matthew (USA)	I have **one brother and one sister**.

b ● **2.35** Ask SS *How old are his brothers and sisters?* Play the CD once for SS to answer the question.
- Play the CD again to check the answer (see listening script 2.35). Replay as necessary.

2.35	CD1 Track 87
Interviewer	Do you have brothers and sisters?
Matthew	I have one brother and one sister.
Interviewer	How old are they?
Matthew	My **sister is 23**, and my **brother is 17**.

c ● Focus on the instructions. Tell SS they are going to listen to the six people in the photos answer the same questions.
- **2.36** Play the CD for SS to complete the information for Joanna. Replay as necessary and pause. Check answers (see listening script 2.36).
- Repeat this process for the other five people.

2.36		CD1 Track 88
Interviewer	Do you have brothers and sisters?	
Joanna (POL)	Yes, I have **two brothers**.	
Interviewer	How old are they?	
Joanna	One is **21** and the other is **24**.	
Interviewer	Do you have brothers and sisters?	
Sohail (UK)	Yes, I have **three sisters**.	
Interviewer	How old are they?	
Sohail	**36, 28**, and **39**.	
Interviewer	Do you have brothers and sisters?	
Chris (UK)	I have **one brother**.	
Interviewer	How old is he?	
Chris	He's **29**.	
Interviewer	Do you have brothers and sisters?	
Lauren (USA)	I have **one brother**.	
Interviewer	How old is he?	
Lauren	He is **17** years old.	
Interviewer	Do you have brothers and sisters?	
Hampton (USA)	I have **one sister**.	
Interviewer	How old is she?	
Hampton	She's **13**.	
Interviewer	Do you have brothers and sisters?	
Anna (USA)	I have **four brothers**.	
Interviewer	How old are they?	
Anna	**46, 44, 43**, and **36**.	

Extra support

If you have time, let SS listen again with the listening script on *p.83*. Go through the dialogues line by line with SS and elicit/explain any words or phrases that they don't understand.

d • Explain to SS that they are going to interview each other using the questions from the interview.
   • Model and drill the two questions.
   • Demonstrate with a good student. Get SS to ask and answer the questions in pairs.

4 PERSONAL INFORMATION

a • Focus on questions 1–9. Remind SS that in English we stress (= say more strongly) the words that carry the meaning.
   • Go through the questions one by one and elicit/explain any words or phrases that SS don't understand, e.g. *address, postcode, home phone number, mobile number, email address.*
   • **2.37** Play the CD once for SS to repeat the questions in chorus copying the rhythm.

2.37	CD1 Track 89
1 What's your name? How do you spell it?	
2 Where are you from?	
3 What's your address?	
4 What's your postcode?	
5 How old are you?	
6 Are you married?	
7 What's your home phone number?	
8 What's your mobile number?	
9 What's your email address?	

b • Focus on the form and explain/show how the nine questions correspond to the spaces in the form. Highlight that SS might be asked some of these

questions in real life, e.g. at Immigration at an airport.
   • Elicit/explain the meaning of *age* and *single*.
   • Point out that for **Nationality** we normally ask *Where are you from?* not *What's your nationality?* If somebody answers with the country, e.g. *I'm from Spain*, you would still put *Spanish* (the nationality word) on the form.
   • Explain also the meaning of *title* and the difference between *Mr, Ms*, and *Mrs* which is explained at the bottom of the form. Model and drill the pronunciation of *Mr* /ˈmɪstə/, *Ms* /məz/, and *Mrs* /ˈmɪsɪz/.
   • Explain that men always use the title *Mr*, but women can choose between *Mrs* and *Ms*. *Ms* refers to all women, but married women can use *Mrs* if they want to. However, you would not normally be asked *What's your title?*, which is why there is no question for this bit of information.
   • Now get SS to cover the questions and just look at the form. Elicit the questions from the class, or from individual SS, encouraging them to use the correct stress. Then get them to try to remember the questions with a partner.

c • Now tell SS to complete the form for themselves. Give SS a few minutes to complete it, and walk round checking that they are doing it correctly.

d • Put SS in pairs, **A** and **B**. Tell them to go to **Communication** *Personal information*, **A** on *p.77* and **B** on *p.79*.
   • Go through the instructions and make sure SS understand what they have to do. They take the role of a person, and then answer the questions in that role. The first names (Alex and Chris) can be male or female in English.
   ⚠ We have not asked SS to use personal information, as questions like *How old are you?* or *Are you married?* can be sensitive. If this is not an issue for your class, you could always get them to interview each other after they have done the **Communication**.
   • Tell SS to go back to the main lesson on *p.21*.

WORDS AND PHRASES TO LEARN

Focus on the words and phrases to learn. Make sure SS understand the meaning of each phrase. If necessary, remind SS of the context in which they came up in the lesson. If you speak your SS' L1, you might like to elicit a translation for the words/phrases for the SS to write next to them.

Study Link SS can find more practice of these words and phrases on the MultiROM and on the *New English File Beginner* website.

Extra photocopiable activities

Communicative
Missing information *p.169* (instructions *p.155*)

HOMEWORK

Study Link **Workbook** *pp.18–19*

For instructions on how to use these pages, see *p.29*.

What do you remember?

GRAMMAR

1 a 2 b 3 a 4 b 5 a 6 a 7 b 8 a 9 b
10 a

VOCABULARY

a 2 a bag
3 an umbrella
4 keys
5 a pen
6 glasses

b 1 mother
2 husband
3 daughter
4 brother
5 girlfriend

c 1 women
2 children
3 people

d 1 cheap
2 small
3 bad
4 short
5 short

e 1 40
2 67
3 99
4 56
5 82

f 1 This
2 old
3 Fine
4 over
5 address

PRONUNCIATION

a vowels: up, computer, cat, train, car, horse
   consonants: snake, zebra, mother
c ex<u>pe</u>nsive   a<u>dd</u>ress   <u>f</u>amily   <u>mo</u>bile   umb<u>re</u>lla

What can you do?

1 CAN YOU UNDERSTAND THIS TEXT?

a 2 She's from Venice in Italy.
3 He's 15.
4 Her name's Chiara.
5 He's Polish.
6 She's his sister./She's Piotr's sister.
7 She's married.
8 She's 19.

3 CAN YOU UNDERSTAND THESE PEOPLE?

1 a 2 a 3 b 4 a 5 a 6 a 7 b 8 a 9 a
10 b

2.38   CD1 Track 90

1 A What's your brother's name?
   B Alex.

2 A Are those your glasses?
   B No. My glasses are blue, not red.

3 A What's your address?
   B 90 Park Street.

4 A Is your hotel nice?
   B Yes, but my room's very small.

5 A How old's your father?
   B He's 67 and my mother's 63.

6 A What's your new mobile number?
   B Er…it's 077170641.

7 A Is that tall girl your sister?
   B No, it's my friend Ella. My sister's blonde and she's not very tall.

8 A What's that? Is it a DVD or a CD?
   B Let's see. It's a CD.

9 A What's your email address?
   B susie@hotmail.com.
   A Is that S-U-S-I-E or S-U-Z-Y?
   B S-U-S-I-E.

10 A Is that your new car? The white BMW?
   B No, that's my car over there. It's black.

Extra photocopiable activities

Grammar
2 revision *p.131*
Vocabulary
Word search *p.194* (instructions *p.191*)

Test and Assessment CD-ROM

File 2 Quicktest
File 2 Test

3 **A**

G present simple: *I* and *you*
V common verbs 1
P /uː/, /w/, and /v/; linking

A bad hair day

File 3 overview

The focus in File 3 is on the present simple form of common verbs. The *I* and *you* forms are presented in **3A** and in **3B** SS learn the *we*, *you*, and *they* forms. Finally, in **3C** SS are introduced to the *he*, *she*, and *it* forms and the minor complication in English grammar of the 3rd person *s* ending. In the **Practical English** lesson SS learn the days of the week and how to tell the time.

Lesson plan

A typical conversation between a hairdresser and his customer provides the context for SS to learn the first two forms (*I* and *you*) of the present simple in positive and negative sentences and questions. After the grammar presentation and practice, SS go to the Vocabulary Bank to learn a group of common verb phrases which are then recycled in the listening. In Pronunciation SS practise linking words together and also practise a new vowel sound and two consonants. Finally, all the language is brought together in the speaking activity where SS ask and answer questions about lifestyle.

Optional lead-in (books closed)

- Bring into class some photos from magazines of famous people with different haircuts. Elicit *short/long hair* and *dark/blond(e) hair*. Model and drill pronunciation, in chorus and individually. Try to avoid using *He/She has...* and just focus on the adjective and nouns.

- Then for each photo ask SS *Do you like his hair? Do you like her hair?* (you could indicate the meaning of *like* with a thumbs up/thumbs down gesture if this is culturally appropriate).

1 LISTENING & READING

a ● **3.1** Focus on the pictures and get SS to cover the dialogue. Elicit/teach the words <u>hairdresser</u> and <u>customer</u>, and write them on the board. Model and drill the word.

- Play the CD once for SS to listen and number the pictures. Replay as necessary. SS will get help here from the sound effects and from words they know like *coffee*, *Madonna*, etc., which they should be able to pick out from the dialogue. Get SS to compare their answers and then play the CD again to check. Make it clear to SS that they are not expected to understand the dialogue, just to get a rough idea of what is being said.

A 4	**B** 1	**C** 2	**D** 3	**E** 5

3.1   CD1 Track 91

H = Hairdresser, C = Customer
H Hello. Is this your first time here?
C Yes, it is.
H Do you live near here?
C No, I don't. I live in the centre.
H Oh, nice. How do you want your hair?
C I don't know. Something different.
H Do you want a coffee?
C No, thanks. I don't drink coffee.
H Do you want a magazine?
C Yes, please. Ah look. Madonna's children.
H Do you have children?
C Yes, I do. I have two boys.
H How old are they?
C Eight and ten.
***
C It's very short.
H Don't worry. Wait.
***
H OK. Do you like it?

---

b ● Get SS to uncover the dialogue and focus on the instructions. Elicit/explain the meaning of the words in the list.

- Give SS time to read the dialogue and then tell them to work in pairs to try and complete the spaces using the words from the list. There is quite a lot of new vocabulary in the dialogue, so SS will need to use the pictures to help them.

c ● Play the CD again, pausing after each space to check the answer.

2	in the centre	**5**	magazine
3	coffee	**6**	children
4	coffee	**7**	boys

- Play the CD again and go through the dialogue with SS line by line. Elicit/explain any words or phrases that SS don't understand, e.g. *first time, live near here/in the centre, How do you want your hair?* etc.

⚠ SS may ask about the meaning of *do* and *don't* here. Explain that these words have no translation, but that we use *do* in English to make a question and *don't* to make a negative in the present simple, and that it will be explained later in the **Grammar** section.

⚠ The question *Do you have children?* can also be asked *Do you have **any** children?* but at Beginner level we think it is easier to teach the question <u>without</u> *any*.

- Highlight that at this stage we do not hear the woman's answer to the hairdresser's question *Do you like it?* But SS will find out in the next activity.

d ● Put SS in pairs, **A** and **B**. Tell them to go to **Communication** *A new haircut* on p.81.

- Focus on the picture and ask *Do you like her haircut?* (*Yes, it's nice/beautiful*; *No, it's awful*, etc.).

- Tell SS to go back to the main lesson on p.24.

e ● **3.2** Focus on the last lines of the dialogue. Tell SS that we are going to hear if the woman likes her haircut. Ask the class what they think. Play the CD for SS to complete the space. Check the answer (see listening script 3.2).

> **3.2** CD1 Track 92
>
> **H** OK. Do you like it?
> **C** No, I don't. It's terrible.

f ● Get SS to repeat the dialogue line by line after the CD or after you before they practise.
  ● Put SS in pairs, **A** and **B**. Assign roles and get them to practise the dialogue. Tell whoever is reading the customer to add in the last line.
  ● Monitor and help with pronunciation. Correct any mistakes on the board.

2 GRAMMAR present simple: *I* and *you*

a ● Focus on the instructions and give SS time to complete the chart.
  ● Check answers on the board.

> ⊞ I live near here. ⊟ I *don't* live near here.
> ⑦ *Do* you live near here? ☑ Yes, I *do*. ☒ No, I *don't*.

b ● Tell SS to go to **Grammar Bank 3A** on *p.92*.
  ● **3.3** Play the CD and ask SS to listen and repeat the example sentences. Use the pause button as necessary.

> **3.3** CD2 Track 02
>
> I live in the city centre.
> You live near here.
>
> I don't live in the city centre.
> You don't live near here.
>
> Do you live near here? Yes, I do. No, I don't.

  ● Go through the rules with the class using the expanded information in the **Grammar notes** below to help you. You may want to use L1 here if you know it.

Grammar notes

  ● The *I* and *you* forms of the present simple are the same – *I live*, *you live*, i.e. the verb endings don't change, unlike in many languages. Highlight that it is the subject pronoun *I/you* which changes, not the verb (*live*). For this reason it is essential to always use the pronoun, otherwise it wouldn't be clear which person you were talking about.
  ● In the present simple we use *don't* before the infinitive of another verb to form negatives. *Don't* is the contraction of *do not*. *Do* and *don't* are called **auxiliary verbs** – they are used to help form negatives and questions. Remind SS that native speakers nearly always use contracted forms in spoken English.
  ● We use the verb *do* + the infinitive form of the verb to make questions. *Do* in this context cannot be translated. It simply indicates to the other person that you are going to ask a question in the present simple.
  ● Highlight the use of the short answers *Yes, I do* and *No, I don't*, which can be used as an alternative to just answering *Yes* or *No*.

● Highlight the simplicity of **imperatives** in English. There are only two forms – positive and negative, e.g. *Wait*, *Don't wait*. Elicit/give a few more examples of imperatives, encouraging SS to give the negative forms, e.g. *Sit down*, *Look*, *Listen*, *Don't write*, *Don't look*, etc.

● Focus on the exercises for **3A** on *p.93* and get SS to do them individually or in pairs. If they do them individually, get them to compare answers with a partner.
● Check answers.

> **a 1** A Do B don't   **4** don't
> **2** don't   **5** A do B don't
> **3** A Do B don't   **6** B do
>
> **b 1** I don't like football.
> **2** Do you want a magazine?
> **3** I live in a small house.
> **4** Do you study English?
> **5** I have two sisters.
> **6** I don't want a British car.
> **7** Do you live near here?
> **8** I don't have a mobile phone.

Study Link SS can find more practice of this grammar on the MultiROM and on the *New English File Beginner* website.

● Tell SS to go back to the main lesson on *p.24*.

3 VOCABULARY common verbs 1

a ● Focus on the instructions. Give SS a few minutes to match the phrases in pairs. Check answers.

> **2** c **3** a **4** e **5** d

b ● Tell SS to go to **Vocabulary Bank** *Common verbs 1* on *p.107*.
  ● **3.4** Focus on the instructions for **a.** Play the CD and get SS to repeat the phrases in chorus and individually as necessary. Use the pause button as necessary.
  ● Highlight the irregular pronunciation of the verb *live* /lɪv/. SS might expect /laɪv/, especially as *like* /laɪk/ is taught here too. You could remind SS that *i* + consonant + *e* is usually /aɪ/. Highlight also the silent *t* in *listen*.
  ● Highlight also the use of the preposition *to* in *listen to music*, but remind SS that if there is no object after *listen*, you don't use *to*. Compare *Please listen!* and *Now listen to the CD*.

> **3.4** CD2 Track 03
>
> live in a flat   drink coffee
> have children   speak English
> watch TV   want a new car
> listen to the radio like dogs
> read magazines   work in a bank
> eat fast food   study Spanish

● **3.5** Focus on the instructions for **b.** Demonstrate by saying part of a phrase and eliciting the complete phrase from the class, e.g. *in a flat* (*live in a flat*). Then play the CD and pause after the first item and elicit the phrase from the class. Make sure SS are clear what they have to do before continuing.

- Play the rest of the CD and give SS time to say the phrase in chorus.
- Repeat the activity, this time getting individual SS to respond.

3.5	CD2 Track 04
in a flat… live in a flat	coffee… drink coffee
children… have children	English… speak English
TV… watch TV	a new car… want a new car
the radio… listen to the radio	dogs… like dogs
magazines… read magazines	in a bank… work in a bank
fast food… eat fast food	Spanish… study Spanish

- Focus on the instructions for **c**. Demonstrate the activity by completing the first two sentences on the board about yourself. Elicit alternative answers from one or two SS.
- Give SS a few minutes to complete the sentences about themselves. Monitor and help.
- Put SS in pairs and ask them to read out their sentences to each other. Monitor and correct any pronunciation mistakes on the board.
- Get feedback by asking SS if they had any sentences the same.

> **Study Link** SS can find more practice of these verbs on the MultiROM and on the *New English File Beginner* website.

- Tell SS to go back to the main lesson on *p.24*.

4 LISTENING

a ● **3.6** Focus on the picture and establish the context for the listening by asking
Who is she? (She's the woman from the hairdresser's),
Who is the man? (He's a taxi driver).

- Focus on the instructions and check that SS understand the words *happy* and *sad*. Play the CD once or twice for SS to answer the question. (She's happy at the end of the conversation.)

3.6	CD2 Track 05

T = taxi driver, W = woman
T Good morning! Where to?
W Oxford Street, please.
T OK. The traffic is bad this morning.
W Yes. It's terrible.
T Do you live in London?
W Yes, I do.
T Are you OK? What's the problem?
W I don't like my new haircut.
T Why not? I like it.
W Really? Do you like it?
T Yes, I do.
W Thanks.
T Where do you want to stop?
W Over there, Topshop. I want a new bag.
T OK. That's 15.20.
W Here's 16. Keep the change.
T Thanks very much. Have a nice day.

b ● Focus on sentences 1–10. Give SS time to read them and ask you about any words they don't understand.
- Focus on the task and make it clear that SS have to choose which of the two alternative phrases was said.

- Play the CD for SS to circle the right phrase. Replay and use the pause button as necessary.
- Get SS to compare answers in pairs. Check answers.

> **1** a **2** a **3** a **4** a **5** b **6** a **7** b **8** b **9** a **10** b

- Now let SS have a final listen with the listening script on *p.83*. Elicit/explain any words or phrases SS don't understand, e.g. *Keep the change*. Focus on useful phrases such as *Are you OK? What's the problem?* and *Really?*

5 PRONUNCIATION /uː/, /w/, and /v/; linking

- Read the **Pronunciation notes** and decide how much of the information you want to give your SS.

Pronunciation notes

- Remind SS that the two dots in the symbols /uː/ mean that it's a long sound.
- You may want to highlight the following sound–spelling patterns:
  /uː/ the letters *oo* are often pronounced /uː/, e.g, *food*. but not always, e.g. *book, look* /ʊ/.
  /w/ the letter *w* (without *h*) is always pronounced /w/ at the beginning of a word, e.g. *watch*. The letters *wh* are usually pronounced /w/, e.g. *what, where* but there are some exceptions, e.g. *who* /huː/.
  /v/ the letter *v* is always pronounced /v/, e.g. *live*.
  Linking It is very common in English to link words together, especially when one word finishes with a consonant sound and the next word begins with a vowel sound. Being aware of this will not only help SS pronounce better, but also help them to 'separate' words in their head when people speak to them.

a ● **3.7** Focus on the sound picture *boot* and write the word on the board. Play the CD to model and drill the word and sound (pause after the sound).
- Now focus on the words after *boot*. Remind SS that the pink letters are the /uː/ sound. Play the CD pausing after each word for SS to repeat.
- Repeat for the other two sounds and words (*witch* and *vase*).
- Focus especially on sounds that are difficult for your SS and model them so that SS can see your mouth position. Get SS to repeat these sounds a few more times.

3.7		CD2 Track 06
boot	/uː/	do, you, food, too
witch	/w/	watch, want, where, what, work
vase	/v/	have, live, very, TV

> **Study Link** SS can find more practice of these sounds on the MultiROM and on the *New English File Beginner* website.

b ● **3.8** Focus on the sentences and play the CD just for SS to listen.
- Highlight the linked words and model and drill the separate phrases.
- Play the CD for SS to listen and repeat.

3.8 CD2 Track 07

A Do you live in a flat?
B No, I don't. I live in a house.

A Do you have children?
B Yes, I do. I have a boy and a girl.

- You could give SS extra practice by writing some more phrases on the board with word-linking marked, e.g.
  Do you want a coffee?
  Have a nice day!
  The traffic is terrible.
  I live in the centre.
  Get SS to practise saying the phrases trying to link the words.

6 SPEAKING

a • Focus on the instructions. Give SS time to complete the phrases in pairs.
- Check answers by asking individual SS to read out the two phrases.

2	have	7	drink
3	watch	8	speak
4	listen	9	want
5	read	10	like
6	eat		

b • Focus on the instructions and speech bubbles. Elicit the questions for the first verb (*Do you live near here? Do you live in a house?*). Remind SS we use *do* to make questions in the present simple. Elicit the possible answers (*Yes* or *Yes, I do/No* or *No, I don't*).
- Elicit the question for the second verb (*Do you have brothers and sisters? Do you have a cat or a dog?*).
- Model and drill some or all of the questions. Encourage SS to use the correct sentence rhythm.
- Demonstrate the activity by getting the class to interview you first, asking you some or all of the questions. Give true answers and where possible try to give some extra information (but using language within the SS' range).
- Put SS in pairs and get them to ask and answer questions with the phrases. Encourage them to give extra information in their answers.
- Monitor and help with pronunciation and sentence stress. Correct any mistakes on the board.

WORDS AND PHRASES TO LEARN

Focus on the words and phrases to learn. Make sure SS understand the meaning of each phrase. If necessary, remind SS of the context in which they came up in the lesson. If you speak your SS' L1, you might like to elicit a translation for the words/phrases for the SS to write next to them. You may also like to ask SS to test each other on the phrases.

Study Link SS can find more practice of these words and phrases on the MultiROM and on the *New English File Beginner* website.

Extra photocopiable activities

Grammar
present simple: *I* and *you p.132*
Communicative
Do you...? *p.170* (instructions *p.155*)

HOMEWORK

Study Link Workbook *pp.20–21*

G present simple: *we, you, they*
V food and drink
P word stress; /tʃ/, /dʒ/, and /g/

3B What do you have for breakfast?

Lesson plan

The context of this lesson is what people in different parts of the world have for breakfast. SS begin by learning the vocabulary for basic food items, e.g. *meat*, and the words for different meals (*breakfast*, etc.). After reading about different breakfasts, SS learn the *we, you,* and *they* forms of the present simple. In Pronunciation SS have more practice in word stress and pronouncing consonant sounds. The lesson builds up to a speaking activity where SS talk about what people eat in their country and also their family's eating habits. They also have extra writing practice with a paragraph to complete about breakfast in their country. The word *usually* is taught in this lesson as a vocabulary item. Adverbs of frequency are taught fully in lesson **4A**.

Optional lead-in (books closed)

- Write the names of some 'international' food words on the board, e.g. *pasta, pizza, sushi, dim sum, hamburgers, croissants, paella, burritos,* etc. Choose words which are the same or very similar in your SS' L1. You might be able to elicit some more from the class.
- Ask SS *Where are they from?* and elicit, e.g. *Pasta and pizza are from Italy,* etc.
- Finally, get SS in pairs to ask each other *Do you like...?*
- Get feedback to find out what some SS like /don't like.

1 VOCABULARY food and drink

a • Focus on the picture and the title of the article. Ask SS *Where is she from?* (France).
  - Give SS time to read the text and label the picture.
  - Check answers (hot chocolate, croissant). Model and drill the pronunciation of the food and drink words: *bread* /bred/, *butter* /ˈbʌtə/, *croissant* /ˈkrwæsɑ̃/, *milk* /mɪlk/, *chocolate* /ˈtʃɒklət/
  - Go through the text and focus on any other new words, e.g. *at home, a café* /ˈkæfeɪ/, *typical,* etc. Model and drill the pronunciation.

b • Tell SS to go to **Vocabulary Bank** *Food and drink* on *p.108*. There is quite a heavy vocabulary load, so you may need to spend longer on the drilling stage here.
  - **3.9** Focus on the instructions for **a**. Play the CD and get SS to repeat the words in chorus. Use the pause button as necessary.
  - Drill the pronunciation of all the words with phonetics. You may want to highlight that:
    - *ea* is pronounced /iː/ in *tea* and *meat,* but /e/ in *bread* and *breakfast,* and /ɪə/ in *cereal.*
    - *vegetables* and *chocolate* both have a syllable which is not pronounced.
    - the *d* in *sandwich* is not usually pronounced. The word can also be pronounced in two different ways – /ˈsænwɪtʃ/ or /ˈsænwɪdʒ/.
    - the *s* in *sugar* is pronounced /ʃ/.

3.9			CD2 Track 08
fish	salad	bread	coffee
meat	vegetables	a sandwich	tea
pasta	potatoes	butter	milk
rice	fruit	cheese	water
eggs		cereal	orange juice
		sugar	beer
		chocolate	wine

- Focus on the **Meals** box and go through the information. Elicit/explain that *breakfast* is a meal in the morning, *lunch* is at midday, and *dinner* is usually in the evening (although some people call the midday meal *dinner* if it is their main meal of the day).

⚠ Make sure SS are clear about the difference between *have* and *eat. Have* can be used with both food and drink (e.g. *have a sandwich, have coffee*) and is normally used when we talk about specific meals, e.g. *have breakfast, have lunch, have dinner. Eat,* e.g. *eat fast food,* can only be used for food.

- Focus on the instructions for **b**. Ask SS to cover the words with a piece of paper and look only at the pictures (they do this for each block of pictures). Give them time to remember the words with a partner.
- Monitor and help. Make a note of any pronunciation problems they are still having to focus on at the end of the activity.
- Focus on the instructions for **c**. Put SS in pairs to practise asking about food and drink they like and don't like. Monitor and help as before.

Study Link SS can find more practice of these words on the MultiROM and on the *New English File Beginner* website.

- Tell SS to go back to the main lesson on *p.26*.

2 READING

a • Focus on the two photos and the instructions and elicit the food SS can see. Don't teach the new words (*soup, green tea, sausage*) as SS will learn them when they read the text.

> The photos include rice, fish, miso soup, and green tea; eggs, cheese, cold meat, sausage, bread, coffee, and orange juice.

b • Focus on the two texts. Remind SS that when they read they should focus on the words they know, and try to guess the meaning of each sentence. Give them time to read both texts.
  - Now go through sentences 1–5 and make sure SS understand them. Give them time to read the text again and mark the sentences T or F. Get them to compare their answers with a partner. Monitor and help, then check answers.

1 F	**2** F	**3** T	**4** T	**5** T

c ● Focus on the highlighted words and give SS time in pairs to guess their meaning. SS can check their answers in a dictionary or you can use SS' L1 if you know it. Go through both texts and deal with other new vocabulary, e.g. *traditional, today, a lot of, I prefer*, etc.

● You may want to point out the difference between *sausage* (dry meat generally served cold in thin slices) and *sausages* (cooked meat eaten hot and whole).

Extra support

Alternatively, you could do exercises **b** and **c** together in a more teacher-led and interactive way. Read the texts aloud to your class, stopping after each sentence to check understanding. Focus especially on the highlighted words and ask SS to try and guess their meaning. You can also elicit comparisons with breakfast habits in your SS' country as you go along, e.g after eliciting/teaching the meaning of *traditional,* you could ask *What is a traditional breakfast in* (your SS' country)? Finally, go through sentences 1–5 in exercise **b** and give SS time to mark the sentences T or F. Leave out exercise **c** as the vocabulary will have been dealt with already.

d ● Focus on the question. Tell SS what you have for breakfast. Give them time to ask and answer the question in pairs. Monitor and help and teach any new words SS may need, e.g. *toast.*

● Get feedback by asking some SS to tell the class what their partner has for breakfast. Write *He has…/She has…* on the board.

3 GRAMMAR present simple: *we, you, they*

a ● Focus on the sentences and the instructions. Ask *Are the verbs the same or different?* (the same).

b ● Tell SS to go to **Grammar Bank 3B** on *p.92.*

● **3.10** Play the CD and ask SS to listen and repeat the example sentences. Use the pause button as necessary.

3.10		CD2 Track 09
We have coffee for breakfast.		
You have rice for lunch.		
They have fish for dinner.		
We don't have tea for breakfast.		
You don't have pasta for lunch.		
They don't have meat for dinner.		
Do you have coffee?	Yes, we do.	No, we don't.
Do they have tea?	Yes, they do.	No, they don't.

● Go through the rules with the class using the expanded information in the **Grammar notes** below to help you. You may want to use L1 here if you know it.

Grammar notes

● The *I, we, you,* and *they* forms of the present simple are the same, i.e. the verb doesn't change.

● Remind SS that we use *don't* before the infinitive of another verb to form negatives.

● Remind SS that we use *do* to form questions.

● Focus on the exercises for **3B** on *p.93* and get SS to do them individually or in pairs. If they do them individually, get them to compare answers with a partner.

● Check answers.

a 1 Do you want coffee or tea?
  2 They don't have cereal for breakfast.
  3 Do you like chocolate?
  4 We eat a lot of rice in Japan.
  5 Do you drink coffee in the evening?
  6 We don't like Chinese food.
  7 They have salad for lunch.
  8 Do they drink tea in Russia?

b 1 don't listen   **2** have   **3** Do, watch
  4 don't speak   **5** drink   **6** Do, work   **7** like
  8 Do, read

Study Link SS can find more practice of this grammar on the MultiROM and on the *New English File Beginner* website.

● Tell SS to go back to the main lesson on *p.27.*

4 LISTENING

a ● **3.11** Focus on the instructions, the title of the programme *You are what you eat*, and the question *What's his favourite meal?* Tell SS they are going to listen to William talking and for the moment they just have to answer this one question.

● Play the CD once all the way through and check the answer (Breakfast, at the weekend).

3.11	CD2 Track 10
I = interviewer, W = William	
I	What do you usually have for breakfast?
W	I usually have cereal and a cappuccino.
I	Not tea?
W	No, I prefer coffee. Not very English, I know!
I	Isn't the typical English breakfast eggs and bacon, and sausages?
W	Yes, but I only have that at the weekend.
I	What do you have for lunch?
W	I have a sandwich at work, in my office, and juice or water.
I	Do you have dinner at home?
W	Yes, with my family.
I	What do you usually have?
W	We have meat or fish with potatoes and vegetables, or maybe pasta. It depends.
I	What's your favourite meal, breakfast, lunch, or dinner?
W	Breakfast at the weekend. Eggs and bacon.

b ● Focus on the task and give SS time to read the words. Elicit/teach *bacon.*

● Play the CD again for SS to tick the things he has.

c ● Tell SS to turn to the listening script on *p.83.* Play the CD again for SS to listen and read.

● Give SS time to check their answers to **b.**

● Check answers by asking individual SS to read out what William has for each meal.

● Focus on the new vocabulary in the listening script, especially *usually* /ˈjuːʒuəli/, *at the weekend, at work, it depends.* Model and drill pronunciation of these words and phrases.

Breakfast: cereal, coffee
Breakfast at the weekend: eggs, bacon, sausages
Lunch: a sandwich, water, juice
Dinner: meat, pasta, fish, vegetables, potatoes

d ● Focus on the question. Tell SS what your favourite meal is and why. Give them time to ask and answer the question in pairs. Monitor and help.

● Ask SS to tell the class what their partner's favourite meal is.

5 PRONUNCIATION word stress; /tʃ/, /dʒ/, and /g/

a ● **3.12** Focus on the instructions. Do an example with the class. Write *coffee* on the board and ask *How many syllables?* (two). Now ask *Where's the stress?* (on syllable one). Underline the first syllable, i.e. *coffee*.

● Get SS to underline the stressed syllables in the words in pairs. Monitor and help.

● Play the CD for SS to repeat, and check their answers (see listening script 3.12).

● Check answers by writing the words on the board and eliciting the stressed syllable from individual SS.

3.12		CD2 Track 11
vegetables	sugar	chocolate
potatoes	salad	
butter	cereal	

⚠ The word *vegetables* has only three syllables, and *chocolate* has only two syllables, because they contain silent letters. Write the words on the board, say them and ask *Which letter is silent?* (the second *e* in *vegetables*, the second *o* in *chocolate*). Cross out these letters, i.e. *vegetables, chocolate* and drill the two words in chorus and individually.

● Read the **Pronunciation notes** and decide how much of the information you want to give your SS.

Pronunciation notes

● The sounds in this lesson are all consonant sounds. SS may find the symbols /dʒ/ and /tʃ/ difficult to remember.

● You may want to highlight the following sound–spelling patterns:

/tʃ/   *ch* and *tch* are usually pronounced /tʃ/, e.g. *children, watch*.

/dʒ/   *j* is always pronounced /dʒ/, e.g. *juice*. Also *g* can sometimes be /dʒ/, e.g. *German, orange*, especially before *e* (though there are exceptions, e.g. *get*).

/g/   the letter *g* is always pronounced /g/ at the end of a word, e.g. *bag, dog*, and often at the beginning and in the middle, e.g. *glasses, sugar*.

b ● **3.13** Focus on the sound picture *chess* and write the word on the board. Play the CD to model and drill the word and sound (pause after the sound).

● Now focus on the words after *chess*. Remind SS that the pink letters are the /tʃ/ sound. Play the CD pausing after each word for SS to repeat.

● Repeat for the other sounds and words (*jazz* and *girl*).

3.13		CD2 Track 12
chess	/tʃ/	cheese, lunch, chocolate, sandwich
jazz	/dʒ/	juice, Japan, orange, vegetables
girl	/g/	sugar, eggs, go, bag

Study Link SS can find more practice of these sounds on the MultiROM and on the *New English File Beginner* website.

c ● **3.14** Focus on the sentences and play the CD just for SS to listen. Then play the CD for SS to listen and repeat. Then get SS to practise the sentences in pairs.

3.14	CD2 Track 13
I'm Charles. I have a cheese sandwich for lunch. I'm Jane. I drink orange juice for breakfast. I'm Grace. I have eggs, and tea with sugar.	

6 SPEAKING & WRITING

a ● Focus on the questionnaire and give SS time to think about their answers. Deal with any problems with vocabulary. As well as food words, the questionnaire also recycles several expressions that have already come up in the lesson, e.g. *a lot of, at the weekend*, etc.

b ● If you are not from your SS' country, you could get them to interview you first. Try to give answers using words SS will understand.

⚠ If your SS are from the same country, get them to just answer the questions together in the **In your country** section, and then to interview each other with the **In your family** section.

● Give SS time to ask and answer the questions in the questionnaire with a partner. Monitor and help. Before they start, remind SS of the useful expression *It depends*. Encourage SS to give as much information as they can.

Extra challenge

You could get Student **A** to close their book while Student **B** interviews them, and then swap roles.

c ● Focus on the task and make it clear that in the first space SS have to write the name of their country. Give SS time to complete the spaces.

● Get SS to read out their sentences to a partner.

WORDS AND PHRASES TO LEARN

Focus on the words and phrases to learn. Make sure SS understand the meaning of each phrase. If necessary, remind SS of the context in which they came up in the lesson. If you speak your SS' L1, you might like to elicit a translation for the words/phrases for the SS to write next to them. You may also like to ask SS to test each other on the phrases.

Study Link SS can find more practice of these words and phrases on the MultiROM and on the *New English File Beginner* website.

Extra photocopiable activities

Grammar
present simple: *we, you, they p.133*
Communicative
Food and drink *p.171* (instructions *p.155*)

HOMEWORK

Study Link Workbook *pp.22–23*

G present simple: *he, she, it*
V jobs and places of work
P 3rd person *s*; word and sentence stress

3C

He speaks English at work

Lesson plan

In this lesson the 3rd person singular (*he, she, it*) of the present simple is introduced. This is the only verb form in the present simple which is different, as there is a change to the verb ending (+ *s* or *es*, e.g. *works, teaches*) and a different auxiliary is used (*does/doesn't*). For this reason a whole lesson has been devoted to this point and beginners will need time to assimilate it.

The lesson context is people who use English at work (when it is not their first language). The new grammar point is presented through a dialogue between a British and Spanish woman at a gym in Madrid. This leads into Vocabulary where SS learn the words for some common jobs and places of work (e.g. *in an office*), and Pronunciation where SS practise word and sentence stress. Then SS talk about their jobs and those of other family members, and about whether they use English. Finally, SS read about the use of English as a *lingua franca* in companies around the world.

Optional lead-in (books closed)

- Write seven blanks on the board and play *hangman* with the word TEACHER (see *p.26* for how to play hangman). Tell SS that the word is a job, making sure SS know what *job* means.
- When the word has been guessed ask SS if they know any other English words for jobs, e.g *doctor*, and write them on the board.

1 GRAMMAR present simple: *he, she, it*

a ● **3.15** Focus on the two women in the photo. Ask SS where they are (at the gym). Tell SS their names are Emily and Sofia. Focus on the task and give SS time to read the questions 1–3. Elicit/teach and drill *tourist guide*, and also *job* if you didn't do the **lead-in**.

- Ask SS to cover the dialogue. Play the CD for SS to circle the correct answer. Replay as necessary.
- Find out with a show of hands how many SS have put *a* or *b* for each question, but <u>don't give the right answers at this point</u> as SS will check their own answers in **b**.

3.15   CD2 Track 14

E = **Emily**, S = **Sofia**
E Your English is fantastic. What do you do?
S I'm a teacher. I teach English at the University here in Madrid.
E Do you like your job?
S Yes, I like it very much.
E What does your husband do?
S He's a tourist guide. He works at the Prado museum.
E Does he like his job?
S Yes, very much. He likes art and history. And he doesn't work in the morning, only in the afternoon.
E Does he speak English too?
S Yes, he does. He speaks it very well. He meets a lot of British and American tourists.
E Do you speak English together?
S Only when we don't want our children to understand!

---

b ● Now focus on the dialogue. Play the CD for SS to listen again and tell them to read the dialogue as they listen. Tell them to check their answers to **a** as they listen and read.
- Check answers.

---

1 b   **2** b   **3** a

- Go through the dialogue with SS line by line and elicit/ explain any words or phrases that SS don't understand, e.g. *museum, art,* and *history*. Teach/elicit that the question *What do you do?* = What's your job? Focus too on the use of *very much* (= a lot) and the use of *very well* in *He speaks it very well.*

⚠ The final line of the dialogue is quite complicated grammatically, but SS should be able to understand it as they know all the individual words.

c ● **3.16** Focus on the highlighted phrases. Play the CD for SS to listen and repeat, encouraging them to copy the rhythm. Replay as necessary.

- Focus on the question *How do the verbs change when they talk about Sofia's husband?* Elicit the answer that *do* changes to *does* in questions, and you add an *s* or *es* to the ⊞ verbs. SS may also notice that *don't* changes to *doesn't* (e.g. *He doesn't work in the morning*).

Extra support

If SS find it difficult to answer the question, get them to complete the chart first.

3.16   CD2 Track 15

E What do you do?
S I'm a teacher.
E Do you like your job?
S Yes, I like it very much.
E What does your husband do?
S He's a tourist guide. He works at the Prado museum.
E Does he like his job?
S He likes art and history. And he doesn't work in the morning, only in the afternoon.

- Focus on the chart and give SS time to find the phrases in the dialogue and complete the spaces.

I/you	*he/she*
What do you do?	What *does* your husband do?
Do you like your job?	*Does* he like his job?
Yes, I like it very much.	Yes, he *likes* art and history.

---

d ● Tell SS to go to **Grammar Bank 3C** on *p.92*.

- **3.17** Play the CD and ask SS to listen and repeat the example sentences. Use the pause button as necessary. After repeating the positive and negative forms write *does* and *doesn't* on the board and elicit the pronunciation /dʌz/ and /ˈdʌznt/.
- When SS repeat the sentences in **Spelling rules 3rd person s**, remind them that the *-es* and *-ies* endings are pronounced /ɪz/.

3.17	CD2 Track 16

He works.
She works.
It works.
He doesn't work.
She doesn't work.
It doesn't work.

Does he work?	Yes, he does.	No, he doesn't.
Does she work?	Yes, she does.	No, she doesn't.
Does it work?	Yes, it does.	No, it doesn't.

He works in an office.
He lives in Spain.
She watches CNN.
The film finishes at 8.00.
He studies history.

- Go through the rules with the class using the expanded information in the **Grammar notes** below to help you. You may want to use L1 here if you know it.

Grammar notes

- The *he, she,* and *it* forms of the present simple are different from the other forms. The positive form of the verb always finishes with an *s* (or *es*).
- We form negatives by putting *doesn't* /ˈdʌznt/ (not *don't*) before an infinitive. *Doesn't* is the contracted form of *does not*. Remind SS that native speakers usually use contractions in spoken English.
- We use *does* (not *don't*) with *he, she,* or *it* and an infinitive to make questions.
- ⚠️ If SS ask about the meaning of *does,* tell them that, like *do,* it is a word we need in the present simple to help make negatives and questions and it cannot be translated.

Spelling rules 3rd person *s*

- Most verbs make the *he/she/it* form by adding *s*, e.g. *eats, drinks.*
- Verbs ending in -*ch,*-*sh, -s, -ss,* and -*x* make the *he/she/it* form by adding *es*, e.g. *watches, finishes, kisses.*
- Verbs ending in a consonant + *y* make the *he/she/it* form by changing the *y* to *i* and adding *es*, e.g. *studies.* This change does not occur when the verb finishes in a vowel + *y,* e.g. *plays.*
- The spelling rules are the same for verbs in the 3rd person singular as for plural nouns (see Student's Book *p.90* **2A** and **Pronunciation notes**).
- *have, do,* and *go* are irregular in the *he/she/it* form and change to *has, does,* and *goes.* Highlight that *goes* /gəʊz/ and *does* /dʌz/ are pronounced differently.

- Focus on the exercises for **3C** on *p.93* and get SS to do them individually or in pairs. If they do them individually, get them to compare answers with a partner.
- Check answers.

a 1 He reads magazines.
2 My sister teaches small children.
3 Does he speak English?
4 My brother doesn't eat fish.
5 Does she like cats?
6 Andrew has two brothers.
7 My mother doesn't watch TV.
8 Simon studies French at school.

b 1 She *listens* to Radio 1.
2 *Do* you *eat* meat?
3 Where *does* she *live?*
4 My husband *doesn't like* big cars.
5 What *do* they *have* for breakfast?
6 He *watches* TV at the weekend.
7 *Does* he *want* tea or coffee?
8 The restaurant *doesn't open* at the weekend.

Study Link SS can find more practice of this grammar on the MultiROM and on the *New English File Beginner* website.

- Tell SS to go back to the main lesson on *p.28.*

2 PRONUNCIATION 3rd person *s*

- Read the **Pronunciation notes** and decide how much of the information you want to give your SS.

Pronunciation notes

- The rules for pronouncing the *s* of the *he/she/it* form are the same as the rules for pronouncing the *s* of plural nouns (see **Pronunciation notes** *p.32*).
- The difference between the /z/ and /s/ endings is small and you may not want to focus on it too much at this level.
- We suggest you highlight the /ɪz/ pronunciation of the *es* ending in verbs which end in -*sh* and -*ch,* e.g. *watches, teaches.*

a ● **3.18** Focus on the sound pictures for *zebra* and *snake,* and the /ɪz/ symbol. Elicit the words and the sounds, and write the words on the board.

- Now focus on the example words after each sound picture. Remind SS that the pink letters are the same sound as the picture word.
- Play the CD for SS to listen to all three groups, to hear the difference. Then play it again, pausing after each group for SS to repeat.

3.18		CD2 Track 17
zebra	/z/	does, has, lives, listens, reads
snake	/s/	likes, speaks, works, eats, drinks
	/ɪz/	finishes, watches, teaches

Study Link SS can find more practice of these sounds on the MultiROM and on the *New English File Beginner* website.

b ● **3.19** Focus on the instructions. Tell SS they will hear a sentence with *I,* and then they will hear either *he, she,* or *it,* or a name. They have to say the sentence again beginning with *he, she, it,* or the name.

- Play the CD and pause after the first sentence (*I like art. He…*). Elicit *He likes art.* Make sure SS are clear what they have to do before continuing.
- Play the rest of the CD and give SS time to say the 3rd person sentences in chorus. Correct any wrong pronunciation of the 3rd person *s* ending.
- Repeat the activity, this time getting individual SS to respond.

3.19	CD2 Track 18

1 I like art. He... He likes art.
2 I speak English. She... She speaks English.
3 I live in Rome. My brother... My brother lives in Rome.
4 I watch MTV. She... She watches MTV.
5 I want a coffee. He... He wants a coffee.
6 I have a dog. John... John has a dog.
7 I don't eat meat. My sister... My sister doesn't eat meat.
8 I don't read books. My son... My son doesn't read books.
9 Do you work? He... Does he work?
10 Do you drink tea? She... Does she drink tea?

3 VOCABULARY jobs and places of work

a • Focus on the questions and elicit the answers from the class (*Sofia is a teacher. Her husband is a tourist guide.*).

b • Tell SS to go to **Vocabulary Bank** *Jobs and places of work* on *p.109*. Focus on the first section **What do they do?**

• **3.20** Focus on the instructions for **a**. Play the CD and get SS to repeat the words in chorus or individually. Use the pause button as necessary.

3.20	CD2 Track 19
a teacher	an administrator
a doctor	a lawyer
a nurse	a policeman
a shop assistant	a policewoman
a waiter	a factory worker
a waitress	a student

• Highlight that:
  – in English we always use *a* or *an* before singular jobs, e.g. *He's a teacher* NOT ~~He's teacher~~.
  – *waiter* is used for a man and *waitress* for a woman.
  – an *administrator* is someone whose job is to organize and manage an office in a company, school, hospital, etc.

• Focus on the instructions for **b**. Ask SS to cover the words and look at the questions *What does he do?/What does she do?* Model and drill the examples in chorus and individually.

• Give SS time to ask and answer questions about the pictures in pairs. Monitor and help, correcting pronunciation where necessary.

• **3.21** Focus on the instructions for **c**. Play the CD for SS to listen and repeat.

3.21	CD2 Track 20
He works for Microsoft.	He doesn't have a job.
He's at school.	She's retired.
She's at university.	
She studies economics.	

• Focus on the box and go through the information.

• Highlight that we say *work **for** a company*, *at school*, and *at university*. Elicit/explain the meaning of *She's retired*.

• Focus on the instructions for **d**. If SS are working, check that they know how to say their job and get them to write it in the space. Deal with any vocabulary problems and write any new jobs on the board. Get SS to underline the stress on these words.

⚠ If SS are not working, get them to write whichever is true for them from *I'm at school / I'm a student / I don't have a job / I'm retired*.

• Focus on the second section **Where do they work?**

• **3.22** Focus on the instructions for **a**. Play the CD and get SS to repeat the words in chorus.

3.22	CD2 Track 21
in the street	in an office
in a hospital	in a school
in a shop	in a factory
in a restaurant	at home

• Highlight that we use usually say *work **in** a place*, but with *home* we use the preposition *at*, i.e. *at home*.

• Focus on the instructions for **b**. Ask SS to cover the pictures and say the phrases in pairs.

• Focus on the instructions for **c** and the speech bubbles. Model and drill the example question and answer, in chorus and individually.

• Then get SS to ask and answer questions about the jobs in pairs. Monitor and help, correcting pronunciation where necessary.

• Focus on the instructions for **d** and help SS to complete the sentence with their place of work. Write any new places on the board. If your SS are students, you could get them to write *I study at ... school/university*.

Study Link SS can find more practice of these words and phrases on the MultiROM and on the *New English File Beginner* website.

• Tell SS to go back to the main lesson on *p.29*.

c • Focus on the instructions. Tell SS to stand up and mingle and ask at least five other SS *What do you do?*

⚠ If your SS are mainly school or university students, you may want to skip this stage, or ask them to choose a job from the **Vocabulary Bank**.

4 PRONUNCIATION word and sentence stress

a • This exercise focuses on word stress. Focus on the words and get SS to underline the stress in pairs.

b • **3.23** Play the CD once for SS to listen and check. Pause after each word and ask individual SS to say which syllable is stressed (syllable one/syllable two, etc.). Highlight that the final *-er/or* is never stressed and is pronounced /ə/.

1 a <u>tea</u>cher 2 a <u>doc</u>tor 3 a <u>wai</u>ter
4 a <u>fac</u>tory worker 5 an ad<u>min</u>istrator
6 a po<u>lice</u>man 7 a <u>shop</u> assistant 8 a <u>law</u>yer

• Ask SS to practise saying the words in pairs, encouraging them to copy the /ə/ pronunciation. Monitor and help.

3.23	CD2 Track 22
1 a teacher	5 an administrator
2 a doctor	6 a policeman
3 a waiter	7 a shop assistant
4 a factory worker	8 a lawyer

c • **3.24** This exercise focuses on sentence stress. Focus on the sentences and remind SS that:

– we stress the information words in sentences (e.g. *works...hospital*) and we don't usually stress pronouns, articles, and prepositions.

– we link words together where one ends in a consonant sound and the next starts with a vowel, e.g. *in a hospital*.

• Play the CD just for SS to listen. Then play the CD for SS to listen and repeat.

3.24   CD2 Track 23

She's a nurse. She works in a hospital.
Does he work in a shop? Yes, he does.
Is he a shop assistant? Yes, he is.

---

5 SPEAKING & WRITING

a • Focus on the instructions. Demonstrate the activity by writing a person from your family on the board, e.g. your mother.

• Focus on the question prompts and ask *What's missing?* and elicit that it is *does she* or *does he*. Elicit the full questions from SS to ask about your mother and write them on the board:

What does she do?

Where does she work?

Does she speak English at work?

Does she like her job?

Elicit the sentence stress and underline the words.
Get SS to ask you the questions, and answer them about your family member.

• Put SS in pairs, **A** and **B**. Get **A** to tell **B** who his/her first person is, and **B** then asks the four questions. Then **B** tells **A** who his/her first person is. They then repeat for their second person. Monitor and help with vocabulary.

• Get feedback and find out about some of the SS' friends' or relatives' jobs.

b • Focus on the instructions. Ask SS to read the model. Point out that the sentences are the answers to the questions in **a**.

• Give SS time to write about their two people. Monitor and help. Correct any mistakes on the board.

Extra idea

If most of your class have jobs, finish this part by getting them to ask the questions to each other.

6 READING

a • Focus on the instructions and ask individual SS to give their score (1–5) for the first job (a waiter). Then tell SS, in pairs, to try to agree a score for the other jobs and write a number in the space.

• Get feedback from the class.

b • Focus on the text and ask SS to read it once. Ask them to underline three jobs in the first paragraph (a banker, a waiter, and a worker in an electronics factory). Remind SS that when they read they should try to focus on the words they know, and try to guess the meaning of new words.

• Focus on the questions and ask SS to read them. Tell SS to read the text again and answer the questions. They could do this orally or write the answers. Get SS to compare their answers in pairs.

• Check answers.

---

1 They speak English at work.
2 He works for an IT company.
3 He works in Paris.
4 He speaks French and English.
5 He speaks English. No, it isn't.

---

c • Focus on the highlighted words and get SS to guess their meaning with a partner. SS can check the meaning in their dictionaries or you can use SS' L1 if you know it.

• Go through the text and deal with any other vocabulary problems.

d • Focus on the question and do it as an open-class question with those of the SS who have jobs.

• Get feedback from individual SS.

WORDS AND PHRASES TO LEARN

Focus on the words and phrases to learn. Make sure SS understand the meaning of each phrase. If necessary, remind SS of the context in which they came up in the lesson. If you speak your SS' L1, you might like to elicit a translation for the words/phrases for the SS to write next to them. You may also like to ask SS to test each other on the phrases.

Study Link SS can find more practice of these words and phrases on the MultiROM and on the *New English File Beginner* website.

Extra photocopiable activities

Grammar
present simple: *he, she, it p.134*
Communicative
What do they do? Where do they work? *p.172 (instructions p.156)*

HOMEWORK

Study Link Workbook *pp.24–25*

Telling the time
Days of the week
Silent consonants

Lesson plan

In this lesson SS learn how to tell the time. There are two possible ways of telling the time in English – digital, e.g. *six thirty*, and analogue, e.g. *half past six*. SS will hear both if they travel to an English-speaking country. To avoid confusing SS with two forms the focus here is on the more common analogue time. Teachers may want to point out the easy digital alternative as a 'fall-back' option.

After SS have learnt and practised telling the time, they listen to people in the street saying what they do, and what time they start and finish work. SS then learn the days of the week, and there is a pronunciation focus on silent consonants as in *half*, *Wednesday*, etc. The lesson finishes with the song *Friday I'm in love* which recycles the days of the week.

Optional lead-in (books closed)

- Revise numbers 1–30. Get SS to count round the class, first normally, then in twos (*2, 4, 6*, etc.), in threes (*3, 6, 9*, etc.), and finish with fives (*5, 10, 15*, etc.).

1 TELLING THE TIME

a ● **3.25** Books closed. Show SS your watch and ask *What is it?* (a watch). Then point to the clock in the classroom (or draw one on the board) and ask *What is it?* (a clock).

- Books open. Ask SS to cover the dialogues with a piece of paper and look at the pictures and clocks. Ask *Where are they?* (picture 1 – at home, picture 2 – in the street).
- Play the CD for SS to match the dialogues to the pictures. Replay as necessary. Check answers (A1, B2).
- Now tell SS to uncover the dialogues and play the CD again while SS read the dialogues. Tell SS to look at the clock in picture A and ask *What time is it?* (It's half past six). Do the same for picture B (It's quarter to seven).
- Play the CD again and explain/elicit new vocabulary, e.g. *go back to sleep, just a moment.* Highlight the typical response of *You're welcome* to *Thanks.*

3.25 / 3.26	CD2 Tracks 24/25

1 A What time is it?
   B It's half past six. Go back to sleep.
   A OK. Have a nice day.
   B You too.

2 A Excuse me. What time is it?
   B Sorry, I don't know. I don't have a watch.
   A Excuse me. What time is it?
   C Just a moment. It's quarter to seven.
   A Thanks.
   C You're welcome.

b ● **3.26** Play the CD again for SS to repeat. Get SS to practise the dialogues in pairs. In the second dialogue **B** can take the part of both **B** and **C**.

⚠ There are two common ways of asking the time: *What's the time?* and *What time is it?* Here *What time is it?* is taught as it is easier for SS to move from this to questions with the present simple like *What time do you finish work?*

c ● Tell SS to go to **Vocabulary Bank** *The time and ordinal numbers* on *p.110*. Focus on part **A What time is it?**

- **3.27** Focus on the instructions for **a**. Play the CD and get SS to repeat the words in chorus.
- Highlight the pronunciation of *past* /pɑːst/, *half* /hɑːf/, and *quarter* /ˈkwɔːtə/.

⚠ In some parts of Britain *past* is pronounced /pæst/ and teachers from these areas may wish to model the pronunciation themselves.

3.27	CD2 Track 26
It's one o'clock.	It's half past one.
It's five past one.	It's twenty-five to two.
It's ten past one.	It's twenty to two.
It's quarter past one.	It's quarter to two.
It's twenty past one.	It's ten to two.
It's twenty-five past one.	It's five to two.

- Focus on the instructions for **b**. Tell SS to cover the words and look at the clocks. Give them time to practise saying the times to themselves. Monitor and help, correcting pronunciation as necessary. Note any general problems and focus on them on the board at the end.
- With the first line of clocks covered ask individuals *Clock number 1 – What time is it?* and elicit the answer. Do the same for all the clocks.

Study Link SS can find more practice of times on the MultiROM and on the *New English File Beginner* website.

- Tell SS to go back to the main lesson on *p.30*.

d ● **3.28** Focus on the instructions. Play the CD and pause after the first time. Get SS to draw the hands on the clock. Continue, pausing for SS to draw the times on the clocks.

- Play the CD again for SS to check the times. Get SS to compare their answers with a partner. Check answers by doing a drawing of a clock on the board and drawing the hands in for each time.

3.28	CD2 Track 27
1 It's nine o'clock.	5 It's quarter past nine.
2 It's twenty past three.	6 It's twenty-five to twelve.
3 It's half past nine.	7 It's five past eight.
4 It's ten to ten.	8 It's quarter to six.

e ● Focus on the instructions and the speech bubbles. Model and drill the question *What time is it?*

- Demonstrate by asking the class: *Number 2 – What time is it?* and elicit *It's twenty past three.*
- Get SS to ask and answer with a partner using all the clocks but in random order. Monitor and help, correcting pronunciation.

f ● Put SS in pairs, **A** and **B**. Tell them to go to **Communication** *What time is it?* **A** on *p.77* and **B** on *p.79*.

- SS each have ten clocks, five of which are complete and five of which have no clock hands. SS share information and draw in the missing clock hands.
- Go through the instructions with SS.
- Monitor and help. When SS have finished get them to compare their clocks to check the times.
- Tell SS to go back to the main lesson on *p.30*.

2 PEOPLE IN THE STREET

Study Link This exercise is also on the *New English File Beginner* DVD, which can be used instead of the class audio (see **Introduction** *p.11*). SS can get more practice on the MultiROM, which contains more of the short street interviews with a listening task and scripts.

- Focus on the photo of Heidi and the three questions in the box. Explain that SS are going to hear Heidi being asked these questions.

a ● **3.29** Focus on the instructions. Ask *What does she do?* Play the CD for SS to write her job. Check answers (see listening script 3.29).

3.29	CD2 Track 28
Interviewer	What do you do?
Heidi (UK)	I'm a **doctor**.

b ● **3.30** Ask *Does she like her job?* Play the CD again for SS to answer. Check the answer (see listening script 3.30).

3.30	CD2 Track 29
Interviewer	What do you do?
Heidi	I'm a doctor.
Interviewer	Do you like it?
Heidi	**Yes**, I do.

c ● **3.31** Focus on the instructions. Ask *What time does she start and finish?* Play the CD for SS to answer the question. Check answers (see listening script 3.31).

3.31	CD2 Track 30
Interviewer	What do you do?
Heidi	I'm a doctor.
Interviewer	Do you like it?
Heidi	Yes, I do.
Interviewer	What time do you start and finish?
Heidi	I start work at **half past eight** and I finish work at **six o'clock**.

d ● **3.32** Focus on the instructions and explain that SS are going to hear four more people answering the same questions.

- Play the CD for SS to complete the information for Chris. Replay as necessary and use the pause button if SS are finding it hard. Check answers (see listening script 3.32).
- Repeat this process for the other three speakers.

3.32	CD2 Track 31
Interviewer	What do you do?
Chris (UK)	I'm a **factory worker**.
Interviewer	Do you like it?
Chris	**No**, no, I don't.
Interviewer	What time do you start and finish?
Chris	I start at **six in the morning** and finish at **two in the afternoon**.
Interviewer	What do you do?
Pamela (USA)	I'm a **nurse**.
Interviewer	Do you like it?
Pamela	Of course (= **yes**).
Interviewer	What time do you start and finish?
Pamela	I work **nine** to **four**.

Interviewer	What do you do?
Sam (AUS)	I'm a **waiter**.
Interviewer	Do you like it?
Sam	**Yeah** (= **yes**), I do.
Interviewer	What time do you start and finish?
Sam	I start at **four o'clock in the afternoon**, and finish at **11.30 at night**.
Interviewer	What do you do?
Ana (SPA)	I am an **administrator**.
Interviewer	Do you like it?
Ana	**Yes**, I do.
Interviewer	What time do you start and finish?
Ana	I start at **nine o'clock** and finish at **five in the afternoon**.

e ● Focus on the activity and model and drill the three questions the people were asked, one by one. Then get SS in pairs to interview each other.

⚠ If you have SS in your class who are at school or university, *Do you like your job?* can be changed to *Do you like your school/university?* and the third question can be changed to *What time do you start and finish class?*

- Finally, you could get some quick feedback from a few SS about their partner to revise the 3rd person, e.g. *Jan is a shop assistant. He likes his job. He starts at 9.00*, etc.

3 VOCABULARY days of the week

a ● **3.33** Focus on the days of the week in the diary. Play the CD once for SS to listen. Then play it again for SS to listen and repeat.

- Get SS to practise saying the words in pairs. Remind them that the underlined syllable is the stressed syllable. Monitor and help. Model and drill any problem words. Highlight especially the pronunciation of *Wednesday* /ˈwenzdeɪ/ (in which the *d* and second *e* are silent) and the difference between *Tuesday* /ˈtjuːzdeɪ/ and *Thursday* /ˈθɜːzdeɪ/.
- Get SS to practise saying all the days of the week on their own, then practise them round the class.

3.33	CD2 Track 32
Monday Tuesday Wednesday Thursday Friday Saturday Sunday	

- Focus on the information box. Highlight that days of the week are always written with a capital letter.

b ● **3.34** Focus on the dialogues. Play the CD for SS to complete the days of the week. Replay as necessary. Check answers by playing the CD again, pausing after each answer.

> 1 Tuesday 2 Friday 3 Wednesday 4 Thursday
> 5 Wednesday

- Play the CD again and go through the dialogues with SS line by line. Elicit/explain any words that SS may not understand, e.g. *today, Why...? Because* /bɪˈkɒz/... *birthday, present, tomorrow*.
- Model and drill the dialogues line by line. Get SS to practise them in pairs, then change roles.

3.34	CD2 Track 33
1 A	What day is it today?
B	It's Tuesday. Why?
A	Because it's my wife's birthday on Friday and I don't have a present!

> **2 A** Is it Wednesday tomorrow?
> **B** No, Thursday. Today is Wednesday.

c • **3.35** Focus on the phrases. Elicit/explain the meaning. Remind SS that *Bye* is a little more informal than *Goodbye*.
• Play the CD once for SS to listen and then play it again for them to listen and repeat.

> **3.35** CD2 Track 34
> **A** Goodbye.
> **B** See you on Monday.
> **A** Bye.
> **B** See you tomorrow.

• SS now practise saying goodbye with different days of the week. Say *Monday* and elicit *Goodbye. See you on Monday.* Continue with the other days of the week, and *tomorrow*.

d • Focus on the questions. Get SS to ask and answer the questions in pairs. Monitor and help. Then get feedback from the class.

4 PRONUNCIATION silent consonants

• Read the **Pronunciation notes** and decide how much of the information you want to give your SS.

Pronunciation notes

• In English many words have a 'silent' consonant, i.e. a consonant which is not pronounced. SS have already met and learnt to pronounce many of these words, but have not focused specifically on the silent consonant. In some combinations there is a rule which you may want to point out to SS, e.g. *kn-* at the beginning of a word is always /n/, and *wr-* is always /r/.
• Encourage SS to cross out silent letters, as in exercise **a**, when they learn new words with them.
• You could show SS how looking at the phonetic transcription of words in a dictionary can help them check if a word has a silent letter, e.g. *listen* /ˈlɪsn/.

a • **3.36** Focus on the words. Play the CD once for SS to listen. Point out that the highlighted consonant which is crossed through is a silent consonant, i.e. a consonant that isn't pronounced.
• Play the CD again for SS to listen and repeat.
• Get SS to practise saying the words in pairs. Monitor and help. Make a note of any problems and write any problematic words on the board. Model and drill the difficult words again in chorus and individually.

> **3.36** CD2 Track 35
> half Wednesday know listen white school
> talk write

b • **3.37** Focus on the sentences and play the CD just for SS to listen. Then play the CD for SS to listen and repeat.
• Give SS time to practise saying the sentences by themselves. Finally, get a few individual SS to say the sentences.

> **3.37** CD2 Track 36
> Don't write on the whiteboard.
> I don't know the school.
> See you on Wednesday at half past four.

5 **3.38** SONG *Friday I'm in love*

• This is one of the best-known songs by the band The Cure. It was released in 1992 and reached number six in the UK charts. For copyright reasons this is a cover version of the song. The activity for this song focuses on rhyming words.
• If you want to do this song in class, use the photocopiable activity on *p.204*.

> **3.38** CD2 Track 37
> ***Friday I'm in love***
>
> I don't care if Monday's blue
> Tuesday's grey and Wednesday too
> Thursday I don't care about you
> It's Friday I'm in love
>
> Monday you can fall apart
> Tuesday, Wednesday break my heart
> Thursday doesn't even start
> It's Friday I'm in love
>
> **Chorus**
> Saturday, wait
> And Sunday always comes too late
> But Friday, never hesitate
>
> I don't care if Monday's black
> Tuesday, Wednesday – heart attack
> Thursday, never looking back
> It's Friday I'm in love
>
> Monday, you can hold your head
> Tuesday, Wednesday stay in bed
> Or Thursday – watch the walls instead
> It's Friday I'm in love
>
> **Chorus**
>
> Repeat verses 1 and 2

WORDS AND PHRASES TO LEARN

Focus on the words and phrases to learn. Make sure SS understand the meaning of each phrase. If necessary, remind SS of the context in which they came up in the lesson. If you speak your SS' L1, you might like to elicit a translation for the words/phrases for the SS to write next to them. You may also like to ask SS to test each other on the phrases.

Study Link SS can find more practice of these words and phrases on the MultiROM and on the *New English File Beginner* website.

Extra photocopiable activities

Communicative
Time bingo *p.173* (instructions *p.156*)
Song
Friday I'm in love p.204 (instructions *p.200*)

HOMEWORK

Study Link **Workbook** *pp.26–27*

For instructions on how to use these pages, see *p.29*.

What do you remember?

GRAMMAR

1 b 2 b 3 a 4 a 5 a 6 b 7 b 8 b 9 a
10 b

VOCABULARY

a	1	listen	c	1	half past two
	2	speak		2	five to six
	3	live		3	quarter to ten
	4	read		4	twenty past ten
	5	have/eat		5	twenty-five to four
b	1	bread	d	1	time
	2	twenty		2	depends
	3	waiter		3	know
	4	fruit		4	please
	5	bank		5	lot

PRONUNCIATION

a	vowels:	boot
	consonants:	witch, vase, chess, jazz, girl
c	breakfast potatoes administrator policeman
	Saturday

What can you do?

1 CAN YOU UNDERSTAND THIS TEXT?

a	1	fruit
	2	meat
	3	salads
	4	butter
	5	fish
	6	bacon
	7	wine

2 CAN YOU WRITE THIS IN ENGLISH?

a	1 Selma 2 Emre 3 Selma 4 Selma 5 Emre

3 CAN YOU UNDERSTAND THESE PEOPLE?

First name	Ania
Surname	Nowak
Nationality	Polish
Age	19
Occupation	student
Brothers/Sisters at school	No ✗ Yes ✓
Name/Class number	Maria, class 5
Phone number	07981 663745

3.39 CD2 Track 38

R = receptionist, A = Ania
R Hello. Are you a new student?
A Yes, I am.
R OK. First I need some information. What's your first name?
A Ania. That's A-N-I-A.
R And what's your surname?
A Nowak.
R Sorry, can you spell that, please?
A Yes, N-O-W-A-K.
R Where are you from, Ania?
A I'm from Poland, from Katowice.
R Oh you're Polish. And how old are you?
A I'm 19.
R What do you do?
A I'm a student at the University of Warsaw.
R Do you have brothers or sisters at this school?
A Yes, I have a sister. Her name's Maria and she's in class 5.
R OK. Do you have a phone number?
A Yes, my mobile is 07981663745.
R 07981…
A 663745.
R Thanks. Now please go to room 8 to do the entry test…

Extra photocopiable activities

Grammar
3 revision *p.135*
Vocabulary
Categories *p.195* (instructions *p.191*)

Test and Assessment CD-ROM

File 3 Quicktest
File 3 Test

4 A

G adverbs of frequency, present simple
V a typical day
P sentence stress

Do you like mornings?

File 4 overview

File 4 gives SS more practice with the present simple, first in **4A** with adverbs of frequency, and then in **4B** with questions, where present simple questions are contrasted with questions with *be*. **4C** introduces the verb *can*, and in the **Practical English** lesson SS learn to ask and answer how much things cost, and to buy food and drink in a coffee shop.

Lesson plan

This lesson begins with the context of a questionnaire *Do you like mornings?* about typical morning activities. This leads into learning the vocabulary to talk about your daily routine. The grammar focus is on using adverbs of frequency. We have deliberately limited the choice of adverbs to the four most common ones – *always, never, usually,* and *sometimes,* and focus on their position with the present simple. (Other adverbs of frequency, and their position after *be,* are taught in *New English File Elementary.*) SS then consolidate the grammar and vocabulary by reading an adapted magazine article about a day in the life of the singer James Blunt, and the lesson builds up to a speaking activity where SS tell a partner about their own daily routine.

Optional lead-in (books closed)

- Write the following questions on the board:
  Are you a 'morning person'?   Are you a 'late night person'?
- Ask the questions to each student, and write their names under the questions, to see what the majority of the class consider themselves to be.

1 LISTENING & SPEAKING

a • Books open. Focus on the two pictures. Ask SS *Does the man like mornings?,* etc.
- Now focus on the questionnaire **Do you like mornings?** Give SS time to read the questions. Then go through the questions making sure SS understand them.
- Now get SS to write their answers on a piece of paper. Tell them they only have to write the numbers for the times, or *yes/no,* not full sentences. Monitor and help.

b • **4.1** Focus on the instructions. Tell SS that they are going to hear Anna answering the seven questions in the questionnaire.
- Play the CD for SS to listen only and then play it again for SS to write the answers to the questions. They can write the question number and a short answer on a piece of paper. Replay as necessary.
- Check answers by playing the CD again and pausing after Anna answers each question.

1 at six o'clock
2 yes
3 fruit or cereal, and coffee
4 sitting down
5 at seven
6 No, because I get up at six.
7 Yes

Extra support

You could ask SS to turn to the listening script on *p.84* and listen and read while you play the CD again. Elicit/explain any new vocabulary, e.g. *very early.*

> **4.1**   CD2 Track 39
>
> **I = interviewer, A = Anna**
> **I** What time do you get up?
> **A** Very early! At six o'clock.
> **I** Do you have a shower?
> **A** Yes.
> **I** What do you have for breakfast?
> **A** Fruit or cereal. And coffee.
> **I** Do you have breakfast sitting down or standing up?
> **A** Sitting down.
> **I** What time do you go to work?
> **A** At seven. I start work at eight, but my office isn't very near where I live.
> **I** Are you in a hurry in the morning?
> **A** No, because I get up at six! I have time for everything.
> **I** Do you like mornings?
> **A** Yes I do. I like my job. I don't get up and think 'Oh no! Work…'

c • **4.2** Focus on the questions. Play the CD for SS to listen and repeat, encouraging them to copy the rhythm. Replay as necessary.

> **4.2**   CD2 Track 40
>
> 1 What time do you get up?
> 2 Do you have a shower?
> 3 What do you have for breakfast?
> 4 Do you have breakfast sitting down or standing up?
> 5 What time do you go to work?
> 6 Are you in a hurry in the morning?
> 7 Do you like mornings?

d • Demonstrate the activity by getting SS to ask you the questions in the questionnaire. Give simple answers that SS can understand.
- Put SS in pairs, **A** and **B**. Ask the **B**s to close their books. Tell **A** to ask **B** the questions and to write down his/her answers on a piece of paper. Then swap roles. Monitor and help.
- When SS finish get some feedback. Ask a few SS to tell you any things about their partner, e.g. *Lina gets up at 7.30. She doesn't have breakfast.*

Extra challenge

You could get SS to change pairs and tell another student what they know about their partner, e.g. *Amy gets up at 7.30, she has a shower*, etc.

2 VOCABULARY A typical day

a • Tell SS to go to **Vocabulary Bank** *A typical day* on *p.111*.

• **4.3** Focus on the instructions for **a**. Play the CD and get SS to repeat the phrases. Use the pause button as necessary. Remind SS that the underlined syllables are stressed more strongly. Replay as necessary.

4.3	CD2 Track 41
get up	go home
have breakfast	go shopping
have a shower	go to the gym
go to work	make dinner
go to university	have dinner
have a coffee	do housework
have a sandwich	watch TV
have lunch	go to bed
finish work	

• Focus on the box and go through the information. Highlight that the verb *make* is used when we make a meal or a drink, e.g. *make dinner, make coffee*, whereas we use *do* with housework (*do the housework*).

⚠ Stress that *housework* means cooking, cleaning, etc. SS may confuse this with *homework* (= exercises a teacher gives you to do at home).

• Focus on the different constructions with *go*. Highlight that *go* usually uses the preposition *to*, e.g. *go to the gym, go to the cinema*. Point out that *go home* is an exception. Highlight that we **don't** use *the* with *work, school*, and *bed*.

• **4.4** Focus on the instructions for **b**. Demonstrate the activity by playing the first two sentences and asking SS to point to the picture. Ask them *What number is the picture?* each time.

• Now play the CD from the beginning pausing after each sentence for SS to listen and point to the picture.

4.4	CD2 Track 42

They have lunch at two o'clock.
She finishes work at half past five.
He goes to the gym.
They watch TV.
She goes shopping.
He goes to university at half past eight.
They do housework.
They go to bed at eleven o'clock.
He makes dinner.
She has a coffee.

• Focus on the instructions for **c**. Elicit the first four sentences, i.e. *They get up at half past seven. They have breakfast. He has a shower. She goes to work.*

• Then get SS to continue in pairs. Remind them to add an *s* to the verb (or use *has*) if the picture shows just the man or just the woman doing something. Monitor and help. Make a note of any mistakes and correct them on the board later.

• Finally, elicit the man and woman's day from the whole class, picture by picture.

Study Link SS can find more practice of these phrases on the MultiROM and on the *New English File Beginner* website.

• Tell SS to go back to the main lesson on *p.34*.

b • Focus on the instructions and demonstrate the activity.

⚠ If you are happy to act in front of your class, you can mime a few verbs for SS to guess. However, if you are not comfortable acting, you might prefer to draw the verbs instead.

• Get SS to continue miming or drawing in pairs. Monitor and help. Correct any mistakes on the board.

Extra support

You could let SS refer to **Vocabulary Bank** *A typical day* on *p.111* if they can't remember all the verbs.

3 PRONUNCIATION sentence stress

a • **4.5** Focus on the questions and answers. Remind SS that the words that are underlined are important information words, and are stressed.

• Play the CD once for SS just to listen. Then play the CD again for SS to listen and repeat. Encourage them to try and copy the rhythm by stressing the underlined words more strongly and the other words less strongly. Replay as necessary.

4.5	CD2 Track 43

A What time do you get up?
B At seven o'clock.
A What time do you have breakfast?
B At half past seven.
A What time do you go to work?
B At eight o'clock.

Extra challenge

To revise **linking**, which SS studied in **3A**, ask them to find pairs of words in **a** that are linked (*get up, seven o'clock, at eight o'clock*). Model and drill these. Ask SS to think about linking when doing **b**, and give encouragement to SS you hear using it.

b • Focus on the question *What time do you...?* and the verbs, and elicit the questions from the class.

• Demonstrate the activity by getting SS to ask you the questions and answer them. Try to use *about* in your answers, e.g. *I get up at about 7.00*, and teach that *about* = more or less; approximately. You can also use *I usually...*, which SS learnt in **3B**.

• Now tell SS they are going to ask and answer the questions about a typical week day. Put SS in pairs and get them to ask and answer the questions, paying special attention to sentence stress. Monitor and help. Make a note of any general problems SS are having and deal with these on the board at the end.

4 GRAMMAR adverbs of frequency

a • Focus on the chart and elicit the days of the week from the letters.

• Elicit the meaning of the highlighted words by looking at the ticks and crosses and asking *How many days?* (*always* = five days, *never* = no days, *usually* = four days, *sometimes* = two days).

If you speak your SS' L1, you may want to elicit a translation of these words.

- Tell SS that 1–4 are the first parts of a sentence and a–d are the second parts. Tell SS they have to read the sentences and match the two parts. Demonstrate the activity by doing the first example with the class (*I always get up at 7.30…because I start work at 8.30*).
- Ask SS to continue individually. Get them to compare their answers in pairs and then check answers by asking individual SS to read out the complete sentence.

> 1 c   2 d   3 a   4 b

b ● Tell SS to go to **Grammar Bank 4A** on *p.94*.
  ● **4.6** Play the CD and ask SS to listen and repeat the example sentences. Use the pause button as necessary. Elicit the stressed syllable by asking *Where's the stress?* for each adverb and get SS to underline it (<u>al</u>ways, <u>u</u>sually, <u>some</u>times, <u>nev</u>er). Replay as necessary.

> **4.6**   CD2 Track 44
>
> I always have breakfast.
> They usually finish work at 5 o'clock.
> She sometimes watches TV in the evening.
> He never eats meat.

- Go through the rules for adverbs of frequency with the class using the expanded information in the **Grammar notes** below to help you. You may want to use L1 here if you know it.

Grammar notes

- With all verbs except *be*, adverbs of frequency go <u>before</u> the main verb. At this level we have not focused on adverbs of frequency with *be*.
- In ⊞ sentences they usually go between the pronoun and the verb, e.g. **I always have** *coffee for breakfast*.

⚠ *Sometimes* and *usually* can also be used at the beginning of a sentence, but it is probably best to just give SS a simple rule at this level.

- You may want to tell SS that in a negative sentence the adverbs go between *don't/doesn't* and the main verb, e.g. **I don't usually have** *breakfast*. However, this is not tested in the exercises.
- Highlight that we always use a positive verb with *never*, e.g. *I never eat meat*.

- Focus on the exercises for **4A** on *p.95* and get SS to do them in pairs or individually. If they do them individually, get them to compare answers with a partner.
- Check answers.

> **a** 1 I never go to bed before 12.
>   2 My husband sometimes makes dinner.
>   3 I always have a shower in the morning.
>   4 He usually has breakfast at home.
>   5 They always go to work by bus.
>   6 We sometimes have a sandwich for lunch.
>   7 The restaurant usually closes late.
>   8 She never goes shopping after work.
>
> **b** 1 sometimes goes   2 always do   3 usually have
>   4 never drink   5 always gets   6 never speak
>   7 sometimes watch   8 usually finishes

Study Link SS can find more practice of this grammar on the MultiROM and on the *New English File Beginner* website.

- Tell SS to go back to the main lesson on *p.34*.

c ● Focus on the instructions. Demonstrate the activity by telling SS about yourself, e.g. *I always listen to the radio in the car. I never read a newspaper in the morning.* You may want to add a bit of extra information (e.g. *I listen to Kiss FM*), or a reason to encourage SS to do the same.

- Ask a few SS to make a true sentence with the first prompt. If they respond with *always* or *usually*, you could ask them *Which radio station?*
- Now put SS in pairs and tell them to make true sentences.
- Monitor and help. Make a note of any general problems and deal with them at the end.

Extra support

You could ask SS to write the sentences and then read them out to a partner.

Extra challenge

At the end you could get SS to tell the class a sentence about their partner, e.g. *Ivan always drinks black coffee.*

5 READING

a ● Focus on the photos and the title and ask *Who's James Blunt?* and elicit/teach *He's a singer.* Ask SS if they know any of his songs (SS may have listened to a cover version of his song, *You're beautiful*, in lesson **2C**).

- Tell SS that this article is adapted from a newspaper, so it will have some words they don't know. Remind them that when they read they should try to focus on the words they know, and try to guess the meaning of new words. Point out that they also have a glossary at the end of the article to help them.
- Go through the **Glossary** and make sure SS understand all the new words.
- Set a time limit and tell SS to read the article once (fast readers may have time to read it twice).
- When you can see that they have all finished, focus on the questions and get SS to answer them orally with a partner, or to write short answers. Monitor and help.
- Check answers.
- Finally, go through the text line by line and elicit/explain/demonstrate new vocabulary (but without focusing on the highlighted words), e.g. *view, sea, hungry, sofa, village, tin of tuna, ham, work in the garden* (= e.g. plant trees), *music system, music collection, singer-songwriter, club, look out of, sky*.

⚠ SS may find the two meanings of *like* confusing in this sentence: *I* **like** *singer-songwriters from the 1970s,* **like** *Lou Reed and Leonard Cohen.* Point out that the second *like* = for example.

> 1 He lives in a beautiful old house in Ibiza.
> 2 He usually gets up at about 9.30.
> 3 He always wears jeans and a T-shirt.
> 4 No, he doesn't./No, he never has breakfast.
> 5 He makes a fire and cleans the house. Then he plays the piano, or he sits on the sofa and plays the guitar.
> 6 He has bread and a tin of tuna, or maybe ham or cheese.
> 7 He sometimes works in the garden.
> 8 No, he doesn't.
> 9 He usually goes out with friends.

Extra support

Alternatively, you could read the article aloud to the class, eliciting/explaining the meaning of new words as they come up or directing them to the glossary. Then ask the questions to the whole class. If you do this, you don't need to do exercise **b**.

Extra challenge

You could ask the class more comprehension questions on the text, e.g. *How old is his house? Why doesn't he have breakfast?*, etc.

b • Focus on the highlighted words in the article and point out that they all refer to time. Put SS in pairs to guess their meaning.

⚠ If SS have dictionaries, they could check their own answers here. If not, use your SS' L1 if you know it.

c • Focus on the instructions and ask SS to complete the sentences with one of the highlighted words. SS could do this activity in pairs or individually.

  • Check answers.

> 1 Then
> 2 When
> 3 after
> 4 before
> 5 about

d • Focus on the question. Write on the board *It's typical because…* and *It isn't typical because…*

  • Elicit ideas from the class and write them on the board, e.g. *It's typical because he plays the guitar. It isn't typical because he lives in a small village/doesn't have a TV.*

  • Finally, ask SS if they think he has a nice day.

6 SPEAKING & WRITING

a • Tell SS to go to **Vocabulary Bank** *A typical day* on *p.111*. Then write on the board: *My typical morning,* and write about it on the board, e.g. *I usually get up at 7 o'clock.*

  • Ask SS to copy the title and write the first sentence for them. Then tell them to use the other verb phrases (*have breakfast, have a shower,* etc.) to write about their typical **morning** (during the week). Monitor and help while they do so.

  • Get SS to swap their paragraphs and read their partner's text.

b • Tell SS they are going to use the verbs to tell a partner about their typical **afternoon** and **evening**. Elicit the first sentences from two or three SS, e.g. *I usually have lunch at half past one. I have a salad and then a coffee.*

• Get SS to continue describing their typical weekday afternoon and evening in pairs, and to use adverbs of frequency whenever appropriate. **A** could talk about his/her afternoon, then **B** could, and then repeat for the evening, or you could give **A** a long turn speaking about both afternoon and evening, and then swap roles.

• Monitor and help. Make a note of any mistakes and correct them on the board.

• Tell SS to go back to the main lesson on *p.35*.

Extra challenge

Get fast finishers to talk about their typical Saturday or Sunday.

WORDS AND PHRASES TO LEARN

Focus on the words and phrases to learn. Make sure SS understand the meaning of each phrase. If necessary, remind SS of the context in which they came up in the lesson. If you speak your SS' L1, you might like to elicit a translation for the words/phrases for the SS to write next to them. You may also like to ask SS to test each other on the phrases.

> **Study Link** SS can find more practice of these words and phrases on the MultiROM and on the *New English File Beginner* website.

Extra photocopiable activities

Grammar
adverbs of frequency *p.136*
Communicative
What about you? *p.174* (instructions *p.156*)

HOMEWORK

> **Study Link** **Workbook** *pp.28–29*

G word order in questions; question words
V common verbs 2
P /eə/, /ɒ/, /aʊ/, and /j/

Life at the top of the world

Lesson plan

In this lesson SS focus on word order in questions. The context for presenting the grammar is an interview with the Tourist Information Officer in the town of Hammerfest in Norway, which is the most northern town in the world. He talks about life in a town which has 24 hours daylight in the summer, but is dark most of the day in winter. In Vocabulary, SS learn some more common verbs, and the pronunciation focus is on vowel sounds /eə/, /ɒ/, and /aʊ/, and the consonant sound /j/. The lesson builds up to a speaking activity where SS talk about what they do in their free time.

Optional lead-in (books closed)

*   Write the following information about you on the board:
1   **your name**
2   **the town where you live**
3   *No, I'm not. I'm* (your nationality).
4   *I'm a teacher.*
5   **the time you get up** (e.g. *at 7*)
6   **what you have for breakfast** (e.g. *coffee and cereal*)
*   Tell SS they have to ask the right questions for the answers on the board. Demonstrate the activity by pointing to your name and eliciting the question (*What's your name?*).
*   Put SS in pairs and give them a few minutes to decide on the questions.
*   Elicit the questions from individual SS by pointing to the answers on the board.

> 1   What's your name?
> 2   Where do you live?
> 3   Are you (American, etc.)?
> 4   What do you do?
> 5   What time do you get up?
> 6   What do you have for breakfast?

1 READING

a • Books open. Focus on the instructions and the photos of Hammerfest. Elicit the meaning of *winter* and *summer* and write the words on the board and underline the stress (*winter, summer*). Use the photos to pre-teach *snow*.
   • Ask SS *Who prefers the winter?* and get a show of hands. Do the same for the summer.

b • Focus on the introduction and the two questions. Give SS time to read it and answer the questions with a partner.
   • Check answers, and explain/elicit/demonstrate the meaning of *town, north, Norway, kilometres* /kɪˈlɒmɪtəz/ or /ˈkɪləˌmiːtəz/, *the Arctic Circle, light* (opposite = *dark*), *hours* /ˈaʊəz/, *midnight,* and *sun.* Model and drill the pronunciation.
   ⚠ There are two high numbers in the text – 1,000 and 9,407. In this book SS only learn how to *say* numbers 1–100 so don't ask them to say these numbers. Saying high numbers is taught in *New English File Elementary*.

> 1   It's in the north of Norway.
> 2   In the winter it is light for only two or three hours. In the summer it is light for 24 hours.

c • Focus on the photo of Knut-Arne Iversen (/ˌknʊt ɑːnə ˈiːvəsən/) and read the information about him aloud. Show SS that the questions are missing.
   • Focus on the instructions for exercise **c** and go through the questions, dealing with any new vocabulary.
   • Focus on the interview and the first question, which has been done. Tell SS to read the interview and write 2–7 in the boxes next to the questions. Give SS time to match the questions to the answers. Get them to compare answers with a partner.

d • **4.7** Play the CD once for SS to check their answers. Pause after Knut's second answer, and elicit what the question was. Get SS to write the question in the space. Check the meaning of any new vocabulary in Knut's answer. Repeat with the other questions and answers.

> 7, 6, 3, 1, 5, 4, 2

> **4.7**   CD2 Track 45
> **N = narrator, I = interviewer, K = Knut**
> **N** Hammerfest is a small town in the north of Norway. It is about 1,000 km north of the Arctic Circle. Only 9,407 people live here. In the winter it is light for only two or three hours. People have breakfast, lunch, and dinner in the dark. In the summer, it is light for 24 hours, and people go to bed very late. Some people play golf in the midnight sun! Knut-Arne Iversen is from Hammerfest. He works for the Tourist Information Office.
> **I** Do a lot of tourists come to Hammerfest?
> **K** Yes, about 175,000 a year.
> **I** When do they usually come?
> **K** In the summer. We don't have a lot of tourists in the winter!
> **I** Is the winter very cold?
> **K** No, not very, about –3 degrees. But we sometimes have a lot of snow, and the streets and schools are closed.
> **I** What do people do in the winter?
> **K** We do a lot of sports – we ski a lot and we have snowmobiles. Children usually play outside, but if it's very cold, they play inside on their computer or watch TV. In the evening we usually stay at home and relax, or go and see friends. But the winter is difficult for old people.
> **I** What do people do in the summer?
> **K** Life is completely different. It's light for 24 hours a day, and the weather is sometimes very hot. People are outside all the time. We fish, and walk, and have barbecues. We don't swim because the water is very cold – maybe only 10 degrees. People don't sleep a lot, and young children say 'I don't want to go to bed. It isn't dark.'
> **I** Do you prefer the summer or the winter?
> **K** In the winter it's nice to be at home with your family and friends. But I prefer the summer.
> **I** Do you like life in Hammerfest?
> **K** Yes. Life here is easy. It's quiet and beautiful, and the air is clean. But the winter is very long, and the summer is very short. I'm not sure if I will stay here forever.

e ● Tell SS to read the interview again, with the questions now in. Tell them to stop when they come to a highlighted word, and match it to its opposite in the list. Get SS to compare with a partner and check answers. Check meaning, model and drill pronunciation, and get SS to underline the stressed syllables.

> **1** hot **2** difficult **3** dark **4** short **5** inside
> **6** winter **7** different **8** closed

● Get SS to cover half of the list and try to remember the eight opposite words. Then they cover the other half of the list and remember the other eight. Then test their memory by asking, e.g. *What's the opposite of (outside)?*

● Put SS in pairs, **A** and **B**, and get **A**s to test **B**s (book closed) on either of the adjectives in the pairs, asking *What's the opposite of...?* Then they swap roles.

f ● Tell SS to cover the interview. Ask the class the questions and get them to try to remember Knut's answer from memory.

● Ask them *Do you think Hammerfest is a nice place to live?* and elicit responses.

● Put SS in pairs and tell them they are going to ask the same questions about their town. Elicit the first question, e.g. *Do a lot of tourists come to...?*

● Get SS to ask and answer in pairs.

● Get feedback by finding out who prefers the summer and who the winter in their country.

⚠ If all your class are from the same town, you could ask the first five questions to the whole class, and get SS to ask each other the last two.

2 GRAMMAR word order in questions

a ● Focus on the task. Elicit the first question and write it on the board.

● Give SS time to write the other questions in pairs.

● Check answers.

> Where is Knut-Arne from?
> Is Hammerfest in Norway?
> Where does Knut-Arne work?
> Do people swim in the sea?

● Elicit answers from individual SS.

b ● Tell SS to go to **Grammar Bank 4B** on *p.94*.

● (4.8) Play the CD and ask SS to listen and repeat the example sentences. Use the pause button as necessary.

(4.8)	CD2 Track 46
Are they American?	Do you speak English?
Is this your coat?	Where do you live?
How old are you?	What does your sister do?
Where are you from?	What music do you like?
What time is it?	When does Jane go to the gym?
	How do you spell it?

● Go through the rules for word order in questions, using the information in **Grammar notes**. You may want to use L1 here if you know it.

Grammar notes

● With the verb *be*, in ⊞ and ⊟ sentences the subject (person or thing) always comes before the verb. To make a question you simply invert the subject and the verb, so *They are American* becomes *Are they American?* and *This is your coat* becomes *Is this your coat?*, etc.

● With other main verbs in the present simple, you need to first put the auxiliary verb (*do* or *does*) then the subject and then the main verb in the infinitive, so *She likes chocolate* becomes *Does she like chocolate?*

● If a question has a question word, e.g. *What, Where*, etc. then this always comes first.

● The acronyms **ASI** (**A**uxiliary verb + **S**ubject + **I**nfinitive) and **QUASI** (**Qu**estion word + **A**uxiliary verb + **S**ubject + **I**nfinitive) will help SS remember the correct word order in questions in the present simple (with verbs other than *be*).

● Focus on the exercises for **4B** on *p.95* and get SS to do them individually or in pairs. If they do them individually, get them to compare answers with a partner.

● Check answers.

> **a 1** Where is the city centre?
>   **2** How is your mother?
>   **3** Are we late for class?
>   **4** Is this your coat?
>   **5** Where does Kate live?
>   **6** Does your brother speak English?
>   **7** Do your family like sushi?
>   **8** What time does the film start?
>
> **b 1** When **2** What **3** How **4** What **5** Who
>   **6** When **7** Where **8** How

Study Link SS can find more practice of this grammar on the MultiROM and on the *New English File Beginner* website.

● Tell SS to go back to the main lesson on *p.36*.

3 VOCABULARY common verbs 2

a ● This exercise revises verb noun collocations SS already know. Focus on the instructions. Give SS time to complete the sentences in pairs then check answers.

> **1** go **2** watch **3** read **4** listen **5** do **6** go
> **7** have **8** eat

b ● Tell SS to go to **Vocabulary Bank** *Common verbs 2* on *p.112*. Focus on part **A**.

● (4.9) Focus on the instructions for **a**. Play the CD and get SS to repeat the phrases in chorus. Use the pause button as necessary.

(4.9)	CD2 Track 47
go to the cinema	play computer games
go to the theatre	do sport
go to the beach	ski
play tennis	walk
play the piano	swim

- Highlight that:
  - we say *play **the** piano* (*the* with musical instruments) but *play tennis*, *play computer games* (i.e. we don't use *the* with sports or games).
  - we say *do sport* (general) and *do exercise/yoga, aerobics*, etc. but *play* + names of sports, e.g. *golf, football, tennis*, etc.
- Focus on the instructions for **b**. Ask SS to cover the words and look at the pictures. Give them time to remember the words with a partner. Monitor and help. Correct any mistakes on the board.
- Focus on the instructions for **c**. Write *sometimes* and *never* on the board. Demonstrate the activity by making sentences about yourself, e.g. *I sometimes go to the cinema.* Elicit the first sentence from two or three SS, and then ask SS to continue in pairs.
- Monitor and help. Make a note of any mistakes and correct them on the board.

Study Link SS can find more practice of these verbs on the MultiROM and on the *New English File Beginner* website.

- Tell SS to go back to the main lesson on *p.37*.

4 PRONUNCIATION /eə/, /ɒ/, /aʊ/, and /j/

- Read the **Pronunciation notes** and decide how much of the information you want to give your SS.

Pronunciation notes

- The sounds /eə/, /ɒ/, and /aʊ/ are all vowel sounds whereas /j/ is a consonant sound. Highlight that the sound /j/ is **not** pronounced the same as the letter *j*.
- You may want to highlight the following sound–spelling patterns:
  /eə/ *air* and *eir* are always pronounced /eə/, e.g. *hair, their*. The letters *ere* are sometimes /eə/, e.g. *where*, but can also be /ɪe/ as in *here*.
  /ɒ/ remind SS that the typical spelling of this sound is *o* between two consonants, e.g. *hot, long, not,* etc. *What* and *watch* (and *want*) are exceptions.
  /aʊ/ *ou* and *ow* are often pronounced /aʊ/, e.g. *house, brown*.
  /j/ the letter *y* at the beginning of a word is pronounced /j/, e.g. *yes*. The letter *u* is sometimes pronounced /juː/, e.g. *music, student, university*.

a ● **4.10** Focus on the sound picture *chair* and write the word on the board. Play the CD to model and drill the word and sound (pause after the sound).
- Now focus on the example words after *chair*. Remind SS that the pink letters are the /eə/ sound. Play the CD pausing after each word for SS to repeat. Replay as necessary.
- Repeat for the other three sounds and words.

4.10		CD2 Track 48
chair	/eə/	where, there, their, hairdresser
clock	/ɒ/	what, watch, hot, long
owl	/aʊ/	how, town, mountains, outside
yacht	/j/	you, yes, usually, music, computer, newspaper

Study Link SS can find more practice of these sounds on the MultiROM and on the *New English File Beginner* website.

b ● **4.11** Focus on the sentences and play the CD for SS to just listen. Remind SS that the underlined words are the ones that are stressed more strongly. Then play the CD for SS to listen and repeat. Give SS time to practise saying the sentences.

4.11	CD2 Track 49
Where do you live? Over there.	
What TV programmes do you watch?	
What music do you usually listen to?	
How do you relax? I walk in the mountains.	

5 SPEAKING

- Focus on the question prompts and the speech bubbles. Elicit that *Do you* has been added where the slash (/) is. Highlight that SS need to add this every time there is a slash.
- Model and drill some of the questions, reminding SS to stress question words, verbs, and nouns, but not pronouns or prepositions.
- Focus on the information box. Remind SS of the preposition usage: **at** with times, **on** with days of the week, and **in** with months, years, and seasons. You might want to point out that we say *in the morning, afternoon*, etc.
- Demonstrate the activity by getting SS to ask you some or all of the questions.
- Put SS in pairs, **A** and **B**, and ask **B**s to close their books. Tell **A** to ask **B** the questions, and then get SS to swap roles.
- Monitor and help. Make a note of any problems they are having and deal with these at the end.
- Get feedback from a few pairs.

Extra support

You could let both SS look at the questions while one is asking.

WORDS AND PHRASES TO LEARN

Focus on the words and phrases to learn. Make sure SS understand the meaning of each phrase. If necessary, remind SS of the context in which they came up in the lesson. If you speak your SS' L1, you might like to elicit a translation for the words/phrases for the SS to write next to them. You may also like to ask SS to test each other on the phrases.

Study Link SS can find more practice of these words and phrases on the MultiROM and on the *New English File Beginner* website.

Extra photocopiable activities

Grammar
word order in questions *p.137*
Communicative
Find the people *p.175* (instructions *p.156*)

HOMEWORK

Study Link Workbook *pp.30–31*

4 C

G *can/can't*: permission and possibility
V common verbs 2
P sentence rhythm

You can't park here

Lesson plan

Can is a very versatile verb in English and is used to express ability, possibility, permission, and to make requests. This lesson focuses on two of the most common uses, **permission** and **possibility**.

Can for ability (e.g. *Can you swim?*) is not taught here, as for many beginner SS it is confusing, since in many languages permission and possibility are expressed with one verb, but ability with another. *Can* for ability is taught in *New English File Elementary*.

Can is presented through two dialogues which illustrate permission and possibility. Special attention is given to the pronunciation of *can/can't* which sometimes causes communication problems. In Vocabulary SS learn some more common verbs, especially ones which are used in the context of permission/possibility, e.g. *pay, park, come*. Finally, SS talk about what people can/can't do in their town, and what they personally can/can't do at work or school.

Optional lead-in (books closed)

- Draw these phonetic symbols on the board: 1 /æ/ 2 /ɑː/ 3 /ə/ and elicit the picture words (*cat, car,* and *computer*).
- Now write the following words on the board:
  about   dark   after   sandwich   half   address   black   stand   start
- Get SS, in pairs, to say the words and decide if the **a** is sound 1, sound 2, or sound 3.
- Check answers and write the words on the board under the symbol.

/æ/	/ɑː/	/ə/
sandwich	dark	about
black	after	address
stand	half	
	start	

1 GRAMMAR *can/can't*: permission and possibility

a ● **4.12** Books open. Focus on the instructions. Ask SS to cover the dialogues. Elicit answers to the question, and accept any possible ideas, e.g. *Don't park here!* Some TT may prefer to use L1 here.

- Play the dialogues once or twice for SS to get the gist of what's happening.
- Get feedback asking SS for any words or phrases they understood.

4.12   CD2 Track 50

P = policeman, W = woman
1 **P**   Excuse me. You can't park there.
   W   No? Why not?
   P   You're on a double yellow line.
   W   Oh – I'm sorry, officer. Where can I park near here?
   P   You can park over there, madam, in the car park.
   W   Thank you, officer.

E = Ellie, M = Matt
2 **E**   Hi Matt.
   M   Hi. Who's that?
   E   It's me, Ellie. How are you?
   M   Oh, fine thanks.
   E   Matt, can you come to dinner on Friday?
   M   On Friday? Oh I'm really sorry. I can't come. It's my girlfriend's birthday.
   E   Your girlfriend?
   M   Yes, Lucy, from work.
   E   Oh. Lucy.
   M   Sorry about the dinner.
   E   That's OK. Bye.

---

b ● Play the CD again for SS to listen to and read dialogue 1.

- Focus on the questions. Give SS time to read them and deal with any problems. Get SS to answer them in pairs.
- Check answers with the whole class. Then repeat the process for dialogue 2.

---

1 Because she/her car is on a double yellow line.
2 In the car park.
3 Yes, he is.
4 To have dinner with Matt.
5 He says no, because it's his girlfriend's birthday.
6 She's sad.

- Finally, go through the two dialogues line by line and focus on any new phrases, e.g. (dialogue 1) *double yellow line, officer, over there, madam* (you may also want to teach *sir* for a man) and (dialogue 2) *Who's that? It's me, I'm really sorry, birthday, from work, Sorry about..., That's OK.*

⚠ Highlight the difference between *there* and *over there*.

⚠ Highlight *That's OK* as a common response to *Sorry!*

c ● Tell SS to look at the highlighted phrases in the dialogues.

- Focus on the questions and elicit that the first dialogue is about **permission** (parking on a double yellow line is not permitted), and the second is about a **possibility** (it's not possible for Matt to have dinner with Ellie).

d ● Tell SS to go to **Grammar Bank 4C** on *p.94*.

- **4.13** Play the CD and ask SS to listen and repeat the example sentences. Use the pause button as necessary.

4.13   CD2 Track 51

You can park here.
He can come to dinner tonight.
We can have lunch outside.

You can't park here.
He can't come to dinner tonight.
We can't have lunch outside.

| Can I park here? | Yes, you can. | No, you can't. |
| Can they come to dinner? | Yes, they can. | No, they can't. |

- Go through the rules for *can* with the class, using the expanded information in **Grammar notes** to help you. You may want to use L1 here if you know it.

Grammar notes

- *can/can't* are used to talk about permission (*You can park there* = It is permitted) and possibility (*I can come tomorrow* = It is possible for me to come tomorrow). Many other languages use the same verb for these two uses. *Can* for ability is taught in *New English File Elementary* (see **Lesson plan** at the start of this lesson).

- There are only two possible forms, *can* or *can't* (there is no change for the 3rd person).

- The negative *can't* is a contraction of *cannot*. *Can't* is almost always used in both conversation and informal writing.

- Questions with *can* are formed by inverting the subject and the verb, NOT with *do*.

- The verb after *can* is the infinitive without *to*, e.g. *You can park here* NOT ~~You can to park here~~.

- Focus on the **You** box and go through the information. Highlight that *you* can be singular or plural in English. Explain the third use of *you* (= people in general).

- Focus on the exercises for **4C** on *p.95* and get SS to do them individually or in pairs. If they do them individually, get them to compare answers with a partner.

- Check answers.

> **a 1** Can we watch TV after dinner?
> **2** I can't see the board.
> **3** James can help us tomorrow.
> **4** Can you come to class tomorrow?
> **5** You can read my newspaper.
> **6** We can't park here.
> **7** Can I sit here?
> **8** She can't go to the cinema tomorrow.
> **b 1** Can, swim **2** can't read **3** can't remember
> **4** can have **5** can, speak **6** can walk
> **7** can't hear **8** Can, open

Study Link SS can find more practice of this grammar on the MultiROM and on the *New English File Beginner* website.

- Tell SS to go back to the main lesson on *p.38*.

2 PRONUNCIATION sentence rhythm

- Read the **Pronunciation notes** and decide how much of the information you want to give your SS.

Pronunciation notes

- There are two main pronunciation problems related to *can/can't*:
  - *can* is usually unstressed = /kən/ in ⊞ sentences like *You can take photos*. Your SS may find this difficult to hear and to say. If they stress *can*, the listener may think they are saying a ⊟ sentence.
  - The negative *can't* is always stressed. Not stressing it can cause a communication problem (the listener may understand *can* not *can't*). The pronunciation of *can't* varies among different groups of native English speakers, e.g. in American English it is pronounced /kænt/. In standard British English it is usually pronounced /kɑːnt/ but there are regional variations.

If your own pronunciation of *can't* is different from what is on the CD, you may want to model the sentences yourself. The important thing is for SS to make sure that they stress *can't* quite strongly.

- *can* is stressed in *yes/no* questions, e.g. *Can I sit here?*, but not in questions beginning with a question word, e.g. *Where can I sit?*

a ● **4.14** Focus on the sound picture *cat* and write the word on the board. Play the CD to model and drill the word and sound (pause after the sound).

- Now focus on the sentences after *cat*. Remind SS that the pink letters are the /æ/ sound, and that the underlined words are stressed. Play the CD pausing after each sentence for SS to repeat, encouraging them to copy the rhythm.

- Repeat for the other two sounds and sentences.

4.14		CD2 Track 52
cat	/æ/	Can I park here? Yes, you can.
computer	/ə/	Where can I park? You can park here.
car	/ɑː/	You can't park there.

Study Link SS can find more practice of these sounds on the MultiROM and on the *New English File Beginner* website.

b ● **4.15** This section gives SS practice in distinguishing between *can* and *can't*. Focus on the sentences. Play the CD for SS to hear the difference between the sentences.

4.15		CD2 Track 53
1 a We can park here.		**b** We can't park here.
2 a I can help you.		**b** I can't help you.
3 a We can stop here.		**b** We can't stop here.
4 a You can sit here.		**b** You can't sit here.
5 a Mark can go with me.		**b** Mark can't go with me.
6 a I can walk home.		**b** I can't walk home.
7 a We can come tonight.		**b** We can't come tonight.
8 a You can write in the book.		**b** You can't write in the book.

c ● **4.16** Now tell SS that they are going to hear only <u>one</u> of the sentences (**a** or **b**) and they have to circle the letter of the one they hear.

- Play the CD, pausing for SS to circle **a** or **b**.
- Play the CD again for SS to check their answers.

> **1** a **2** b **3** b **4** b **5** a **6** a **7** b **8** a

4.16		CD2 Track 54
1 We can park here.	**5** Mark can go with me.	
2 I can't help you.	**6** I can walk home.	
3 We can't stop here.	**7** We can't come tonight.	
4 You can't sit here.	**8** You can write in the book.	

Extra challenge

Put SS in pairs, **A** and **B**. Get **A**s to say either sentence **a** or **b** for sentences 1–8 to **B**, who listens and says *a* or *b* depending on which sentence he/she understands. **A** says *yes* or *no*. Then they swap roles.

d ● Focus on the dialogues in exercise **1**. Put SS in pairs and assign roles. Ask SS to practise the dialogues and then swap roles. Monitor and make a note of any pronunciation problems. Correct any mistakes on the board.

Extra support

Model and drill the dialogues line by line or play the CD for SS to repeat.

3 VOCABULARY common verbs 2

a ● Focus on the two signs. Write *You can't …* and *You can …* on the board. Elicit the meaning of the signs and complete the sentences (*You can't park here. You can have a coffee here.*).

b ● Tell SS to go to **Vocabulary Bank** *Common verbs 2* on *p.112*. Focus on part **B**.

   ● **4.17** Focus on the instructions for **a**. Play the CD and get SS to repeat each verb (phrase) in chorus and individually. Use the pause button as necessary.

4.17	CD2 Track 55
smoke	pay by credit card
change money	park
use the Internet	come
take photos	see
drive	hear

   ● Focus on the instructions for **b**. Ask SS to cover the words and look at the pictures. Give them time to remember the words with a partner. Monitor and help.

Study Link SS can find more practice of these verbs on the MultiROM and on the *New English File Beginner* website.

   ● Tell SS to go back to the main lesson on *p.39*.

c ● Focus on the signs. Elicit the verb to complete the first sentence (smoke). Give SS time to complete the rest of the sentences in pairs.

   ● Check answers by asking SS to read out complete sentences. Correct any errors of pronunciation with *can* and *can't*.

1	smoke	4	pay	7	drive
2	change	5	take	8	play
3	use	6	use		

d ● Ask SS to cover sentences 1–4 with a piece of paper and look at the signs. Give them time to remember the sentences with a partner. Then get them to do the same for 5–8. Monitor and make a note of any pronunciation problems and drill any sentences that SS are mispronouncing.

Extra challenge

Ask SS *Where do you see these signs?* and elicit places.

Possible answers
1 in schools, offices, restaurants, etc.
2 outside a bank
3 in a classroom, a hospital
4 in a shop window
5 in a museum
6 in an airport, a station
7 in the street
8 in a park

4 SPEAKING & WRITING

a ● Focus on the questions. Give SS time to read through them and deal with any problems.

   ● Tell SS they are going to interview each other using these questions. Put SS in pairs, **A** and **B**. Give them time to ask the questions and then swap roles. SS should ask their partner either the questions in **At work** or **At university/school** according to whether their partner has a job or is at school/university.

   ⚠ If all your SS are from the same town, you could ask them the questions for **In your town/city** and elicit answers from different SS. They then interview each other with either **At work** or **At university/school**.

   ● Get some general feedback from the class.

Extra support

Get SS to interview you about *your* home town (if it is different from theirs) and your workplace.

Extra challenge

Get the student who is answering in each pair to have their book closed so that they just hear but don't read the questions.

b ● Focus on the instructions and the model. Write the first sentence on the board *In (e.g. Rome) you can…and you can…*

   ⚠ Elicit the start of the second paragraph and write it on the board (*At work/school/university I can…*).

   ● Give SS time to write their paragraph. Monitor and help.

WORDS AND PHRASES TO LEARN

Focus on the words and phrases to learn. Make sure SS understand the meaning of each phrase. If necessary, remind SS of the context in which they came up in the lesson. If you speak your SS' L1, you might like to elicit a translation for the words/phrases for the SS to write next to them. You may also like to ask SS to test each other on the phrases.

Study Link SS can find more practice of these words and phrases on the MultiROM and on the *New English File Beginner* website.

Extra photocopiable activities

Grammar
can / can't p.138
Communicative
What's missing? *p.176* (instructions *p.157*)

HOMEWORK

Study Link Workbook *pp.32–33*

Saying and understanding prices
Buying a coffee
/ʊə/, /s/, and /k/

Lesson plan

In this lesson SS learn how to ask how much something is, and to say prices in pounds, dollars, and euros. At this level SS need more practice in understanding prices than in saying them, as they are likely to have to understand prices if they travel. They go on to practise buying a coffee and something to eat in a coffee shop. In the **People in the street** section, SS hear people talking about where they have lunch and how much it costs. The lesson finishes with the song *Money, money, money*.

Optional lead-in (books closed)

- Revise numbers 10–99 by giving SS a dictation. Dictate ten numbers and ask SS to write them down. Make sure you write the numbers down as you say them. Get them to compare answers with a partner and then check answers.

- Tell SS to choose ten numbers of their own and to write them on a piece of paper. Put SS in pairs, **A** and **B**, and ask **A** to dictate their numbers for **B** to write them down. Then get SS to swap roles. Monitor and make a note of any problems.

- Ask SS to check answers by comparing the numbers they wrote with the numbers their partner wrote.

- Correct any mistakes on the board.

1 UNDERSTANDING PRICES

a ● **4.18** Books open. Focus on the three money pictures and elicit where they are from (Britain, the United States, and the EU). You may want to point out that not all countries in the EU use the euro.

- Play the CD once for SS just to listen and then again for SS to listen and repeat. Highlight that *pence* can be shortened to *p* /piː/.

4.18	CD2 Track 56
twenty pounds	fifty cents
fifty pence / fifty p	twenty euros
twenty dollars	fifty cents

b ● Draw the symbols for pounds, dollars, and euros on the board and elicit what currency they refer to.

- Focus on the instructions. Demonstrate the task by eliciting the first answer, i.e. 1 H (twelve pounds seventy-five). Ask SS to continue matching the words and prices in pairs. Monitor and deal with any problems.

1 H	2 C	3 D	4 A	5 F	6 G	7 E	8 B

c ● **4.19** Play the CD once for SS to listen and check. Then play it again for SS to listen and repeat.

- Highlight that we don't use *and* between pounds and pence or dollars/euros and cents (e.g. NOT ~~two pounds and twenty~~), and that we normally only use the word *pence/cents* for an amount that is less than a pound/dollar/euro (e.g. *fifty cents*, but NOT ~~one dollar fifty cents~~).

4.19	CD2 Track 57
1 twelve pounds seventy-five	
2 fifteen dollars ninety-nine	
3 fifty euros ninety-nine	
4 a hundred and twenty pounds	
5 thirteen dollars twenty-five	
6 three euros twenty	
7 sixty p	
8 eighty cents	

d ● Tell SS to cover the words in A–H and look at the prices 1–8. Give them time to practise saying the prices. Monitor and correct any mistakes SS are making. Then with the prices in words still covered elicit the prices one by one from the class.

e ● **4.20** Focus on the pictures and ask SS what they can see (a newspaper, a phone card, a memory card/stick, and a train ticket). Drill the pronunciation of the four items.

- Now focus on the two prices in each picture and get SS to practise saying them in pairs.

- Play the CD, repeating each dialogue twice for SS to circle the right price. Get them to compare their answers with a partner.

- Check answers.

1 $1.25	2 £15	3 $4.99	4 £30.20

4.20	CD2 Track 58
1 A *The New York Times*, please. B Here you are. A How much is that? B It's one dollar twenty-five.	
2 A Can I have a phone card, please? B How much for? A Fifteen pounds, please. B Here you are. A Thanks.	
3 A Can I have a memory card, please? B Four gig or eight? A Four, please. How much is that? B Four ninety-nine. A Can I pay with Mastercard? B Sure.	
4 A A ticket to Oxford, please. B Single or return? A Return. B Thirty pounds twenty. A Oh! OK.	

f ● Get SS to turn to the listening script on *p.84* and go through the dialogues line by line, eliciting and explaining any other words or phrases SS don't understand, e.g. *Can I pay with Mastercard?*, *Sure*, *A ticket to Oxford, please*, *Single or return?*

⚠ Highlight especially the use of *Can I have...?* to buy something in a shop (or ask for something in a restaurant).

- You may want to point out to SS that if you say the name of the credit card, e.g. Visa, then you say *pay with Visa*, NOT ~~pay by Visa~~.

Extra support

You could get SS to practise the dialogues in pairs. Before they start, play the CD again and get SS to listen and repeat the dialogues.

2 PRONUNCIATION /ʊə/, /s/, and /k/

- Read the **Pronunciation notes** and decide how much of the information you want to give your SS.

Pronunciation notes

- Very few words in English have the /ʊə/ sound. You might like to point out that the sound is a diphthong, i.e. two sounds, if you think it will help your SS.
- The aim of the section on /s/ and /k/ is to help SS with two pronunciations of the letter *c*.
- You may want to highlight the following sound–spelling rules:

  /ʊə/   *eu* is usually pronounced /ʊə/, e.g. *euro* but it is not a common vowel combination.

  /s/   the letter *c* is pronounced /s/ before the vowels *e* and *i*, e.g. *centre, city, rice* (*ci* can also be /ʃ/ in endings such as *-cion* or *-cial* but it's probably best to simplify the rule at this level).

  /k/   the letter *c* is pronounced /k/ before consonants and before the letters *a*, *o*, and *u*, e.g. *class, cat, computer, cup.*

a • **4.21** Focus on the sound picture *tourist* and write the word on the board. Play the CD to model and drill the word and sound (pause after the sound).

- Now focus on the words after *tourist*. Remind SS that the pink letters are the /ʊə/ sound. Play the CD pausing after each word for SS to repeat.
- Repeat for the other two sounds and words (*snake* and *key*).

4.21		CD2 Track 59
tourist	/ʊə/	euro, Europe, sure, tour
snake	/s/	cent, pence, cinema, price
key	/k/	coffee, can, credit card

Study Link SS can find more practice of these sounds on the MultiROM and on the *New English File Beginner* website.

b • **4.22** Focus on the sentences and play the CD for SS just to listen. Then play the CD for SS to listen and repeat.

4.22	CD2 Track 60
In Europe a lot of countries use the euro.	
The cinema ticket is six euros and sixty cents.	
Can I have a cup of coffee, please?	

3 BUYING A COFFEE

a • **4.23** Focus on the menu and deal with any vocabulary problems. Model the words and ask SS to underline the stressed syllable (es<u>pre</u>sso, Ameri<u>ca</u>no, cappu<u>cci</u>no, <u>la</u>tte, <u>cho</u>colate <u>brow</u>nie, <u>muf</u>fin, <u>coo</u>kies). Then drill the words in chorus and individually.

- Tell SS to cover the dialogue and focus on the questions. Play the CD once or twice for SS to answer the questions.

> The woman asks for a coffee (a single espresso) and a chocolate brownie. It's two pounds forty-five.

4.23 / **4.24**		CD2 Tracks 61/62
Barman	Can I help you?	
Woman	Yes, can I have a coffee and a chocolate brownie, please?	
Barman	Espresso, Americano, cappuccino?	
Woman	An espresso, please.	
Barman	Single or double?	
Woman	Single. How much is that?	
Barman	Two pounds forty-five.	
Woman	Here you are.	
Barman	Thanks.	

b • Focus on the dialogue and the instructions. Give SS, in pairs, time to think what the missing words are, but tell them not to write them in yet. Then play the CD again for SS to complete the spaces.

- Check answers by playing the CD again and pausing after each answer.

> **1** coffee **2** please **3** double **4** How **5** Here

- Go through the dialogue line by line eliciting/explaining any words or phrases SS don't know. Focus especially on *Can I have…? Can I help you? Single or double?* and *How much is that?* Highlight that *How much is that?* is the normal way to ask how much you need to pay when you order things in a café or restaurant or buy something in a shop.

c • **4.24** Play the CD for SS to listen and repeat, encouraging them to copy the rhythm.

- Focus on the box and go through the information. Highlight that *Can I have…, please?* is the normal polite way to ask for things in a café, restaurant, or shop.
- Put SS in pairs and assign roles. Give SS time to practise the dialogue and then tell them to swap roles. Monitor and correct any pronunciation mistakes.

d • Focus on the instructions and the example. Demonstrate the activity by asking *How much is a single espresso?* (one pound twenty-five). Ask two or three more questions to individual SS. Remind them that *single, regular, double,* and *large* are adjectives, so have to go before the noun.

- Model and drill the question *How much is a single espresso?* in chorus and individually. Then get SS to ask you the prices of some items from the menu.
- Put SS in pairs and give them time to ask and answer questions about prices. Monitor and help. Make a note of any problems and correct any general mistakes on the board afterwards.

e • Focus on the instructions and the speech bubbles. Demonstrate the activity with a good student. The student is the barman and you order a different coffee and a different cake.

- Put SS in pairs and assign roles. Give them time to practise the dialogue ordering different coffees and drinks. Then swap roles. Monitor and help.

Extra idea

You could get a pair or pairs of SS to act out the roleplay in front of the class.

4 PEOPLE IN THE STREET

Study Link This exercise is also on the *New English File Beginner* DVD, which can be used instead of the class audio (see **Introduction** *p.11*). SS can get more practice on the MultiROM, which contains more of the short street interviews with a listening task and scripts.

a ● **4.25** Focus on the photo of Brandy and the three questions. Ask *Where does she usually have lunch?* Play the CD then check the answer (see listening script 4.25).

4.25	CD2 Track 63
Interviewer	Where do you usually have lunch?
Brandy (USA)	**In my office**.

b ● **4.26** SS will hear Brandy say what she had. Play the CD for SS and check the answer (see listening script 4.26).

4.26	CD2 Track 64
Interviewer	Where do you usually have lunch?
Brandy	In my office.
Interviewer	What do you have?
Brandy	**Salad.**

c ● **4.27** SS will hear Brandy say how much it is. Play the CD for SS and check the answer (see listening script 4.27).

4.27	CD2 Track 65
Interviewer	Where do you usually have lunch?
Brandy	In my office.
Interviewer	What do you have?
Brandy	Salad.
Interviewer	How much is it?
Brandy	**$4.**

d ● **4.28** Focus on the chart and the four people. Explain that SS are going to hear the people answering the questions.

● Play the CD for SS to complete the information for Bridget. Replay and pause as necessary. Check answers (see listening script 4.28).

● Repeat this process for the other three speakers.

4.28	CD2 Track 66
Interviewer	Where do you usually have lunch?
Bridget (UK)	Er, I have lunch **in my office**.
Interviewer	What do you have?
Bridget	I have a **sandwich**.
Interviewer	How much is it?
Bridget	**2.75.**
Interviewer	Where do you usually have lunch?
Joshua (USA)	I eat lunch **at the student cafeteria**.
Interviewer	What do you have?
Joshua	I have a **chicken sandwich** or sometimes I have **pizza**.
Interviewer	How much is it?
Joshua	I'd say about **$5 or $6.**

Interviewer	Where do you usually have lunch?
Helen (UK)	I usually have lunch **in a café**.
Interviewer	What do you have?
Helen	I have a **sandwich** and some **fruit**.
Interviewer	How much is it?
Helen	It's about **£2.70**.
Interviewer	Where do you usually have lunch?
Dax (USA)	Usually **at a restaurant near my house**.
Interviewer	What do you have?
Dax	Usually **chicken, rice, and beans**.
Interviewer	How much is it?
Dax	About **$7.**

Extra support

If you have time, let SS listen again with the listening script on *p.85*. Go through the dialogues line by line with SS and elicit/explain any words or phrases that they don't understand.

e ● Get SS to ask you questions 1–3 in the box. Then get SS to ask and answer the questions in pairs. Tell them to give simple answers for question 2, i.e. not try to go into great detail. You may want to pre-teach *It's free* as an answer to 3.

● Monitor and help with any other vocabulary they may need.

● Get feedback from different SS.

5 **4.29** SONG ♫ *Money, money, money*

● This song was originally recorded by the Swedish pop group Abba and was sung by Meryl Streep in the film musical *Mamma Mia!* For copyright reasons this is a cover version. As usual there is quite a lot of new vocabulary in the song, but SS should be able to understand the basic message of the song.

● If you want to do this song in class, use the photocopiable activity on *p.205*.

4.29	CD2 Track 67

Money, money, money

I work all night, I work all day
To pay the bills I have to pay
Ain't it sad?
And still there never seems to be
A single penny left for me
That's too bad
In my dreams I have a plan
If I got me a wealthy man
I wouldn't have to work at all
I'd fool around and have a ball

Chorus
Money, money, money
Must be funny
In the rich man's world
Money, money, money
Always sunny
In the rich man's world
Aha-ahaaa
All the things I could do
If I had a little money
It's a rich man's world
It's a rich man's world

A man like that is hard to find
But I can't get him off my mind
Ain't it sad?
And if he happens to be free
I bet he wouldn't fancy me
That's too bad
So I must leave, I'll have to go
To Las Vegas or Monaco
And win a fortune in a game
My life will never be the same

Chorus

WORDS AND PHRASES TO LEARN

Focus on the words and phrases to learn. Make sure SS understand the meaning of each phrase. If necessary, remind SS of the context in which they came up in the lesson. If you speak your SS' L1, you might like to elicit a translation for the words/phrases for the SS to write next to them. You may also like to ask SS to test each other on the phrases.

Study Link SS can find more practice of these words and phrases on the MultiROM and on the *New English File Beginner* website.

Extra photocopiable activities

Communicative
Can I have…? *p.177* (instructions *p.157*)
Song
Money, money, money p.205 (instructions *p.200*)

HOMEWORK

Study Link Workbook *pp.34–35*

For instructions on how to use these pages, see *p.29.*

What do you remember?

GRAMMAR

1 a	2 b	3 a	4 b	5 b	6 a	7 a	8 a	9 b
10 a								

VOCABULARY

a	1	breakfast	d	1	twenty dollars
	2	shower		2	eight euros twenty-five
	3	work		3	nine pounds ninety-nine
	4	home		4	seventy cents
	5	gym		5	eighty p / pence
b	1	go	e	1	much
	2	pay		2	That's
	3	take		3	have
	4	do		4	difficult
	5	park		5	Single
c	1	in			
	2	at			
	3	on			
	4	for			
	5	in			

PRONUNCIATION

a	vowels:	chair, owl, car, cat, computer, tourist
	consonants:	yacht, key, snake
c	piano housework dollar before sometimes

What can you do?

1 CAN YOU UNDERSTAND THIS TEXT?

a	1 F	2 T	3 F	4 F	5 F	6 F	7 T	8 F

3 CAN YOU UNDERSTAND THESE PEOPLE?

1 a	2 b	3 a	4 a	5 a	6 a	7 b	8 a

4.30 CD2 Track 68

1 A What time do you usually get up?
   B During the week I get up at a quarter to seven.

2 A Do you always have bacon and eggs for breakfast?
   B No, only on Saturdays. I usually have cereal and fruit.

3 A What time do you finish work?
   B It depends. Monday to Thursday I finish at 6.00.
      But on Friday I finish early at 5.00.
   A Oh, that's good.

4 A When do you usually go shopping?
B It depends. Sometimes after work, but usually on Saturday. Never on Sunday.

5 A Can I park here?
B No, you can't park in this street. It's no parking.
A Where's the car park?
B Over there.
A OK. We can park there.

6 A What languages do you speak?
B I speak Spanish.
A What about Italian?
B No. And you?

7 A Hello. Can I help you?
B Hi. Two cappuccinos, please.
A Regular or large?
B Er...regular.
A Anything else?
B Yes, a brownie.
A Just one?
B Yes, one please. How much is that?

8 A Can I help you?
B Yes. Can I have a pen, please?
A Black or blue?
B Black.
A Here you are.
B How much is it?
A Two pounds sixty.
B Sorry?
A Two pounds sixty.

Extra photocopiable activities

Grammar
4 revision *p.139*
Vocabulary
Verb circles *p.196* (instructions *p.191*)

Test and Assessment CD-ROM

File 4 Quicktest
File 4 Test
Progress test 1–4

G past simple: *be*
V *in, at, on*: places
P /ɜː/ and *was/were*

Before they were famous...

File 5 overview

File 5 introduces SS to the past simple. In **5A** the past simple of the verb *be* is presented and in **5B** SS learn the past simple of three common irregular verbs: *have, go,* and *get.* **5C** focuses on the past of regular verbs and presents SS with more irregular past verb forms. The **Practical English** lesson introduces ordinal numbers and goes on to teach SS how to say the date.

Lesson plan

What some well-known actors and singers did before they were famous provides the context to introduce and practise the past simple of the verb *be.* First SS try to guess the previous jobs of eight actors and singers and then they listen to see if they were right. In Pronunciation SS practise a new vowel sound /ɜː/ and the strong and weak forms of *was* and *were.* The vocabulary focus in the lesson is on prepositions with places, *in, at,* and *on* (e.g. *at the airport, on a bus*) and in the final speaking activity grammar, pronunciation, and vocabulary are brought together when SS ask and answer questions about where they were at various times the previous day.

Optional lead-in (books closed)

● Tell SS that you are going to say a sentence about a person, and they have to say what the person's job is.
● Say the sentences below to elicit the jobs from the class. Jobs 4, 7, and 8 are new, so you may need to mime a bit and then teach the words. Write the new jobs on the board.

1 This woman works in a shop and says *Can I help you?* (She's a shop assistant.)
2 This man works in a restaurant and says *A table for two?* (He's a waiter.)
3 This person works in a hospital. She helps the doctors. (She's a nurse.)
4 This person works in a garage. He says *What's the problem with your car?* (He's a mechanic.)
5 This man cuts your hair. (He's a hairdresser.)
6 This person works in a school. He helps you with your English. (He's an English teacher.)
7 This person works in a gym. She says *1 and 2 and 3 and 4.* (She's an aerobics teacher.)
8 This person walks like this (mime soldier walking up and down with a rifle). (He's a soldier.)

1 GRAMMAR past simple: *be*

a ● Books open. Focus on photo 1 of James Blunt and ask *Who is he?* (James Blunt). Ask *What does he do?* (He's a singer).
● Write on the board the words *singer* and *actor.* Model and drill the words in chorus and individually. Highlight that the *-er* and *-or* endings are pronounced /ə/.

⚠ You may want to teach the word *actress* here to describe a female actor. Nowadays many actresses prefer to be called *actors* but the word *actress* is still widely used.

● Now ask about the other nine people. Ask *Who is he/she? Is he/she a singer or an actor?*

⚠ Numbers 4 and 7 refer in each case to **two** people.

1 James Blunt – singer
2 Sting – singer and actor
3 Jack Nicholson – actor
4 Jennifer Aniston – actor; Barbra Streisand – singer and actor
5 Morgan Freeman – actor
6 Danny DeVito – actor
7 Lucy Liu and Calista Flockhart – both actors
8 Tina Turner – singer

b ● Focus on the title of the lesson and the title on the photos and see if SS can work out what it means. Use L1 to check if you know it.
● Focus on the list of jobs. If you didn't do the **lead-in**, make sure SS know what all the words mean. Remind SS of the male and female form of *waiter/waitress.*
● Now focus on the instructions and sentences 1–8. Make sure SS understand that 'old jobs' means their jobs before they were famous.
● Give SS, in pairs, time to guess the old jobs of the people in the photos. Tell SS to only write in sentences 1–8 jobs that they are sure about. If SS ask what *was/were* means tell them it is the past of *is/are.* (This is focused on later.) Monitor and help.

c ● 🔊 **5.1** Play the CD, pausing after each sentence to check answers and giving SS time to complete the sentences. Find out if any pairs guessed all the jobs correctly.

1 soldier 2 English teacher 3 shop assistant
4 waitresses 5 mechanic 6 hairdresser
7 aerobics teachers 8 nurse

5.1   CD2 Track 69

1 James Blunt was a soldier.
2 Sting was an English teacher.
3 Jack Nicholson was a shop assistant.
4 Jennifer Aniston and Barbra Streisand were waitresses.
5 Morgan Freeman was a mechanic.
6 Danny DeVito was a hairdresser.
7 Lucy Liu and Calista Flockhart were aerobics teachers.
8 Tina Turner was a nurse.

---

d ● Copy sentences 1 and 4 on the board and underline *was* and *were.* Elicit/explain that *was* is the past of *is* and *were* is the past of *are.* Establish a gesture to indicate the past tense, e.g. pointing backwards over your shoulder with your thumb.

- Now focus on the chart (**Present**) and establish that *Sting is a singer* and *They are actors* are the present simple, i.e. these things are true now.
- Focus on **Past** in the chart. Give SS a moment to think which two words are missing, then check answers.

Present	Past
Sting is a singer.	He *was* a teacher.
They are actors.	They *were* aerobics instructors.

e • Tell SS to go to **Grammar Bank 5A** on *p.96*.

- 5.2 Play the CD and ask SS to listen and repeat the example sentences. Use the pause button as necessary.

5.2   CD2 Track 70

I was a teacher.
You were at school yesterday.
He was at home last night.
It was hot last week.
We were at work.
You were in a hurry.
They were in Canada.

I wasn't a teacher.
You weren't at school yesterday.
He wasn't at home last night.
It wasn't hot last week.
We weren't at work.
You weren't in a hurry.
They weren't in Canada.

Were you late?	Yes, I was.	No, I wasn't.
Was she a singer?	Yes, she was.	No, she wasn't.
Were they in Mexico last week?	Yes, they were.	No, they weren't.

- Go through the rules with the class using the expanded information in the **Grammar notes** below to help you. You may want to use L1 here if you know it.

Grammar notes

- *was* is the past of *am* and *is*. *Were* is the past of *are*. Like *is* and *are*, *was* and *were* can be used to describe permanent and temporary states, e.g. *I was a teacher / I was at home last night*.
- *was* and *were* are used exactly like *is* and *are*, i.e. they are inverted to make questions (e.g. *he was → was he?*) and *not (n't)* is added to make negatives (*wasn't, weren't*).
- The past simple is used to talk about finished time, especially with past time expressions, e.g. *last night, last week*.
- ⚠ Highlight that past time expressions do **not** have an article, i.e. *last week* NOT ~~the last week~~.
- ⚠ Some SS have a tendency to remember *was* and forget *were*.

- Focus on the exercises for **5A** on *p.97* and get SS to do them in pairs or individually. If they do them individually, get them to compare answers with a partner.
- Check answers by asking individual SS to read out the complete sentences.

---

a 1 Were you at school yesterday?
2 James wasn't in the meeting.
3 We were on the plane at 4.00.
4 Were they in class yesterday?
5 David wasn't very happy last night.
6 I was at work until 8.00 today.
7 Was your sister in Boston last week?
8 It was a terrible film.

b 2 was 3 weren't 4 were 5 wasn't 6 Was
7 wasn't 8 was 9 Were 10 weren't 11 were
12 Was 13 wasn't 14 was

Study Link SS can find more practice of this grammar on the MultiROM and on the *New English File Beginner* website.

- Tell SS to go back to the main lesson on *p.44*.

2 PRONUNCIATION /ɜː/ and *was / were*

- Read the **Pronunciation notes** and decide how much of the information you want to give your SS.

Pronunciation notes

/ɜː/

- Remind SS that the two dots mean that this sound is long.
- You may want to highlight the following sound–spelling pattern:
  /ɜː/   *er, ir,* and *ur* are usually pronounced /ɜː/, e.g. *verb, first, nurse*.

was and **were**

- *was* and *were* have different pronunciations depending on whether they are stressed or not, i.e. they can have a strong or weak pronunciation.
- *was* and *were* have a strong pronunciation in *yes/no* questions, short answers, and negatives. The pronunciation is /wɒz/ and /wɜː/.
- *was* and *were* tend to have a weak pronunciation in positive sentences and are pronounced /wəz/ and /wə/, e.g. *He was a teacher* /wəz/, *They were waitresses* /wə/.
- Pronunciation of strong and weak forms tends to occur quite naturally when there is good sentence stress and rhythm. Tell SS to focus on this, and not to worry too much about getting the sound right as they will gradually pick this up.

---

a • 5.3 Here SS practise a new vowel sound which occurs in the stressed pronunciation of *were* and will be used in exercise **b**.

- Focus on the sound picture *bird* and write the word on the board. Play the CD to model and drill the word and sound (pause after the sound).
- Now focus on the words after *bird*. Remind SS that the pink letters are the /ɜː/ sound. Play the CD pausing after each word for SS to repeat. Model and drill the words yourself if you see SS are having problems. Give more practice as necessary.

<table>
<tr><td>

5.3   CD2 Track 71

bird   /ɜː/   nurse, work, her, word, first
</td></tr>
</table>

b • **5.4** Focus on the three sound pictures and try to elicit the second and third words (*clock* and *computer*). Write *clock* and *computer* on the board.

• Focus on the sound picture *bird*. Play the CD to model and drill the word and sound (pause after the sound).

• Now focus on the three sentences. Remind SS that the pink letters are the /ɜː/ sound and that the underlined words in the sentences are the ones that are stressed. Play the CD pausing after each sentence for SS to repeat. Give more practice as necessary.

• Repeat the process for *clock*. Get SS to repeat the sounds and sentences.

• Highlight that in the sentences after *bird* and *clock*, *was* and *were* are stressed and have a strong pronunciation.

• Now focus on the *computer* picture and elicit the word and sound. Tell SS that in ⊞ sentences *was* and *were* are not stressed and the sound is /ə/. Play the CD for SS to listen and repeat the picture word and sound, and then the two sentences.

• Tell SS that if they get used to getting the stress right in sentences with *was/were*, they will get the sounds right.

<table>
<tr><td colspan="3">

5.4   CD2 Track 72
</td></tr>
<tr><td>bird</td><td>/ɜː/</td><td>Were they famous?
Yes, they were.
No, they weren't.
They weren't famous.</td></tr>
<tr><td>clock</td><td>/ɒ/</td><td>Was she a teacher?
Yes, she was.
No, she wasn't.
She wasn't a teacher.</td></tr>
<tr><td>computer</td><td>/ə/</td><td>He was a soldier.
They were waitresses.</td></tr>
</table>

Study Link SS can find more practice of these sounds on the MultiROM and on the *New English File Beginner* website.

c • **5.5** Focus on the instructions and the example. Play the first sentence to demonstrate the activity. Pause the CD after the prompt (*He's a teacher*) and elicit the past form from the class (*He was a teacher*). Then take off the pause button and SS will hear the correct answer.

• Repeat with the other prompts, getting SS to respond together. Make sure they stress the sentences correctly.

• Repeat the activity asking individual SS to respond.

<table>
<tr><td>

5.5   CD2 Track 73

1 He's a teacher… He was a teacher.
2 Is she at school?… Was she at school?
3 They aren't happy… They weren't happy.
4 It isn't cold… It wasn't cold.
5 We're late… We were late.
6 Are you tired?… Were you tired?
7 I'm very hungry… I was very hungry.
8 You aren't at home… You weren't at home.
</td></tr>
</table>

3 VOCABULARY *in, at, on*: places

a • Focus on the instructions and get SS to complete the sentences in pairs. These four prepositional phrases all came up earlier in the book.

• Check answers.

   1 in   **2** at   **3** at   **4** on

b • **5.6** Write *in*, *at*, and *on* on the board and highlight that we often use these prepositions with places.

• Focus on the chart. Deal with any vocabulary problems, e.g. *a meeting*. Get SS in pairs to complete the spaces with *at*, *in*, or *on*. They should be able to do this quite easily.

   1 at   **2** in   **3** on

• Play the CD once for SS to check their answers.

• Play the CD again for SS to listen and repeat.

• Explain that the best way to learn prepositions in English is by learning and remembering them in phrases, e.g. *at home, in the office*. However, you may want to give SS this very simplified rule:

– Use **at** for buildings, e.g. *at the airport* and for *home*, *work* and *school* (*at home, at work, at school*).

– Use **in** for towns, countries, rooms (in a house or building), the street, bed, or a meeting.

– Use **on** for transport (*bus, car, plane*) but not *car* (**in** *a car*).

⚠ In some circumstances you use *in* with a building when you want to emphasize *inside* the building, e.g. *You can't smoke in a cinema* not ~~at a cinema~~, but it is better at this level to give SS a clear (if incomplete) rule rather than confuse them with subtleties of meaning.

<table>
<tr><td colspan="3">

5.6   CD2 Track 74
</td></tr>
<tr><td>**1** at home
at work
at school
at the gym
at the airport
at the cinema
at a restaurant
at the hairdresser's</td><td>**2** in bed
in the
  bedroom
in a car
in London
in a meeting
in the street
in the park</td><td>**3** on a bus
on a train
on a plane</td></tr>
</table>

c • Focus on the instructions and the examples. Demonstrate the activity by saying a word from the chart and eliciting the correct prepositional phrase. Repeat with four or five more words.

• Put SS in pairs, **A** and **B**. Tell **A** to look at the chart and tell **B** to close their books. **A** tests **B** on the phrases. After a few minutes get them to swap roles.

d • **5.7** Focus on the instructions and the exercise. Explain that SS are going to hear sounds on the CD which will tell them where Mike was yesterday at the times in the exercise. They have to complete the sentences with the place.

• Play the CD and stop after the first example. Elicit the answer and write it on the board (He was in bed). Make sure SS understand what they have to do before continuing. Pause after each sound to give SS time to write.

- Get SS to compare with a partner, and then play the CD again. Check answers, playing the CD one more time, pausing after each sound and eliciting the answers from individual SS.

> 2 He was in a/his car.
> 3 He was at the airport.
> 4 He was on a plane.
> 5 He was at a hotel.
> 6 He was in a meeting.
> 7 He was in a taxi/in the street.
> 8 He was at the gym.
> 9 He was at a restaurant.
> 10 He was in bed.

> **5.7**   CD2 Track 75
> 1 6.00 (sound effect – man snoring)
> 2 7.00 (sound effect – in car)
> 3 8.00 (sound effect – airport)
> 4 10.00 (sound effect – plane taking off, *Tea or coffee, sir?*)
> 5 12.00 (sound effect – hotel reception, *You're in room 214 on the first floor.*)
> 6 2.00 (sound effect – in a meeting, *Can we start, please?*)
> 7 6.00 (sound effect – in taxi, *Where to? The Sheraton hotel, please.*)
> 8 7.00 (sound effect – gym)
> 9 8.00 (sound effect – restaurant)
> 10 10.00 (sound effect – man snoring again)

4 SPEAKING

a ● Focus on the pictures and the instructions. Give SS one minute to look at the pictures and remember where the people were yesterday. You may want to elicit who is where in the pictures before SS try to memorize the picture. Ask *Who is in bed?* (Morgan Freeman), *Who's at the gym?* (Jack Nicholson), etc. (The other pictures show Lucy Liu on a bus, Barbra Streisand on a plane, Sting at the cinema, Danny DeVito at the hairdresser's, James Blunt in a meeting, Calista Flockhart in a car, Tina Turner in the park, and Jennifer Aniston at a restaurant.)

b ● Tell SS to go to **Communication** *Where were they?* **A** on *p.77*, **B** on *p.80*.

  ● Focus on the instructions and make sure SS understand that they have the answers to the questions in brackets. Demonstrate the activity by taking the role of **A** and asking a **B** the first question.

  ● When SS have tested each other's memory find out who remembered most answers in each pair.

  ● Tell SS to go back to the main lesson on *p.45*.

c ● Focus on the questions. Demonstrate the activity by getting SS to ask you the questions. SS should ask two separate questions for each part of the day (morning, afternoon, etc.), e.g. *Where were you yesterday at 6.30 in the morning? Where were you at 10.00 in the morning?*

  ● Give SS a few minutes to ask and answer the questions in pairs. Monitor and help, making a note of any problems they are still having.

  ● Get feedback by asking individual SS to tell the whole class a sentence about their partner. e.g. *Maria was in bed at 6.30 in the morning.*

WORDS AND PHRASES TO LEARN

Focus on the words and phrases to learn. Make sure SS understand the meaning of each phrase. If necessary, remind SS of the context in which they came up in the lesson. If you speak your SS' L1, you might like to elicit a translation for the words/phrases for the SS to write next to them. You may also like to ask SS to test each other on the phrases.

Study Link SS can find more practice of these words and phrases on the MultiROM and on the *New English File Beginner* website.

Extra photocopiable activities

Grammar
past simple: *be p.140*
Communicative
Find someone who was at/in/on... *p.178* (instructions *p.157*)

HOMEWORK

Study Link **Workbook** *pp.36–37*

5 B

G past simple: *have, go, get*
V irregular verbs; revision of daily routine verbs
P sentence stress

A perfect day?

Lesson plan

This lesson introduces the past simple of the three most common irregular verbs in English: *go, get,* and *have.* The lesson begins by revising the vocabulary of daily routine. The new grammar is presented through the context of a phone conversation where a father asks his teenage daughter what she did earlier in the day, and begins to suspect she is not alone at home. SS learn how to make ⊞ and ⊟ sentences and questions, and interview each other about the previous day. SS then read three blogs from a UK history website which was set up to record what people did on one particular day in the early 21st century. Finally, SS listen to a song, *Perfect day.*

Optional lead-in (books closed)

- Test SS on the verb phrases they know using *have* and *go* from **Vocabulary Bank** *A typical day* on *p.111* like this:

  T *breakfast*   SS *have breakfast*

  T *work*   SS *go to work,* etc.

1 VOCABULARY revision of daily routine verbs

- Books open. SS revise the daily routine verbs they learnt in **4A**. Focus on the instructions and the speech bubbles. Tell SS to go to **Vocabulary Bank** *A typical day* on *p.111*.
- Put SS in pairs, **A** and **B**, and give them a few minutes to test each other on the pictures. Monitor and help.
- Tell SS to go back to the main lesson on *p.46*.

2 LISTENING

a ● 5.8 Focus on the lesson title *A perfect day?* and explain/elicit the meaning.

- Focus on the instructions and the photos. Highlight that the man's name is Ben and tell SS that he is a businessman, and that the girl is his daughter Linda. Ask *Where's Ben?* (in Paris), *Where's Linda?* (at home).
- Focus on the list of places (*at school, at the gym,* etc.).
- Get SS to cover the dialogue with a piece of paper. Play the CD once for SS to tick the places where Linda was during the day. Replay as necessary. Get SS to compare answers with a partner before checking answers as a whole class. Ask SS *Was Linda at school?* (Yes, she was). *Was she at the gym?* (No, she wasn't).

✓ at school	✓ at a café
✗ at the gym	✗ at a restaurant
✓ at a museum	✓ at a shopping centre
✗ at the hairdresser's	✗ at the cinema

5.8	CD2 Track 76

Linda	Hi.
Ben	Hi, darling.
Linda	Oh hi Dad. How's Paris?
Ben	Fine. A lot of work. Did you have a good day?
Linda	It was OK.

Ben	What did you do?
Linda	I got up early. I went to school.
Ben	How was it?
Linda	Great! We didn't have classes. We went to the British Museum.
Ben	Oh nice. Did you have lunch there?
Linda	Yes, we had lunch at the café. And then I went shopping with Katy.
Ben	Did you do your homework?
Linda	Yes, of course. I always do my homework.
(Boy	Where's the coffee?)
Ben	Who's that, Linda?

b ● Now focus on the dialogue and the instructions. Replay the CD as necessary for SS to complete the spaces.

- Get SS to compare their answers. Check answers by playing the CD again, pausing after each answer. Write the words on the board.

1 day 2 up 3 Great 4 British 5 lunch
6 shopping 7 always

- Go through the dialogue with SS and elicit/explain any new words or phrases, e.g. *darling, a lot of work, Who's that?* Explain/elicit that *did* is the past of *do, got up* of *get up, had* of *have,* and *went* of *go.*

c ● 5.9 Focus on the instructions and the questions. Play the CD for SS to answer the questions. Replay as necessary. Get SS to compare answers then check with the whole class.

1 at the cinema   2 her boyfriend

5.9	CD2 Track 77

Ben	Who's that, Linda?
Linda	What?
Ben	I can hear somebody.
Linda	Oh, it's just the TV.
Ben	Can I speak to your mother?
Linda	Mum? She's out. She went to the cinema with her friends.
Ben	Are you alone?
Linda	Yes. I am.
Ben	Linda, is somebody with you?
Linda	Yes, Dad. Simon is here.
Ben	Simon? Who's Simon?
Linda	He's my boyfriend, Dad. He's very nice.

Extra support

You could get SS to listen to the dialogue again with the listening script on *p.85.* Explain/elicit the meaning of any new words/phrases e.g. *alone, somebody.*

3 GRAMMAR past simple: *have, go, get*

a • Elicit/teach the meaning of *early* (= opposite of *late*, i.e. before the usual time).

• Focus on the chart. Highlight that the sentences in the first column are in the present and those in the second column are in the past.

• Focus on the dialogue in **2b** and elicit the word that is missing from the first sentence in the chart *(did)*.

⚠ SS may ask about the meaning of *did* here. Explain that *did* is the past of *do* and, like *do*, it has no translation. We use *did* in English to make a question and *didn't* to make a negative in the past simple.

• Give SS time to complete all the sentences in the chart and get them to check their answers with a partner.

b • **5.10** Focus on the chart again. Play the CD for SS to check their answers (see **bold** in listening script 5.10).

• Play the CD again, pausing for SS to repeat.

5.10	CD2 Track 78
What do you do?	What **did** you do?
I get up early.	I **got** up early.
We don't have classes.	We **didn't** have classes.
We go to the British Museum.	We **went** to the British Museum.
We have lunch at the café.	We **had** lunch at the café.

c • Tell SS to go to **Grammar Bank 5B** on *p.96*.

• **5.11** Play the CD and ask SS to listen and repeat the example sentences. Use the pause button as necessary.

5.11		CD2 Track 79
I got up early yesterday.		
You had breakfast in bed.		
He went to work by car.		
We got up late today.		
You went to school.		
They had dinner at home.		
I didn't get up early yesterday.		
You didn't have breakfast in bed.		
He didn't go to work by car.		
We didn't get up late today.		
You didn't go to school.		
They didn't have dinner at home.		
Did you go to school yesterday?	Yes, I did.	No, I didn't.
Did she get up early?	Yes, she did.	No, she didn't.
Did they have lunch at work?	Yes, they did.	No, they didn't

• Go through the rules with the class using the expanded information in the **Grammar notes** below to help you. You may want to use L1 here if you know it.

Grammar notes

• The past simple is used for finished actions and states in the past however distant or recent. For example, we can say *I got up early yesterday* and *I got up early today*. This may be different in your SS' L1.

• A small number of verbs (several of which are very common) are irregular in the past simple. The change of form can be just one or two letters, e.g. *get → got*, or can be a completely new word, e.g. *go → went*.

• Irregular verbs are only irregular in ⊞ sentences. In ⊟ sentences *didn't* is used with the infinitive (not the past) and questions are formed using *did* + the infinitive.

• There is no complication with the 3rd person singular in the past – all forms are the same.

• The word order in questions is the same as in the present simple, i.e. **ASI** (**A**uxiliary + **S**ubject + **I**nfinitive) and **QUASI** (**Qu**estion + **A**uxiliary + **S**ubject + **I**nfinitive). See *p.66* **4B Grammar notes**.

• Focus on the exercises for **5B** on *p.97* and get SS to do them in pairs or individually. If they do them individually, get them to compare with a partner.

• Check answers by getting individual SS to read the sentences and questions aloud.

> **a** 1 She had cereal for breakfast yesterday.
> 2 Did you go to the cinema yesterday?
> 3 We didn't have lunch yesterday.
> 4 They went home at 8.00 yesterday.
> 5 What time did you get up yesterday?
> 6 She didn't go to school by bus yesterday.
> 7 Jack got up late yesterday.
> 8 What did you have for dinner yesterday?
>
> **b** 1 A did, have B had   2 didn't go
> 3 A did, go B went   4 A did, get up B got up
> 5 didn't have

Study Link SS can find more practice of this grammar on the MultiROM and on the *New English File Beginner* website.

• Tell SS to go back to the main lesson on *p.46*.

4 PRONUNCIATION & SPEAKING sentence stress

a • **5.12** Focus on the questions and the instructions. Play the CD for SS to answer the questions *What two words are missing? Are they stressed?*

• Check answers. (The missing words are *did you*, and they are not stressed.)

5.12	CD2 Track 80
1 What time did you get up?	
2 Did you have breakfast? What did you have?	
3 Did you go to work?	
4 Where did you have lunch? What did you have?	
5 Did you go to the gym?	
6 Did you go shopping?	
7 Did you have dinner at home? What did you have?	
8 Did you watch TV? What did you watch?	
9 What time did you go to bed?	

b • Play the CD again for SS to repeat the questions.

c • Focus on the chart and the instructions. Demonstrate the activity by asking the first question to a good student. Write the time he/she says on the board.

• Put SS in pairs, **A** and **B**, and get **A** to interview **B** about yesterday. Then swap roles.

• Get feedback by asking SS to tell the class one thing their partner did yesterday, e.g. *Kim had lunch in a Japanese restaurant, Mina went to bed very late*, etc.

Extra support

You could get the class to interview you with the questions before they interview each other.

5 READING

a • Focus on the instructions and the introduction to the article. Give SS time to answer the questions.

• Check answers. (They wrote a blog about what they did the day before, to give a picture of life at the beginning of the 21st century.)

b • Focus on the instructions and the photos. Highlight that SS can find the meaning of some new words/ phrases in the glossary.

• Give SS time to read the three blogs and match two photos to each one. They should write 1, 2, or 3 in the boxes. Get SS to compare their answers with a partner and then check answers with the whole class.

> 1 C, E
> 2 A, F
> 3 B, D

c • Focus on the sentences. Give SS time to read them and deal with any vocabulary problems, e.g. *teenager, early*.

• Focus on the instructions. Demonstrate the activity by eliciting the answer to the first sentence (R). Give SS time to read the article again and complete the rest of the sentences with a letter. Check answers.

> 1 R 2 P 3 N 4 R 5 N 6 P 7 N
> 8 P 9 P, R 10 N

Extra challenge

Drill the pronunciation of the three names (Pauline /ˈpɔːliːn/, Nick /nɪk/, Rachel /ˈreɪtʃl/). When you check answers get SS to say the full sentences starting with the names, e.g. *Rachel is a teenager.*

d • Focus on the highlighted words in the article. Put SS in pairs to guess their meaning.

⚠ If SS have access to dictionaries, they could check their own answers here. If not, elicit/explain the words/phrases using L1 if you know it.

• Deal with any other new/unknown vocabulary items in the article, e.g. *trip, a present, history*, etc.

e • Focus on the instructions. Give SS time to read the blogs again and underline three things that *they* did yesterday. Get them to compare with a partner.

• Get some feedback from individual SS.

⚠ When SS reach the end of the File (**Revise & Check** p.53) and have learnt how to form regular verbs and more irregular verbs, they write a blog about what they did the previous Saturday.

⚠ The website *History Matters* is no longer open.

6 5.13 SONG 🎵 *Perfect day*

• *Perfect day* was written and recorded by Lou Reed in 1972. It was featured in the 1996 film *Trainspotting*. The activity for this song focuses on intensive listening. For copyright reasons this song is a cover version. If you want to do this song in class, use the photocopiable activity on *p.206*.

5.13   CD2 Track 81

Perfect day

Just a perfect day
Drink sangria in the park
And then later when it gets dark
We go home
Just a perfect day
Feed animals in the zoo
Then later a movie too
And then home

Chorus
Oh it's such a perfect day
I'm glad I spent it with you
Oh such a perfect day
You just keep me hanging on
You just keep me hanging on

Just a perfect day
Problems all left alone
Weekenders on our own
It's such fun
Just a perfect day
You made me forget myself
I thought I was someone else
Someone good

Chorus

WORDS AND PHRASES TO LEARN

Focus on the words and phrases to learn. Make sure SS understand the meaning of each phrase. If necessary, remind SS of the context in which they came up in the lesson. If you speak your SS' L1, you might like to elicit a translation for the words/phrases for the SS to write next to them. You may also like to ask SS to test each other on the phrases.

Study Link SS can find more practice of these words and phrases on the MultiROM and on the *New English File Beginner* website.

Extra photocopiable activities

Grammar
past simple: *have, go, get p.141*
Communicative
Did you do the same as me yesterday? *p.179* (instructions *p.157*)
Song
Perfect day p.206 (instructions *p.201*)

HOMEWORK

Study Link Workbook *pp.38–39*

5C

G past simple: regular verbs
V common verbs 3; more irregular verbs
P regular past simple endings

It changed my life

Lesson plan

This lesson introduces the past simple of regular verbs in the context of a student's real experience of the Erasmus programme (a European study programme where SS do part of their course in another country). These are presented through a short picture story about a Polish student, Joanna, who went to Rome to do part of her university course. SS then focus closely on the different pronunciations of the *ed* ending and go on to practise this in a speaking activity. In Vocabulary SS learn some more common verbs and the lesson finishes with SS reading about Joanna's time in Rome. The information about Joanna was adapted from an Erasmus website. Note that Joanna has a Polish accent, but a native-speaker model is provided for drilling grammar and vocabulary.

Optional lead-in (books closed)

- Write *It changed my life* on the board and tell SS it's the title of this lesson. Write *Joanna, Gdansk, Rome, Erasmus* on the board and tell them these are the names and places in the story.
- Elicit ideas from the class as to what the lesson might be about.

1 GRAMMAR past simple: regular verbs

a • Books open. Focus on the instructions and read the information with SS. Deal with any vocabulary problems, e.g. *thousands, foreign*. Highlight the silent *g* in *foreign* and model and drill the pronunciation.
- Ask SS these questions about the information:
  Where is Joanna from? (Gdansk)
  Where did she go? (Rome)
  When did she go? (last September)

⚠ The months of the year are taught later in this File in Practical English on *p.50*.

- Focus on picture 1 and ask *Where's Joanna?* (in a taxi). Repeat the question for picture 2 (at the airport) and picture 8 (on the plane/in Rome). Elicit the meaning of *kissed, check-in, cried,* and *arrived*, and deal with any other vocabulary problems.
- Focus on the sentences below the pictures and establish that they are all in the past simple and that all the ones with blue highlighting are **regular** verbs. Don't deal with vocabulary problems at this stage.
- Put SS in pairs and give them some time to try and match pictures 1–8 to the sentences. SS should be able to do this from words they know/recognize and using a bit of imagination. Monitor and help.

b • **5.14** Play the CD once for SS to listen and check their answers (see listening script 5.14). Check answers with the whole class by asking individual SS to read out the sentences in order.

⚠ The pronunciation rules for *ed* endings will be dealt with in Pronunciation.

5.14 / 5.17   CD3 Tracks 02/05

1 I went to the airport with my mother.
2 My friends went to the airport too.
3 They helped me with my cases.
4 It was early. We waited at the check-in.
5 I kissed my mother goodbye.
6 My mother cried.
7 My friends were sad too. They wanted to come.
8 I arrived in Rome at 11 o'clock.

c • Focus on the instructions and elicit the past simple of the first example, *help* (helped). Give SS time to write the other past simple forms.
- Check the answers by copying the present and past forms on the board like this:

present   **past**
help   helped

- Ask SS to look at the verbs again and elicit the basic rule for regular verbs in the past simple (we add *ed*).

1 helped   2 waited   3 kissed   4 cried
5 wanted   6 arrived

d • Tell SS to go to **Grammar Bank 5C** on *p.96*.
- **5.15** Play the CD and ask SS to listen and repeat the example sentences. Use the pause button as necessary. You may want to drill the sentences with individual SS as well.

⚠ Encourage SS to copy the pronunciation on the CD. Some TT may want to go through the pronunciation rules at this point (see **Pronunciation notes** on *p.84*).

5.15   CD3 Track 03

I arrived early.
You finished the book.
He wanted a coffee.
The film ended at 7.00.
We studied Spanish at school.
You worked late.
They stopped at a café.

I didn't arrive early.
You didn't finish the book.
He didn't want a coffee.
The film didn't end at 7.00.
We didn't study Spanish at school
You didn't work late.
They didn't stop at a café.

Did you watch TV
   yesterday?   Yes, I did.   No, I didn't.
Did she walk to work?   Yes, she did.   No, she didn't.
Did they play tennis?   Yes, they did.   No, they didn't.

- Go through the rules with the class using the expanded information in the **Grammar notes** to help you. You may want to use L1 here if you know it.

Grammar notes

- The past simple of regular verbs is very easy. There is no 3rd person change. The basic rule is add *ed* to the infinitive.
- There are some small spelling changes in some past simple forms of regular verbs:
  - verbs ending in *e*: just add *d*, e.g. *change → changed, live → lived, like → liked.*
  - verbs ending in **consonant + y**: change *y* to *i* and add *ed*, e.g. *cry → cried, study → studied.*
    (Verbs ending in **vowel + y** do NOT change the *y* to *i*, e.g. *play → played* NOT ~~plaied.~~)
  - verbs ending in **consonant + one vowel + consonant**: double the final consonant and add *ed*, e.g. *stop → stopped* NOT ~~stoped.~~
    (Verbs ending in **vowel + w** or **x** do NOT double the final consonant, e.g. *relax → relax**ed*** NOT ~~relaxxed.~~)
  - ⊟ sentences and questions are the same as for irregular verbs, i.e. the infinitive is used after *didn't* or *did.*
- Most verbs in English are regular, although some of the most common ones happen to be irregular, e.g. *go, have, see.*

- Focus on the exercises for **5C** on *p.97* and get SS to do them individually or in pairs. If they do them individually, get them to compare with a partner.
- Monitor while SS are doing the exercises. If you see they are having problems with word order in **b**, remind them of **QUASI** and **ASI** (see **4B** *p.66*).
- Check answers to **a** by getting individual SS to read the sentences and questions aloud, and **b** by asking different pairs to read out the mini dialogues.

> **a** 1 We worked in a bank.
>   2 He finished work late.
>   3 They lived in Brazil.
>   4 I worried a lot.
>   5 She walked to work.
>   6 The train stopped in Barcelona.
>   7 We played tennis.
>   8 You talked a lot!
> **b** 1 A did, park B parked
>   2 A Did, finish B didn't finish
>   3 A did, study B studied
>   4 A Did, like B didn't like
>   5 A Did, watch B watched
>   6 A Did, close B closed

Study Link SS can find more practice of this grammar on the MultiROM and on the *New English File Beginner* website.

- Tell SS to go back to the main lesson on *p.48*.

2 PRONUNCIATION regular past simple endings

- Read the **Pronunciation notes** and decide how much of the information you want to give your SS.

Pronunciation notes

- The regular past simple ending *ed* can be pronounced in three different ways:
  1 *ed* is pronounced /d/ with verbs which end in a **voiced*** sound , e.g. *arrive → arrived*, change → changed.
  2 *ed* is pronounced /t/ with verbs which end in these **unvoiced*** sounds: /k/, /p/, /f/, /s/, /ʃ/, /tʃ/, e.g. *cook → cooked* /kʊkt/, *kiss → kissed* /kɪst/, *watch → watched* /wɒtʃt/.
  3 *ed* is pronounced /ɪd/ after verbs ending in the sounds /d/ or /t/, e.g. *want → wanted* /'wɒntɪd/, *need → needed* /'niːdɪd/.

* For the difference between **voiced** and **unvoiced** sounds see **Pronunciation notes 2A** *p.32*.

In practice, the difference between /t/ and /d/ is very small and at this level we recommend you do not spend too much time on this. However, the difference between /ɪd/ and the other two is significant (it is an extra syllable), and SS tend to use this ending for all regular verbs.

⚠ You may want to give SS this simplified rule: Only pronounce the *e* in *ed* endings when there's a *t* or a *d* before it.

---

a ● **5.16** Explain that there are three different ways of pronouncing *-ed*: /d/, /t/, and /ɪd/. Focus on the first sound picture *dog* and write the word on the board. Play the CD pausing after the word and sound and get SS to repeat it.
- Now focus on the two example sentences. Play the CD for SS to listen. Then play it again pausing for SS to repeat the sentences.
- Repeat this process for the /t/ and /ɪd/ sounds.
- Point out that /d/ and /t/ are very similar, but /ɪd/ is very different (see **Pronunciation notes**).
- Give SS more practice listening and repeating as necessary. You could model the sounds if you think this will help.

5.16		CD3 Track 04
dog	/d/	My mother cried. I arrived in Rome at 11.00.
tie	/t/	I kissed my mother goodbye. They helped me with my cases.
	/ɪd/	We waited at the check-in. They wanted to come.

b ● **5.17** Focus on the instructions then on the sentences in **1a**. Play the CD for SS to repeat. Check that SS are pronouncing the *-ed* ending correctly.
- Tell SS to cover the sentences and focus on the pictures in **1a**. Elicit the story picture by picture from the whole class.
- Put SS in pairs and get them to retell the story. They can either say alternate sentences, or **A** can tell the whole story while **B** helps and prompts, and then they swap roles.
- Monitor and correct any pronunciation errors focusing on where SS pronounce the *e* in *ed* and where they shouldn't, e.g. /helpt/ NOT /~~helpɪd~~/ for *helped*.

3 WRITING & SPEAKING

a ● Focus on the instructions. Give SS time to read the phrases and deal with any vocabulary problems, e.g. *check my emails.*

● Demonstrate the activity by writing a few true positive and negative sentences about yourself on the board using the phrases in the chart, e.g. *I didn't play a computer game yesterday, I used the Internet yesterday.*

● Then give SS time to write nine true sentences about themselves using the phrases. Monitor and help.

b ● Focus on the instructions. Put SS in pairs, **A** and **B**. Tell **A** to tell **B** his/her sentences while **B** listens. Tell **B** to remember what **A** did. Then they swap roles. Monitor and correct pronunciation.

● Give SS time to agree on which things they both did before getting some feedback from a few pairs. Elicit sentences like *We played a computer game/We didn't play a computer game.*

4 VOCABULARY common verbs 3

a ● Focus on the task. Give SS a few minutes to match the verbs and the phrases in pairs. Check answers.

1 h	2 c	3 f	4 g	5 a	6 d	7 e	8 b

● Quickly test SS' memory by saying the nouns at random for them to say the whole phrase, e.g.

T *noise*

SS *hear a noise*

b ● Tell SS to go to **Vocabulary Bank** *Common verbs 3* on *p.113*.

● Focus on part **A**. Go through the verbs one by one and make sure SS know what they mean. If there is any doubt, SS can use a dictionary or you can explain or use SS' L1.

● (5.18) Focus on the instructions for **a**. Play the CD and get SS to repeat the words in chorus or individually as necessary and highlight pronunciation. Use the pause button as necessary.

(5.18)	CD3 Track 06
arrive at the airport	learn a language
break your leg	meet a friend
buy a ticket	rent a car
come back from holiday	say hello
find a job	stay at a hotel

● Focus on the information box for *arrive* and go through the information with SS. Highlight that we use *arrive **in*** for countries and cities, and *arrive **at*** for buildings.

● Now focus on the information box for ***meet*** and highlight the different meanings of *meet*, i.e. meet someone for the first time (e.g. *Nice to meet you*) and meet somebody by arrangement (e.g. *We can meet at the cinema at 7.00*), or by accident (*meet somebody in the street*). You could elicit a translation for each meaning if you think it would help your SS.

● Focus on the instructions for **b**. Tell SS to cover the verb phrases and look at the pictures. Give them a few minutes to say the verb phrases in pairs. Monitor and help.

Study Link SS can find more practice of these verbs on the MultiROM and on the *New English File Beginner* website.

● Tell SS to go back to the main lesson on *p.48.*

5 READING & SPEAKING

a ● SS are now going to read what happened when Joanna, the Polish girl from **1a**, arrived in Rome and did her Erasmus programme.

● Revise the first part of Joanna's story. Get SS to cover the sentences and look at the pictures. Elicit the eight sentences from the class, encouraging them to pronounce the *ed* endings correctly.

b ● Focus on the question and instructions and make sure SS understand them. You could get SS to cover the text so that they are not tempted to read it before you want them to.

● Give SS time to read the possible problems and deal with any questions about vocabulary, e.g. *the weather, different customs.*

● Focus on the **My guess** column. Explain that a tick means they think this was a problem and a cross means they think it wasn't a problem. Give SS, in pairs, time to tick or cross the boxes. Monitor and help.

● Get feedback from the class but don't tell them at this point whether their guesses are right or not.

c ● Focus on the instructions. Tell SS they are going to read what Joanna wrote on a website after her year in Rome. Remind SS that when they read they should try to focus on the words they know, and try to guess the meaning of new words. Give SS time to read the text.

● Focus on the **What Joanna said** column. Give SS a few minutes to read the text again, and tick or cross the boxes. Get them to check with a partner and try to agree on the sentences which need ticking.

● Check answers and as you check each one ask *Were you right?* Find out which pairs guessed the problems correctly.

● Go through the text line by line and elicit/explain the meaning of new words and phrases, e.g. *through the city, made friends, broke my heart, speak Italian quite well, the best in the world, I feel European, a year ago,* etc.

⚠ *Ciao bella! = Hello, beautiful!* in Italian.

What Joanna said			
where to live	✗	the language	✓
making friends	✗	Italian men	✗
the weather	✗	money	✓
the food	✗	different customs	✗

d ● Focus on the instructions and the example. Tell SS that the verbs come in the same order in the text, i.e. *stay* is the first verb. Get SS to find the past simple of the second verb *buy* (bought), and tell them to write it in.

● Give SS a few minutes to read the text again and find the other past simple forms. Get them to compare their answers with a partner.

● Write *R = regular verbs* and *I = irregular verbs* on the board. Remind SS that all regular verbs end in *ed*. Give SS time to complete the boxes with *R* or *I* in pairs.

e • **5.19** Play the CD for SS to listen and check their answers.
- Check answers by asking individual SS to spell some of the past forms while you write them on the board. Then ask them if the verb is regular or irregular.

> **2** bought (I) **3** rented (R) **4** said (I) **5** liked (R)
> **6** spoke (I) **7** could/couldn't (I) **8** started (R)
> **9** made (I) **10** found (I) **11** learnt (I)
> **12** changed (R) **13** lived (R) **14** met (I)
> **15** broke (I) **16** came back (I)

5.19		CD3 Track 07
1 stay stayed	**9** make made	
2 buy bought	**10** find found	
3 rent rented	**11** learn learnt	
4 say said	**12** change changed	
5 like liked	**13** live lived	
6 speak spoke	**14** meet met	
7 can/can't could/couldn't	**15** break broke	
8 start started	**16** come back came back	

- Play the CD again for SS to listen and repeat. Focus especially on the forms SS may have problems with, e.g. *bought* /bɔːt/. Model them yourself so that SS can see the position of your mouth. Then drill in chorus and individually.
- With the regular verbs remind SS not to pronounce the *e* in the *ed* ending in *stayed*, *liked*, *changed*, and *lived*, but to pronounce it as /ɪd/ in *rented* and *started*.

f • Do this as an open-class question and get any SS who know people to tell the rest of the class about their experiences.

WORDS AND PHRASES TO LEARN

Focus on the words and phrases to learn. Make sure SS understand the meaning of each phrase. If necessary, remind SS of the context in which they came up in the lesson. If you speak your SS' L1, you might like to elicit a translation for the words/phrases for the SS to write next to them. You may also like to ask SS to test each other on the phrases.

Study Link SS can find more practice of these words and phrases on the MultiROM and on the *New English File Beginner* website.

Extra photocopiable activities

Grammar
past simple: regular and irregular verbs *p.142*
Communicative
Guess how many *p.180* (instructions *p.158*)

HOMEWORK

Study Link Workbook *pp.40–41*

5 PRACTICAL ENGLISH WHAT'S THE DATE TODAY?

Ordinal numbers
Months
Saying the date

Lesson plan

In this lesson SS learn how to say the date in English. This involves teaching SS ordinal numbers, which are presented through a general knowledge quiz. SS then learn the months, and finally how to say the date.

We have focused on one way of saying the date, i.e. *the first of May* (as opposed to *May the first*) and have not focused on how to say the year, which is taught in *New English File Elementary*. In **People in the street** SS listen to five people saying when their birthday is and what they did on their last birthday. SS then answer the same questions themselves.

Optional lead-in (books closed)
- Revise numbers by playing Bingo. Draw a Bingo card on the board like this:

- Tell SS to write six numbers from 1 to 31 in the chart. Elicit the rules of the game from the class.
- Read out numbers in random order, crossing them out with a pencil as you say them, until a student shouts *Bingo!*
  1 2 3 4 5 6 7 8 9 10 11 12 13 14 15 16 17
  18 19 20 21 22 23 24 25 26 27 28 29 30 31
- Get the winning SS to read out their numbers to check that all the numbers have been called.

1 ORDINAL NUMBERS

a • Focus on the quiz and give SS a minute or so to read the quiz but not to answer the questions at this point.
- Tell SS to look at the words in red. Focus on FIRST (question 1) and elicit/explain that it is the ordinal number for the number *one*. Do the same for SECOND and THIRD. Then show SS that from then onwards the ordinal number is the normal number + *th*. Highlight that these numbers are called *ordinal* numbers because they tell us the *order* of something.
- Put SS in pairs and give them time to circle the answers. Monitor and help, then check answers.

> **1** c **2** c **3** b **4** c **5** c **6** c **7** b **8** a **9** a

- Tell SS to cover the quiz. Write the number *1* on the board and elicit the corresponding ordinal number (*first*). Do the same for 2–9.

b • Tell SS to go to **Vocabulary Bank** *The time and ordinal numbers* on *p.110*. Focus on part **B Ordinal numbers**.
- **5.20** Focus on the instructions for **a**. Play the CD and get SS to repeat the words in chorus. Replay as necessary. Model and drill problem numbers, e.g. *fifth* /fɪfθ/, *eighth* /eɪtθ/, and *twelfth* /twelfθ/.

5.20		CD3 Track 08
the first	the eighth	the fifteenth
the second	the ninth	the sixteenth
the third	the tenth	the seventeenth
the fourth	the eleventh	the eighteenth
the fifth	the twelfth	the nineteenth
the sixth	the thirteenth	the twentieth
the seventh	the fourteenth	

- Highlight that:
  - we put the two small letters after the number to distinguish it from a normal (cardinal) number, e.g. *first* → *1st.* Remind SS that the two letters are the last two letters of the ordinal number.
  - *first, second,* and *third* are irregular in that they are completely different in form from the cardinal numbers *one, two,* and *three.*
  - all the other ordinals are formed by adding *th* to the cardinal number, pronounced /θ/.
  - the following ordinals are slightly irregular in their full written form:
    fifth /fɪfθ/, *ninth* /naɪnθ/, *twelfth* /twelfθ/.
- Point out that we say *twenty-first, twenty-second, twenty-third* NOT ~~twenty-oneth, twenty-twoth, twenty-threeth.~~
- ⚠ Before ordinals which start with a vowel, e.g. *eighth, eleventh,* the pronunciation of *the* is not /ðə/ but /ðiː/. You may want to point this out to your SS.
- Focus on the instructions for **b.** Give SS time to practise saying the ordinal numbers. Note any general problems and focus on these on the board when SS finish.

Study Link SS can find more practice of these numbers on the MultiROM and on the *New English File Beginner* website.

- Tell SS to go back to the main lesson on *p.50.*

c • Read the **Pronunciation notes** and decide how much of the information you want to give your SS.

Pronunciation notes

- *th* is pronounced in two ways – as in *thumb* /θʌm/ or as in *mother* /ˈmʌðə/ – and there are no easy rules to give SS. It is hard for many SS to produce either sound correctly, and depending on their nationality they tend to pronounce *th* as /d/, /z/, or /s/.
- Show your SS that both sounds are made by touching the tip of your tongue very lightly against the tips of your top teeth. However, the /θ/ sound in *thumb* is **unvoiced**, while the /ð/ sound in *mother* is **voiced**. (For the difference between **voiced** and **unvoiced** sounds see **Pronunciation notes 2A** *p.32.*)
- Mispronouncing *th* as /θ/ when it should be /ð/ does not usually cause communication problems, and the priority is to help SS to produce these sounds approximately and intelligibly. However, it is worth making SS aware of the two pronunciations of *th* and encouraging them to try to hear the difference, even if they find it very difficult at first to make these sounds.

- **5.21** Play the CD for SS just to listen to the two sounds and words.
- Now focus on the sound picture *thumb* and write the word on the board. Play the CD for SS to listen and repeat the word and the sound /θ/. Then pause the CD.

- Now focus on the example words after *thumb.* Remind SS that the pink letters are the same sound as the picture word.
- Play the CD for SS to listen and repeat the words, pausing after each word to give them time to respond chorally. Then ask a few individual SS to pronounce each word before moving on to the next one.
- Then repeat this process for the *mother* sound. Write *mother* on the board before you start.
- Play the CD again for both sounds and give SS time to practise the sounds themselves for a few moments.

5.21		CD3 Track 09
thumb	/θ/	think, Thursday, three, third, seventh, ninth
mother	/ð/	the, they, then, their

Study Link SS can find more practice of these sounds on the MultiROM and on the *New English File Beginner* website.

d • **5.22** Focus on the instructions. Play the CD and pause after the first number (*one*). Ask SS what the ordinal number is and elicit *the first.* Play the CD so SS can hear the correct answer. Make sure SS are clear what they have to do before continuing. Remind SS that *the* is the /ð/ sound and that the final *th* in the ordinals is the /θ/ sound.
- Play the rest of the CD and give SS time to say the ordinal numbers in chorus. You may need to pause the CD if the repeat time is not long enough.
- Repeat the activity, getting individual SS to respond.

5.22		CD3 Track 10
one… the first	twenty… the twentieth
two… the second	nine… the ninth
five… the fifth	twenty-one… the twenty-first
eighteen… the eighteenth	twenty-four… the twenty-fourth
eleven… the eleventh	thirty… the thirtieth
three… the third	

2 MONTHS

a • **5.23** Focus on the exercise and drill the pronunciation of *months* /mʌnθs/.
- Play the CD once for SS to listen. Replay as necessary, getting SS to repeat in chorus and asking some individual SS. Model and drill problem words, e.g. *January* /ˈdʒænjuəri/ and *February* /ˈfebruəri/. Note that *February* is often pronounced /ˈfebuəri/.
- Practise the months round the class two or three times.

5.23		CD3 Track 11
January	May	September
February	June	October
March	July	November
April	August	December

b • Focus on the instructions. Give SS two minutes to remember the months.
- Get SS to cover the months and look at the abbreviations, e.g. JAN, FEB, and try to remember the months.

- Test SS by telling them to close their books, and writing abbreviations of the months on the board, e.g. SEP, and eliciting the month from the class.

Extra idea

Get SS to test each other in pairs. **A** says a number, e.g. *three*, and **B** says the corresponding month (March).

c • Ask SS to cover **a** and focus on the questions. Give SS time to answer in pairs, then check answers.

> *February* sometimes has 29 days.
> *September, October, November,* and *December* end in *-er.*
> *May* has only three letters.
> *January, June,* and *July* begin with the letter *J.*
> *January, February, May,* and *July* end with the letter *y.*

3 SAYING THE DATE

a • **5.24** Focus on the instructions and the dialogues. Highlight that the words in the spaces are ordinal numbers.
- Play the CD once for SS to listen. Replay as necessary for SS to complete the spaces. Check answers.

> **1** fifth, fourth **2** twentieth

5.24	CD3 Track 12

1 A What's the date today?
B It's the fifth of May.
A Is it? I thought it was the fourth.
2 B When's your birthday?
A On the twentieth of July.

- Focus on the box **Saying the date** and go through the information.
- Highlight the use of the words *the* and *of* in the **We say** column, and the different ways of writing the date.
- ⚠ The date can also be said as, e.g. *May the fourth,* but don't confuse SS by pointing this out. They will have no problems understanding a date said like this.
- ⚠ In US English they both write and say the date in a different way. When they write it, they give the month first and then the day, i.e. 9/11 = the 11th of September, NOT the 9th of November. When they say the date they normally also give the month first and don't use *the,* e.g. 4th May would be *May fourth.*

b • **5.25** Focus on the instructions and the dates. Play the CD for SS to listen and repeat.
- Focus on the first date again. Elicit how to say it (*the first of January*) and write it on the board.
- Give SS time to practise saying the dates in pairs. Note any problems and focus on them at the end.
- Ask individual SS around the class to say the dates.

Extra challenge

Alternatively, you could get SS to close their books and listen and write down the dates. Replay each date twice, then check answers and practise saying the dates.

5.25	CD3 Track 13

the first of January
the third of February
the fifth of March
the twelfth of April
the fifteenth of May
the twenty-second of June
the thirty-first of July
the tenth of August
the fourteenth of September
the ninth of October
the thirtieth of November
the twenty-fifth of December

c • Focus on the instructions. Model and drill the two questions. Then put SS in pairs and get them to ask each other the questions.

Extra challenge

Write on the board *tomorrow, the day after tomorrow, the day before yesterday,* and elicit the questions. Get SS to ask and answer.

d • Focus on the instructions. Model and drill *When's your birthday?* Get SS to write down their birthday on a piece of paper.
- Elicit the answer by asking a good student *When's your birthday?* (e.g. the 22nd of September).
- Tell SS to write down the names of all the SS in the class.
- ⚠ If your class is very large, tell them just to choose ten SS.
- Get SS to stand up and ask other SS *When's your birthday?* Tell them to write down the date on their list of names.
- Write a list of SS' names on the board. Get feedback by asking individual SS about a different student, e.g. *When's Maria's birthday?* Write the date on the board.
- Focus on the list of birthdays on the board and see what is the most popular month.

e • Focus on the instructions and the speech bubble. Demonstrate the activity by writing three birthdays on the board and saying whose birthdays they are.
- Give SS a few minutes to write down their important birthdays. SS, in pairs, tell each other whose the important birthdays are.

4 PEOPLE IN THE STREET

Study Link This exercise is also on the *New English File Beginner* DVD, which can be used instead of the class audio (see **Introduction** *p.11*). SS can get more practice on the MultiROM, which contains more of the short street interviews with a listening task and scripts.

a • **5.26** Focus on the photo of Helen. Ask *When's her birthday?* Play the CD for SS to answer the question. Replay as necessary and check answers (see listening script 5.26).

5.26	CD3 Track 14
Interviewer	When's your birthday?
Helen (UK)	It's **the 25th of April**.

b • **5.27** Ask *What did she do on her last birthday?* Play the CD again for SS to answer the question and check answers (see listening script 5.27).

5.27	CD3 Track 15
Interviewer	When's your birthday?
Helen	It's the 25th of April.
Interviewer	What did you do on your last birthday?
Helen	I had **a party**.

c ● **5.28** Focus on the four people and the gapped sentences. Explain that SS are going to hear the people answering the questions.

● Play the CD for SS to complete the information for Aidan. Replay and pause as necessary. Check answers (see listening script 5.28).

● Repeat this process for the other three speakers.

5.28	CD3 Track 16
Interviewer	When's your birthday?
Aidan (UK)	My birthday is on **the 19th of September.**
Interviewer	What did you do on your last birthday?
Aidan	On my last birthday I went **shopping** with some friends.
Interviewer	When's your birthday?
Heidi (UK)	My birthday is on **the 15th of December.**
Interviewer	What did you do on your last birthday?
Heidi	I went to the **cinema** with my **boyfriend.**
Interviewer	When's your birthday?
Sam (AUS)	**The second of March.**
Interviewer	What did you do on your last birthday?
Sam	I went to **a club** in the evening with some **friends.**
Interviewer	When's your birthday?
Michael (GER)	It's **the 21st of October.**
Interviewer	What did you do on your last birthday?
Michael	I think I had **lunch** or **dinner** with my **wife.**

d ● Get SS to ask you questions 1 and 2. Then get SS to ask and answer the questions in pairs. Monitor and help with vocabulary where necessary.

WORDS AND PHRASES TO LEARN

Focus on the words and phrases to learn. Make sure SS understand the meaning of each phrase. If necessary, remind SS of the context in which they came up in the lesson. If you speak your SS' L1, you might like to elicit a translation for the words/phrases for the SS to write next to them. You may also like to ask SS to test each other on the phrases.

Study Link SS can find more practice of these words and phrases on the MultiROM and on the *New English File Beginner* website.

Extra photocopiable activities

Communicative
Famous birthdays *p.181* (instructions *p.158*)

HOMEWORK

Study Link **Workbook** *pp.42–43*

5 REVISE & CHECK

For instructions on how to use these pages, see *p.29.*

What do you remember?

GRAMMAR

1 a	2 b	3 a	4 b	5 b	6 a	7 b	8 b	9 a
10 b								

VOCABULARY

a	1	at	**d**	1	the third
	2	at		2	June
	3	in		3	the twentieth
	4	on		4	February
	5	at			
b	1	find	**e**	1	last
	2	arrived		2	have
	3	stay		3	usual
	4	come back		4	date
	5	buy		5	best
c	1	broke			
	2	made			
	3	played			
	4	came			
	5	worked			

PRONUNCIATION

a	vowels:	bird, clock, computer
	consonants:	dog, tie, thumb, mother
c	<u>c</u>inema	a<u>rrive</u> seven<u>teen</u>th Sep<u>tem</u>ber Ju<u>ly</u>

What can you do?

1 CAN YOU UNDERSTAND THIS TEXT?

a	1 F	2 T	3 F	4 T	5 T	6 T	7 F	8 T
	9 T	10 F						

3 CAN YOU UNDERSTAND THESE PEOPLE?

1 b	2 a	3 b	4 b	5 b	6 a	7 a	8 b

1 **A** Where were you last night? I phoned at eight o'clock and at nine o'clock but your phone was off.
   B I was at the cinema with my girlfriend.

2 **A** Was the hotel good?
   B It was OK. The rooms were very nice, but the breakfast wasn't very good.

3 **A** What time did you finish work yesterday?
   B I didn't go to the office yesterday. I worked at home in the morning, and in the afternoon I was with the children.

4 **A** Did you go out last night?
   B Yes. We had dinner at an Italian restaurant, and then we went to see a French film.
   A Was it good?
   B Yes, it was fantastic.

5 **A** Where did you go for your last holiday?
   B We went to Venice with my sister and her husband.
   A Did you stay at a hotel?
   B No, we rented a flat.

6 **A** I went to the new shopping centre yesterday.
   B Did you? I went there last week. I bought some boots. Did you buy anything?
   A No, I couldn't find anything I liked.

7 **A** Did you have a good weekend?
   B No, I didn't. It was awful.
   A Why? What did you do?
   B I stayed at home on Saturday and helped my wife do housework. And on Sunday her mother and father came to lunch.

8 **A** Hi Liam. Happy birthday!
   B It's not my birthday today, it's tomorrow. The 11th of June.
   A Oh.

Extra photocopiable activities

Grammar
5 revision *p.143*
Vocabulary
What is *floppit? p.197* (instructions *p.192*)

Test and Assessment CD-ROM

File 5 Quicktest

File 5 Test

6A

G *there is/there are*
V hotels; *in, on, under*
P /eə/ and /ɪə/

On an island in Scotland

File 6 overview

File 6 presents and practises the construction *there is/there are* and its past form *there was/there were*. **6A** introduces this construction in the present and the use of *some* and *any* with plural nouns, and in **6B** SS learn how to use it in the past. **6C** shows SS how to understand and use object pronouns and revises the past simple. In the **Practical English** lesson SS learn how to ask for and give opinions about music and films.

Lesson plan

The topic of this lesson is unusual hotels. First SS learn vocabulary related to hotels and hotel rooms. The presentation of *there is* and *there are* is a dialogue between a hotel receptionist and a young footballer and his wife. When the couple arrive at a hotel on a remote Scottish island they are upset to find that there is no TV, Internet, etc.

In Pronunciation the focus is on the sounds /eə/ and /ɪə/. In the second half of the lesson SS read some authentic website information about three very unusual hotels. This also provides a context for SS to learn the prepositions *in*, *on*, and *under*. The lesson finishes with an information gap speaking activity where SS ask about what there is in a hotel room, and where it is. *Some* and *any* with uncountable nouns (e.g. *some bread*) is not actively taught in *New English File Beginner* but is presented in *New English File Elementary*.

Optional lead-in (books closed)

- Write on the board A HOTEL ROOM and give SS three minutes in pairs to brainstorm words for things you might find in a hotel room, e.g. *table, chair, bed, shower, phone, minibar, door, window*, etc.
  Feed back ideas onto the board, and model and drill pronunciation.

1 VOCABULARY hotels

a
- Books open. Focus on the instructions and the pictures, and tell SS they are all things you can usually find in a hotel room. Elicit the first word (*chair*). Then give SS, in pairs, a few minutes to write the other words.
- Check answers by asking individual SS and writing the words on the board. Get them to spell some of the words to you to revise spelling.

1 a chair	5 a shower
2 a table	6 a TV/television
3 a window	7 a phone/telephone
4 a door	

⚠ You may want to skip this stage if you did the optional **lead-in**.

b
- Tell SS to go to **Vocabulary Bank** *Hotels* on *p.114*.
- Focus on the first section **In a hotel bedroom**.
- **6.1** Focus on the instructions for **a**. Play the CD and get SS to repeat the words in chorus and individually. Use the pause button and replay as necessary.
- Focus especially on any words that SS are having

difficulty with. Highlight that *ow* is /aʊ/ in *towel* but /əʊ/ in *pillow*. Highlight the silent *p* in *cupboard*. Remind SS that we usually use *the* with *bedroom*, *bathroom*, and *floor* because there is usually only one or it is clear which one you are talking about.

6.1	CD3 Track 18
the bathroom	the floor
a bath	a pillow
a shower	a lamp
a towel	a remote control
a bed	a cupboard

- Focus on the instructions for **b**. Tell SS to cover the words and look at the picture. Give them a few minutes to say the words in pairs. Monitor and correct any pronunciation mistakes.
- Focus on the second section **In a hotel**.
- **6.2** Focus on the instructions for **a**. Play the CD and get SS to repeat the words in chorus. Highlight pronunciation, especially the /ɑː/ sound in *bar, car park, garden*, and *spa*.

6.2	CD3 Track 19
a bar	reception
a car park	a restaurant
a garden	a spa
a gift shop	a swimming pool
a gym	toilets
a lift	

- Focus on the instructions for **b**. Tell SS to cover the words and look at the picture. Give them a few minutes to say the words in pairs. Monitor and correct any pronunciation mistakes.
- Focus on the instructions for **c** and the examples. Look at the drawing of the hotel and highlight that we use ordinal numbers to talk about the floors of a hotel and *ground floor* for the floor which is at street level.
- Model and drill *the ground floor, the first floor, the second floor*, etc. in chorus and individually. Highlight that we use the preposition *on* to talk about the floors of a building.
- Demonstrate the activity by asking a good student *Where's the swimming pool?* (It's on the fourth floor). Elicit a question from the same student and answer the question yourself.
- Give SS a few minutes to ask and answer questions about the hotel in pairs. Monitor and help. Make a note of any problems they are having and correct any mistakes on the board.

Study Link SS can find more practice of these words on the MultiROM and on the *New English File Beginner* website.

- Tell SS to go back to the main lesson on *p.54*.

2 GRAMMAR *there is / there are*

a ● **6.3** Focus on the pictures and the instructions. Teach the pronunciation of *island* /ˈaɪlənd/ and highlight the silent *s*. Make sure SS have covered the dialogue, and write the question *Are they happy with the hotel and their room? Why (not)?* on the board.

● Play the CD once or twice for SS to answer the question. Get SS to compare what they think and check answers with the whole class. Establish that the couple aren't happy, and elicit a couple of ideas as to why not, e.g. the room is small/they wanted a double bed/no TV, etc.

⚠️ You may want to point out to your SS that the receptionist speaks with a Scottish accent.

Extra support

Alternatively, you could write on the board (without the answers given in brackets):

The room is very _____. (small)

Their room doesn't have a _____ *bed or a* _____. (double/TV)

The bathroom doesn't have a _____. (bath)

They can't use _____. (the Internet)

Play the CD twice and SS try to complete the spaces.

6.3   CD3 Track 20

M = man, R = receptionist, W = woman

M Hello. We have a reservation.
R Let's see, yes Mr and Mrs Robson. Welcome to the island. Your room's upstairs, number seven.
M <u>Is there a lift?</u>
R No, I'm sorry <u>there isn't</u>. But I can help you with your cases.
***
R This is your room.
W It's very small.
R Yes, but <u>there's a beautiful view</u>.
M <u>There are two beds</u>. We wanted a double bed.
R I'm sorry, <u>there aren't any rooms</u> with a double bed.
W Where's the TV?
R <u>There isn't one</u>. <u>There are some books</u> over there.
W Books!
R This is the bathroom.
W <u>There isn't a bath</u>.
R No, <u>there's a shower</u>. It uses less water.
M Can I use the Internet here?
R No, I'm sorry you can't.
W <u>Are there any shops</u> near here?
R No, madam, <u>there aren't</u>. Enjoy your stay.

---

b ● Focus on the dialogue and the instructions. Play the CD for SS to complete the missing words. Pause after each space to give SS time to write.

● Get SS to compare with a partner.

● Check answers by playing the CD again, pausing after each space to elicit the correct word.

2 lift   **3** beautiful   **4** two beds   **5** books   **6** bath
7 shower   **8** shops

c ● Focus on the first example of *there is/there are* in the dialogue (*Is there a lift?*). Elicit the meaning (in SS' L1 if you know it, or by writing on the board *Is there a lift in the hotel? = Does the hotel have a lift?*).

● Give SS a few minutes to underline the examples of *there is/there are* in the dialogue.

● Check answers by asking individual SS to read out the complete sentence (answers are underlined in listening script 6.3).

d ● Tell SS to go to **Grammar Bank 6A** on *p.98*.

● **6.4** Play the CD and get SS to listen and repeat the example sentences. Use the pause button as necessary. Focus on and drill the elision in *There's a TV, There isn't a phone, There aren't any towels,* etc. Highlight too the pronunciation of *isn't* /ˈɪznt/ and *aren't* /ɑːnt/.

6.4   CD3 Track 21

There's a TV.
There's a bath.

There isn't a phone.
There isn't a garden.

There are two beds.
There are some pictures.

There aren't any towels.
There aren't any pillows.

Is there a car park?   Yes, there is.
Is there a gym?   No, there isn't.

Are there any lifts?   Yes, there are.
Are there any cupboards?   No, there aren't.

● Go through the rules for *there is/there are* with the class using the expanded information in the **Grammar notes** below to help you. You may want to use L1 here if you know it.

Grammar notes

there is/there are

● *There is* is used with singular nouns, *there are* with plural nouns.

● *There is* contracts to *there's*, but we write *there are* NOT ~~there're~~.

● *There is* isn't contracted in short answers, i.e. *Yes, there is* NOT ~~Yes, there's~~.

● ⊟ sentences are formed with the negative of *be*, i.e. *isn't* and *aren't*.

● Questions are formed by inverting *there* and *is/are*, e.g. *There is* ➔ *Is there…?/There are* ➔ *Are there…?*

● When giving a list of things we use *There is* if the first word in the list is singular, e.g. *There's a bed, a table, and two chairs.*

a/an, some, **and** ***any***

● We use *a/an* after *there is* with singular nouns, e.g. *There's a TV, There isn't a phone, Is there a car park?* A typical error is to omit the article, e.g. ~~There isn't phone~~.

● We use *some* in ⊞ plural sentences, e.g. *There are some pictures,* and *any* in ⊟ plural sentences and questions, e.g. *There aren't any towels, Are there any lifts?*

⚠️ The use of *some* and *any* with uncountable nouns, e.g. *There's some bread,* is not actively taught here, but SS should recognize it if they encounter this use of *there is/are* elsewhere. This grammar point is taught in *New English File Elementary.*

● Focus on the exercises for **6A** on *p.99* and get SS to do them individually or in pairs. If they do them individually, get them to compare answers with a partner. Monitor and help. Check answers, getting SS to read the full sentences and questions.

a 1 any **2** some **3** a **4** any **5** a **6** a
    7 any **8** some
b 1 Are there **2** There aren't **3** There's
    4 Is there **5** There isn't **6** There aren't
    7 Is there **8** There are

Study Link SS can find more practice of this grammar on the MultiROM and on the *New English File Beginner* website.

- Tell SS to go back to the main lesson on *p.54*.

e ● Go through the dialogue line by line with SS and elicit/explain any other words or phrases that they don't understand. Focus especially on *Welcome to the island*, *upstairs* (teach SS *downstairs* here, too), *a beautiful view*, *Enjoy your stay*, etc. Model and drill pronunciation.

- Get SS to practise the dialogue in groups of three.
- ⚠ If your class doesn't divide into threes, have one or two pairs, and get one student to read the receptionist and the other the man and the woman.
- If there is time, SS can swap roles. You could get one group to act out the dialogue in front of the class.

f ● Now tell SS they are going to hear what happened after the man and woman saw their room. Focus on the question *Do they leave? Why (not)?* and write it on the board.

- **6.5** Play the CD once for SS to answer the question. Get SS to compare their answers in pairs and then play the CD again for them to check the answer. (They don't leave because the boat left five minutes ago. There isn't another boat until tomorrow afternoon.)
- Tell SS to turn to the listening script on *p.86*. Play the CD again and explain/translate any unknown vocabulary.
- Focus on the question *Do <u>you</u> like this hotel? Why (not)?* and elicit answers from the class.

6.5	CD3 Track 22

W = woman, M = man, R = receptionist
W We don't like the room and we don't like the hotel.
M We want to go back to Edinburgh. When's the next boat?
R I'm very sorry, sir. There's only one boat a day in the winter – and it left five minutes ago. There isn't another boat until tomorrow afternoon.
W 24 hours here! There's isn't a TV. There aren't any shops. What can we do?

3 PRONUNCIATION /eə/ and /ɪə/

- Read the **Pronunciation notes** and decide how much of the information you want to give your SS.

Pronunciation notes

- You could point out that /eə/ and /ɪə/ are diphthongs, i.e. two sounds, if you think this will help SS.
- You may want to highlight the following sound–spelling patterns:

/eə/ *air* is always pronounced /eə/, e.g. *hair, chair*.
/ɪə/ *eer* is always pronounced /ɪə/, e.g. *beer*.
    ere and *ear* are sometimes pronounced /ɪə/, e.g. *here, near*, but are also sometimes pronounced /eə/, e.g. *there, wear*. SS need to learn these examples.

a ● **6.6** Focus on the sound picture *chair* and write it on the board. Play the CD to model and drill the word and sound (pause after the sound).

- Now focus on the example words after *chair*. Remind SS that the pink letters are the /eə/ sound. Play the CD pausing after each word for SS to repeat.
- Repeat the process for *ear*. Write *ear* on the board before you play the CD.
- Replay as necessary and get SS to practise saying the words.

6.6		CD3 Track 23
chair	/eə/	where, there, airport, upstairs
ear	/ɪə/	near, here, beer, idea

Study Link SS can find more practice of these sounds on the MultiROM and on the *New English File Beginner* website.

b ● Focus on the instructions and the words. Demonstrate the activity by eliciting a true sentence with the first word, *a board* (*There's a board in our classroom/There isn't a board in our classroom*).

- Choose individual SS to make a ⊞ or ⊟ sentence with each word. Correct pronunciation.

Extra idea

Get SS to write two sentences about their classroom (one ⊞ and one ⊟) and two about their school.

4 READING

a ● Focus on the photos and the title. Establish that the photos show three very unusual hotels (they are from a website called *Unusual Hotels*). Now focus on paragraphs **A**, **B**, and **C**. Set a short time limit and tell SS to read them and match them to the photos. Remind them to focus on the words they know, and try to guess the meaning of new words.

- Check answers.

A = right **B** = top left **C** = bottom left

b ● Focus on the instructions and the sentences. Go through them with the class and deal with any vocabulary problems, e.g. *massage, meal*. Focus on the first sentence (*You can go with children*) and show SS that the correct hotels are B and C, so they have been ticked. Give SS time to read the information about the three hotels again and tick the boxes. Monitor and help.

- Get SS to compare their answers in pairs and then check answers.

2 C **3** A **4** A **5** A and C **6** A
7 B **8** B and C

- Now go through each text and deal with any new vocabulary, e.g. *floating, underwater, aquarium, ancient caves, side, private terrace, luxury, gourmet, cuisine*, etc.

Extra challenge

Give SS a minute or so to read the texts again and try to memorize the key information. Then get them to close or cover their books. Write **Utter Inn, Elkep Evi**, and **Kamalame Cay** on the board and see how much SS can remember about each hotel. Starting with Utter Inn elicit anything they can remember and write it on the board under the name of the hotel, e.g. *You arrive by boat, you sleep in an aquarium, there's only one room, there are two single beds*, etc.

Then do the same for the other two hotels.

c ● Do this as an open-class question and elicit opinions about the three hotels. You could find out which hotel the class prefers by saying *Who prefers hotel A?* and getting a show of hands.

● Finally, tell SS which hotel you prefer and why.

5 SPEAKING

a ● Focus on the photos and the titles of the paragraphs in **4**. Ask *Where is hotel A? Where is hotel B? Where is hotel C?*, and elicit *under (the) water, in a mountain, on an island*. Make sure SS understand that hotel A is under the surface of the lake and only the entrance is above water, and B is inside the mountain rather than built on the mountainside. Check this by drawing a simple diagram of a mountain and a lake surface, and getting SS to put crosses where the hotels are.

● Now focus on the pictures and give SS time to write the correct preposition in pairs. Check answers.

> **1** in　**2** under　**3** on

● Try to get across the difference between *in* = inside something and *on* = on the surface of something.

Extra idea

You could practise these prepositions further by placing an object, e.g. your mobile phone, in different places in the classroom and asking *Where's my phone? (It's on the table, it's under the chair, it's in your bag,* etc.*)*.

b ● Focus on the pictures. In each one the remote control is in a different place.

● Focus on the speech bubbles and picture 1. Model and drill the question and answer in chorus and individually.

● Now ask the whole class the questions for pictures 2–6.

● Get a pair of SS to demonstrate the activity. Then give SS time to ask and answer the question with a partner. Monitor and help.

> **1** It's on the TV.　　　　**4** It's in the cupboard.
> **2** It's in the case.　　　　**5** It's on the table.
> **3** It's under the bed.　　　**6** It's under the chair.

c ● Put SS in pairs, **A** and **B**. Tell them to go to **Communication** *Is there a TV? Where is it?* **A** on *p.77* and **B** on *p.80.*

● Focus on the instructions and make sure SS are clear about what they have to do. Establish that **A** is going to first ask **B** questions about picture 1. For each object or set of objects, if **B** answers *Yes, there is/are,* **A** then has to ask *Where is it?/Where are they?* and draw the object(s) in the right place or write the word there.

● Demonstrate by taking the role of **A** and asking one of the **B**s *Is there a laptop?* and eliciting *Yes, there is.* Then ask *Where is it?* and elicit *It's on the bed.* Then tell all the **A**s to draw a laptop on the bed. Now do the same choosing a plural object, e.g. *towels.*

● Get the **A**s to continue with the questions and then to swap roles.

● As soon as a pair has finished tell them to compare their pictures.

Extra idea

You could get fast finishers to write sentences about their picture, e.g. *There's a laptop on the bed, There's a lamp on the big table,* etc.

● Tell SS to go back to the main lesson on *p.55.*

WORDS AND PHRASES TO LEARN

Focus on the words and phrases to learn. Make sure SS understand the meaning of each phrase. If necessary, remind SS of the context in which they came up in the lesson. If you speak your SS' L1, you might like to elicit a translation for the words/phrases for the SS to write next to them. You may also like to ask SS to test each other on the phrases.

> **Study Link** SS can find more practice of these words and phrases on the MultiROM and on the *New English File Beginner* website.

Extra photocopiable activities

Grammar
there is / there are p.144
Communicative
Is there a...? Where is it? *p.182 (instructions p.158)*

HOMEWORK

> **Study Link** **Workbook** *pp.44–45*

6
B

G *there was/there were*
V places
P the letters *ea*

Dream town?

Lesson plan

This lesson presents *there was/there were* through the context of a well-known Spanish tourist resort called Benidorm. Until the 1950s Benidorm was a small fishing village, but now it is so built-up that it has been nicknamed 'the Manhattan of the Mediterranean'. Before the grammar presentation SS revise and extend their vocabulary for places. The pronunciation focus is on the different possible pronunciations of the letters *ea*. SS then go on to listen to a conversation between an American tourist and her English friend talking about a weekend away in the UK. The lesson builds up to a speaking activity where SS exchange information about a holiday. Finally, SS write an email about a disastrous stay in a hotel.

Optional lead-in (books closed)

- Write the following sentences on the board:
  1 *There's hospital in my town.*
  2 *There is a university here?*
  3 *There is some good restaurants.*
  4 *There aren't some parks in the centre.*
- Tell SS there is a mistake in each sentence. Give them a few minutes in pairs to find the mistakes, and check answers.

  > 1 There's **a** hospital in my town.
  > 2 **Is there a** university here?
  > 3 There **are** some good restaurants.
  > 4 There aren't **any** parks in the centre.

1 VOCABULARY places

a • Books open. Focus on the quiz. Go through the questions. Elicit/explain *have an accident* in question 2 and *something* in 4, 5, and 6. Then elicit the first answer from SS (to a restaurant).
- Give SS a few minutes to do the quiz in pairs. Monitor and help.
- Check answers and get individual SS to spell the words to you and write them on the board.

  > 1 to a restaurant   2 to a hospital   3 to a car park
  > 4 to a shop   5 to a school   6 to a bar/café
  > 7 to a hotel

Extra challenge

Alternatively, to give extra listening practice you could tell SS to close their books and read out the 'clues' in the places quiz one by one for SS to write down the answers.

b • Tell SS to go to **Vocabulary Bank** *Places* on *p.115*.
- **6.7** Focus on the instructions for **a**. Play the CD and get SS to repeat the words in chorus and individually. Use the pause button and replay as necessary. Remind SS that the underlined syllables have extra stress. Model and drill any problem words yourself. Make sure SS are clear about the meaning of all the vocabulary items.

- Draw SS' attention to the apostrophe in *chemist's*. Explain that some words for places end in *'s* (e.g. *hairdresser's*) because they were originally *a hairdresser's shop*, etc. You may also want to teach the word *pharmacy* as this is becoming more widely used in the UK.

⚠ SS may want to know the difference between a *road* and a *street*: a *road* connects villages, towns, and cities; a *street* is a road with houses and buildings on both sides. Both words are used in addresses, e.g. *Oxford Street, Park Road*.

> **6.7**   CD3 Track 24
>
> a city   a town   a village   an airport   a bank
> a beach   a chemist's   a church   a cinema
> a hospital   a museum   a park   a petrol station
> a post office   a river   a road   the sea   a shop
> a station   a supermarket

- Focus on the instructions for **b**. Get SS to cover the words and look at the pictures. Give them time to remember the words with a partner. Monitor and help.
- Focus on the instructions for **c**. Go through the prompts with SS and highlight the alternative expressions with *there is/there are*. Remind SS that *some* = an unspecified but small number, *a lot of* = a large number.
- Focus on the example. Give SS time in pairs to tell each other about their town/city. Monitor and help, correcting any pronunciation mistakes.
- Get feedback by eliciting a sentence for each prompt.

⚠ If all your SS live in the same town, just elicit sentences from the class about their town, e.g. *Bologna is a big town. There's an airport…*

Extra support

Get SS to write sentences about their town/city before telling a partner about it.

> **Study Link** SS can find more practice of these words on the MultiROM and on the *New English File Beginner* website.

- Tell SS to go back to the main lesson on *p.56*.

2 READING & LISTENING

a • Focus on the lesson title and make sure SS know what it means. Tell SS to look at the photos and ask *Where's Benidorm?* (in Spain). Find out if any SS have been there.
- Elicit from SS the difference between Benidorm in the 1950s and today. (In the 1950s it was small. Now there are a lot of hotels.)
- Focus on the text and give SS a few minutes to read it. Then focus on the questions and go through them. Deal with any vocabulary problems, e.g. *build, rule*.
- Then give SS time to answer the questions with a partner.
- Check answers with the whole class and elicit the meaning of *mayor* /meə/ and *bikini*.

> 1 small   2 the mayor of Benidorm
> 3 a big tourist town   4 hotels   5 the bikini rule

- Go through the text and deal with any further vocabulary problems, e.g. *south-east*.

b ● **6.8** Focus on the instructions and the chart. Highlight that the first column has information about Benidorm today and the second column about Benidorm in the 1950s. Give SS time to read the information in the chart.

- Focus on the first number, *65,000,* and teach that this is said *sixty-five thousand.* Teach the meaning of *million* and *km = kilometres.* Show also that 128 is said *a hundred **and** twenty-eight,* 600 = *six hundred,* 264 = *two hundred **and** sixty-four.*

⚠ These high numbers are taught here for recognition only and are taught formally in *New English File Elementary.*

- Tell SS first just to listen and not to write anything. Play the CD once. Then play it again for SS to complete the chart. If necessary pause after each answer is given to give SS time to write. Get SS to compare their answers with a partner.

- Check answers by playing the CD again, pausing after each answer.

> There are four million *tourists* a year.
> There's an *airport* 50 km from Benidorm.
> There are 128 *hotels*.
> There are 600 *bars*.
> There are 264 *supermarkets*.

6.8   CD3 Track 25

I = interviewer, S = Mr Soriano
I Mr Soriano, what differences are there between Benidorm today and Benidorm in the 1950s?
S There are very big differences. For example, today there are 65,000 people who live in Benidorm. In the 1950s there were only about 3,000 people.
I Wow! That's a big difference! What about tourists?
S Today there are four million tourists a year. In the 1950s there were only maybe 300 tourists. And they were Spanish. Now tourists come from all over the world.
I Was there an airport near Benidorm in the 1950s?
S No, there wasn't an airport then. Today there is a big international airport in Alicante, which is only 50 km from Benidorm.
I How many hotels are there now?
S There are 128 hotels in the town.
I That's a lot! And in the 1950s?
S In the 1950s there were only three.
I Benidorm is famous for its nightlife. How many bars are there?
S About 600! In the 1950s I think there were maybe only ten bars in the village, and there wasn't a supermarket, only some little shops. Today there are 264 supermarkets and hundreds of shops.
I Thank you, Mr Soriano.
S You're welcome.

Extra support

Tell SS to go to the listening script on *p.86*. Play the CD again for them to have a final listen as they read. Deal with any vocabulary problems.

---

c ● Focus on the questions. Ask the questions one by one to the whole class, and elicit opinions.

3 GRAMMAR *there was/there were*

a ● Focus on the instructions and the chart in **2b**. Elicit the past forms of *there is/there are*. Write them on the board like this:

Present		Past
there is	→	there was
there are	→	there were
there isn't	→	there wasn't
there aren't	→	there weren't

b ● Tell SS to go to **Grammar Bank 6B** on *p.98*.
- **6.9** Play the CD and ask SS to listen and repeat the example sentences. Encourage SS to get the stress right, i.e. not to stress *was* and *were* in the ⊞ sentences. Use the pause button as necessary and replay as necessary.

6.9   CD3 Track 26

There was a station.
There was a road.

There wasn't an airport.
There wasn't a swimming pool.

There were some hotels.
There were ten bars.

There weren't any big shops.
There weren't any tall buildings.

Was there a park?	Yes, there was.
Was there a shopping centre?	No, there wasn't.
Were there any hotels?	Yes, there were.
Were there any restaurants?	No, there weren't.

- Go through the rules for *there was/there were* with the class using the expanded information in the **Grammar notes** below to help you. You may want to use L1 here if you know it.

Grammar notes

- *There is/there are* can be used in different forms by changing the form of *be*, thus the past simple is *there was/there were*.
- Although it works in exactly the same way as *there is/there are*, SS have a tendency to forget the past plural form *there were*.
- The rules for using *a/an, some,* and *any* after *there was/were* are the same as for *there is/are*.

- Focus on the exercises for **6B** on *p.99* and get SS to do them individually or in pairs. If they do them individually, get them to compare answers with a partner. Remind them to use *some* and *any* in plural sentences where no number is mentioned.
- Check answers, getting SS to read the full sentences.

a 1 Was there an airport?
  2 There weren't any restaurants.
  3 There were a lot of shops.
  4 There weren't any bars.
  5 Were there any tourists?
  6 There wasn't a spa.
  7 Was there a cinema?
  8 There was a hospital.

b 2 there weren't   6 Were there
  3 Was there   7 Was there
  4 there wasn't   8 there was
  5 There was

Study Link SS can find more practice of this grammar on the MultiROM and on the *New English File Beginner* website.

- Tell SS to go back to the main lesson on *p.57*.

4 PRONUNCIATION the letters *ea*

- Read the **Pronunciation notes** and decide how much of the information you want to give your SS.

Pronunciation notes

- The combination of vowels *ea* has several possible pronunciations. In this exercise we focus on the most common pronunciation of this spelling: /iː/, e.g. *dream*, and the less common /e/, e.g. *weather*.

⚠ The /eɪ/ pronunciation of *ea* is very rare. It occurs in the words *great*, *steak*, and *break* – this pronunciation will be pointed out when the words come up.

a ● **6.10** Focus on the words and elicit that they all have the vowels *ea*, but the pronunciation is not the same.

- Focus on the sound pictures. Write the words on the board and model and drill the words and sounds (*tree* /iː/, *egg* /e/). Then elicit the pronunciation of the two words (*dream* and *weather*).

- Give SS a few minutes in pairs to put the words in the right column. Get them to say the words aloud each time.

- Play the CD, pausing for SS to check answers (see listening script 6.10).

6.10		CD3 Track 27
tree	/iː/	dream, beach, please, eat, sea, speak
egg	/e/	weather, bread, breakfast

Study Link SS can find more practice of these sounds on the MultiROM and on the *New English File Beginner* website.

b ● **6.11** Focus on the sentences and play the CD just for SS to listen. Then play the CD for SS to listen and repeat. Then give SS time to practise the sentences in pairs.

6.11	CD3 Track 28
My dream is to speak perfect English!	
Please eat your breakfast!	
The weather at the beach was terrible.	

5 LISTENING

a ● **6.12** Focus on the photo. Tell SS it shows a popular UK holiday destination, but don't tell them where it is.

- Now focus on the instructions and establish the situation. Play the CD once for SS to answer the question. Get SS to compare with a partner and check the answer (No, Jeff and Kelly had a terrible weekend).

6.12	CD3 Track 29

F = friend, K = Kelly
F How was your weekend, Kelly? What did you do?
K We went to Blackpool.
F Blackpool? Why Blackpool?
K Well, somebody told us that Blackpool was like Benidorm… in Spain. Well, maybe it is in the summer, but it certainly isn't in April. The weather was terrible! And a lot of places were closed, you know the restaurants and cafés. There was nothing to do.
F Where did you stay? In a hotel?
K I wanted to stay in a good hotel, but Jeff wanted something typically English so we stayed in a bed and breakfast.
F How was it?
K Well, the room was really small. And the breakfast was terrible!
F Terrible? English breakfasts are usually very good!
K Yes, and that's what we wanted, a typical English breakfast, you know bacon and eggs, sausages. But there was only cereal, cold toast, and tea. There wasn't any coffee! I tell you, the weekend was a complete disaster.

b ● Focus on the instructions. Tell SS they are going to listen to the CD again and they have to circle the right answer. Give SS time to read the sentences. Elicit/teach *bed and breakfast* (= a private house which has rooms where you can pay to stay the night and have breakfast).

- Play the CD for SS to circle the answers. Replay as necessary.

- Check answers by playing the CD again, pausing after each answer.

1 b   **2** a   **3** a   **4** b   **5** b   **6** a

- Get SS to go to the listening script on *p.86* and play the CD again while they read so that they can see exactly what was said and how much they understood. Translate/explain any new words or phrases. Focus especially on useful phrases such as *How was your weekend?*, *a complete disaster*, and *typically English*.

6 SPEAKING & WRITING

a ● Put SS in pairs, **A** and **B**. Tell them to go to Communication *Good or bad holiday?* **A** on *p.78* and **B** on *p.80*. SS do a roleplay about a holiday.

- Focus on the instructions for **a** and give SS a few minutes to read about their hotels.

- Focus on the instructions for **b**. Elicit that in the first two questions, what's missing (where the slash (/) is) is *did*, and in the other questions *was*.

- Focus on the instructions for **c** and **d**. **B** interviews **A**. Then get them to swap roles. Monitor and help, correcting any errors that cause a breakdown in communication.

Extra support

You could elicit the questions and write them on the board and leave them there for SS to refer to if they need to.

Extra idea

Finally, you could ask SS to use the questions to ask each other about a real holiday. Stress that it should be a holiday where they stayed in a hotel.

- Tell SS to go back to the main lesson on *p.57*.
b - Focus on the instructions. Give SS time to read the feedback form and deal with any problems.
- Now focus on the email. Elicit how the third sentence should continue (*The room **was very small and cold***).
- Give SS time to continue the email in pairs, using the information on the feedback form. Monitor and help with any problems.
- In a small class, go round and check what SS are writing. In a large class, elicit the sentences and write them on the board.

> **Possible answer**
> The room was very small and cold. There wasn't a TV and there weren't any towels in the bathroom.
> And it wasn't only the room. The receptionist wasn't very friendly, and there wasn't a restaurant. There was a gym but it was closed.

WORDS AND PHRASES TO LEARN

Focus on the words and phrases to learn. Make sure SS understand the meaning of each phrase. If necessary, remind SS of the context in which they came up in the lesson. If you speak your SS' L1, you might like to elicit a translation for the words/phrases for the SS to write next to them. You may also like to ask SS to test each other on the phrases.

Study Link SS can find more practice of these words and phrases on the MultiROM and on the *New English File Beginner* website.

Extra photocopiable activities

Grammar
there was / there were p.145
Communicative
Memory test *p.183* (instructions *p.158*)

HOMEWORK

Study Link Workbook *pp.46–47*

G revision of past simple; object pronouns: *me*, *him*, etc.
V common verbs 3
P sentence stress

6C Strangers on a train

Lesson plan

In this lesson SS learn how to use object pronouns through the context of a short story. At the start of the lesson previously-taught verb phrases are revised and SS learn some new ones, which will be recycled in the story. SS then read and listen to the story in sections, answering questions on each part. The story also serves to revise and introduce more regular and irregular past forms. The object pronouns in the story, which SS will probably have recognized passively, are then focused on. The pronunciation focus is on sentence stress in sentences with object pronouns. The lesson finishes with the song *I'm a believer*.

Optional lead-in (books closed)

- Write the following on the board:
  THE LAST TIME I TRAVELLED BY TRAIN
  Where did you go?
  When did you go?
  Who did you go with?
  What did you do on the train?
- Give SS a few minutes to answer the question in pairs. Monitor and help with past verbs.
- Get feedback by asking some SS to tell the class about their partner, e.g. *Sabina went to Prague last week with her friend. She listened to music on the train.*

1 VOCABULARY more verb phrases

a • Books open. Focus on the instructions and give SS a few minutes to complete the questions in pairs.
- Check answers by getting SS to read out the full questions. Correct any pronunciation mistakes.

> 1 learn 2 meet 3 arrive 4 say 5 rent
> 6 stay 7 buy

b • Focus on the instructions. Demonstrate by getting SS to ask you the first three questions. Then give SS a few minutes to ask and answer questions in pairs. Monitor and help, making sure that SS use the past simple in question 6.
- Get feedback by finding out about a few SS.

c • Tell SS to go to **Vocabulary Bank** *Common verbs 3* on p.113. Focus on part **B**.
- **6.13** Focus on the instructions for **a**. Play the CD and get SS to repeat the phrases in chorus or individually. Use the pause button as necessary.

6.13	CD3 Track 30
call a friend	send an email
get a letter	take an umbrella
give a present	tell somebody a story
leave the cinema	turn on the light
lose your keys	turn off the light

- Elicit/explain/demonstrate the meaning of the phrases, using L1 if necessary.

- Focus on the instructions for **b**. Ask SS to cover the words and look at the pictures. Give them time to remember the words with a partner. Monitor and help.

Study Link SS can find more practice of these verb phrases on the MultiROM and on the *New English File Beginner* website.

- Tell SS to go back to the main lesson on p.58.

d • Focus on the exercise. Demonstrate by eliciting the opposite of the first sentence *(The plane leaves at 6.00)*.
- Give SS a few minutes to continue completing the sentences. Monitor and help.
- Check answers by getting SS to read out the full sentence. Then quickly check SS' memory of these four pairs of verbs by asking *What's the opposite of (e.g. lose)?*

> 1 leaves 2 find 3 get 4 give 5 turn off

2 READING & LISTENING

a • Pre-teach the following vocabulary to help SS with the story. Draw a train on the board and elicit the word *train*. Now elicit/teach words connected with travelling by train, e.g. *platform, seat, station, get on/get off (a train)*. Write them on the board and drill pronunciation.
- Focus on the title of the story and elicit/explain that *a stranger* = a person you don't know, NOT a person from another country (= *foreigner* – *stranger* is a 'false friend' for some nationalities).
- Now focus on **Part 1**. Tell SS that they are going to read and listen at the same time. Tell SS that they should try to guess the meaning of the verbs which are highlighted in blue. They are all past simple forms of verbs which SS know in the present.
- **6.14** Play the CD for SS to read and listen to **Part 1**.

⚠ The man in the story has a light American accent.

- Focus on questions 1–4. Get SS to answer them in pairs. Tell them to use the pictures to help them. Check answers.

> 1 At the station.
> 2 Chanel Number 5.
> 3 They talked about books.
> 4 They had coffee.

- Elicit/teach the meaning of any words in the story you think SS may not have understood, e.g, *full* (elicit the opposite here = *empty*), *next to*.

6.14	CD3 Track 31

N = narrator, **W** = woman
Strangers on a train
Part 1
N When the train stopped, I opened my eyes and looked out of the window. I saw her on the platform. A tall, blonde woman with dark blue eyes. The train left the station. As usual the 6.20 was full.
W 'Excuse me. Can I sit here?'

N I opened my eyes again. It was the tall, blonde woman.
'Sure.' I said. She sat down next to me. There was a nice smell. Chanel Number 5, I thought. I opened my book and started to read.
W 'I loved that book.'
N 'Sorry?' I said.
W 'I said I loved that book.'
N We chatted about books until the train arrived at Victoria station.
W 'Coffee?'
N she said. I looked at my watch. 'OK,' I said.

- **6.14** Play the CD for SS to read and listen to **Part 2**.
- Focus on questions 5–8. Get SS to answer them in pairs and then check answers. Elicit/teach the meaning of any words or phrases you think SS may not have understood, e.g. *That's interesting, Time to go, she smiled.*

5 She works in property – flats and houses.
6 He works for Citibank.
7 He lives in London, near the river.
8 She lives near him.

Part 2
N We sat at the station coffee bar, and we drank coffee and talked. Her name was Olivia. She told me that she worked in London.
'What do you do?' I asked.
W 'I work in property – flats and houses. What do you do?'
N 'I work for Citibank.'
W 'That's interesting!'
N said Olivia.
W 'Do you live in London?'
N 'Yes. I have a flat near the river.' I told her the street.
W 'Wow! That's an expensive part of London!'
N I looked at my watch. 'It's late. Time to go.'
W 'I can take you,'
N she said.
W 'I live near you.'
N She smiled. Her eyes were very blue.

- **6.14** Play the CD for SS to read and listen to **Part 3**.
- Focus on questions 9–12. Get SS to answer them in pairs and then check answers. Elicit/explain that the text message in 10 means *I really want to see you again*; in text messages people often use *c u* instead of *see you*.
- Elicit/teach the meaning of any words you think SS may not have understood, e.g. *text message, show*.

 9 An Audi TT.
10 I really want to c u again! Friday?
11 *Chicago*.
12 At the Cambridge Theatre at 7.30.

Part 3
N Her car was in the station car park. It was an Audi TT.
'Nice car,' I said.
She drove fast. Very fast.
She stopped outside my flat. We said goodbye, and I gave her my phone number.
Next morning there was a text message from Olivia.
W *I really want to see you again! Friday?*
N On Friday morning she called me.
W 'I have two tickets for *Chicago* tonight at the Cambridge Theatre! Can you get them from the box office at 7.15? We can meet in the theatre bar at 7.30. The show starts at 8.00.'

- **6.14** Play the CD for SS to read and listen to **Part 4**.
- Focus on questions 13–16. Get SS to answer them in pairs and then check answers. Elicit/explain that the man's text says *Where are you?* and that the letter *r* is often used in text messages instead of *are*.
- Elicit/teach the meaning of any words you think SS may not have understood, e.g. the use of *get* in *got the tickets*, *interval, angry*.

13 He arrived at 7.00.
14 He got a text message from Olivia. It said she was in a meeting. He found his seat in the theatre.
15 He called Olivia and sent her a text message.
16 He left the theatre and went home.

Part 4
N I arrived at the theatre at 7.00. I got the tickets and I waited in the bar. I read the evening paper. Olivia didn't come. I looked at my watch. It was 7.45. I looked at my phone. There was a text message.
W *Sorry! In a meeting. See you in the theatre. Leave my ticket at the box office.*
N I left her ticket at the box office and found my seat. The show started but Olivia didn't arrive. In the interval I called her but her phone was off. I sent her another text: *Where are you?* I was angry. I left the theatre and went home. I opened the door of my flat and turned on the light…

b • **6.15** Focus on the question and elicit possible answers, but <u>don't</u> give away the end of the story. Then play the CD for SS to find out what happened. Get them to compare with a partner and then play the CD again. Check answers.

His TV, hi-fi, pictures, and laptop weren't there. Olivia went to his flat when the man was at the theatre and took/stole them.

6.15   CD3 Track 32
I opened the door of my flat and turned on the light. Oh no! My flat looked very different. There was no TV, no hi-fi. There weren't any pictures on the walls. I went into my bedroom. My laptop wasn't there! But there was a nice smell. Chanel Number 5.

Extra idea

You could give SS extra listening practice by getting them to close their books and listen to the whole story again.

c • **6.16** Focus on the verbs and elicit that they are all **irregular**. Check that SS understand their meaning.

- Give SS a few minutes to find the past forms in the story. Check answers and get SS to spell the words to you as you write them on the board.

⚠ Highlight that although the spelling of *read* is the same in the present and past, the pronunciation is different, i.e. present /riːd/, past /red/.

Part 1	see	*saw*	leave	*left*	think	*thought*
Part 2	drink	*drank*	tell	*told*		
Part 3	drive	*drove*	give	*gave*		
Part 4	read	*read*	send	*sent*		

- Play the CD for SS to listen to the pronunciation of the past forms. Then play the CD again for SS to listen and repeat. Replay as necessary.

6.16					CD3 Track 33
see	saw	leave	left	think	thought
drink	drank	tell	told		
drive	drove	give	gave		
read	read	send	sent		

d ● Tell SS to go to **Vocabulary Bank** *Irregular verbs* on *p.116*.

● Quickly go through the verbs in the **PRESENT** list and check SS remember their meaning.

● **6.17** Focus on the instructions for **a**. Demonstrate by playing the first two pairs of verbs so that SS realize that at this stage they are just repeating the present and past forms, not the sentences.

● Play the CD from the beginning and get SS to repeat the verbs in chorus and individually, pausing and replaying as necessary. Focus especially on any verbs SS are having difficulty with, and model and drill these verbs yourself.

6.17				CD3 Track 34
is	was	leave	left	
are	were	lose	lost	
begin	began	make	made	
break	broke	meet	met	
buy	bought	pay	paid	
can	could	read	read	
come	came	say	said	
do	did	see	saw	
drink	drank	send	sent	
drive	drove	sit	sat	
eat	ate	sleep	slept	
find	found	speak	spoke	
get	got	swim	swam	
give	gave	take	took	
go	went	tell	told	
have	had	think	thought	
hear	heard	wear	wore	
know	knew	write	wrote	
learn	learnt			

● Focus on the instructions for **b** and on the sentences. Make sure that SS understand that the missing word in the sentences is the past simple verb. Ask SS to cover the past verbs with a piece of paper and look at the present verbs and the sentences. Elicit the first two sentences, i.e. *It was very hot yesterday, They were in Rome last week.*

● Give SS time to try to say the other sentences in the past with a partner. Monitor and help, correcting any pronunciation mistakes. If SS can't remember a past form, they can quickly uncover the **PAST** column and check.

● Finally, with the **PAST** column still covered go through the list asking individual SS to say the complete sentence with the verb in the past.

> **Study Link** SS can find more practice of these verbs on the MultiROM and on the *New English File Beginner* website.

● Tell SS to go back to the main lesson on *p.59*.

3 GRAMMAR object pronouns: *me, him,* etc.

a ● Focus on the four sentences from the story. Give SS time to complete them in pairs. Check answers.

> **1** me **2** you **3** them **4** her

Extra support

Let SS find the sentences in the story if they can't remember them.

b ● Focus on the chart and the words **Subject pronoun** and **Object pronoun**.

● Write the sentence *I love John but he doesn't love me* on the board, and get SS to identify which are the subject pronouns (*I* and *he*) and which is the object pronoun (*me*). You could explain that a subject pronoun is used for a person who <u>does</u> an action, and an object pronoun is used for the person who <u>receives</u> the action.

● Get SS to complete the chart with the words from **a**. Check answers.

Subject pronoun	Object pronoun
I	*me*
you	*you*
he	him
she	*her*
it	it
we	us
they	*them*

c ● Tell SS to go to **Grammar Bank 6C** on *p.98*.

● **6.18** Play the CD and ask SS to listen and repeat the example sentences. Use the pause button and replay as necessary.

6.18	CD3 Track 35
I'm your teacher.	Do you want to speak to me?
You're lost.	Can I help you?
He was at the party.	I saw him.
She never listens.	Don't talk to her.
It's a beautiful coat!	I want it for Christmas.
We aren't friends.	They don't speak to us.
They're good books.	Why don't you read them?

● Go through the rules for object pronouns using the expanded information in the **Grammar notes** below to help you. You may want to use L1 here if you know it.

Grammar notes

● Both subject and object pronouns are used to refer to people and things when we don't want to repeat the noun, e.g.
subject pronoun: **Olivia** *got on the train and* **she** *sat down.*
object pronoun: *The man liked* **Olivia** *and he gave* **her** *his phone number.*

● *it* is used for things, *him* for a man, and *her* for a woman. The plural *them* is used for both people (men and women) and things.

⚠ *her* is both the object pronoun for a woman and also the possessive adjective, e.g. *Her car was fast.*

● Focus on the exercises for **6C** on *p.99* and get SS to do them individually or in pairs. If they do them individually, get them to compare answers with a partner. Check answers, getting SS to read the full sentences.

> **a 1** him **2** us **3** them **4** it **5** them **6** him
> **7** her **8** us **9** it **10** her
> **b 1** it **2** him **3** them **4** her **5** me **6** us
> **7** you

> **Study Link** SS can find more practice of this grammar on the MultiROM and on the *New English File Beginner* website.

● Tell SS to go back to the main lesson on *p. 59*.

4 PRONUNCIATION sentence stress

a • Focus on the exercise. Demonstrate by eliciting the answer to the first question (e). Then give SS time to match the other questions and answers in pairs.

b • **6.19** Play the CD once for SS to check their answers.

> 1 e 2 a 3 b 4 d 5 c

• Play the CD again for SS to repeat a–e, encouraging them to copy the rhythm.

⚠ They don't have to repeat the questions, just the answers.

6.19	CD3 Track 36
1 Did you see the film? Yes, I saw it yesterday.	
2 Did you buy the books? Yes, I bought them yesterday.	
3 Did you meet Ana? Yes, I met her yesterday.	
4 Did John call you? Yes, he called me yesterday.	
5 Did Silvia tell you about the party? Yes, she told us yesterday.	

c • Put SS in pairs, **A** and **B**. Tell **A** to ask the questions and **B** to answer them from memory. Monitor and help with sentence stress.

• They then swap roles.

5 **6.20** SONG 🎵 *I'm a believer*

• *I'm a believer* was originally recorded in 1966 by the American group The Monkees. However, today it is perhaps better known in the cover version by the Californian group Smash Mouth which featured in the 2001 film *Shrek*. The activity for this song focuses on past forms. For copyright reasons this is a cover version.

• If you want to do this song in class, use the photocopiable activity on *p.207*.

6.20	CD3 Track 37

I'm a believer

I thought love was only true in fairy tales
Meant for someone else but not for me
Love was out to get me
That's the way it seemed
Disappointment haunted all my dreams

Chorus
Then I saw her face
Now I'm a believer
Not a trace
Of doubt in my mind
I'm in love
And I'm a believer
I couldn't leave her if I tried

I thought love was more or less a givin' thing
Seems the more I gave, the less I got
What's the use in tryin'?
All you get is pain
When I wanted sunshine, I got rain

Chorus

What's the use in tryin'?, etc.

Chorus

WORDS AND PHRASES TO LEARN

Focus on the words and phrases to learn. Make sure SS understand the meaning of each phrase. If necessary, remind SS of the context in which they came up in the lesson. If you speak your SS' L1, you might like to elicit a translation for the words/phrases for the SS to write next to them. You may also like to ask SS to test each other on the phrases.

Study Link SS can find more practice of these words and phrases on the MultiROM and on the *New English File Beginner* website.

Extra photocopiable activities

Grammar
object pronouns *p.146*
revision of past simple *p.147*
Communicative
Question and answer match *p.184* (instructions *p.159*)
Song
I'm a believer p.207 (instructions *p.201*)

HOMEWORK

Study Link **Workbook** *pp.48–49*

Asking for opinions
Giving opinions
Strong stress

Lesson plan

In this lesson SS learn to ask for and give opinions. The context is music and singers, and in the **People in the street** section the people interviewed talk about the last film they saw and what they thought of it.

Optional lead-in (books closed)

- Elicit some different types of music from SS and write their ideas on the board. The list could include: *blues, classical music, heavy metal, hip hop, country, jazz, pop music, reggae, rock*, etc. Model and drill the pronunciation.
- Tell SS you want them to find out what music their partner likes. They have to take turns to ask *Do you like…?* (*Yes, I do/No, I don't*) and try to remember the answers. You could teach the *agreeing* expressions *Me too* and *Me neither*.
- Give SS a few minutes to ask and answer questions. Monitor and help.
- Get feedback by asking a few to tell the class about their partner's musical tastes, e.g. *Katya likes rock and pop, but she doesn't like hip hop.*

1 ASKING FOR & GIVING OPINIONS

a ● **6.21** Books open. Focus on the drawing and tell SS that a boy is giving his headphones to a girl because he wants her to listen to some music.

- Get SS to cover the dialogue and play the CD for SS to listen. Then ask the whole class the questions *Who's the singer?* (Shakira) and *Who likes the music?* and elicit that the boy likes it.

6.21 / **6.22**	CD3 Tracks 38/39
A Listen to this. What do you think of it?	
B I don't like it. It's <u>awful</u>. Who is it?	
A Shakira. I really like her. She's <u>great</u>.	

b ● **6.22** Ask SS to uncover the dialogue and focus on the instructions.

- Play the CD for SS just to listen for the words which have extra stress (*awful* and *great*).
- Play the CD again, pausing for SS to listen and repeat. Encourage them to copy the stress.
- Go through the dialogue checking understanding. Elicit/explain that *it* in the question *What do you think of it?* refers to the music they are listening to, *awful* = very bad, *great* = very good, *really* in *I really like her* = very.
- Then get SS in pairs to read the dialogue aloud, swapping roles.

c ● **6.23** Focus on **Giving opinions: What do you think of…?** and on column 1 of the chart. Elicit/explain that if you are asking someone's opinion about some music, the question is *What do you think of this music?* or *What do you think of **it**?* Highlight the possible answers

---

using the smiley faces to aid meaning. Emphasize that *It's OK* (or *It's all right*) is a neutral answer (= It's not very good or very bad).

- Play the CD for SS to repeat.

6.23		CD3 Track 40
What do you think of this music?		
I really like it.	It's OK.	
It's fantastic. / It's great.	I don't like it.	
I like it.	It's terrible. / It's awful.	

d ● **6.24** Tell SS they are going to hear some music extracts. Tell them they have to use one of the phrases in column 1 to say what they think of the extract.

- Play the CD, pausing after each extract to elicit an opinion from individual SS, using the question, *What do you think of it?* Encourage them to use extra stress in their response.

6.24		CD3 Track 41
1 heavy metal	5 classical	
2 jazz	6 techno	
3 country	7 pop	
4 blues	8 opera	

e ● Focus on column 2 of the chart. Highlight that this column refers to a female singer and that the question is *What do you think of* (e.g. Shakira)? or *What do you think of her?*

- Look at the first example with SS, *I really like her*. Then focus on the first space. Elicit the missing word (*She's*). Give SS time to complete the spaces in the chart in pairs. Check answers.
- Explain that column 3 refers to a male singer (e.g. Ricky Martin) and give SS time to complete the spaces in the chart. Check answers. Then establish that column 4 refers to a group (e.g. The Rolling Stones) and that a group is plural. Elicit from the class what the missing words are in the chart. Check answers.
- Model and drill the sentences with *like* + pronoun, making sure SS stress *like* and not the pronoun, e.g. *I really like it, I don't like her*, etc.

I really like <u>*her*</u>.	I really like <u>*him*</u>.	I really like <u>*them*</u>.
She's fantastic/ *She's* great.	*He's* fantastic/ *He's* great.	*They're* fantastic/ *They're* great.
I like <u>*her*</u>.	I like <u>*him*</u>.	I like <u>*them*</u>.
She's OK.	*He's* OK.	*They're* OK.
I don't like <u>*her*</u>.	I don't like <u>*him*</u>.	I don't like <u>*them*</u>.
She's terrible/ *She's* awful.	*He's* terrible/ *He's* awful.	*They're* terrible/ *They're* awful.

Extra support

Get SS to cover the chart and use prompts (*What do you think of this music/Shakira/Sting/the Beatles?*) to elicit some of the possible answers from the class.

f ● Focus on the photos and the questions and answers in the speech bubbles.

- Drill the pronunciation of the two questions and also of the singers or groups for SS to repeat. Demonstrate the activity by getting SS to ask you what you think of some of them.

- Put SS in pairs and give them time to ask and answer questions about the singers and groups in the photos. Monitor and help. Note any general problems and deal with them on the board at the end.

g • Focus on the categories and spaces in the 'iPods'. Elicit the name of a very famous female singer for the first space to give SS the idea. Give SS time to complete the other 'iPods' individually.

- In a monolingual class tell SS they can use famous people/songs from their country if they like, and that they shouldn't translate the names of songs.

- Monitor and help SS with ideas if necessary.

h • Put SS in pairs and give them time to ask their partner's opinion of the singers and groups using *What do you think of...?* Monitor and help.

2 PEOPLE IN THE STREET

Study Link This exercise is also on the *New English File Beginner* DVD, which can be used instead of the class audio (see **Introduction** *p.11*). SS can get more practice on the MultiROM, which contains more of the short street interviews with a listening task and scripts.

a • **6.25** Focus on the photo of Helen and the two questions in the box. Explain that SS are going to hear her being asked these questions.

- Focus on the film titles A–F. If you know your SS' L1, try to help them to translate the film titles. Tell them each person saw one of these films.

- Now ask *What's the last film she saw?* Play the CD once or twice if necessary. Check the answer (see listening script 6.25 and answer key).

> F

6.25		CD3 Track 42
Interviewer	What's the last film you saw?	
Helen (UK)	*Indiana Jones.*	

b • **6.26** Ask *What did she think of the film?* Play the CD for SS to answer the question. Elicit/explain the meaning of *exciting*. Check the answer (see listening script 6.26).

6.26		CD3 Track 43
Interviewer	What's the last film you saw?	
Helen	*Indiana Jones.*	
Interviewer	What did you think of it?	
Helen	It was **great.** It was really exciting.	

c • **6.27** Focus on the instructions. Tell SS they are going to listen to five more people answering the questions.

- Play the CD for SS to complete the information for Lauren. Replay and pause as necessary. Check answers (see listening script 6.27).

- Repeat this process for the other four speakers.

Lauren C		**Heidi** A	
Tom B		**Joshua** E	
Suzy D			

6.27		CD3 Track 44
Interviewer	What's the last film you saw?	
Lauren (USA)	I saw *The Visitor.*	
Interviewer	What did you think of it?	
Lauren	I thought it was **great.**	
Interviewer	What's the last film you saw?	
Tom (CAN)	The last film I saw was *WALL•E.*	
Interviewer	What did you think of it?	
Tom	I thought it was **fantastic.**	
Interviewer	What's the last film you saw?	
Suzy (UK)	I went to see *Mamma Mia!*	
Interviewer	What did you think of it?	
Suzy	I **loved** it. It was **great.**	
Interviewer	What's the last film you saw?	
Heidi (UK)	*Female Agents.*	
Interviewer	What did you think of it?	
Heidi	It was **OK.**	
Interviewer	What's the last film you saw?	
Joshua (USA)	I saw *Wanted* with Angelina Jolie.	
Interviewer	What did you think of it?	
Joshua	I thought it was **terrible.**	

d • Get SS to ask you the two questions in the box. Then get SS to ask and answer the questions in pairs. Monitor and help.

- Get feedback from different SS.

Extra support

If you have time, let SS listen again with the listening script on *p.86*. Go through the dialogues line by line with SS and elicit/explain any words or phrases that they don't understand.

WORDS AND PHRASES TO LEARN

Focus on the words and phrases to learn. Make sure SS understand the meaning of each phrase. If necessary, remind SS of the context in which they came up in the lesson. If you speak your SS' L1, you might like to elicit a translation for the words/phrases for the SS to write next to them. You may also like to ask SS to test each other on the phrases.

Study Link SS can find more practice of these words and phrases on the MultiROM and on the *New English File Beginner* website.

Extra photocopiable activities

Communicative
What do you think of...? *p.185* (instructions *p.159*)

HOMEWORK

Study Link Workbook *pp.50–51*

6 REVISE & CHECK

For instructions on how to use these pages, see *p.29*.

What do you remember?

GRAMMAR

1 b 2 b 3 a 4 b 5 b 6 a 7 a 8 b 9 b
10 b

VOCABULARY

a 1 remote control	d 1 drank
2 pillow	2 took
3 double	3 told
4 towels	4 said
5 car park	5 left
b 1 petrol station	e 1 floor
2 village	2 view
3 airport	3 wear
4 post office	4 time
5 supermarket	5 of
c 1 give	
2 leave	
3 call	
4 turn off	
5 send	

PRONUNCIATION

a vowels: chair, ear, owl, tree, egg, boot
consonants: jazz

c be<u>d</u>room <u>re</u>staurant mu<u>s</u>eum <u>air</u>port
fan<u>ta</u>stic

What can you do?

1 CAN YOU UNDERSTAND THIS TEXT?

a 1 F 2 F 3 F 4 T 5 T 6 T 7 F

2 CAN YOU WRITE THIS IN ENGLISH?

1 She went to Mexico.
2 Last year.
3 By plane.
4 In (a hotel in) Cancún.
5 She swam every day. She travelled around by bus
6 She saw Chichen Itza.
7 Yes, because it's beautiful, the people are friendly, and
   the weather is great.

3 CAN YOU UNDERSTAND THESE PEOPLE?

a 1 b 2 b 3 b 4 a 5 b 6 a 7 b 8 a

6.28   CD3 Track 45

A Good afternoon. Holiday Homes Limited. Can I help
   you?
B Good afternoon. I saw an advertisement in the
   newspaper about a holiday house to rent. It's reference
   4795. Can you give me some more information,
   please?
A Yes, absolutely. What do you want to know?
B Where is it exactly?
A It's in a village called Langon, about 50 kilometres
   from Bordeaux.
B 15?
A No, 50.
B Is there a beach near the house?
A Not very near. The village is in the mountains. It's
   about an hour from the beach by car. But there's a
   swimming pool in the garden.
B How many bedrooms are there? Three?
A Four. Three big ones and one very small bedroom.
B Ah, yes. How many bathrooms are there?
A There are two, one upstairs and one downstairs.
B Is it free in September? We want to go on holiday from
   the 10th to the 20th of September.
A Yes, I think that's a possibility. Can you come to our
   office one day this week? Then I can show you more
   photos and we can talk about dates.
B Is Thursday afternoon OK?
A Just a moment. Yes, that's OK. At quarter past five?
B Yes, that's fine.
A Do you know our address?
B It's Cowley Road, isn't it?
A Yes, number 86. OK. See you on Thursday at quarter
   past five.
B Thank you very much. Goodbye.

Extra photocopiable activities

Grammar
6 revision *p.148*
Vocabulary
Draw it *p.198* (instructions *p.192*)

Test and Assessment CD-ROM

File 6 Quicktest
File 6 Test

7A

G *like* + verb + *-ing*
V activities
P /ʊ/, /uː/, and /ŋ/

What do you like doing?

File 7 overview

In File 7 the focus is on the use of the *-ing* form after *like*, and the future with *be going to*. In **7A** SS learn how to use *like* with the *-ing* form to talk about free-time activities. In **7B** they are introduced to the future with *be going to* to discuss future plans. Lesson **7C** continues with *be going to* and focuses on its use to express predictions. There are several ways of expressing the future in English, but at this level we have chosen to teach one form, *be going to*, which can be used for both plans and predictions. Finally, in the **Practical English** lesson SS learn to ask for and give simple directions.

Lesson plan

This lesson focuses on free-time activities. After learning the vocabulary, the grammar (*like* + verb + *-ing*) is presented through the context of a dating website. In Pronunciation, SS practise the long and short vowel sounds /uː/ and /ʊ/, and the /ŋ/ sound. SS then read an article about the different ways people enjoy spending their free time all over the world, and then write and speak about what they like doing.

Optional lead-in (books closed)

- Write FREE TIME on the board. Elicit/explain the meaning if necessary.
- Ask SS *What do you do when you have free time?* and elicit verbs onto the board, e.g. *I read, I watch TV*, etc.
- Now show SS that if you add *-ing* to the verbs, you have the word for the activity (grammatically a noun), e.g. *reading, watching TV*, etc. Show how you can change *I read, I watch TV*, etc. to *I like reading, I like watching TV*, etc.

1 VOCABULARY activities

a ● Focus on the task and on picture 1. Ask *What's the activity?* and elicit *swimming*. Tell SS to write 1 in the box next to *swimming*. Give SS a few minutes to match the rest of the activities and the pictures. Get them to compare answers in pairs.

b ● **7.1** Play the CD once for SS to check their answers (see listening script 7.1). Using the pause button elicit the answer for each picture before releasing the pause button to hear the right answer.
- Make sure SS are clear about the meaning of all the activities.
- Play the CD again, pausing for SS to listen and repeat the activities. Elicit that the *-ing* ending is not stressed.

7.1	CD3 Track 46

1 swimming 2 shopping 3 chatting online
4 flying 5 reading 6 going to the cinema
7 cooking 8 running 9 travelling
10 camping 11 watching DVDs 12 cycling

c ● Focus on the instructions. Ask SS to cover the words and give them time to look at the pictures and remember the activities with a partner. Monitor and correct any mistakes in pronunciation. Then, with SS looking only at the pictures, elicit all the activities from the class, helping them with pronunciation.

2 GRAMMAR *like* + verb + *-ing*

a ● Focus on the instructions. Tell SS they are going to read information on a dating website (a website where people can find a new partner).
- Focus on the website, and on the verb *love*. Explain that in English we use *love* to say, e.g. *I love you*, but we also use *love* to say we like something very much, e.g. *I love playing the piano*.
- Give SS time to read the information about the six people and deal with any vocabulary problems. Highlight the difference between *shopping* and *buying*. *Shopping* = going to (usually several) shops to buy food, clothes, etc. and *buying* = giving money in exchange for something. We always put a noun (thing) after *buying*, e.g. *buying CDs*, etc., but not after *shopping*.
- Now ask SS to read the information again and, in pairs, match the men and women.
- Focus on the speech bubble and encourage them to use the phrases to say what they think.
- Get feedback by asking pairs to explain their choices. Encourage them to begin *We think…* and then ask the rest of the class if they agree.

> 1 Isabella and William, because she loves playing the piano and he likes classical music, and she likes doing sport and he loves running and cycling.
> 2 Sharon and Luke because she loves buying clothes and he loves shopping, and she likes the cinema and he likes watching DVDs.
> 3 Adriana and Daniel because she loves walking in the mountains and he likes camping, and she likes good food and he loves cooking.

Extra idea

You could ask SS if they think it's a good way to find a partner, and if they know anyone who met their partner through a dating website.

b ● Focus on the task. Give SS time to correct the sentences in pairs. Check answers by asking individual SS to read out the sentence correctly.

> 1 My father likes **cooking**.
> 2 Do you like **flying**?
> 3 Vicky loves **reading**.

c
- Tell SS to go to **Grammar Bank 7A** on *p.100*.
- **7.2** Play the CD and ask SS to listen and repeat the example sentences. Use the pause button and replay as necessary.

7.2	CD3 Track 47

What do you like doing at the weekend?
I like walking in the mountains.
I love cooking.
I don't like studying.

- Go through the rules for *like* + verb + *-ing* using the expanded information in the **Grammar notes** below to help you. You may want to use L1 here if you know it.

Grammar notes

like (+ verb + -ing)

- When another verb follows *love*, *like*, or *don't like*, the *-ing* form is normally used, e.g. *camping, cooking,* **not** the infinitive without *to*, e.g. NOT ~~I like camp~~.
- ⚠ The infinitive with *to* after *like* and *love* is sometimes used (especially in US English), but it is easier for SS at this level to just learn the most common form.

Spelling rules

- most verbs simply add *-ing* to the infinitive to make the *-ing* form, e.g. *reading, watching*.
- verbs ending in *y* don't change the *y* to an *i* as they do in 3rd person singular (e.g. *fly – flying* NOT ~~fliing~~).
- verbs ending in *e* drop the *e* before adding *-ing*, e.g. *cycle – cycling*.
- verbs ending in consonant + one vowel + consonant: double the final consonant and add *-ing*, e.g. *running, swimming*.

- Focus on the exercises for **7A** on *p.101*. SS do them individually or in pairs. If they do them individually, get them to compare answers with a partner. Tell SS to refer to the spelling rules if they're not sure how to spell the *-ing* forms.
- Check answers. When you check the *-ing* forms in **a** get SS to spell them to you, and check that they remember the meaning of the verbs. Check the spelling of the *-ing* forms in **b** too.

a 1 meeting 2 stopping 3 buying 4 going
5 crying 6 writing 7 running 8 losing

b 1 She likes cooking.
2 Do you like travelling?
3 I love getting presents.
4 They don't like watching TV.
5 Does your father like playing chess?
6 I don't like waiting at the doctor's.
7 My mother loves working in the garden.
8 We don't like going to bed late.

Study Link SS can find more practice of this grammar on the MultiROM and on the *New English File Beginner* website.

- Tell SS to go back to the main lesson on *p.64*.

d
- Focus on the task. Demonstrate by telling SS three things about you.
- Give SS time to write three true sentences about themselves. Monitor and help.
- Get them to compare sentences with a partner, and see if they have any the same.
- Get feedback from individual SS.

Extra idea

You could get SS to stand up and say their sentences to the other SS in the class to find the person who is most similar to them.

3 PRONUNCIATION /ʊ/, /uː/, and /ŋ/

- Read the **Pronunciation notes** and decide how much of the information you want to give your SS.

Pronunciation notes

- Remind SS that the two dots in the symbol /uː/ mean that it's a long sound.
- You may want to highlight the following sound–spelling rules:
  - the most common pronunciation of *oo* is the long sound /uː/, e.g. *food, school, soon*. However, *oo* is sometimes pronounced using the short /ʊ/, e.g. *good, book, look, took*.
  - letters *-ng* at the end of a word (and without an *e* after them) are always pronounced /ŋ/ in English, e.g. *thing, wrong*. However, *-nge* is usually pronounced /ndʒ/, e.g. *change*.

a
- **7.3** Focus on the sound picture *bull* and elicit the word from the class, writing it on the board. Play the CD to model and drill the word and sound /ʊ/ (pause after the sound). Now focus on the words after *bull*. Remind SS that the pink letters are the /ʊ/ sound. Play the CD pausing after each word for SS to repeat.
- Repeat for the other two sounds and words (*boot* and *singer*).
- Focus especially on sounds that are difficult for your SS and model them yourself so that SS can see your mouth position. Get SS to repeat these sounds a few more times.

7.3		CD3 Track 48
bull	/ʊ/	cook, book, look, took, good
boot	/uː/	too, food, soon, school, choose
singer	/ŋ/	going, doing, swimming, thing, single

b
- **7.4** Focus on the dialogue. Play the CD once for SS to read and listen. Then play the CD again, pausing after each line for them to repeat the sentence. Encourage SS to copy the sounds and rhythm.
- Get SS to read the dialogue out in pairs. Then get them to swap roles.

A I like cooking. Do you?
B Yes, I like cooking too.
A Do you like reading books?
B Yes, I love reading good books.
A Do you like cycling?
B Yes, I do. I love cycling!
A Are you single?
B No, sorry!

c ● Focus on the instructions and the pictures in **1a**.
Demonstrate the activity by telling SS whether you like
or don't like the first three or four activities.

● Put SS in pairs and give them a few minutes to talk about
the rest of the pictures. Monitor and make a note of any
difficulties SS are having. Correct any mistakes on the
board.

4 READING & SPEAKING

a ● Focus on the introduction to the article and read it
through with the class. Now focus on the pictures
which illustrate some of the things people in the article
like doing.

● Read the first paragraph aloud with the class, and elicit
that *having a long bubble bath* is picture D and *going
window shopping* is picture B. Highlight that *window
shopping* = looking but not buying.

● Get SS to continue reading and matching the highlighted
phrases to the pictures. Set a time limit, e.g. five minutes.

● Check answers by saying a phrase and eliciting the
number of the picture. Make sure SS are clear about the
meaning of the highlighted phrases.

> **A** 4　**B** 2　**C** 3　**D** 1　**E** 5　**F** 6　**G** 7

● Go through the article point by point and deal with any
vocabulary problems, e.g. *sunny, going for a run, novel,
music playlist, in order*, etc.

b ● Focus on the instructions and make sure SS are clear
about what they have to do. Demonstrate by reading
the first paragraph and writing *Teresa* on the board and
either ticking or crossing, according to whether you like
or don't like the same activities. Give SS a few minutes
to read the article again, and tick and cross the people.

c ● Put SS in pairs and get them to compare their answers.

● Get feedback first by asking individual SS who they
ticked. Then ask some SS who they crossed.

d ● Focus on the title and introduction again. Tell SS to
write their own answer to the question on a piece of
paper, but not to put their name on it. Monitor and
help with vocabulary and spelling.

● Collect the answers and shuffle them. Read out each
answer in turn and then ask the class *Who do you think
wrote that?* Elicit from the class the name of the student
who wrote it.

Extra idea

With a small class you could number the answers and pin
them on the wall for SS to read and guess the name of the
student who wrote each one. Then check answers to find
out who guessed the most correctly.

WORDS AND PHRASES TO LEARN

Focus on the words and phrases to learn. Make sure SS
understand the meaning of each phrase. If necessary, remind
SS of the context in which they came up in the lesson. If you
speak your SS' L1, you might like to elicit a translation for
the words/phrases for the SS to write next to them. You may
also like to ask SS to test each other on the phrases.

Study Link SS can find more practice of these words
and phrases on the MultiROM and on the *New English File
Beginner* website.

Extra photocopiable activities

Grammar
like + verb + -ing p.149
Communicative
I think you like it *p.186* (instructions *p.159*)

HOMEWORK

Study Link **Workbook** *pp.52–53*

G *be going to* (plans)
V future time expressions
P sentence stress

Trip of a lifetime

Lesson plan

This lesson is based on the real journey of two amateur cyclists, Liz Evans and her boyfriend Clive Salisbury, who decided to cycle from Ecuador to Argentina. Their trip provides the context for the presentation of *be going to* for future plans, through an interview with Liz before she started her trip. SS practise sentence stress in *going to* sentences, and go on to talk about their own plans for the future. Vocabulary focuses on future time expressions. SS then listen to Liz, after the trip, describing their adventures, and finally, in a speaking activity, SS plan their own dream trip.

Optional lead-in (books closed)

- Write these questions on the board:
  Can you ride a bike?
  Do you like cycling?
  When was the last time you cycled?
  Where did you go?
- Get SS to ask you the questions.
- Then give them time, in pairs, to ask and answer the questions.
- Get SS to talk about their partner.

1 GRAMMAR *be going to* (plans)

a ● **7.5** Focus on the lesson title and elicit/explain the meaning.
  - Now focus on the photo and the map and tell SS the woman's name is Liz. Explain that Liz is planning the trip of a lifetime.
  - Tell SS to cover the dialogue. Liz's friend Jerry is asking her about the trip. Write on the board:
    Where? From _____ to _____
    When? From _____ to _____
    Then play the CD once. Elicit answers from the class (From Ecuador to Argentina; From October to April).
  - Uncover the dialogue. Now focus on the verbs in the list and the spaces. Play the CD again for SS to listen and complete the spaces. Get SS to compare with a partner and then check answers by playing the CD again and pausing after each space.

2 go 3 go 4 stay 5 camp 6 start
7 come back 8 be

7.5   CD3 Track 50

J = Jerry, L = Liz
J What exactly are your plans, Liz?
L I'm going to cycle from Ecuador to Argentina.
J Wow! How far is that?
L It's about 7,500 kilometres.
J Are you going to go alone?
L No, I'm not. I'm going to go with my boyfriend.
J Where are you going to stay?
L We're going to camp, and maybe sometimes stay in small hotels.
J When are you going to start your trip?
L In October. And we aren't going to come back until April.
J Six months – that's a long time! Are you excited?
L Yes, I am. It's going to be a fantastic trip!

---

b ● Focus on the dialogue again and get SS to read it again. Elicit the answer to the question (the highlighted sentences are about the future).
  - Now go through the dialogue line by line eliciting and explaining any words or phrases that SS don't understand, e.g. *How far is that?*, *until April*, *That's a long time*, and *Are you excited?*

c ● Focus on the chart and elicit the words to complete the first sentence (going to).
  - Give SS time to look at the dialogue and complete the other two sentences in pairs. Check answers.

  > I'm *going to* cycle from Ecuador to Argentina.
  > *Are you* going to go alone?
  > We *aren't going to* come back until April.

d ● Tell SS to go to **Grammar Bank 7B** on *p.100*.
  - **7.6** Play the CD and ask SS to listen and repeat the example sentences. Use the pause button and replay as necessary. Point out that *to* is pronounced in its weak form /tə/ here, not as /tuː/. Get SS to put the stress on *going* and the main verb – the *to* should sound almost like a small /t/ attached to the main verb. To show this, write an example sentence on the board, underlining the stressed syllables and crossing out the *o* of *to*, e.g. *We're going to fly*. Model and drill the sentence.

7.6   CD3 Track 51

I'm going to come to class on Friday.
You're going to go to Paris this weekend.
He's going to buy a new car.
We're going to fly.
They're going to stay with us.

I'm not going to come to class on Friday.
You aren't going to go to Paris this weekend.
He isn't going to buy a new car.
We aren't going to fly.
They aren't going to stay with us.

Are you going to travel?	Yes, I am.	No, I'm not.
Is she going to see them?	Yes, she is.	No, she isn't.
Are they going to swim?	Yes, they are.	No, they aren't.

- Go through the rules for *be going to* (plans) with the class using the expanded information in the **Grammar notes** below to help you. You may want to use L1 here if you know it.

Grammar notes

- *be going to* + infinitive is the most common way to express future plans. It is often used with time expressions like *tonight, next week*, etc. SS don't usually find the concept of *be going to* a problem, but the form needs plenty of practice. A typical error is the omission of the auxiliary *be*, i.e. ~~I going to have dinner.~~

⚠ In song lyrics *going to* is sometimes spelt *gonna*, e.g. *I'm gonna leave you*. You may want to point this out, but discourage SS from using this when they write.

- Focus on the exercises for **7B** on *p.101*. SS do them individually or in pairs. If they do them individually, get them to compare answers with a partner.
- Check answers by getting SS to read the full sentences.

> **a** 1 They're going to take the train to London.
> 2 She isn't going to go to university.
> 3 We're going to get married next summer.
> 4 Are you going to go out for dinner?
> 5 Is he going to pay you the money?
> 6 I'm not going to study this evening.
> 7 Are you going to meet us at the airport?
> 8 She's going to make pasta for lunch.
>
> **b** 1 're going to buy   2 Are, going to send
> 3 are, going to do   4 aren't going to have
> 5 aren't going to stay   6 'm going to go
> 7 Are, going to take   8 's going to meet

Study Link SS can find more practice of this grammar on the MultiROM and on the *New English File Beginner* website.

- Tell SS to go back to the main lesson on *p.66*.

2 PRONUNCIATION   sentence stress

a • **7.7** For notes on the pronunciation of *going to*, see **Grammar** section **d** on *p.109* and the **Grammar notes** above.

- Focus on the instructions. Play the CD once for SS just to listen. Write the sentences on the board. Then play the CD again, pausing after each sentence for SS to underline the stressed words. Get SS to compare with a partner.
- Check answers by eliciting the underlined words from SS and underlining them on the board.
- Now get SS to read the full sentences with correct stress. Remind SS to use the weak form of *to* /tə/.

> **7.7**   CD3 Track 52
>
> I'm <u>going</u> to <u>cycle</u> from <u>Ecuador</u> to <u>Argentina</u>.
> <u>Are</u> you <u>going</u> to <u>go</u> <u>alone</u>?
> <u>Where</u> are you <u>going</u> to <u>stay</u>?

b • **7.8** Focus on the highlighted sentences in the dialogue in **1a**. Play the CD pausing for SS to listen and repeat. Encourage them to copy the rhythm. Replay as necessary.

> **7.8**   CD3 Track 53
>
> I'm going to cycle from Ecuador to Argentina.
> Are you going to go alone?
> I'm going to go with my boyfriend.
> Where are you going to stay?
> We're going to camp.
> When are you going to start your trip?
> We aren't going to come back until April.
> It's going to be a fantastic trip!

c • Put SS in pairs and assign roles. Give SS time to practise the dialogue and then swap roles. Monitor and make a note of any problems SS are having. Deal with any general problems on the board.

Extra support

Before you begin you could model and drill the whole dialogue with SS repeating in chorus after you or after the CD.

d • **7.9** Focus on the instructions and the speech bubble. Tell SS they are going to hear verb phrases. They then have to make ⊞ sentences with *be going to* about tomorrow.

- Play the first verb phrase on the CD (*go to work*) and elicit the sentence from the class, i.e. *I'm going to go to work tomorrow*.
- Continue getting the whole class to make the sentences, pausing the CD as necessary. Encourage them to use correct sentence stress. Repeat the activity for SS to do it with more fluency.

> **7.9**   CD3 Track 54
>
> go to work… I'm going to go to work tomorrow.
> watch TV… I'm going to watch TV tomorrow.
> get up early… I'm going to get up early tomorrow.
> go shopping… I'm going to go shopping tomorrow.
> make lunch… I'm going to make lunch tomorrow.
> come to class… I'm going to come to class tomorrow.
> go to the gym… I'm going to go to the gym tomorrow.
> see my friends… I'm going to see my friends tomorrow.

Extra idea

Tell SS that now they have to make true sentences about tomorrow, so they may be ⊞ or ⊟. For ⊟ sentences they need to say *I'm not going to….* Play the CD and elicit true sentences from individual SS. Demonstrate yourself first.

e • Focus on the instructions. Demonstrate the activity yourself by writing four true sentences and one false one on the board. Read out your sentences and elicit guesses from the whole class on which is the false sentence.

- Give SS time to write the sentences. Monitor and help.
- Put SS in pairs, **A** and **B**, and tell **A** to read their sentences for **B** to guess which one is false. Then they swap roles.

3 VOCABULARY & SPEAKING

a • Focus on the expressions in the box and the time line. Elicit/remind SS of the meaning of *now, tonight,* and *the future*.

• Give SS a few minutes in pairs to complete the rest of the time line. Check answers, and model and drill pronunciation. Highlight that we do not usually use *the* with these expressions.

now – tonight – tomorrow – tomorrow night – next week – next month – next year – the future

b • Focus on the **Today** part of the questionnaire and ask SS what words are missing in the questions *(are you going to)*.

• Give SS a few minutes to read through the questionnaire and think about their answers to the questions. They could jot down ideas to help them. Monitor and help.

Extra support

You could get SS to write some of the questions first, but tell them not to refer to these when they ask their partner the questions.

c • Demonstrate the activity by getting SS to ask you the questions for, e.g. **Today**. Give clear, simple answers.

• Put SS in pairs, **A** and **B**. Tell **A** to ask **B** the questions in the questionnaire and make notes of **B**'s answers. Then they swap roles. Monitor and help.

Extra challenge

Get **B** to close his/her book when **A** is asking the questions. Get **A** to do the same when it's his/her turn to answer.

Extra challenge

Put SS in new pairs, and get SS to tell their new partner about their old partner's plans. Elicit that they need to change the verb from *I'm going to…* to *He/She's going to….* Get feedback by asking a few questions to different SS.

4 LISTENING

a • Focus on the instructions and get SS to cover the dialogue. Focus on the prompts. Highlight the sentence in the speech bubble and give SS a few minutes to remember Liz's plans for her trip.

• Get feedback by asking SS to say the full sentence *(She's going to go with her boyfriend, They're going to camp, They're going to start the trip in October, They're going to come back in April).*

b • **7.10** Tell SS that Liz came back from her trip last week and they are going to look at some photos she or friends took. Focus on the photos and get SS, in pairs, to say what they can see.

• Tell SS they are going to listen to an interview with Liz after her trip and they have to number the photos in the order she mentions them.

• Before they listen go back to the map of South America on *p.66* and elicit the names of the countries they went through: *Ecuador, Peru, Bolivia, Chile, Argentina.*

• Play the CD for SS to number the photos. Replay as necessary. Get them to compare with a partner and then check answers.

1 Argentina! **2** The bus in Chile
3 Camping with an alpaca! **4** Bike problems

7.10 CD3 Track 55

J = Jerry, L = Liz
J So, how was the trip, Liz?
L It was great, fantastic! We had a great time!
J Did you cycle to the South of Argentina?
L Yes, we did. 7,500 kilometres.
J Wow! That's amazing. And did you cycle all the way?
L Almost. One day in Chile we took a bus, because I wasn't well and I couldn't cycle.
J Did you camp?
L We camped in Ecuador and Peru, and we sometimes stayed in small hotels. In Chile and Argentina we usually camped.
J Did you have any problems?
L Not big problems no. We had one problem with a bike.
J What happened?
L Well, my boyfriend's bike broke.
J Where were you when it broke?
L We were near La Paz, in Bolivia.
J What did you do?
L We were very lucky. A Bolivian man stopped to help us. He took us to La Paz in his car. We took the bike to a mechanic there and he repaired it.
J What was your favourite place?
L We loved all the countries we visited. The people were fantastic. But my favourite place was probably Patagonia, in the South of Argentina and Chile. It was very beautiful.
J Do you have any plans for your next trip?
L Yes, we're going to cycle around India.

---

c • Focus on the task and give SS time to read through the questions. Deal with any vocabulary problems.

• Tell SS when they listen again, just to mark the sentences T or F. Play the CD again and get SS to compare their answers.

• Now tell SS to listen again and to try and correct the false information. Play the CD again, pausing as necessary to give SS time to write.

• Check answers.

1 T
2 F (One day in Chile they took a bus.)
3 F (They sometimes stayed in small hotels.)
4 F (Her boyfriend's bike broke.)
5 F (A mechanic repaired the bike.)
6 T
7 F (They're going to go to India.)

Extra support

If you have time, you could get SS to have a final listen with the listening script on *p.87* and deal with any words or phrases they didn't understand.

• Finally, ask SS *Would you like to cycle from Ecuador to Argentina?*

5 SPEAKING

a • Write *dream trip* on the board and elicit possible destinations from SS, e.g. *India, the Greek Islands, South Africa, China*, etc.

   • Now tell SS they are going to plan their dream trip. Focus on the questions and give SS time to complete the spaces. Monitor and help, especially with country names.

b • Go through the instructions with SS and focus on the example in the speech bubbles. Highlight the use of *be going to* in the question. Elicit the other questions from SS *(When are you going to go? How are you going to travel? Who are you going to go with? Where are you going to stay?)*.

   • Demonstrate the activity by thinking up your own dream trip and get SS to interview you before they start.

   • Put SS in pairs, **A** and **B**. Tell **A** to ask **B** about his/her dream trip and **B** to answer the questions. Then swap roles. Monitor and help.

   • Get feedback by finding out where as many SS as possible want to go.

Extra idea

You could bring in travel ads from British magazines or newspapers, and get SS to use these to plan their trip.

WORDS AND PHRASES TO LEARN

Focus on the words and phrases to learn. Make sure SS understand the meaning of each phrase. If necessary, remind SS of the context in which they came up in the lesson. If you speak your SS' L1, you might like to elicit a translation for the words/phrases for the SS to write next to them. You may also like to ask SS to test each other on the phrases.

Study Link SS can find more practice of these words and phrases on the MultiROM and on the *New English File Beginner* website.

Extra photocopiable activities

Grammar
be going to (plans) *p.150*
Communicative
Adventure holidays *p.187* (instructions *p.160*)

HOMEWORK

Study Link **Workbook** *pp.54–55*

7C

G *be going to* (predictions)
V the weather; revision: verb collocation
P revision of sounds

What's going to happen?

Lesson plan

This lesson continues with *be going to*, but this time focuses on how the structure is used to express predictions (what we think is going to happen in the future, especially when we have some kind of evidence). SS first learn some basic weather vocabulary, and then see how *be going to* is often used to predict the weather. They then practise the grammar orally by looking at a picture and predicting what the people in it are going to do (they have the answers in Communication). In Pronunciation SS revise six common vowel sounds, and finally they revise some high-frequency verb phrases. The lesson ends with the song *Three little birds*.

Optional lead-in (books closed)

- Revise *be going to* for plans. Write the following prompts on the board:
  AFTER CLASS   TOMORROW NIGHT
  NEXT WEEKEND   NEXT SUMMER
- Elicit the question *What are you going to do after class?* and repeat with the other three prompts.
- Get SS to ask you the questions. Then give them a few minutes to ask and answer in pairs.

1 GRAMMAR *be going to* (predictions)

a • Books open. Focus on the pictures and establish that these are weather symbols. Model and drill the phrase *the weather* in chorus and individually and write it on the board.
- Now focus on the task. In pairs SS match the sentences and pictures. Check answers, and model and drill pronunciation.

> It's going to be hot. = 4
> It's going to be sunny. = 3
> It's going to be cold. = 5
> It's going to snow. = 2
> It's going to rain. = 1

- Get SS to test each other's memory by covering the phrases and pointing at the pictures.

b • **7.11** Focus on the map. Tell SS they are going to hear a weather forecast for England, and they have to draw the symbols on the map.
- Highlight the words *north*, *south*, *east*, and *west* on the map, and model and drill them.
- Write the word *degrees* on the board and elicit/explain the meaning. You could also use the symbol °. Model and drill the pronunciation /dɪˈɡriːz/.
- Ask SS *How many degrees is 'cold' in your country? How many degrees is 'hot'?*
- Play the CD once for SS just to listen, without writing anything.
- Then play the CD again for SS to draw the symbols on the map, pausing after each section (North, East, etc.), to give them time to draw. Replay as necessary. Highlight that SS have to draw two symbols on each part of the map.

- Get them to compare their answers with a partner.
- Draw a quick, rough outline of England on the board. Check answers by getting SS to say full sentences, e.g. *It's going to be very cold in the north of England.* Draw the relevant symbols onto the outline map on the board.

> north: cold, snow
> east: cold, rain
> west: cold, sunny
> south: hot, sunny

> **7.11**   CD3 Track 56
>
> **R = radio presenter, W = weather forecaster**
> **R** And here's Mark with the weather.
> **W** Well tomorrow is going to be a very mixed day. In the north of England it's going to be cold, maybe no more than three or four degrees, and it's probably going to snow. In the east it's also going to be cold, but it isn't going to snow, it's going to rain. So remember to take an umbrella if you live in the east of England. In the south and the west the weather is going to be very different. In the west it's going to be a beautiful day. It's going to be cold, but it's going to be sunny. And in the south it's going to be sunny too, and it's going to be hot, maybe twenty degrees. So I hope you all have a good day...

Extra support

If you have time, you could get SS to have a final listen with the listening script on *p.87* and deal with any words or phrases they didn't understand.

c • Focus on the instructions. Give SS, in pairs, time to write two sentences about tomorrow's weather in their country. Monitor and help.
- Get one pair of SS to read out their answers and ask the rest of the class if they agree.

d • Tell SS to go to **Grammar Bank 7C** on *p.100*.
- **7.12** Play the CD and ask SS to listen and repeat the example sentences. Use the pause button and replay as necessary.

> **7.12**   CD3 Track 57
>
> It's going to rain.
> I think you're going to like it.
> What's going to happen next?
> They're going to have a fantastic time in New York.

- Go through the rules for *be going to* (predictions) using the expanded information in the **Grammar notes** to help you. You may want to use L1 here if you know it.

Grammar notes

- SS learnt the use of *be going to* to express future plans in the previous lesson. Here it is used to make predictions, often based on evidence, e.g. what we can see or know is going to happen (from information we have).

- Focus on the exercise for **7C** on *p.101*. SS do it individually or in pairs. If they do it individually, get them to compare answers with a partner.
- Check answers, getting SS to read out the full sentences.

> **Possible answers**
> 2 She's going to make a pizza.
> 3 The train is going to leave soon.
> 4 He's going to tell them a story.
> 5 It's going to rain tomorrow.
> 6 They're going to swim in the river.
> 7 He's going to break his leg.
> 8 He's going to be late for school.

Study Link SS can find more practice of this grammar on the MultiROM and on the *New English File Beginner* website.

- Tell SS to go back to the main lesson on *p.68*.

2 SPEAKING

a • In this activity SS make logical predictions based on visual evidence as to what various people are going to do in a park scene. Later they go to a second picture (in **Communication**) and find out what actually happened.
- Focus on the instructions and the picture. Demonstrate the exercise by focusing on number 1 and elicit a possible prediction, e.g. *It's going to rain.*
- Give SS a few minutes to write more predictions in pairs.

b • Change the pairs, e.g. by moving a student from one end of a row to another. Then get SS (now with a different partner) to compare their sentences aloud.
- Elicit predictions from SS. Accept all reasonable possibilities.

> **Possible answers**
> 1 It's going to rain.
> 2 He's going to read the newspaper.
> 3 He's going to kiss her.
> 4 He's going to sit down.
> 5 They're going to fly a plane.
> 6 He's going to play the guitar.
> 7 The child is going to swim.
> 8 She's going to call someone/She's going to answer her phone/She's going to send a text.

- Now tell SS they are going to find out if their predictions were right. Tell them to go to **Communication 7C** on *p.81* and look at the picture.
- Elicit (in the past simple) what really happened.

> 1 It didn't rain, the sun came out.
> 2 The man didn't read the paper, he made a fire.
> 3 The man didn't kiss the woman, she hit the man.
> 4 The man didn't sit down, he did tai chi/danced.
> 5 The little boy didn't play with the plane, his father did.
> 6 The man didn't play the guitar, he had a sandwich and a drink.
> 7 The child cried because she didn't want to swim.
> 8 The woman didn't phone a friend, she took a photo with her phone.

3 PRONUNCIATION revision of sounds

a • Focus on the six sound pictures and elicit the words and sounds (*train* /eɪ/, *egg* /e/, *boot* /uː/, *phone* /əʊ/, *cat* /æ/, and *tree* /iː/). Write the words on the board.
- Now focus on the words in the list and elicit that they are all verbs. Focus on the first verb, *camp*, and elicit that it's like *cat*. Then get SS to continue in pairs. Encourage them to say the words out loud to help them decide what the sound is.

b • **7.13** Play the CD for SS to listen and check. Check answers (see listening script 7.13). Then play it again, pausing after each word or group of words for SS to repeat. Replay as necessary.

7.13		CD3 Track 58
train	/eɪ/	make, play, rain
egg	/e/	get, rent, send
boot	/uː/	do, lose, use
phone	/əʊ/	go, know, snow
cat	/æ/	camp, have, relax
tree	/iː/	meet, see, speak

4 VOCABULARY & SPEAKING revision: verb collocation

a • Focus on the verbs in the list and the boxes. Explain that in each box there are two or three phrases which are all often used with the same verb.
- Focus on box 1 and ask SS *Which verb can you use with 'an umbrella' and 'a photo'?* (take).
- Give SS a few minutes in pairs to write the other verbs in the boxes.
- Check answers and elicit the meanings of each verb phrase. Highlight that sometimes one verb in English may have different translations in their L1.

> 1 take 2 get 3 go 4 have 5 do 6 play
> 7 make 8 meet

b • Go through the instructions with SS and elicit the verb for the first space (play).
- Elicit the verb for the second space (playing), and remind SS that after *like* and *love* we use an *-ing* form.
- SS continue to complete the sentences in pairs. Monitor and help.
- Check answers by getting SS to read out the full questions. Encourage them to stress the questions correctly.

> 1 play, playing 2 have, have 3 doing, do
> 4 make, make 5 go, go 6 get, get 7 meet, meet
> 8 taking, take

c • Demonstrate the activity by getting SS to ask you a few of the questions.
- Get SS to ask and answer the questions in pairs. Monitor and help.
- Get feedback from individual SS.

5 7.14 SONG ♫ *Three little birds*

- *Three little birds* is one of the most popular songs by Bob Marley & The Wailers. It was released in 1980, but since then has appeared in a number of films, including *Shark Tale, The Little Mermaid,* and *I Am Legend.* The activity for this song focuses on matching the halves of lines, and the song revises *be going to* for predictions. This is the original version of the song.
- If you want to do this song in class, use the photocopiable activity on *p.208.*

7.14	CD3 Track 59

Three little birds

Chorus
Don't worry about a thing
'cause every little thing is gonna be all right
(Singing) Don't worry about a thing,
'cause every little thing is gonna be all right

Rise up this morning
Smiled with the rising sun
Three little birds pitch by my doorstep
Singing sweet songs of melodies pure and true
Saying: This is my message to you

(Singing) Don't worry about a thing,
'cause every little thing is gonna be all right
(Singing) Don't worry about a thing
'cause every little thing is gonna be all right

(repeat verse and chorus)

WORDS AND PHRASES TO LEARN

Focus on the words and phrases to learn. Make sure SS understand the meaning of each phrase. If necessary, remind SS of the context in which they came up in the lesson. If you speak your SS' L1, you might like to elicit a translation for the words/phrases for the SS to write next to them. You may also like to ask SS to test each other on the phrases.

Study Link SS can find more practice of these words and phrases on the MultiROM and on the *New English File Beginner* website.

Extra photocopiable activities

Grammar
be going to (predictions) *p.151*
Communicative
What are they going to do? *p.188* (instructions *p.160*)
Song
Three little birds p.208 (instructions *p.201*)

HOMEWORK

Study Link Workbook *pp.56–57*

PRACTICAL ENGLISH
IS THERE A BANK NEAR HERE?

Asking for and giving directions
Prepositions of place
Polite intonation

Lesson plan

In this lesson SS learn how to understand and give simple directions in the street. They learn four new prepositions of place and basic language for directions, which is practised through a roleplay. The focus is more on understanding directions than giving directions, as the latter is quite challenging for SS at this level. In **People in the street** SS listen to people giving directions.

Optional lead-in (books closed)

- Write the prompt PLACES IN A TOWN on the board. Give SS two minutes in pairs to brainstorm words for places in a town, e.g. *school, bank, theatre,* etc.
- Get SS to tell you their words and write them on the board.

1 ASKING WHERE PLACES ARE

a ● 7.15 Books open. Focus on the four prepositions of place and the diagrams.
- Play the CD once for SS to listen to the prepositions. Play it again, pausing after each preposition for SS to repeat it.
- Highlight that:
  - *opposite* means face-to-face, and is used mainly for people or buildings.
  - some prepositions of place are one word, e.g. *opposite, between,* but others are two, e.g. *next to.*
  - *on the corner* can be followed by *of* + street name, e.g. *on the corner of Oxford Street.*

7.15		CD3 Track 60
1 next to	3 between	
2 opposite	4 on the corner	

Extra idea

You could give more practice with *next to, opposite,* and *between* by asking questions about things/people in the classroom.

b ● 7.16 Focus on the small map.
- Demonstrate the activity by choosing a place and describing its position yourself, e.g. *It's on the corner, next to the post office* for SS to say the place (the supermarket).
- Play the CD, pausing after the first sentence to elicit the answer (the cinema). Make sure SS are clear they have to write number *1* on the cinema.
- Play the rest of the CD, pausing after each one to give SS time to write the number.
- Check answers by playing the CD, pausing after each sentence for SS to say the answer individually or in chorus.

1 the cinema	2 the post office	3 the park
4 the supermarket	5 the chemist's	6 the theatre
7 the bank	8 the school	

7.16 CD3 Track 61

1 It's opposite the theatre. (the cinema)
2 It's between the school and the supermarket. (the post office)
3 It's next to the museum, opposite the school. (the park)
4 It's on the corner opposite the church, next to the post office. (the supermarket)
5 It's between the bookshop and the cinema. (the chemist's)
6 It's next to the music shop, opposite the cinema. (the theatre)
7 It's on the corner opposite the bookshop, next to the music shop. (the bank)
8 It's opposite the park. (the school)

c • Focus on the example in the speech bubbles. Model and drill the question *Where's the cinema?* Then say other places from the map for SS to substitute, e.g.

    T *Bookshop*   **SS** *Where's the bookshop?*

• Demonstrate the activity by asking a few questions to individual SS, e.g. *Where's the supermarket?* (It's next to the post office).

• Get SS to ask and answer questions in pairs about the map. Monitor and help, correcting pronunciation and prepositions as necessary.

d • **7.17** Focus on the map. Give SS time to read the names of the buildings and the street names. Model and drill the street names.

• Now focus on the dialogue. Tell SS that they are going to listen and complete the spaces.

• Play the CD once or twice as necessary for SS to complete the spaces. Check answers.

1 bank   **2 bookshop**

7.17 / **7.18** CD3 Tracks 62/63

A Excuse me. Is there a bank near here?
B Yes there's one in South Street, next to the bookshop.
A Thanks.

• Remind SS that *Excuse me!* /ɪksˈkjuːz miː/ is a polite way of attracting a stranger's attention (we don't use *Please!* or *Sorry!*).

e • **7.18** Play the CD again for SS to listen to the rhythm and intonation. Highlight that polite intonation in English tends to be higher than normal intonation.

• Play the CD again for SS to repeat, encouraging them to copy the rhythm and intonation.

f • Go through the instructions and focus on the example in the speech bubbles.

• Model and drill the question *Is there a bank near here?* Then say other places for SS to substitute, e.g.

    T *Petrol station*   **SS** *Is there a petrol station near here?*

• Demonstrate the activity by asking one student about a place, e.g. *Excuse me. Is there a chemist's near here?* (to elicit *Yes, there's one in South Street, next to the bank*).

• Get SS to ask and answer questions about the places in the map in **d** in pairs. Monitor and help.

2 UNDERSTANDING & GIVING DIRECTIONS

a • **7.19** Focus on the pictures and directions, and give SS a few moments to match them. Then play the CD once for SS to check answers.

1 C   **2 A**   **3 B**

• Play the CD again for SS to repeat.

• Use gestures to elicit the phrases, e.g. *go straight on*, by making an appropriate gesture, e.g. putting both hands together and pointing forwards with them, *turn right* (the gesture could be pointing right with your right hand) and *turn left* (the gesture could be pointing left with your left hand). These gestures will be easier for your SS to see if you turn sideways to the class.

7.19 CD3 Track 64

1 Go straight on.
2 Turn right.
3 Turn left.

Extra idea

If you have room in the classroom, get SS to stand up and follow directions. You could include *Stop!* too.

b • **7.20** Focus on the map and the dialogue. Highlight the starting position, **you are here**. Elicit the meaning of *traffic lights*.

• Tell SS to cover the dialogue. Play the CD twice for SS to follow the directions to the bus station. Get them to compare answers with a partner.

• Check the answer (building 2) by playing the CD again and letting SS read. They can follow the route in their book with their finger.

• Go through the dialogue line by line. Highlight:
  – *sure* = an informal way of saying *yes/of course*.
  – the difference between *Turn left* and *It's on the left*.
  – responding to *Thanks very much/Thanks* with *That's OK* (remind SS of the alternative response *You're welcome*).

7.20 CD3 Track 65

T = tourist, M = man
T Excuse me. Can you help me?
M Sure.
T Where's the bus station, please?
M Go straight on and turn right. Turn right again and it's on the left.
T Thanks very much.
M That's OK.

c • **7.21** Focus on the instructions. Play the first dialogue on the CD twice for SS to follow the directions. Get them to compare answers with a partner, and check the answer.

• Repeat for the second dialogue.

1 The petrol station is 5.   **2** The museum is 10.

7.21	CD3 Track 66

T = tourist, M = man, W = woman

1 T   Excuse me! Is there a petrol station near here?
   M   A petrol station? Let me think. Yes, I know. Go straight on and turn right.
   T   Go straight on and turn right?
   M   Yes, straight on and turn right. Then go straight on about 100 metres and then turn left.
   T   Turn left?
   M   Yes, and the petrol station is on the right. You can't miss it.
   T   Thank you.
   M   No problem.

2 T   Excuse me. Where's the museum?
   W   I'm sorry. I don't know. I don't live here.

* * *

   T   Oh excuse me. Is the museum near here?
   M   Sorry. No speak English.
   T   OK, no problem.

* * *

   T   Excuse me. Can you help me? I want to go to the museum.
   M   The museum?
   T   Yes. Do you know where it is?
   M   Sure. Go straight on down this street and turn left. Then turn right and go straight on. Then turn left and the museum is on the right. It's on the corner.
   T   Thank you very much.
   M   Excuse me!
   T   Yeah?
   M   It's closed on Mondays.
   T   Oh no…

Extra support

If you have time, let SS listen again with the listening script on *p.87*. Go through the dialogues line by line with SS and elicit/explain any words or phrases that they don't understand.

d • Focus on the dialogue in **b** and get SS to practise in pairs.

Extra support

Replay the dialogue (7.20) pausing after each sentence for SS to repeat.

e • Put SS in pairs, **A** and **B**. Focus on the first instruction for **A** and **B**. **A** must not tell **B** which building he/she has chosen.
   • Focus on the example in the speech bubbles with the class. Tell **B** to ask **A** for directions to the Park Hotel. Monitor and make a note of any problems SS are having.
   • Tell SS to swap roles and give **B** time to choose a building for the hospital. Now **A** asks **B** for directions to the hospital. Monitor and help, making a note of any general problems SS are having and deal with these on the board at the end.

Extra support

You could get SS to write the directions down before they give them orally to their partner.

3 PEOPLE IN THE STREET

Study Link This exercise is also on the *New English File Beginner* DVD, which can be used instead of the class audio (see **Introduction** *p.11*). SS can get more practice on the MultiROM, which contains more of the short street interviews with a listening task and scripts.

a • **7.22** Focus on the question in the box and the photo of Suzy. Tell SS that someone is going to ask Suzy for the directions to a place, and she is going to give them.
   • Play the CD once for SS to complete 1 (the place). Then play it again for SS to complete 2 (the directions). Check answers (see listening script 7.22).

7.22	CD3 Track 67
Interviewer	Is there a **post office** near here?
Suzy (UK)	Yes, there's one on London Road, **next to** the **coffee shop**.

b • **7.23** Focus on the instructions. Tell SS they are going to listen to four more people. Play the CD for SS to complete the places and directions, replaying as necessary, then check answers (see listening script 7.23).

7.23	CD3 Track 68
Interviewer Lauren (USA)	Is there a **coffee bar** near here? Yes, turn **right**, it's on the right, **next to** the hotel.
Interviewer Chris (UK)	Is there a **chemist's** near here? There is, yes. Go **straight on**, turn **left**, it's on the **left**.
Interviewer Carolina (MEX)	Is there a **bank** near here? Yes, there is. It's **between** the coffee bar and the **chemist's**.
Interviewer Brittany (CAN)	Is there a **bookshop** near here? Yeah, it's **next to the bank**.

   • You may want to tell SS that *chemist's* is British English and *drugstore / pharmacy* is American English.

WORDS AND PHRASES TO LEARN

Focus on the words and phrases to learn. Make sure SS understand the meaning of each phrase. If necessary, remind SS of the context in which they came up in the lesson. If you speak your SS' L1, you might like to elicit a translation for the words/phrases for the SS to write next to them. You may also like to ask SS to test each other on the phrases.

Study Link SS can find more practice of these words and phrases on the MultiROM and on the *New English File Beginner* website.

Extra photocopiable activities

Communicative
Where are you? *p.189* (instructions *p.160*)
Revision 1–7 *p.190* (instructions *p.160*)

HOMEWORK

Study Link **Workbook** *pp.58–59*

For instructions on how to use these pages, see *p.29*.

What do you remember?

GRAMMAR

1 b	2 a	3 b	4 b	5 b	6 b	7 a	8 a	9 a	
10 b									

VOCABULARY

a
2 camping
3 cooking
4 cycling
5 flying
6 running

b
1 tomorrow
2 next Tuesday
3 year

c
1 get
2 go
3 meet
4 do
5 take
6 take
7 get
8 do
9 meet
10 go

d
1 on
2 time
3 rain
4 opposite
5 turn

PRONUNCIATION

a vowels: b<u>u</u>ll, b<u>oo</u>t
consonants: si<u>ng</u>er
c <u>tr</u>avelling t<u>om</u>orrow <u>s</u>unny after<u>noon</u> <u>o</u>pposite

What can you do?

1 CAN YOU UNDERSTAND THIS TEXT?

a Jesper didn't visit Africa, South America, or Antarctica.
b 1 on 1st January at 7.00 a.m.
2 nearly 45 kilometres
3 in a tent or in hotels
4 in Japan
5 in Australia
6 He's going to start in the north of Europe and finish in North America.

3 CAN YOU UNDERSTAND THESE PEOPLE?

1 b	2 a	3 a	4 b	5 b	6 a	7 b

7.24   CD3 Track 69

1 A Do you like cooking?
   B No, I don't. I love good food but I like having it in a restaurant.
2 A Does your husband like sport?
   B Well, he doesn't like doing sport. He never goes to the gym or runs or anything. But he loves watching it on TV.

3 A So where are you going to go in the summer?
   B Spain.
   A To the beach?
   B No, we're going to go to a small village in the mountains. We wanted to go somewhere where there weren't a lot of people.

4 A Hi Clare, it's Ashley.
   B Hi.
   A Listen, we're going to go to the cinema tonight. Do you want to come?
   B What are you going to see?
   A The new James Bond film.
   B Oh, I saw it last week.
   A Was it good?
   B It was OK. I preferred the last one.

5 And finally tomorrow's weather. It's going to be cold in the north, but sunny, with blue skies, and top temperatures of about five degrees Celsius. In the south, it's going to rain all day, and I don't think we're going to see any blue sky there at all.

6 A Excuse me. Where's the post office?
   B Er, it's in the High Street, on the right, opposite the gift shop.
   A Sorry, did you say the bookshop?
   B No, the gift shop.
   A Thanks.

7 A Excuse me. Is there a bank near here?
   B Yes, there's one in North Street.
   A Sorry, where's North Street?
   B Go straight on and turn right. The bank's on the left, opposite the car park.
   A Thanks very much.

Extra photocopiable activities

Grammar
7 revision *p.152*
Vocabulary
Mime it *p.199* (instructions *p.192*)

Test and Assessment CD-ROM

File 7 Quicktest
File 7 Test
Progress test 5–7
End-of-course test

1–7   THE *Can you...?* GAME

This group board game revises the main language SS have learnt in *New English File Beginner*. As well as providing a final revision, it allows SS to measure their own progress over the course in a fun and motivating way.

> **LANGUAGE**
> Grammar and vocabulary of the book

- Divide the class into groups of three or four. Tell each group to use one copy of the game, and give each group a dice and a counter for each student. If you don't have dice, they can write the numbers 1–6 on pieces of paper and take them out of an envelope or other container. Instead of counters, they can use coins.

- As a demonstration, ask a confident student to throw the dice and move that number of squares from the start. Get another member of their group to read out the *Can you...?* challenge. The student who threw the dice then performs the challenge. Ask the rest of the group *Was that OK?* to encourage SS to listen to and evaluate what the others in their group say. If the rest of the group say no, ask them what the problem is. If they are happy with the performance, pass the dice to the next student. Tell all groups to start in the same way.

- Monitor as the groups play, but don't interfere unless you hear SS fail to pick up on a serious error. You could make notes for dealing with later in class if you like.

- SS continue to play until one student reaches the last square and is the winner. They must throw the exact number needed to land on the last square. If, for example, they need a 3 but throw a 5, they must move to the last square and then 2 back, to number 35.

- Groups that finish fast can look back through the squares, taking turns to do the ones that were not landed on in the game.

PHOTOCOPIABLE ACTIVITIES

CONTENTS

Photocopiable material

- There is at least one **Grammar activity** for each main (A, B, and C) lesson of the Student's Book and a revision activity for each File (1–7).
- There is a **Communicative activity** for each lesson (A, B, C, and Practical English) of the Student's Book.
- There is a **Vocabulary activity** for each File (1–7) of the Student's Book, and a revision activity for the whole book.
- There are seven **Song activities**. These can be used as part of the main lesson in the Student's Book or in a later lesson. The recording of the song can be found in the main lesson on the Class CD.

Using extra activities in mixed ability classes

Some teachers have classes where some SS finish Student's Book activities much more quickly than others. You could give these fast finishers a photocopiable activity (either Communicative or Grammar) while you help the slower students. Alternatively, some teachers might want to give faster SS extra oral practice with a communicative activity while slower students consolidate their knowledge with an extra grammar activity.

Tips for using Grammar activities

The Grammar activities are designed to give SS extra practice in the main grammar point from each lesson. How you use these activities depends on the needs of your SS and the time you have available. They can be used in the lesson if you think all of your class would benefit from the extra practice or you could set them as homework for some or all of your SS.

- All of the activities start with a writing stage. If you use the activities in class, get SS to work individually or in pairs. Allow SS to compare before checking the answers.
- Many of the activities have a final section that gets SS to cover the sentences and to test their memory. If you are using the activities in class, SS can work in pairs and test their partner. If you set them for homework, encourage SS to use this stage to test themselves.
- If SS are having trouble with any of the activities, make sure they refer to the relevant **Grammar Bank** in the Student's Book.
- Make sure that SS keep their copies of the activities and that they review any difficult areas regularly. Encourage them to go back to activities and cover and test themselves. This will help with their revision.

1A   be: I and you

a   3 I   4 you   5 You

b   2 'm   3 Are   4 'm   5 'm   6 're

c   1 Are you   2 I am   3 I'm   4 Am I   5 you aren't

1B   be: he, she, it

a   2 He's from England.   3 It's from Russia.   4 She's from Japan.

b   3 Where's he from? He's from the United States.
4 Where's it from? It's from Italy.   5 Where's she from?
She's from Brazil.   6 Where's it from? It's from Mexico.
7 Where's he from? He's from Turkey.
8 Where's she from? She's from China.

1C   be: we, you, they; negatives

a   2 Are   3 isn't   4 're   5 isn't   6 'm not   7 're   8 aren't

b   3 No, he isn't. He's Mr Rizzi.   4 No, they aren't. They're in Room 109.   5 Yes, it is.   6 No, she isn't. She's Nikoletta.
7 Yes, they are.   8 No, they aren't. They're in Recife.

1   revision

a   3 It   4 He   5 I, you   6 you   7 we   8 I

b   3 're   4 're   5 're   6 aren't   7 isn't   8 's   9 Are   10 are
11 are   12 're   13 Are   14 aren't   15 're

2A   singular and plural nouns; a / an

a   3 a chair   4 hotels   5 dictionaries   6 an umbrella

b   3 What is it? It's a table.   4 What are they? They're watches.   5 What is it? It's a taxi.   6 What are they?
They're pieces of paper.   7 What is it? It's an identity card.   8 What are they? They're buses.

2B1   possessive adjectives

a   2 your   3 his   4 our   5 Their   6 Her   7 its   8 my
9 your   10 his

2B2   possessive s

a   2 They're Helena's books.   3 It's Asima's laptop/computer.
4 They're Max's keys.   5 It's Michelle's umbrella.   6 It's Alex's coat.   7 They're Ali's pens.   8 It's the teacher's mobile.

2C   adjectives

a   2 They're cheap.   3 She's old.   4 They're slow.
5 It's big.   6 He's good-looking.

b   2 They're expensive glasses.   3 He's a tall man.
4 They're long buses.   5 It's a new coat.   6 They're fast cars.

2   revision

a   2 our, His   3 your, Our   4 your, my

b   2 Is this Alison's coat?   3 My husband's train is late.
4 What's your parrot's name?   5 This is my sister's room.   6 Where's Nina's boyfriend from?

c   2 It's an old umbrella.   3 It's an expensive laptop/computer.
4 They're big glasses.   5 They're fast cars.   6 It's a new watch.

3A   present simple: I and you

a   2 Do   3 don't   4 Do   5 don't   6 Do   7 don't
8 do   9 Do   10 do   11 don't   12 Don't   13 Do
14 don't

3B   present simple: we, you, they

a   3 Do you have   4 like   5 Do you read   6 don't like
7 do you listen   8 think   9 do they have   10 drink
11 do they eat   12 eat   13 don't want   14 like

3C   present simple: he, she, it

a   3 She works   4 She eats   5 She doesn't drink
6 She studies/learns   7 She doesn't read
8 She doesn't listen   9 She watches

3   revision

a   3 like   4 don't work   5 do you study   6 studies
7 Does he have   8 does   9 Does he live   10 Do you
know   11 do

c   3 work   4 doesn't read   5 don't have
6 speaks   7 don't drink   8 watches

4A   adverbs of frequency

a   2 sometimes   3 never   4 always

b   2 usually listens   3 sometimes has / eats   4 always goes
5 never plays   6 sometimes goes

4B   word order in questions

a   2 What's your surname?   3 How do you spell it?
4 Where do you work?   5 Are you a doctor?   6 Do you
like your job?   7 What do you do in your free time?
8 What music do you listen to?   9 What time do you
finish work?   10 Are you free after work tonight?

4C   can / can't

a   2 can't   3 Can   4 can't

b   2 can smoke   3 can't take   4 Can, sit   5 can see
6 can't eat

4   revision

a   2 always finish   3 usually drive   4 never do
5 sometimes go

b   2 What time does he finish work?   3 How does he
drive?   4 Does he do housework?   5 Where does he go
with his girlfriend?

d   2 can't have   3 can drive   4 can't pay   5 can use

5A   past simple: be

a   2 wasn't   3 were   4 was   5 Was   6 wasn't   7 was
8 Was   9 was   10 were   11 was   12 weren't
13 were   14 was   15 wasn't   16 was   17 was

5B   past simple: have, go, get

a   2 had   3 did you go   4 went   5 had   6 did you
have   7 had   8 Did you go   9 went   10 got up
11 Did you have   12 didn't have   13 Did they get up
14 Did they have   15 didn't do   16 Did you have lunch
17 didn't have

5C   past simple: regular and irregular verbs

a   2 went to the USA.   3 They arrived in California.
4 They rented a big car.   5 They played golf.   6 They
didn't check their emails.   7 they walked on the
beach.   8 They didn't think about home.   9 They met
new friends.   10 They came back happy!

5 revision

3 Did you pay   4 did   5 were   6 was   7 Did you go
8 Was   9 wasn't   10 was   11 had   12 did you do
13 stayed   14 listened   15 didn't play   16 was
17 went   18 had   19 did you come   20 came
21 didn't come   22 were

6A *there is / there are*

a   3 There isn't a cupboard.   4 There's a shower.
5 There are some lamps.   6 There isn't a minibar.

b   2 Is there a car park? No, there isn't.   3 Are there any
lifts? Yes, there are.   4 Is there a gym? Yes, there is.
5 Are there any shops? Yes, there are.   6 Is there a
swimming pool? No, there isn't.

6B *there was / there were*

a   2 there was   3 Were there   4 there were   5 there
was   6 Were there   7 there weren't   8 There was
9 there wasn't   10 there weren't   11 Was there
12 there wasn't

6C1 object pronouns

a   2 it   3 her   4 us   5 you   6 them   7 him   8 me
9 it   10 us

6C2 revision of past simple

a   3 didn't have   4 stayed   5 watched   6 went out
7 were   8 asked   9 met   10 didn't like   11 liked
12 thought   13 was   14 wanted   15 didn't want
16 were   17 went   18 couldn't   19 got up   20 went
21 had   22 sat   23 saw   24 was   25 asked   26 said
27 began   28 didn't watch   29 called   30 was

b   2 Did, like   3 did, do   4 Were   5 did, meet
6 Did, like   7 did, go   8 did, go   9 did, see   10 was

6 revision

a   2 There weren't any tall buildings.   3 There were some
trees.   4 There was a church.   5 There wasn't an
airport.   6 There weren't any factories.

c   3 ✓   4 They paid   5 Did he drive   6 ✓   7 I read it
8 ✓   9 he doesn't like her   10 I left them

7A *like + verb + -ing*

a   2 loves getting   3 like travelling   4 doesn't like
waiting   5 loves doing   6 likes writing   7 don't like
swimming   8 doesn't like flying   9 loves studying
10 like playing

7B *be going to* (plans)

a   2 are   3 are you going to leave   4 Are you going to go
5 're going to play   6 're going to stay
7 Are you going to come   8 'm not   9 'm going to be
10 are you going to do   11 'm going to learn
12 Are you going to give   13 'm not going to stay
14 'm going to camp   15 are you going to come back
16 'm not going to come   17 'm going to leave

7C *be going to* (predictions)

a   2 's going to buy   3 're going to kiss.
4 're going to fly/go   5 're going to play   6 's going to eat
7 's going to watch   8 's going to snow.   9 's going to
take   10 's going to play

7 revision

a   3 He's going to relax   4 It's going to be   5 I'm not going
to study   6 I'm going to go   7 Are you going to stay
8 am   9 I'm going to clean   10 I'm going to work
11 are you going to make   12 I'm not going to cook
13 We're going to go

b   3 ✓   4 You're going to be late   5 ✓   6 Mary likes
playing   7 are you going to park   8 ✓   9 ✓
10 we don't like skiing

a Complete the conversation with *I* or *you*.

MIKE   Hi, ¹_*I*_'m Mike. Are ²_*you*_ Amanda?

AMANDA Yes, ³_____ am.

MIKE   Nice to meet ⁴_____.

AMANDA ⁵_____'re late!

MIKE   Sorry.

b Complete the conversation with *am*, *'m*, *are*, or *'re*.

STUDENT   Excuse me, ¹_*am*_ I in room 2?

RECEPTIONIST What's your name?

STUDENT   I ²_____ Caroline.

RECEPTIONIST ³_____ you Caroline Herzog?

STUDENT   No, I ⁴_____ not. I ⁵_____ Caroline Fuchs.

RECEPTIONIST You ⁶_____ in room 3.

STUDENT   Thank you.

c Complete the conversation.

CHARLOTTE ¹_____ Enrique González?

ENRIQUE   Yes, ²_____.

CHARLOTTE Hi, ³_____ Charlotte, from the Sydney School of English.

ENRIQUE   Oh, hello!

CHARLOTTE Nice to meet you. ⁴_____ late?

ENRIQUE   No, ⁵_____.

d Practise the conversations with a partner.

a Look at the pictures. Write the answer.

1 Where's she from?   *She's from Spain* .

2 Where's he from?   _____ .

3 Where's it from?   _____ .

4 Where's she from?   _____ .

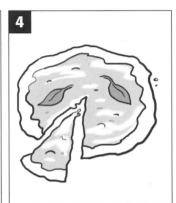

b Write the question and the answer.

1 *Where's he from* ?   *He's from Hungary* .

2 *Where's she from* ?   *She's from Poland* .

3 _____ ?   _____ .

4 _____ ?   _____ .

5 _____ ?   _____ .

6 _____ ?   _____ .

7 _____ ?   _____ .

8 _____ ?   _____ .

c **Test your memory**. Look at the pictures and say the sentences.

A *Where's she from?*

B *She's from Spain.*

a Look at the pictures. Complete the sentences with the correct form of *be*. Use contractions where possible.

1 We *'re* in Paris!

2 _____ they Italian?

3 Nice to meet you, Mr Rossi. — My name _____ Rossi. It's Rizzi.

4 You _____ in room 109.

5 Where's Hollywood? — Hollywood _____ in San Francisco! It's in Los Angeles!

6 Listen and repeat please, Anna. — I _____ Anna. I'm Nikoletta.

7 We _____ in Brazil.

8 Is Rio nice? — We _____ in Rio. We're in Recife.

b Look at the pictures. Write ☐+ or ☐− short answers.
Correct the ☐− answers.

1 Are they in Rome? *No, they aren't. They're in Paris* .

2 Are they Italian? *Yes, they are* .

3 Is he Mr Rossi? _____ .

4 Are they in Room 105? _____ .

5 Is Hollywood in Los Angeles? _____ .

6 Is she Anna? _____ .

7 Are they on holiday? _____ .

8 Are they in Rio? _____ .

a Complete the sentences with a pronoun (*I, you*, etc.).

She's from Brazil.

They're from China.

_____'s from Italy.

_____'s from Japan.

Hi, _____'m Sally. Are _____ Paul?

Nice to meet _____.

Good morning. Are _____ late?

Hello. _____ have a reservation. My name's Fiona Smith.

b Complete the conversations with the correct form of *be*. Use contractions where possible.

RECEPTIONIST What ¹ *'s* your name, please?

EVA I ² *'m* Eva Gomez. And they ³_____ Carlos and Pablo.

RECEPTIONIST You ⁴_____ in room 616 and they ⁵_____ in room 617.

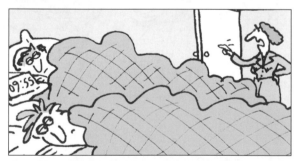

EVA Hurry up. We're late.

CARLOS We ⁶_____ late. Breakfast is from eight to eleven.

EVA No, it ⁷_____. It ⁸_____ from eight to ten!

EVA ⁹_____ you on holiday too?

RADEK Yes, we ¹⁰_____.

EVA Where ¹¹_____ you from?

RADEK We ¹²_____ from Poland. ¹³_____ you Spanish?

EVA No, we ¹⁴_____. We ¹⁵_____ from Mexico.

c Practise the conversations with a partner.

a Look at the pictures. Complete the answers.

1 What is it? It's *a coat* .
2 What are they? They're *keys* .
3 What is it? It's _____ .
4 What are they? They're _____ .
5 What are they? They're _____ .
6 What is it? It's _____ .

HILTON
Plaza
SHERATON

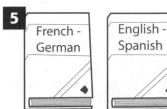

French - German

English - Spanish

b Look at the pictures. Write the questions and answers.

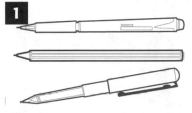

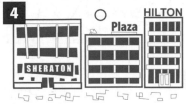

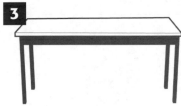

1 *What are they? They're pens.*
2 *What is it? It's a computer.*
3 _____
4 _____
5 _____
6 _____
7 _____
8 _____

c **Test your memory.** Look at the pictures and say the sentences.

A *What are they?*
B *They're pens.*

New English File Teacher's Book Beginner
Photocopiable © Oxford University Press 2009

a Complete the sentence with *my*, *your*, *his*, *her*, *its*, *our*, or *their*.

1 Where's *my* laptop?

2 SECURITY — What's in _____ bag?

3 This is Mark and _____ wife.

4 CLOAKROOM — Where are _____ coats?

5 _____ car is fantastic!

6 _____ husband's English.

7 What's _____ name?

8 Sorry, it's _____ mobile.

9 RECEPTION — Here's _____ key.

10 Hi. I'm Sue. I'm _____ sister.

b **Test your memory**. Cover the sentences. Look at the pictures and say the sentences.

NO MOBILE
PHONES
IN CLASS

a Look at objects 1–8. Whose are they?

1 *It's Nico's dictionary.*

2 _____

3 _____

4 _____

5 _____

6 _____

7 _____

8 _____

b Cover the sentences. Test a partner.

A *Are they Ali's pens?*

B *Yes, they are.*

A *Is it Helena's laptop?*

B *No, it isn't. It's Asima's laptop.*

New English File Teacher's Book Beginner
Photocopiable © Oxford University Press 2009

a Write sentences for the pictures. Use an adjective from the list.

big	cheap	good-looking
old	~~short~~	slow

1 *He's short* .

2 _____ .

3 _____ .

4 _____ .

5 _____ .

6 _____ .

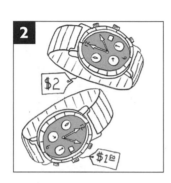

b Complete the sentences for the pictures. Use an adjective from the list and a noun.

expensive	fast	long	new	~~small~~	tall

1 *It's a small table* .

2 They_____ .

3 He_____ .

4 They_____ .

5 It_____ .

6 They_____ .

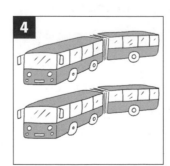

c **Test your memory.** Cover the sentences. Look at the pictures and say the sentences.

New English File Teacher's Book Beginner
Photocopiable © Oxford University Press 2009

a Complete the dialogues with *my, your*, etc.

b Rewrite the sentences with possessive *s*.

1 His new car is fantastic. (Mario)   *Mario's new car is fantastic.*

2 Is this her coat? (Alison)   _____?

3 His train is late. (my husband)   _____.

4 What's its name? (your parrot)   _____?

5 This is her room. (my sister)   _____.

6 Where's her boyfriend from? (Nina)   _____?

c Look at the pictures and write sentences with an adjective from the list and a noun.

big	~~cheap~~	expensive	fast	new	old

1 *It's a cheap mobile.*

2 _____.

3 _____.

4 _____.

5 _____.

6 _____.

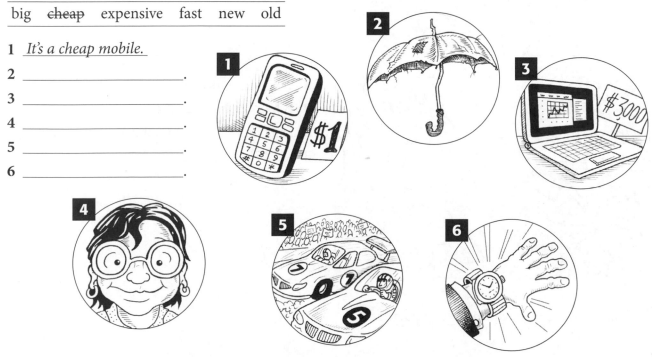

New English File Teacher's Book Beginner
Photocopiable © Oxford University Press 2009

a Complete the conversations with *do* or *don't*.

A ¹ *Do* you live near here?
B No. I live in the centre.
A ² _____ you want a coffee?
B No, thanks. I ³ _____ drink coffee.

A ⁴ _____ you watch MTV?
B No, I ⁵ _____.
A ⁶ _____ you listen to hip hop?
B No. I ⁷ _____ like hip hop. I listen to rock music.

A Where ⁸ _____ you work?
B I work very near here.
A ⁹ _____ you have children?
B Yes, I ¹⁰ _____. I have a girl and two boys.

A I ¹¹ _____ like my new haircut.
B Why not? It's fantastic. ¹² _____ worry!
A Thanks. ¹³ _____ you like my new coat?
B No, I ¹⁴ _____!

b Practise the conversations with a partner.

New English File Teacher's Book Beginner
Photocopiable © Oxford University Press 2009

a Complete the conversations with the correct form of the verb in brackets.

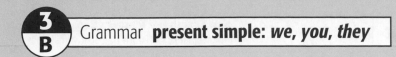

A Where ¹ *do you live* ? (/ you live)

B We ² *live* in the USA, but we're English. (live)

A ³_____ expensive cars? (/ you have)

B Yes. We ⁴_____ fast Italian cars. (like)

A ⁵_____ newspapers? (/ you read)

B No, we don't. We ⁶_____ newspapers or magazines. (not like)

A What music ⁷_____ to? (/ you listen)

B Our music! We ⁸_____ it's fantastic! (think)

A What ⁹_____ for breakfast? (/ they have)

B They ¹⁰_____ milk or orange juice. (drink)

A And what ¹¹_____? (/ they eat)

B They ¹²_____ cereal and fruit. (eat)

A My sons ¹³_____ fruit for breakfast. (not want)

B Really? Why not?

A They only ¹⁴_____ chocolate. (like)

b Practise the conversations with a partner.

New English File Teacher's Book Beginner
Photocopiable © Oxford University Press 2009

a Look at the pictures. Write about Kate.

1 *She lives* in a flat.

2 *She doesn't have* a car.

3 _____ in an office.

4 _____ salad.

5 _____ beer.

6 _____ Spanish.

7 _____ a newspaper.

8 _____ to the radio.

9 _____ TV.

b Make questions and test your partner's memory.

A *Does she work in a shop?*

B *No, she doesn't. She works in an office.*

New English File Teacher's Book Beginner
Photocopiable © Oxford University Press 2009

a Complete the conversation with the correct form of the verb in brackets.

MRS JONES   ¹ _Do you like_ (/ you like) your job?

ANGELA   Yes, I ² _do_ . I ³_____ (like) it very
             much. But I ⁴_____ (not work)
             here a lot. I'm a student.

MRS JONES   What ⁵_____ (/ you study)?

ANGELA   Economics.

MRS JONES   Really? My son ⁶_____ (study)
             economics too. His name's Alex.

ANGELA   ⁷_____ (/ he have) a white car?

MRS JONES   Yes, he ⁸_____.

ANGELA   ⁹_____ (live) in Park Street in the
             big house?

MRS JONES   Yes! ¹⁰_____ (/ you know) my
             son?

ANGELA   Yes, I ¹¹_____. He's my boyfriend! Nice to
             meet you, Mrs Jones.

b Practise the conversation with a partner.

c Complete the sentences with a ⊞ or ⊟ verb.

1 They _live_ in a big
house.

2 We _don't listen_ to
music.

3 I _____ in a
hospital.

4 He _____
newspapers.

5 They _____
a cat.

6 She _____
Japanese.

7 I _____ coffee.

8 He _____ a lot
of TV.

135

a Complete the sentences with an adverb of frequency (*always*, *usually*, *sometimes*, or *never*).

1 He _usually_ goes to university in the morning.

He _____ drinks beer with his friends in the evening.

3 He _____ plays golf.

He _____ goes to bed late.

b Complete the sentences with an adverb of frequency and a verb.

1 She _always gets up_ early.

She _____ to the radio in the morning.

3 She _____ a sandwich at work.

She _____ shopping on Saturday with her children.

5 She _____ computer games.

She _____ to the theatre with her husband.

c **Test your memory.** Cover the sentences. Look at the pictures and say the sentences.

a Order the words to make questions.

WAITER	Good evening. ¹ _Do you have a reservation_? (have / you / do / a reservation)
WOMAN	Yes, we do.
WAITER	²_____? ('s / your surname / what)
WOMAN	It's Lane.
WAITER	³_____? (spell it / how / you / do)
WOMAN	L-A-N-E.
WAITER	Thank you. Your table is by the window.

WOMAN	⁴_____? (you / work / do / where)
MAN	I work in a hospital.
WOMAN	⁵_____? (you / a doctor / are)
MAN	Yes, I am.
WOMAN	⁶_____? (your job / like / do / you)
MAN	Yes, I do. It's fantastic.
WOMAN	⁷_____? (you / what / in your free time / do / do)
MAN	I listen to music.
WOMAN	⁸_____? (listen to / what music / you / do)
MAN	Jazz, and sometimes classical music.

MAN	⁹_____? (finish work / you / what time / do)
WAITRESS	At eleven o'clock.
MAN	¹⁰_____? (free after work tonight / you / are)
WAITRESS	No, I'm not. Good night!

b Practise the conversations with a partner.

New English File Teacher's Book Beginner
Photocopiable © Oxford University Press 2009

a Complete the sentences with *can* or *can't*.

You _can_ leave your bags over there.

I'm sorry. We _____ come to dinner tonight.

_____ you open the window, please?

You _____ park here!

b Now complete sentences with *can* or *can't* and a verb from the list.

eat ~~go~~ sit see smoke take

Can I _go_ to the beach today, please?

You _____ in there.

They _____ photos here.

_____ we _____ here?

The doctor _____ you now.

I'm sorry, but you _____ or drink today.

c **Test your memory.** Cover the sentences. Look at the pictures and say the sentences.

New English File Teacher's Book Beginner
Photocopiable © Oxford University Press 2009

a Complete Dan's sentences using *always*, *never*, *sometimes*, or *usually*, and a verb from the list.

do   drive   finish   go   ~~send~~

1 I *usually send* a lot of emails at work.
2 I _____ work at 10 p.m.
3 I _____ very fast.
4 I _____ housework.
5 I _____ to France with my girlfriend.

b Order the words to make questions.

1 *What does he do at work* ? (do / at work / does / what / he)
2 _____? (he / what time / finish work / does)
3 _____? (drive / does / how / he)
4 _____? (do / housework / he / does)
5 _____? (go / with his girlfriend / where / he / does)

c Test your partner's memory about Dan. Use the questions in **b**.

A *What does he do at work?*

B *He usually sends a lot of emails.*

d Complete the sentences with *can / can't* and a verb.

1 Dan *can't park* there.
2 He _____ dinner with Emma on Friday.
3 He _____ fast on the motorway.
4 He _____ by American Express.
5 He _____ the Internet on the plane.

 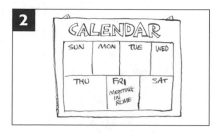

e **Test your memory.** Cover the sentences in **a** and **d**. Look at the pictures and say the sentences.

New English File Teacher's Book Beginner
Photocopiable © Oxford University Press 2009

a Complete the conversations with *was*, *wasn't*, *were*, or *weren't*.

A ¹ <u>Were</u> you at a club last night?

B No, I ² _____.

A Where ³ _____ you?

B I ⁴ _____ at Jane's house.

A ⁵ _____ your mother an actress too?

B No, she ⁶ _____. She ⁷ _____ a nurse.

A ⁸ _____ she tall?

B Yes, she ⁹ _____ very tall and beautiful.

A Why ¹⁰ _____ you late last night?

B I ¹¹ _____ at the gym.

A No, you ¹² _____. You ¹³ _____ with Amanda! This is a message from her on your mobile!

A He ¹⁴ _____ a waiter before he was famous.

B No, he ¹⁵ _____.

A OK, what ¹⁶ _____ he?

B He ¹⁷ _____ an English teacher in Los Angeles.

b Practise the conversations with a partner.

a Complete the conversations with the past form of the verbs in brackets.

A Good morning, Liz. ¹ _Did you go_ out last night? (/ you go)

B Yes, I did. I ²_____ a fantastic time! (have)

A Where ³_____? (/ you go)

B I ⁴_____ to a bar with Beth and Dan. (go)

Then we ⁵_____ dinner at their house. (have)

A What ⁶_____ for dinner? (/ you have)

B We ⁷_____ Japanese food. It was very good! (have)

A ⁸_____ to bed late? (/ you go)

B I ⁹_____ to bed at three o'clock. (go)

And I ¹⁰_____ at six this morning! (get up)

A Do you want a coffee?

B Yes, please. A double espresso!

A Hi, darling. ¹¹_____ a good day? (/ you have)

B No, I ¹²_____ a good day. It was terrible! (not have)

A Why? Are the boys OK? ¹³_____ late again? (/ they get up)

B Yes, very late.

A ¹⁴_____ breakfast? (/ they have)

B Yes, but they ¹⁵_____ their homework and their teacher was angry. (not do)

A ¹⁶_____ at home? (/ you have lunch)

B No. I ¹⁷_____ lunch because I was in a hurry. (not have)

A Don't worry. Tomorrow is Saturday and you can relax.

b Practise the conversations with a partner.

1 want a holiday

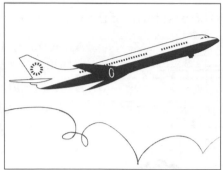

2 go to the USA

3 arrive in California

4 rent a big car

5 play golf

6 not check their emails

7 walk on the beach

8 not think about home

9 meet new friends

10 come back happy

ⓐ Look at the pictures. Write sentences in the past simple.

1 *Jim and Eileen wanted a holiday* .

2 *They* _____.

3 _____.

4 _____.

5 _____ *every day*.

6 _____.

7 *In the evening* _____.

8 _____.

9 _____.

10 _____!

ⓑ Test your memory. Cover the sentences and look at the pictures. Remember the story.

New English File Teacher's Book Beginner
Photocopiable © Oxford University Press 2009

Complete the conversation with the past form of the verbs in brackets and short answers.
Be careful with ⊞ , ⊟ , and ⟨?⟩ .

POLICEMAN   Where ¹ _did you buy_ (/ you buy) that picture, Sir Henry?

SIR HENRY   I ² _bought_ (buy) it in Paris.

POLICEMAN   ³ _____ (/ you pay) a lot of money?

SIR HENRY   Yes, I ⁴ _____.

POLICEMAN   Really? Tell me, Sir Henry, where ⁵ _____ (be) you on the 14th of April?

SIR HENRY   I ⁶ _____ (be) at home with my wife.

POLICEMAN   ⁷ _____ (/ you go) out?

SIR HENRY   I can't remember. ⁸ _____ (be) it Saturday?

POLICEMAN   No, it ⁹ _____ . It ¹⁰ _____ (be) Sunday.

SIR HENRY   Oh, yes. I ¹¹ _____ (have) lunch at home at about one o'clock.

POLICEMAN   What ¹² _____ (/ you do) after that?

SIR HENRY   I ¹³ _____ (stay) at home and ¹⁴ _____ (listen) to the radio. I
¹⁵ _____ (not play) golf because I ¹⁶ _____ (be) tired. At
seven o'clock I ¹⁷ _____ (go) to my favourite restaurant and ¹⁸ _____
(have) dinner alone.

POLICEMAN   What time ¹⁹ _____
(/ you come) home?

SIR HENRY   I ²⁰ _____ (come) home
at about half past ten.

POLICEMAN   No, you ²¹ _____
(not come) home at half
past ten. We know you
²² _____ (be) in the
museum at midnight,
because there are cameras
in the museum.

SIR HENRY   That isn't true!

POLICEMAN   Yes, it is, Sir Henry. Please
come with me...

143

New English File Teacher's Book Beginner
Photocopiable © Oxford University Press 2009

a Write positive or negative sentences about the hotel room with *a/an*, *some*, or *any*.

1 TV   *There's a TV* .

2 chairs   *There aren't any chairs* .

3 cupboard   _____ .

4 shower   _____ .

5 lamps   _____ .

6 minibar   _____ .

b Write questions with *Is there…?/Are there…?* + *a / an*, *some*, or *any*, and a short answer.

1 restaurant?   *Is there a restaurant* ?   *Yes, there is* .

2 car park?   _____ ?   _____ .

3 lifts?   _____ ?   _____ .

4 gym?   _____ ?   _____ .

5 shops?   _____ ?   _____ .

6 swimming pool?   _____ ?   _____ .

c **Test your memory**. Cover the sentences. Look at the pictures and say what there is and isn't in the room and the hotel.

a Complete the conversation with the correct form of *there was / there were*.

A Did you have a good holiday in Brazil?

B Oh yes. It was fantastic. [1] *There were* some beautiful beaches.

A Was the hotel good?

B Yes, and [2]_____ a very nice view.

A [3]_____ any good restaurants?

B Yes, and [4]_____ some very friendly people.

A Did Mike and the children like it?

B Yes, because [5]_____ a swimming pool in the hotel. How was your holiday?

A Terrible.

B Really? Why?

A We went to a village in the mountains. We wanted to ski but there wasn't any snow!

B [6]_____ any good restaurants in the village?

A No, [7]_____. [8]_____ a café, but it was very expensive.

B Was the hotel nice?

A It was OK, but our room was very small and [9]_____ a bath, only a shower. And [10]_____ any towels in the bathroom!

B [11]_____ a spa in the hotel?

A No, [12]_____. The holiday was a complete disaster.

b Practise the conversation with a partner.

New English File Teacher's Book Beginner
Photocopiable © Oxford University Press 2009

a Look at the pictures and complete the sentences with *me, you, him, her, it, us,* or *them.*

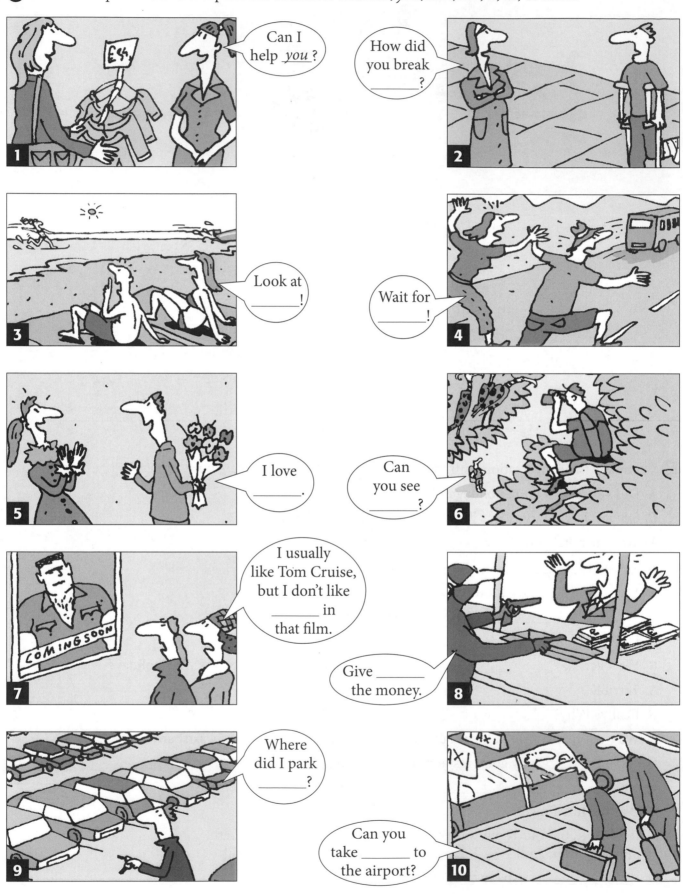

b **Test your memory**. Cover the sentences. Look at the pictures and say the sentences.

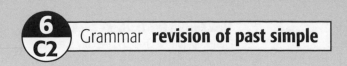
ⓐ Complete the story with the past simple of the verbs in brackets.

Amy ¹ _lived_ (live) alone and she ² _didn't like_ (not like) her life. She ³_____ (not have) a boyfriend. She ⁴_____ (stay) at home and ⁵_____ (watch) TV all evening. She never ⁶_____ (go out). Her friends ⁷_____ (be) worried about her. One evening they ⁸_____ (ask) her to go to the theatre with them.

Amy ⁹_____ (meet) them at the theatre at 7 o'clock. Her friends ¹⁰_____ (not like) the play, but Amy ¹¹_____ (like) it. She ¹²_____ (think) the actor ¹³_____ (be) very good-looking. After the play, Amy ¹⁴_____ (want) to go to a restaurant, but her friends ¹⁵_____ (not want) to go because they ¹⁶_____ (be) tired. Amy ¹⁷_____ (go) home, but that night, she ¹⁸_____ (can't) sleep.

In the morning, Amy ¹⁹_____ (get up) and ²⁰_____ (go) shopping in the city centre. Then she ²¹_____ (have) a coffee in a coffee bar. She ²²_____ (sit) near the window. Suddenly, she ²³_____ (see) a man at the bar. He ²⁴_____ (be) the actor from the theatre! 'Excuse me,' Amy ²⁵_____ (ask), 'Are you an actor?' 'Yes, I am,' the man ²⁶_____ (say). They ²⁷_____ (begin) to talk…

That evening, Amy ²⁸_____ (not watch) TV. When her friends ²⁹_____ (call) her she ³⁰_____ (be) in a restaurant with the actor.

ⓑ Complete the questions about the story.

1 _Did_ Amy _have_ a boyfriend?   No, she didn't.

2 _____ she _____ her life?   No, she didn't.

3 What _____ she _____ all evening?   She watched TV.

4 _____ her friends worried about her?   Yes, they were.

5 What time _____ she _____ her friends?   At 7 o'clock.

6 _____ her friends _____ the play?   No, they didn't.

7 Where _____ Amy _____ after the film?   She went home.

8 Where _____ she _____ in the morning?   She went to the city centre.

9 Who _____ she _____ at the bar?   She saw the actor from the film.

10 Where _____ she when her friends called her?   She was in a restaurant with the actor.

New English File Teacher's Book Beginner
Photocopiable © Oxford University Press 2009

Atford, 1800

Atford today

a Write [+] or [−] sentences about Atford in 1800 with *There was(n't)/There were(n't)* + *a/an*, *some*, or *any*.

1 river   <u>*There was a river*</u> .

2 tall buildings   _____.

3 trees   _____.

4 church   _____.

5 airport   _____.

6 factories   _____.

b Make questions about the same things in Atford today. Test your partner's memory.

   A *Is there a river today?*

   B *No, there isn't.*

c Tick (✔) correct phrases. Correct the wrong ones.

1 We didn't went to the cinema yesterday.   <u>*We didn't go*</u>

2 When did you see John and Sue?   ✔

3 I bought this bag in Milan.   _____

4 They payed by credit card.   _____

5 Did he drove home very fast last night?   _____

6 Mary stayed at home because she was tired.   _____

7 That book is good. I read him yesterday.   _____

8 We're late. Can you take us to the station?   _____

9 Anna likes Bill, but he doesn't like she.   _____

10 I don't have my glasses. I left it on the bus.   _____

New English File Teacher's Book Beginner
Photocopiable © Oxford University Press 2009

a Write sentences with the right form of *like* 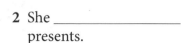, *love* 😀, or *don't like* 🙁 and the activity.

1 He _doesn't like cycling_.

2 She _____ presents.

3 They _____.

4 She _____ for the bus.

5 He _____ exercise.

6 She _____ letters.

7 They _____.

8 He _____.

9 She _____ English.

10 They _____ the piano.

b **Test your memory.** Cover the sentences. Look at the pictures and say the sentences.

a Complete the conversations with the correct form of *be going to* and short answers.

A Are you and Emma OK?

B Yes, Mum, we're fine.

A ¹ *Are you going to go* to bed early tonight? (you / go)

B Yes, we ² _____.

A What time ³ _____ the house tomorrow? (you / leave)

B At eight, as usual. Don't worry!

A ⁴ _____ out after school? (you / go)

B Yes, we are. ⁵ We _____ computer games at Fred's house. (play)

A No, you aren't. ⁶ You _____ at home and do your homework! (stay)

B Oh, Mum!

A ⁷ _____ to the big meeting next Monday? (you / come)

B No, I ⁸ _____. ⁹ I _____ (be) on holiday in Italy.

A What ¹⁰ _____ there? (you / do)

B ¹¹ I _____ Italian, swim in the sea, and eat a lot of good pasta. (learn)

A ¹² _____ us the phone number of your hotel? (you / give)

B ¹³ I _____ in a hotel. (not stay) ¹⁴ I _____. (camp).

A Really? When ¹⁵ _____ to the office? (you / come back)

B ¹⁶ I _____ back. (not come) ¹⁷ I _____ the company. (leave)

b Practise the conversations with a partner.

New English File Teacher's Book Beginner
Photocopiable © Oxford University Press 2009

a Write a prediction for each picture with the correct form of *be going to*.

1 She *'s going to be* cold.

2 He _____ a car.

3 They _____ .

4 They _____ to New York.

5 They _____ tennis.

6 It _____ the cake.

7 She _____ a DVD.

8 It _____ .

9 He _____ a photo.

10 He _____ the violin.

b **Test your memory**. Cover the predictions. Look at the pictures and say the predictions.

New English File Teacher's Book Beginner
Photocopiable © Oxford University Press 2009

a Complete the conversations with the correct form of *be going to* and short answers.

A ¹ *Is Dad going to repair* my bike today?
(Dad / repair)

B No, ² *he isn't* . ³_____ all day
because he's very tired. (he / relax)

A ⁴_____ hot tomorrow. (it / be)

B Yes, I know. ⁵_____ in the
library. (I / not study) ⁶_____ to
the park. (I / go)

A ⁷_____ at home this weekend?
(you / stay)

B Yes, I ⁸_____. ⁹_____ my
house. (I / clean) Then ¹⁰_____
in the garden. (I / work)

A What ¹¹_____ for dinner?
(you / make)

B ¹²_____ tonight. (I / not cook)
¹³_____ out to a restaurant.
(we / go)

b Tick (✔) the correct phrases. Correct the wrong ones.

1 I want to go to Australia but I don't like fly.   *I don't like flying*

2 We're going to go on holiday in August.   ✔

3 They like living in London.   _____

4 Hurry up! You're going be late for work.   _____

5 Jack doesn't like football, but he loves running.   _____

6 Mary likes play golf with her husband.   _____

7 Where you are going to park the car?   _____

8 She has a bike but she doesn't like cycling.   _____

9 Are we going to see a film tonight?   _____

10 We sometimes go to the mountains but we don't like ski.   _____

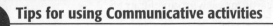

COMMUNICATIVE ACTIVITY INSTRUCTIONS

Tips for using Communicative activities

- We have suggested the ideal number of copies for each activity. However, you can often manage with fewer, e.g. one copy per pair instead of one per student.
- When SS are working in pairs, if possible get them to sit face-to-face. This will encourage them to really talk to each other and also means they can't see each other's sheet.
- If your class doesn't divide into pairs or groups, take part yourself, get two SS to share one role, or get one student to monitor, help, and correct.
- If some SS finish early, they can swap roles and do the activity again, or you could get them to write some of the sentences from the activity.

Classroom language

Copy one sheet per student to keep as a reference.

> **LANGUAGE**
> *Can I have a copy, please?   Thank you.*

- Give each student a copy, and tell them that these are phrases you want them to use in class.
- Go through the phrases one by one, and model and drill the pronunciation. Check SS understand all the phrases.
- Tell SS to keep the sheet at the front of their file and encourage them to use the phrases whenever the opportunity arises rather than using their L1.

 1 A Nice to meet you

A mingle activity

Each student has to find two famous partners. Copy and cut up one sheet per 20 SS.

> **LANGUAGE**
> *Excuse me, are you…?   Sorry, I'm not. / Yes, I am.*
> *Hi / Hello. I'm…   Nice to meet you.*

- Give each student one card. If you have more than 20 SS, have some characters repeated. For smaller groups, tell them that they might only find ONE of the two famous people.
- Tell SS they are the first famous person on their card. They must find the other two famous people and then introduce themselves.
- Write the phrases in **LANGUAGE** on the board and practise the two possible responses. **Highlight that you only introduce yourself if you have found a person you are looking for.** Demonstrate the activity and make sure SS are clear what they have to do.
- Tell SS to stand up and begin the activity.
- As some SS might find their two people very quickly you could set a time limit. In a smaller class you could give out unused cards to fast finishers.

Extra idea Put on some lively party music in the background while SS do this activity.

 1 B Where are they from?

A pairwork activity

SS ask each other where famous people are from. Copy one sheet per pair.

> **LANGUAGE**
> *Where's he from?   He's from Russia.   I don't know.*
> *Where's she from?   She's from Mexico.*

- Quickly revise countries in **Vocabulary Bank** *Countries and nationalities*, p.103.
- Put SS in pairs and give each pair a copy.
- Write the phrases in **LANGUAGE** on the board and drill pronunciation. Give a shrug of the shoulders to remind SS of the meaning of *I don't know.*
- Focus on photo 1 and elicit the question *Where's she from?* Elicit answers from the class and establish that the right answer is *She's from China.*
- SS continue in pairs taking turns to point at one of the photos and ask where the person is from.
- Check answers with the class, telling them the people's nationalities if they don't know them.

> 1 Zhang Ziyi (actress) is from China.
> 2 Roman Polanski (film director) is from Poland.
> 3 Christina Aguilera (singer) is from the USA.
> 4 Ken Watanabe (actor) is from Japan.
> 5 Giorgio Armani (fashion designer) is from Italy.
> 6 Gael García Bernal (actor) is from Mexico.
> 7 Orhan Pamuk (writer) is from Turkey.
> 8 Maria Sharapova (tennis player) is from Russia.
> 9 Javier Bardem (actor) is from Spain.
> 10 Helen Mirren (actress) is from England.
> 11 Gilberto Gil (musician) is from Brazil.
> 12 Agnes Kovacs (swimmer) is from Hungary.

1 C Match the sentences

A pairwork matching activity

SS match sentences. Copy one sheet per pair and cut into **A** and **B**.

> **LANGUAGE**
> *Are you French?   Yes. We're from Paris.*
> *Anna and Toni are from Rome.   We're Italian too!*

- Write up the sentences from **LANGUAGE** on the board but reversing the order of the responses like this:

1 *Are you French?*   a We're Italian too!
2 *Anna and Toni are from Rome.*   b Yes. We're from Paris.

- Elicit from the class which sentence goes with which and draw a line between them (1b, 2a).
- Put SS in pairs, **A** and **B**, and give out their copies. Get SS to sit face-to-face if possible. You may want to pre-teach the meaning of *on business*.
- Get one pair to demonstrate the activity. Student **A** reads the first sentence (*Excuse me. Are you Paola Veroni?*) Student **B** reads the correct response (*No, I'm not. I'm Paola Nardini*). Ask Student **A** if the response is OK.
- SS continue in pairs. **A** says his/her sentences first, and then **B**.

- When all pairs have finished check answers. Then get SS to write the correct response in the space under each question.
- Get SS, in pairs, to practise each of the mini dialogues. Change roles if there is time.

| 1 g | 2 i | 3 j | 4 f | 5 h | 6 c | 7 a | 8 b | 9 d | 10 e |

1 PE How do you spell it?

A pairwork activity

SS spell words for their partner to write down. Copy one sheet per pair and cut into **A** and **B**.

> **LANGUAGE**
> *What's number 1?   It's a train.*
> *How do you spell it?   T-R-A-I-N*

- Before you start, revise spelling by getting SS to spell some items in the classroom.
- Write the questions (**but not the answers**) in **LANGUAGE** on the board and drill pronunciation.
- Put SS in pairs, **A** and **B**. Get SS to sit face-to-face if possible. Give out a sheet to each pair and **tell them not to look at their partner's paper**.
- Get a good pair to demonstrate for the first two words (**B** starts):
  B *What's number 1?*
  A *It's a train.*
  B *How do you spell it?*
  A *T-R-A-I-N* (**B** writes it on his/her sheet). *What's number 2?*, etc.
- SS take turns to ask questions to complete their grid. When their grids are complete SS can look together to see if their spelling is correct.

2 A The same or different?

A pairwork activity

SS find similarities and differences in the contents of a bag. Copy one sheet per pair and cut into **A** and **B**.

> **LANGUAGE**
> *I have three watches in my bag.   Different. I have one.*
> *I have three photos in my bag.   The same. I have three photos too.*

- Quickly revise the vocabulary for **Small things** in **Vocabulary Bank** *Things, p.104*.
- Put SS in pairs, **A** and **B**. Get SS to sit face-to-face if possible. Give out a sheet to each pair and **tell them not to look at their partner's paper**.
- Demonstrate the activity by taking the part of Student **A** and say, e.g. *I have three watches in my bag*, and ask a Student **B**, *The same, or different?* to elicit *Different. I have one*.
- Tell SS to write *D* (= different) in the box next to the watches.
- Now take the part of Student **B** and say *I have three photos*, and elicit from a Student **A** *The same. I have three photos too*, and tell SS to write *S* (= the same) in the box next to the photos.
- Write the sentences in **LANGUAGE** on the board and drill pronunciation.
- Now SS take turns to say what they have in their bag and their partner responds. When all the pairs have finished, check answers by saying each thing (or things) and eliciting *the same* or *different* from the class.

2 B Happy families

A group card game

SS try to collect all members of the same family. Cut up a set of cards for each group of four SS.

> **LANGUAGE**
> *Tom's sister, please.   No, sorry. / Here you are.*

- Tell SS they are going to play a family card game. If SS have a similar game in their language, you may want to refer to this.
- In the game there are five sets of cards. Write on the board: *Tom's family, Carmen's family, Fabio's family, Yuri's family,* and *Chen's family*. Model and drill pronunciation.
- Put SS in groups of four and give each group a pack of cards. One student shuffles and deals the cards face down. Each student should have five cards.
- SS look at their cards. Explain that on each card the small pictures at the bottom is to show them what the other four cards in the family set are. The winner is the first person to collect all four cards in one set.
- To collect a set of cards, SS ask each other for the ones they don't have. They can ask anyone in their group for any card.
- Write the phrases in **LANGUAGE** on the board. Make sure SS understand *Here you are*. Model and drill pronunciation.
- Demonstrate the game by pretending to have a set of cards yourself and asking a student in the group nearest you for a particular card, e.g. *Fabio's son, please,* and elicit the response – *No, sorry* OR *Here you are*.
- SS play the game. S1 asks someone in the group for one of the cards he/she needs. If the student has the card, he/she **must** hand it over. S1 continues asking until a student says *No, sorry*. Then it's the turn of S2 (i.e. the student on the left of S1). When a student has one complete family, he/she puts it on the table and is the winner. SS then shuffle, re-deal and play again.
- Monitor and make sure SS are playing correctly.

Extra idea Alternatively, rather than stopping the game when one person has a set, SS could continue playing until all families have been collected and the winner is the person with the most families.

2 C What is it?

A pairwork activity

SS use adjectives to identify objects. Copy one sheet per pair and cut it into two.

> **LANGUAGE**
> *It's expensive.*
> *Number three.*

- Revise adjectives by saying an adjective and getting SS to say the opposite, e.g. *slow – fast*. (See **Vocabulary Bank** *Adjectives, p.106*).
- Put SS in pairs, **A** and **B**. Get SS to sit face-to-face if possible. Give out the sheets.
- Demonstrate the activity by taking the part of Student **A** and say to a Student **B** *It's expensive*. Elicit the response *number three*.
- Write up the two sentences in **LANGUAGE** on the board as an example.
- SS take turns to say an adjective and their partner says the number of the picture. Make it clear that SS should choose random pictures, not do them in order.

Extra idea When SS finish they could take turns to say a sentence with the adjective and noun together, e.g.
A (points at a picture) *What's number 3?*
B *It's an expensive watch.*

1 fast	**2** tall	**3** expensive	**4** small	**5** old	**6** big
7 new	**8** long	**9** slow	**10** cheap		

2 PE Missing information

An information gap activity

SS ask questions to complete personal information for five people. Copy one sheet per pair and cut into **A** and **B**.

> **LANGUAGE**
> *What's Jack's surname?   How old is he?   Is he married?*
> *Sorry, can you repeat that, please?   Can you spell it, please?*

- Revise personal information questions about a third person by writing on the board:
  Name: David _____   Age: _____
  Nationality: _____   Married: _____
  Address: _____   Mobile number: _____
  Postcode: _____

- Focus on the missing information above and elicit questions from the class to complete it: e.g. *What's David's surname? Where is he from? What's his address? How old is he? Is he married?* etc. Invent answers and write in the information. Repeat the process using a female name to practise questions with *she/her.*

- Then write the phrases, *Sorry, can you repeat that, please? Can you spell it, please?* on the board. Model and drill pronunciation.

- Put SS in pairs, **A** and **B**. Get SS to sit face-to-face if possible. Give out a sheet to each pair and **tell them not to look at their partner's paper.**

- Explain that SS have to complete the missing information on their sheet by asking their partner questions. Tell them to just use the people's first name when they ask questions.

- Focus on the envelope (number 1). Demonstrate the activity with a good pair. Elicit from Student **A** the question, *What's Jack's surname?*, and get **B** to answer (*Gregson*), and then tell **A** to ask for the spelling and write it down. Now elicit **B**'s first question, *What's Jack's address?* etc.

- Now SS take it in turns to ask their partner for the information they need to complete their worksheet.

- When they finish they should put their sheets together to check the information and spelling.

> **A 1** address: 800 West Avenue
>   **2** name: Brown; age: 18; postcode: EH3 0JX
>   **3** address: Alameda 51, Jaen; age: 24;
>   email: BTM23@hotmail.com
>   **4** postcode: 47100; married: yes;
>   home number: 01543-778321
>   **5** name: Williams
> **B 1** name: Gregson
>   **2** email: amanda@btinter.co.uk
>   **3** nationality: Spanish; postcode: 23004; married: no;
>   mobile number: 07640-781234
>   **4** address: Piazza Savonarola 8, Cesena; age: 47; email:
>   marabini@pippo.it; mobile number: 07412-886191
>   **5** address: 2431 South Hall

3 A Do you…?

A group activity

SS ask and answer questions. Copy one sheet per group of three–four SS and cut into cards.

> **LANGUAGE**
> *Do you (live in a big flat)?   Yes, I do. / No, I don't.*
> *Sorry, can you repeat that, please?*

- Revise *Do you…?* questions by asking individual SS and getting them to give you short answers, e.g. *Do you drink tea in the morning? Do you like dogs? Do you speak Spanish?* Say some questions quietly to elicit *Sorry, can you repeat that, please?*

- Write the phrases in **LANGUAGE** on the board. Model and drill pronunciation.

- Put SS in groups of three and give each group a set of cards.

- Demonstrate by getting a student to pick a card and ask you the question.

- SS carry on in their groups, taking turns to pick a card and ask other members of the group the question. You might want to teach SS the expression *What about you?*

  Extra idea As an alternative to the above activity you could copy one sheet per pair, and cut into two columns. **A** and **B** ask each other alternate questions.

3 B Food and drink

A pairwork activity

SS ask and answer questions about their tastes and habits. Copy one sheet per pair and cut into **A** and **B**.

> **LANGUAGE**
> *Do you like fish?   Do you eat a lot of meat?*
> *Do you have breakfast every day?   Do you drink a lot of water?*
> *Sorry, can you repeat that, please?*

- Quickly revise the vocabulary in **Vocabulary Bank** *Food and drink, p.108.*

- Write the questions in **LANGUAGE** on the board. Elicit from SS the meaning of *a lot of* and *every day.* Model and drill pronunciation.

- Put SS in pairs, **A** and **B**. Get SS to sit face-to-face if possible. Give out a sheet to each pair and **tell them not to look at their partner's paper.**

- Tell the groups to look at the pictures of the food/drink and make sure they know the words.

- Demonstrate the activity by taking the part of student **A** and asking a student **B** a question from the sheet and then getting him/her to ask you one of their questions. Remind SS that they can answer *Yes.* or *Yes, I do. / No.* or *No, I don't.*

- SS now take turns to ask and answer each other's questions.

  Extra idea When SS have interviewed each other, you could get them to ask you the questions.

3 What do they do? Where do they work?

C A pairwork information gap activity

SS ask each other about people's jobs and places of work.
Copy one sheet per pair and cut into **A** and **B**.

> **LANGUAGE**
> *What does Gill do?   She's a nurse.*
> *Where does she work?   She works in a school.*

- Put SS in pairs, **A** and **B**. Get SS to sit face-to-face if possible. Give out a sheet to each pair and **tell them not to look at their partner's paper**.
- Explain that their sheet has missing information which their partner has.
- Focus on the question prompts on the left (**What / do?**) and elicit the first question for Gill, *What does Gill do?*
- Elicit from SS **A** the answer (*She's a nurse*) and tell the **B**s to write *a nurse* in the space.
- Elicit from SS **A** the question, *Where does Gill work?* Elicit the answer from **B**s (*She works in a school*) and tell the **A**s to write *in a school* in the space.
- Write the questions and answers in **LANGUAGE** on the board. Model and drill pronunciation. Now ask SS how they would ask the questions for George (*What does George do? Where does he work?* etc.).
- SS continue asking and answering questions. Monitor that they are spelling and pronouncing the words correctly.
- When SS have finished tell them to turn over the sheets and ask quick questions round the class to see if they remember people's jobs and places of work.

3 Time bingo

PE A class game

SS revise the time with Bingo cards. There are ten cards, each card with six times. Copy and cut up as many cards as you need (one per pair of SS).

> **LANGUAGE**
> *twenty past three, quarter to six, eleven o'clock*

- Draw a clock on the board and quickly revise the time.
- Put SS in pairs and give each pair a bingo card.
- Rehearse the shout, *Bingo!*
- Explain you are going to dictate times, and if the time is on their card, they must cross it out (ask SS to cross out in PENCIL so the card can be used again).
- Start calling out times, repeating them once. **Keep a note of all the times you call out.**
- When a pair has crossed out ALL the times on their card they call out *Bingo!*
- Ask SS to read back the times to check they are correct.
- Play again, giving pairs different cards or getting SS to rub out and swap cards with another pair. Call out the times in a different order.

| **Times to dictate:** | 4.15 | 3.20 | 6.25 | 7.50 | 5.25 | 7.30 |
| | 5.45 | 10.55 | 9.35 | 2.50 | 11.10 | 1.05 | 12.10 | 8.40 |

4 What about you?

A A pairwork or small group card activity

SS make sentences using prompts on the cards, then ask each other about their habits. Copy and cut up one sheet of cards per group of three.

> **LANGUAGE**
> *John usually has lunch at 2.30.   What about you?*

- Write up some prompts and ask SS to construct the sentence, e.g. *Martina / usually / lunch at 2.30; Sam / sometimes / to the cinema on Friday afternoon.*
- Get SS to say the full sentences. Model and drill pronunciation.
- Get a good student to say a sentence, then ask him/her *What about you?* to elicit what he/she does, e.g.
  - **S** *Martina usually has lunch at 2.30.*
  - **T** *What about you?*
  - **S** *I never have lunch at 2.30. / I usually have lunch at about one o'clock,* etc.
- Write *What about you?* on the board. Check SS understand it, then model and drill pronunciation.
- Put SS into groups of three and give them a set of cards to put face down. Get a good student in one group to pick a card, make the sentence, and ask *What about you?* to the other SS in the group.
- SS carry on taking turns to pick a card.

Extra idea Alternatively, you could copy one sheet per pair, and cut into two columns. **A** and **B** make sentences to each other and ask *What about you?*

4 Find the people

B A mingle activity

SS mingle and ask each other questions to find people who fit the criteria on their sheet. Copy one sheet per student.

> **LANGUAGE**
> *Do you play a musical instrument?   Yes, I do. / No, I don't.*
> *Are you a teacher?   Yes, I am. / No, I'm not.*

- Write on the board:
  Name:

  _____ *plays tennis.*

  _____ *is a good student.*

- Make it obvious that you're wondering whose name you can write in the first gap. Ask a student *Do you play tennis?* And elicit a short answer from the student – *Yes, I do* or *No, I don't.* If he/she answers *yes*, write his/her name in the sentence, e.g. *Nicolas plays computer games*, or keep asking SS until someone answers *yes* and write their name in. Repeat the process for the second question asking *Are you a good student?*
- Give a sheet to every student and explain they need to write names in the gaps. Elicit the questions SS need to ask, one by one, e.g. *Do you play a musical instrument?* etc.
- Get SS to stand up and mingle, asking each other questions. When a student has answered *yes* to a question, they should write the name in and then move on to someone else. Stop the activity when most SS have completed their sheets.

⚠ If everyone answers *no* to a particular question, you could teach SS the word *nobody*.

- Get feedback by asking questions with *Who…?* and some follow-up questions, e.g.
  T *Who plays a musical instrument?*
  SS *Marga.*
  T *What instrument do you play, Marga?*

Extra idea You could add in some locally relevant sentences, e.g. if you are in Spain _____ *likes flamenco.*

4 C What's missing?
A pairwork activity

SS guess the *can* phrase that's missing from their partner's sentences. Copy and cut up one sheet per pair.

> **LANGUAGE**
> *I can help you.   Can I park here?   You can't smoke in here.*
> *Sorry, try again.   Yes, that's right.*

- Write in large letters on a piece of paper *You can't smoke in the cinema.*
- Then write on the board: *You _____ in the cinema.* [-] Tell SS that you have a sentence on a piece of paper and you want them to guess the sentence. Tell them that what's missing is *can* or *can't* and a verb.
- Elicit ideas. When an incorrect guess is made, say *Sorry, try again.* Eventually someone should suggest *can't smoke* – if not, help by miming. Say *Yes, that's right* and insist that they say the whole sentence before completing it. Then show SS the piece of paper.
- Write on the board *Sorry, try again* and *Yes, that's right,* and model and drill the pronunciation.
- Put SS in pairs, **A** and **B**. Get SS to sit face-to-face if possible. Give out a sheet to each pair and **tell them not to look at their partner's paper.**
- Explain that the bold sentences with gaps are where they have to guess, and the ones without gaps are the ones their partner has to guess.
- Give SS a few minutes to read their sentences.
- Tell **A** to say the first sentence to **B**, who has to say *Yes, that's right* or *Sorry, try again.* Then **B** says the next sentence to **A**, and so on. When they have guessed the sentence correctly, they should write the missing phrase on their sheet.
- When they finish, SS can compare their sheets to check spelling.

4 PE Can I have…?
A roleplay activity

SS roleplay ordering food in a café in groups of three. Copy one sheet per group and cut up the menu and role cards.

> **LANGUAGE**
> **Waiters:**   **Customers:**
> *Can I help you?*   *A table for two, please.*
> *Can I have a cheese sandwich?*   *Anything else?*
> *Here you are.*   *How much is that?*

- Explain that they are going to roleplay ordering food and taking orders in a café. Elicit the phrases in **LANGUAGE** and write them on the board. Model and drill pronunciation.
- Put the SS in groups of three. Make one student the waiter and give him/her the role card and the menu. Give the other two SS the customer card to share. Give SS a few minutes to read their roles. Make sure SS understand *dessert.*

- If possible arrange the chairs and tables to create a café 'feel'. The customers should come into the class and ask the waiter for a table and the menu.
- Waiters should let the customers read the menu before taking their order. They need a piece of paper to take down the orders and later to tell them how much it is. At this point check that SS understand all the items on the menu, e.g. *slices, vegetarian.*
- When the customers have read the menu, tell waiters to take orders and calculate how much it is.
- If you feel you aren't going to put your SS under too much pressure, you could ask a groups or groups to 'perform' in front of the others.

5 A Find someone who was *at*/*in*/*on*…
A mingle activity

SS mingle and ask each other about where they were at particular times in the past. Copy one sheet per student.

> **LANGUAGE**
> Prepositions of place: *at, in, on*
> *Were you at home at 8.30 this morning?*
> *Yes, I was. / No, I wasn't.*

- Revise prepositions of place, e.g. *at work, on the train/bus, in the car, at a restaurant, in bed, at home, in the street, at the gym* (see Student's Book exercise 3 *p.45*).
- Give a sheet to every student and explain they need to write names in the gaps. Elicit the questions SS need to ask one by one, e.g. *Were you at the gym on Saturday morning?*, etc.

> **1** at the gym   **2** on a bus   **3** in bed   **4** in a meeting
> **5** at a restaurant   **6** in the car   **7** in the street   **8** at home
> **9** at work   **10** on the train

- Copy the question and answers from the **LANGUAGE** box on the board.
- Get SS to stand up and mingle, asking each other questions. When a student answers *yes* to a question, they should write the name in and then move on to someone else. Stop the activity when most SS have completed their sheets.
- If everyone answers *no* to a particular question, you could teach SS the word *nobody.*
- Get feedback by asking questions with *Who…?* e.g. *Who was at the gym on Saturday morning?*

5 B Did you do the same as me yesterday?
A mingle activity

SS ask questions to find somebody who did the same things as them. There are ten matching pairs of activity cards on a sheet. Copy enough sheets to ensure that each student will find a student with a matching card.

> **LANGUAGE**
> *Did you go to bed at 10.30 yesterday?*   Yes, I did.
> *Did you have chicken for lunch?*   No, I didn't.

- Write the following on the board:
  went to bed at 10.30
  had chicken for lunch
  got up at 7.00
- Tell SS this is what you did yesterday, and you want to find someone who did exactly the same as you. Elicit the questions you need to ask, i.e. *Did you go to bed at 10.30? Did you have chicken for lunch?* etc.

- Give out cards 1–10 to one half of the class and 11–20 to the other half. If you have fewer than 20 SS, choose the required number making sure there are matching cards (card 1 matches card 11, card 2 matches card 12, etc.). For more than 20 SS, give out duplicate cards. If you have an odd number in the class, you can include yourself.
- Tell SS to read their four sentences, but **not to show their card to anyone**.
- Tell SS that by asking *Did you…?* questions, they have to find somebody in the class who did exactly the same as them yesterday. All four activities must be the same.
- To avoid the risk of some SS finding their match very quickly, tell them there might be more than one person in the class who did the same.
- SS walk around the class asking different SS until they find their matches. When they find a match, they should write the name of the person on the card and continue asking.
- Walk around and monitor the activity.
- Stop the activity when most SS have found a match.

5C Guess how many

A predicting game

SS work in pairs to guess how many people did particular activities. They then do a survey to find out the true numbers. There are ten questions per sheet. Copy sheets and cut into strips so that each pair has one question.

> **LANGUAGE**
> *Did you watch TV last night? Yes, I did.*
> *Did you buy a newspaper yesterday? No, I didn't.*

- Write the verbs used in the activity on the board. Tell SS to say which are regular and which irregular. Elicit the past form of each verb.
- Put SS in pairs and give each pair a questions strip. Tell them that they have to predict the missing numbers and write them where it says **Our guess**.
- Tell SS that now they have to find out if their guess is correct. Tell each pair to write the question they need to ask, and monitor to make sure they have written it correctly.
- Pairs walk around asking their question and keeping note of the answers.
- They could make a list of the names of people in the class before asking their question to make sure they have asked everybody.
- When they have finished, get SS to sit down and ask each pair to report their number like this: *Ten people watched TV last night. Our guess was eight.*

5PE Famous birthdays

A pairwork information gap activity

SS ask each other when famous people's birthdays are in order to complete their sheet. Copy one sheet per pair and cut into **A** and **B**.

> **LANGUAGE**
> *When's Angelina Jolie's birthday? The fourth of June.*

- Write some dates on the board – 3/12, 21/6, 15/5, 31/1, 22/9 – and elicit how to say them (the third of December, the twenty-first of June, etc.).

- Write *Angelina Jolie* on the board. Elicit the question, *When's Angelina Jolie's birthday?* Write 4/6 on the board. Elicit *The fourth of June.* Write the question and answer on the board, and drill pronunciation.
- Give out the copies to SS in pairs, **A** and **B**. **SS must not show each other their worksheet.**
- Explain that SS have to find out the birthdays of the people on their sheet where the birthday is not given.
- Demonstrate the activity with a good pair, getting student **A** to ask *When's Beyoncé's birthday?* and student **B** to answer *The fourth of September* and for **A** to write in the answer on his/her sheet.
- SS take turns to ask and answer the questions and fill in the dates.
- Check answers to make sure SS are saying the date correctly.
- Finally, ask SS if they found a celebrity whose birthday is the same as theirs.

6A Is there a…? Where is it?

A pairwork information gap activity

SS ask each other about facilities/services in two hotels. Copy one sheet per pair and cut up into **A** and **B**.

> **LANGUAGE**
> *Is there a bar in the hotel? Yes, there is.*
> *Where is it? It's on the first floor.*
> *Are there any meeting rooms? No, there aren't.*

- Quickly revise how to say the floors of a hotel by drawing on the board a seven-floor hotel like the ones in the activity and eliciting that 1 = *the first floor*, 2 = *the second floor*, etc.
- Drill pronunciation, including *the ground floor*. Write the questions and answers in **LANGUAGE** on the board, and drill the pronunciation.
- Put SS in pairs, **A** and **B**, and give out the copies. Explain that the hotel on the left is theirs and the one on the right is their partner's.
- Tell SS they have to write one thing from the list of facilities onto each floor of **their** hotel.
- Now tell them they have to fill in their partner's hotel by asking questions like the ones on the board for each facility in the list at the top. Get a good pair to demonstrate the first exchange.
- When SS have finished, get them to compare their hotels.

6B Memory test

A pairwork memory game

SS work in pairs to remember objects missing from a picture. Copy one sheet per pair. Cut the sheet in half, separating the two pictures.

> **LANGUAGE**
> *There was… / There were…*

- Practise the language to be used in the activity. Put a selection of objects on the table, e.g. two books, a dictionary, three pens, a mobile phone, a credit card. Leave them there for 30 seconds and then take them away. Now ask SS *What was there on the table?* and elicit answers with *There was…./There were…* and write the sentences on the board.
- Put SS in pairs. Give each pair a copy of the first picture. Leave it face down on their tables. Get each pair to write the numbers 1–9 in a column on a piece of paper.

- Tell them you are going to give them 30 seconds to look at the picture.
- SS look at the picture and turn it back over when the time is up. Collect the pictures.
- Give out the second picture where some objects and people are missing. SS try to remember what was in the places where the numbers are. Insist that pairs speak to each other in English, using the target language (*There was / There were*), and write the answers together.
- Stop when most pairs have finished. Check answers by reading out the numbers and getting SS to say what there was in each place.

> **1** There was a woman and a child.   **2** There was a man.
> **3** There were two cases and a bag.   **4** There were two people.
> **5** There was a cup.   **6** There was a clock.
> **7** There were some glasses.   **8** There were some magazines.
> **9** There was a bus.

6 C Question and answer match

A pairwork activity

SS revise object pronouns by matching questions and answers. Copy one sheet per pair and cut into **A** and **B**.

> **LANGUAGE**
> *Where did you buy your shoes?   I bought them in a market.*

- To remind SS of object pronouns, write some sentences on the board and underline the object, e.g. *I saw <u>Maria</u> last night, The receptionist helped <u>Tom and Mick</u>, She spoke to <u>you and me</u>, I didn't like <u>the film</u>*, etc.
- Ask students to substitute pronouns for the underlined words (i.e. *her, them, us, it*). Write the pronouns on the board.
- Put SS in pairs, **A** and **B**. Get SS to sit face-to-face if possible. Give out a sheet to each pair and **tell them not to look at their partner's paper**.
- The **A**s and **B**s together read through their sentences and make sure they understand them. Explain that the sentences in the box are the answers for their partner's questions. This needs constant reminding!
- Demonstrate the activity using a good pair. Ask student **A** to ask his/her first question. Student **B** listens to the question and tries to find the answer and reads it to student **A**. If both SS think this is the right answer then **B** dictates it for **A** to write it on his/her paper. Then student **B** asks his first question, etc.
- Now SS in each pair take it in turns to ask each other the questions, and to find and dictate to each other the right answer.
- This activity requires careful monitoring. Fast finishers could practise trying to read their questions and answers as quickly as possible.

> **Answers to A's questions**   **1** f   **2** h   **3** e   **4** c   **5** d   **6** a
> **7** g   **8** b
> **Answers to B's questions**   **1** h   **2** d   **3** e   **4** b   **5** c   **6** g
> **7** f   **8** a

6 PE What do you think of…?

A pairwork activity

SS ask for each others' opinions about singers, actors, etc. Copy one sheet per pair and cut into **A** and **B**.

> **LANGUAGE**
> Object pronouns: *it, her, him, them*
> *What do you think of Brad Pitt?*
> *I love him. He's great.*
> *I don't like him. He's awful.*
> *He's OK. He's nothing special.*

- Write on the board the first four categories on the sheet (a male actor, a female actor, etc.) and write underneath actors/a group/programme you are sure your SS will know. Ask the class *What do you think of … ?* for each person/ group/programme and try to elicit some of the target language.
- Write the questions and answers in **LANGUAGE** on the board, and drill pronunciation. Then elicit how the pronouns change if you replace a male actor with a female actor, a group, and a TV series.
- Put SS in pairs, **A** and **B**, and give out the sheets. Go through the headings in each box and make sure SS understand what they are. Then give SS time to write a name in each box.
- Finally, tell them to complete the two blank boxes with whoever they like (but it should be somebody they think their partner will know).
- Demonstrate by getting a few individual SS to ask you a question from their sheet and answer truthfully.
- SS take turns to ask each other's opinion about the people and things in their boxes. Monitor and correct pronunciation and any errors with pronouns.

7 A I think you like it

A pairwork activity

SS guess their partner's opinion of particular activities. Copy one sheet per pair and cut into **A** and **B**.

> **LANGUAGE**
> *I like swimming. I think you don't like swimming.*
> *You're right. / You're wrong. I love swimming.*

- Write these activities on the board or draw simple pictures, e.g. *playing tennis, travelling, cooking*. Choose a good student and say, e.g. *Mario, I think you like playing tennis. Am I right?* and elicit/teach the answer *You're right / wrong*. Continue guessing other SS' opinions about the activities.
- Write the phrases from **LANGUAGE** on the board and drill pronunciation.
- Ask SS to guess *your* opinion of the three activities, and tell them if they are right or wrong.
- Put SS in pairs, **A** and **B**, and give out the worksheets. **They mustn't look at each other's sheets.**
- SS individually fill in the sentences under each picture, first writing if they like/love/don't like the activity and then writing what they think for their partner.
- SS take turns to read their sentence, e.g.
  A *I don't like camping. I think you love camping.*
  B *You're wrong. I don't like camping.*
- Get feedback to find out who has the most correct guesses.

Adventure holidays

B An information gap activity

SS ask each other questions to complete information about different people's holidays. Copy one sheet per pair and cut the sheet into **A** and **B**.

> **LANGUAGE**
> *Where is he/she going to go?   Who is he/she going to go with?*

- Quickly revise saying some dates, e.g. 11th July, 21st August, 3rd September, etc.
- Put SS in pairs, **A** and **B**. Get SS to sit face-to-face if possible. Give out a sheet to each pair and **tell them not to look at their partner's paper**.
- Tell SS that the information they have is three people's holiday plans. Focus on the first prompt **Where / go ?** and elicit the question *Where is Carlos going to go?* Elicit the answer *On the Trans-Siberian Express.* Repeat for the other two people.
- Tell SS they are going to fill in the missing information by asking their partner questions. Focus on the question prompts on the left and elicit the six questions SS need to ask for Carlos (*Who's he going to go with? Where's he going to stay?*, etc.). Then do the same for Gemma. You could write a couple of the questions on the board as examples to help weaker SS.
- SS now take turns to ask their partner questions to complete their charts. They may have to ask each other to spell some words. When they finish, they can compare their sheets.
- Get feedback and ask SS which holiday plans they like best.

 What are they going to do?

C A pairwork card game

SS use pictures to predict what's going to happen. Copy one sheet per pair and cut up into **A** and **B**.

> **LANGUAGE**
> *He's going to cook the fish.   Sorry, try again.*
> *Is he going to give the fish to his cat?   Yes, that's right.*

- Write on a piece of paper in large letters *Bill's going to give the fish to his cat.* Then draw a simple picture on the board of a man holding a fish and a plate. Tell them his name's Bill. Ask *What's Bill going to do?* Get SS to guess, and tell them whether they were right or wrong.
- Write the sentences from **LANGUAGE** on the board and drill pronunciation.
- Put SS in pairs, **A** and **B**, and give out the sheets. **SS must not show each other their worksheet.**
- Explain that SS have to predict what is going to happen in the spaces with question marks. They mustn't simply read the question.
- Student **B** starts by saying his/her prediction to his/her partner. If it's wrong, student **A** says *Sorry, try again* and **B** keeps guessing until **A** says *That's right.* Student **B** could then write the answer in the square.
- Finally, let SS compare their sheets.

 Where are you?

PE A pairwork or small group activity practising directions

SS follow their partner's instructions on a map and have to say where they are. Make one copy of the map for each pair, and cut up one copy of the direction cards for each pair.

> **LANGUAGE**
> *Go straight on. Turn right / left.*
> *It's the second building on the right.*
> *It's on the corner next to the post office.*

- Revise the language for directions using a simple map and arrows on the board (see Student's Book *p.71* exercise 2).
- Put SS in pairs and give them a map and a set of direction cards.
- Demonstrate the activity with the class. Read one of the cards and ask SS to tell you where they are. You may have to read it several times.
- SS take turns to read the cards for their partner to follow the directions.

Extra idea You could do this in groups. One student picks a card and reads the directions. The first person to correctly identify the place keeps the card, and the person with most cards at the end is the winner.

 Revision 1–7

Questions to revise the language of the book and practise speaking

SS practise the key structures from Files 1–7. This could be used as a final 'pre-test' revision, e.g. before SS have an oral exam. Copy and cut up one set of cards per pair.

> **LANGUAGE**
> Revision Files 1–7.

- Put SS in pairs and give them a set of cards face down.
- Demonstrate the activity with the class. Take a card. Tell SS what the heading is, and ask one student the questions.
- SS take turns to pick a card, tell their partner the heading and ask the questions.
- Monitor and help.

New English File Teacher's Book Beginner
Photocopiable © Oxford University Press 2009

Can I have a copy please?

Thank you.

Sorry? Can you repeat that, please?

I don't understand.

Excuse me. What's *caffè* in English?

What page is it?

I don't know.

Sorry I'm late.

Goodbye.

New English File Teacher's Book Beginner
Photocopiable © Oxford University Press 2009

You're	**Madonna**	You're	**Angelina Jolie**
Find…	**Antonio Banderas**	Find…	**Leonardo DiCaprio**
	Alicia Keys		**Julia Roberts**

You're	**Heidi Klum**	You're	**Carla Bruni**
Find…	**Daniel Craig**	Find…	**Orlando Bloom**
	Shakira		**Scarlett Johanssen**

You're	**Jennifer Aniston**	You're	**Meryl Streep**
Find…	**Bill Gates**	Find…	**Tom Cruise**
	Meryl Streep		**Heidi Klum**

You're	**Shakira**	You're	**Scarlett Johanssen**
Find…	**Madonna**	Find…	**Angelina Jolie**
	George Clooney		**Will Smith**

You're	**Alicia Keys**	You're	**Julia Roberts**
Find…	**David Beckham**	Find…	**Carla Bruni**
	Jennifer Aniston		**Brad Pitt**

You're	**David Beckham**	You're	**Brad Pitt**
Find…	**Madonna**	Find…	**Angelina Jolie**
	Brad Pitt		**Leonardo DiCaprio**

You're	**Leonardo DiCaprio**	You're	**Bill Gates**
Find…	**Bill Gates**	Find…	**Carla Bruni**
	Heidi Klum		**Tom Cruise**

You're	**Tom Cruise**	You're	**Daniel Craig**
Find…	**Daniel Craig**	Find…	**Will Smith**
	Jennifer Aniston		**Meryl Streep**

You're	**Will Smith**	You're	**George Clooney**
Find…	**George Clooney**	Find…	**Antonio Banderas**
	Shakira		**Scarlett Johanssen**

You're	**Antonio Banderas**	You're	**Orlando Bloom**
Find…	**Orlando Bloom**	Find…	**Julia Roberts**
	Alicia Keys		**David Beckham**

New English File Teacher's Book Beginner
Photocopiable © Oxford University Press 2009

1. Zhang Ziyi
2. Roman Polanski
3. Christina Aguilera
4. Ken Watanabe
5. Giorgio Armani
6. Gael García Bernal
7. Orhan Pamuk
8. Maria Sharapova
9. Javier Bardem
10. Helen Mirren
11. Gilberto Gil
12. Agnes Kovacs

New English File Teacher's Book Beginner
Photocopiable © Oxford University Press 2009

A

1 Excuse me. Are you Paola Veroni?

....

2 Are Bill and Tom American?

....

3 Are Anna and Mark on holiday?

....

4 Hi! I'm Marta. I'm from São Paulo.

....

5 Where are Ivan and Alex from?

....

Answers to Student B

a No. I'm from Krakow in Poland.

b Hi! Nice to meet you.

c We're from Venice in Italy.

d Yes. She's from Istanbul.

e You're in room 202.

- -

B

6 Where are you from?

....

7 Are you from Hungary?

....

8 Hello. I'm Sally and this is Karen. We're from England.

....

9 Is Sandra from Turkey?

....

10 Excuse me. Are we in room 201 or 202?

....

Answers to Student A

f Hello, I'm Selma. I'm from Brazil too.

g No, I'm not. I'm Paola Nardini.

h They're from St Petersburg.

i Yes. They're from Ohio.

j No, they aren't. They're on business.

New English File Teacher's Book Beginner
Photocopiable © Oxford University Press 2009

A

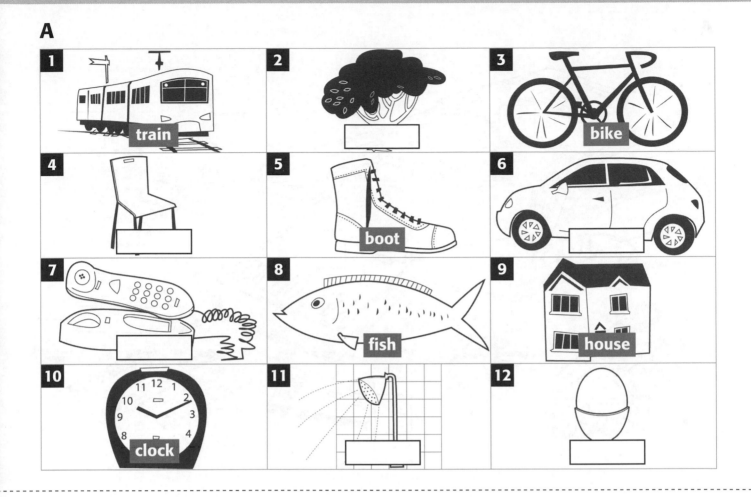

1. train
2.
3. bike
4.
5. boot
6.
7.
8. fish
9. house
10. clock
11.
12.

B

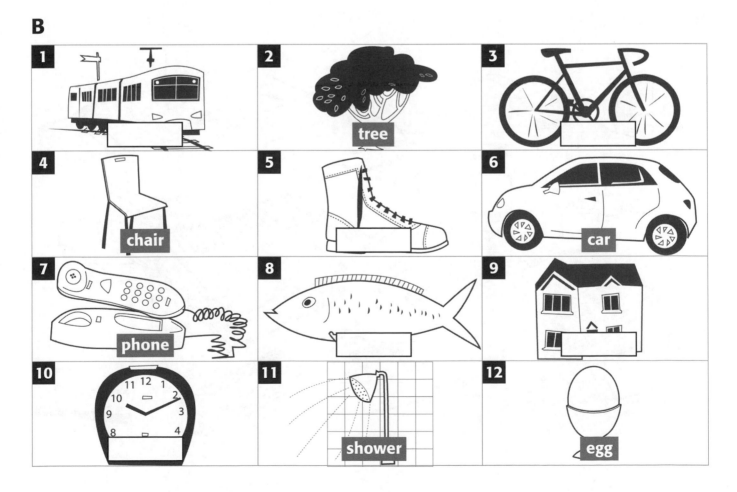

1.
2. tree
3.
4. chair
5.
6. car
7. phone
8.
9.
10.
11. shower
12. egg

New English File Teacher's Book Beginner
Photocopiable © Oxford University Press 2009

A

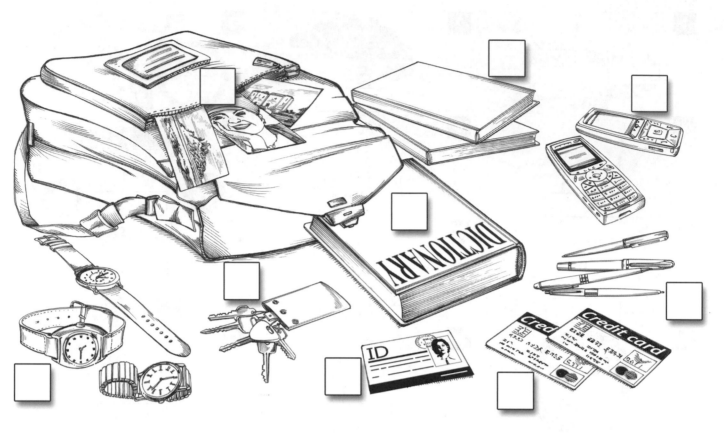

B

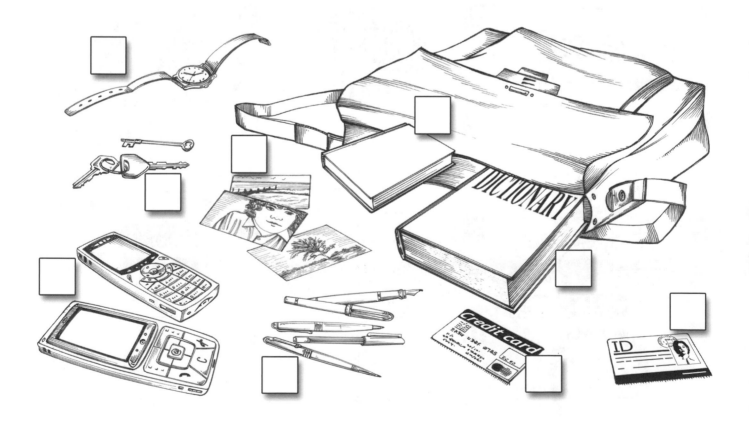

New English File Teacher's Book Beginner
Photocopiable © Oxford University Press 2009

TOM'S FAMILY

SISTER / brother / father / mother

TOM'S FAMILY

sister / BROTHER / father / mother

TOM'S FAMILY

sister / brother / FATHER / mother

TOM'S FAMILY

sister / brother / father / MOTHER

CARMEN'S FAMILY

BROTHER / daughter / sister / husband

CARMEN'S FAMILY

brother / DAUGHTER / sister / husband

CARMEN'S FAMILY

brother / daughter / SISTER / husband

CARMEN'S FAMILY

brother / daughter / sister / HUSBAND

FABIO'S FAMILY

WIFE / brother / sister / son

FABIO'S FAMILY

wife / BROTHER / sister / son

FABIO'S FAMILY

wife / brother / SISTER / son

FABIO'S FAMILY

wife / brother / sister / SON

YURI'S FAMILY

FATHER / wife / son / mother

YURI'S FAMILY

 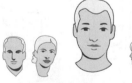

father / WIFE / son / mother

YURI'S FAMILY

father / wife / SON / mother

YURI'S FAMILY

 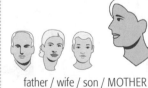

father / wife / son / MOTHER

CHEN'S FAMILY

MOTHER / daughter / husband / son

CHEN'S FAMILY

mother / DAUGHTER / husband / son

CHEN'S FAMILY

mother / daughter / HUSBAND / son

CHEN'S FAMILY

mother / daughter / husband / SON

New English File Teacher's Book Beginner
Photocopiable © Oxford University Press 2009

New English File Teacher's Book Beginner
Photocopiable © Oxford University Press 2009

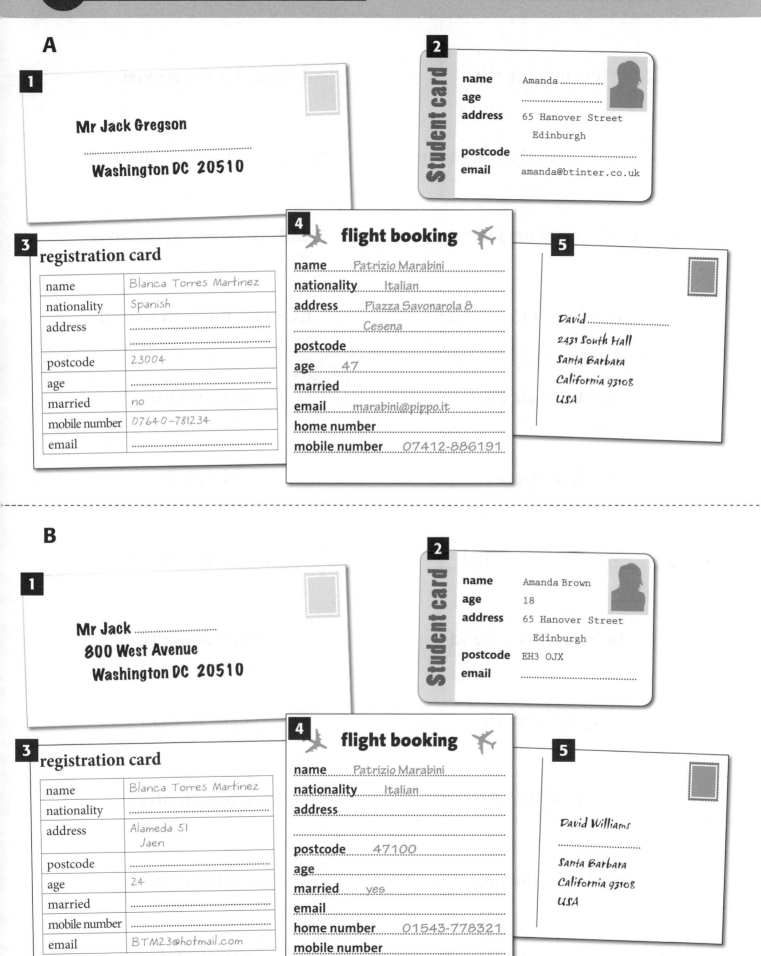

A

1

Mr Jack Gregson

....

Washington DC 20510

2

Student card

name	Amanda ....
age	....
address	65 Hanover Street
	Edinburgh
postcode	....
email	amanda@btinter.co.uk

3 registration card

name	Blanca Torres Martinez
nationality	Spanish
address	....
	....
postcode	23004
age	....
married	no
mobile number	07640-781234
email	....

4 ✈ flight booking ✈

name	Patrizio Marabini
nationality	Italian
address	Piazza Savonarola 8
	Cesena
postcode	....
age	47
married	....
email	marabini@pippo.it
home number	....
mobile number	07412-886191

5

David ....
2431 South Hall
Santa Barbara
California 93108
USA

B

1

Mr Jack ....
800 West Avenue
Washington DC 20510

2

Student card

name	Amanda Brown
age	18
address	65 Hanover Street
	Edinburgh
postcode	EH3 0JX
email	....

3 registration card

name	Blanca Torres Martinez
nationality	....
address	Alameda 51
	Jaen
postcode	....
age	24
married	....
mobile number	....
email	BTM23@hotmail.com

4 ✈ flight booking ✈

name	Patrizio Marabini
nationality	Italian
address	....
	....
postcode	47100
age	....
married	yes
email	....
home number	01543-778321
mobile number	....

5

David Williams
....
Santa Barbara
California 93108
USA

New English File Teacher's Book Beginner
Photocopiable © Oxford University Press 2009

live in a big flat	live near a supermarket
drink coffee in the afternoon	drink water with your lunch
read sports magazines	read computer magazines
listen to the radio in bed	listen to music in the car
eat Chinese food	eat fast food
like opera	like cats
work in a hospital	work with children
study at the weekend	study at night
speak French	speak German
have a blue car	have two children
watch TV in the morning	watch sport on TV
want a new computer	want a holiday

New English File Teacher's Book Beginner
Photocopiable © Oxford University Press 2009

A Do you…?

1 like ?

2 have  on your bread?

3 have  for breakfast?

4 eat  every day?

5 eat a lot of ?

6 have  for breakfast?

7 drink 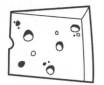 with your dinner?

8 like  ?

9 like  ?

10 have  after lunch?

B Do you…?

1 eat  every day?

2 like  ?

3 like  ?

4 have  every day?

5 have in your coffee?

6 drink with your lunch?

7 have for breakfast?

8 like white  ?

9 eat a lot of  ?

10 have  for breakfast?

3C

Communicative **What do they do? Where do they work?**

New English File Teacher's Book Beginner
Photocopiable © Oxford University Press 2009

A

	Gill	George	Jim	Liz	Julia	Marie
What / do?		_____		_____		_____
Where / work?		_____		_____		_____

B

	Gill	George	Jim	Liz	Julia	Marie
What / do?	_____	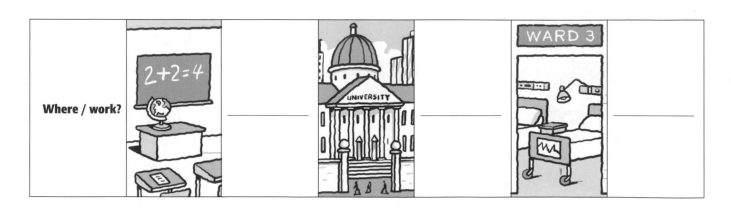				
Where / work?						

New English File Teacher's Book Beginner
Photocopiable © Oxford University Press 2009

New English File Teacher's Book Beginner
Photocopiable © Oxford University Press 2009

✔✔✔✔ / cereal for breakfast

✗✗✗✗✗ / coffee after lunch

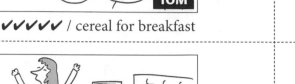

✔✔✗✔✔ / at 7.15

✗✔✗✗✔ / pasta for dinner

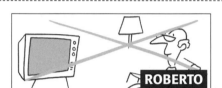

✗✗✗✗✗ / TV in the morning.

✔✔✔✔✔ / shopping on Saturday morning

✔✔✗✔✔ / to bed at 11.30

✗✔✗✗✔ / lunch at a café

✔✔✔✔✔ / a shower in the morning

✔✔✗✔✔ / to the radio in the car

✗✔✗✗✔ / housework on Saturdays

✗✗✗✗✗ / supermarket on Saturday

✗✗✗✗✗ / newspaper

✔✔✔✔✔ / start work at 8.00

✗✔✗✗✔ / gym in the evening

✔✔✗✔✔ / exercise in the evening

NAME

1 _____ plays a musical instrument.

2 _____ is a .

3 _____ has a brother and a sister.

4 _____ goes to bed before .

5 _____ is late for class every day.

6 _____ does a lot of sport.

7 _____ is from a different .

8 _____ has lunch at home.

9 _____ is very today.

10 _____ goes out on Sunday night.

11 _____ drinks tea in the morning.

12 _____ likes .

13 _____ is a slow driver.

14 _____ in the winter.

A

1 _____ you _____ to my birthday party? It's next Saturday.

2 **Can** I **open** the window please? It's very hot in here.

3 **I'm sorry, but you _____ photos in this museum.** [−]

4 Where **can** I **buy** a phone card?

5 _____ I _____ your dictionary for a moment, please?

6 I **can't come** to the next class. I have a meeting.

7 You _____ football here. [−]

8 We **can park** in the car park. It's free.

9 We _____ a pizza in that Italian restaurant. [+]

10 You **can't swim** here. The water's very cold.

11 _____ you _____ me, please? This is very difficult.

12 We **can have** lunch on the beach. It's a beautiful day.

- -

B

1 **Can** you **come** to my birthday party? It's next Saturday.

2 _____ I _____ the window please? It's very hot in here.

3 I'm sorry, but you **can't take** photos in this museum.

4 **Where _____ I _____ a phone card?**

5 **Can** I **use** your dictionary for a moment, please?

6 I _____ to the next class. I have a meeting. [−]

7 You **can't play** football here.

8 We _____ in the car park. It's free. [+]

9 We **can have** a pizza in that Italian restaurant.

10 You _____ here. The water's very cold. [−]

11 **Can** you **help** me, please? This is very difficult.

12 We _____ lunch on the beach. It's a beautiful day. [+]

MENU

cheese / chicken / bacon sandwiches	£3.50
vegetable / chicken soup	£2.95
slice of pizza	£3.10
hamburger and chips	£4.60
vegetarian burger and chips	£4.40
Coke, Fanta, Sprite	£1.80
orange / apple juice	£1.50
water	£1.10
coffee	£1.75
tea	£1.40
chocolate brownie	£1.00
chocolate / vanilla ice cream	£2.00
muffin	£1.20

A You are a waiter

Take your customers to a table and give them the menu.

Useful phrases:

What can I get you?
Here you are.
Anything else?

B You are customers

You want a table for your pair/group.
Look at the menu and choose
- **something to eat**
- **a drink**
- **a dessert**

Useful phrases:

A table for 2 / 3 / 4, please.
Can I have _____?
How much is that?

New English File Teacher's Book Beginner
Photocopiable © Oxford University Press 2009

NAME

1 _____ was on Saturday morning.

2 _____ was  at 8.30 yesterday morning.

3 _____ was  at 11.30 on Sunday morning.

4 _____ was  last Thursday.

5 _____ was  last night.

6 _____ was  at 8.00 yesterday morning.

7 _____ was  at 7.30 this morning.

8 _____ was  on Friday night at 6.00.

9 _____ was  on Saturday morning.

10 _____ was  yesterday.

1

You...
- went to bed at 11.30
- went to the cinema
- had lunch at home
- got up at 8.00

2

You...
- had lunch at work
- got up at 8.00
- went to the cinema
- went to bed at 12.30

3

You...
- had lunch at work
- got up at 8.00
- went shopping
- went to bed at 11.30

4

You...
- had lunch at work
- went to bed at 12.30
- went to the cinema
- got up at 7.30

5

You...
- went to bed at 11.30
- had lunch at work
- went to the cinema
- got up at 7.30

6

You...
- went to bed at 11.30
- went shopping
- had lunch at work
- got up at 7.30

7

You...
- went to the cinema
- went to bed at 11.30
- got up at 7.30
- had lunch at home

8

You...
- went to the cinema
- had lunch at work
- got up at 8.00
- went to bed at 11.00

9

You...
- got up at 7.30
- had lunch at home
- went shopping
- went to bed at 12.30

10

You...
- went shopping
- got up at 8.00
- went to bed at 12.30
- had lunch at home

11

You...
- got up at 8.00
- went to bed at 11.30
- went to the cinema
- had lunch at home

12

You...
- went to bed at 12.30
- had lunch at work
- got up at 8.00
- went to the cinema

13

You...
- went shopping
- had lunch at work
- got up at 8.00
- went to bed at 11.30

14

You...
- had lunch at work
- went to the cinema
- got up at 7.30
- went to bed at 12.30

15

You...
- had lunch at work
- went to bed at 11.30
- went to the cinema
- got up at 7.30

16

You...
- went shopping
- went to bed at 11.30
- had lunch at work
- got up at 7.30

17

You...
- got up at 7.30
- went to the cinema
- went to bed at 11.30
- had lunch at home

18

You...
- had lunch at work
- went to the cinema
- got up at 8.00
- went to bed at 11.00

19

You...
- went shopping
- got up at 7.30
- had lunch at home
- went to bed at 12.30

20

You...
- went to bed at 12.30
- went shopping
- had lunch at home
- got up at 8.00

New English File Teacher's Book Beginner
Photocopiable © Oxford University Press 2009

1 Find out how many people watched TV last night.

Our guess: _____ people   The real number: _____ people

2 Find out how many people had breakfast at home this morning.

Our guess: _____ people   The real number: _____ people

3 Find out how many people used the Internet yesterday.

Our guess: _____ people   The real number: _____ people

4 Find out how many people got up late this morning.

Our guess: _____ people   The real number: _____ people

5 Find out how many people walked to class today.

Our guess: _____ people   The real number: _____ people

6 Find out how many people listened to the radio yesterday.

Our guess: _____ people   The real number: _____ people

7 Find out how many people studied English last night.

Our guess: _____ people   The real number: _____ people

8 Find out how many people waited for a taxi yesterday.

Our guess: _____ people   The real number: _____ people

9 Find out how many people bought a newspaper yesterday.

Our guess: _____ people   The real number: _____ people

10 Find out how many people read in bed last night.

Our guess: _____ people   The real number: _____ people

A

Kanye West 8/6
Beyoncé
Christian Bale 30/1
Penelope Cruz
Robbie Williams
JK Rowling 31/7
Cate Blanchett
Robert De Niro 17/8
Roberto Benigni 27/10
Denzel Washington
Mariah Carey 27/3
Leonardo DiCaprio

B

Kanye West
Beyoncé 4/9
Christian Bale
Penelope Cruz 28/4
Robbie Williams 13/2
JK Rowling
Cate Blanchett 14/5
Robert De Niro
Roberto Benigni
Denzel Washington 28/12
Mariah Carey
Leonardo DiCaprio 11/11

A

a Choose eight things from the list below and write one on each floor of your hotel.

a bar   a café   a restaurant   a spa   a swimming pool   toilets   a gym
a hairdresser's   a gift shop   meeting rooms   a TV room

b Ask **B** about his/her hotel: *Is there a _____ ? Where is it? Are there any _____?*
Where are they?

c Answer **B**'s questions about your hotel.

Your hotel

The Royal Hotel
7
6
5
4
3
2
1
Ground floor

Your partner's hotel

THE AMBASSADOR HOTEL
7
6
5
4
3
2
1
Ground floor

B

a Choose eight things from the list below and write one on each floor of your hotel.

a bar   a café   a restaurant   a spa   a swimming pool   toilets   a gym
a hairdresser's   a gift shop   meeting rooms   a TV room

b Answer **A**'s questions about your hotel.

c Ask **A** about his/her hotel: *Is there a _____ ? Where is it? Are there any _____?*
Where are they?

Your hotel

THE AMBASSADOR HOTEL
7
6
5
4
3
2
1
Ground floor

Your partner's hotel

The Royal Hotel
7
6
5
4
3
2
1
Ground floor

New English File Teacher's Book Beginner
Photocopiable © Oxford University Press 2009

A

1 Where did you buy your shoes? _____
2 Where did Sally meet Harry? _____
3 Did Sonia phone you? _____
4 Did you send the email yesterday? _____
5 Why didn't Andrew say hello to you? _____
6 Sorry. We don't understand this. _____
7 Where did you see Fiona and Kirsty? _____
8 When does Colin usually see his daughter? _____

Answers to Student B

a Because she doesn't like her.
b Yes, he got it on Monday.
c Yes, she told us about it yesterday.
d She calls him every evening.

e Yes, but he found them in his bag.
f I can't do this exercise. Can you help me?
g Can I make you a sandwich?
h I don't know. I couldn't understand him.

B

1 What did the teacher say? _____
2 When does Diana usually call Tim? _____
3 Did Tony lose his keys? _____
4 Did Mark get a letter from the university? _____
5 Do you know about Helen's new job? _____
6 We're very hungry! _____
7 What's the problem? _____
8 Why doesn't Andrea talk to Carolina? _____

Answers to Student A

a Can I help you?
b He sees her every Sunday afternoon.
c No, I sent it this morning.
d Because he didn't see us.

e Yes, she phoned me last night.
f I bought them in the market.
g We saw them on the bus.
h She met him at university.

New English File Teacher's Book Beginner
Photocopiable © Oxford University Press 2009

A

Ask your partner:

What do you think of...?

a male actor	a female actor	a group
_____	_____	_____
a TV series	_a male sportsperson_	a female sportsperson
_____	_____	_____
a TV personality	_____	_____
_____	_____	_____

B

Ask your partner:

What do you think of...?

a male actor	a female actor	a group
_____	_____	_____
a TV series	_a male sportsperson_	a female sportsperson
_____	_____	_____
a TV personality	_____	_____
_____	_____	_____

A   *I love / I like / I don't like ...-ing*

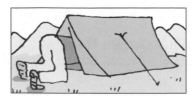

1 I _____
   I think you _____

2 I _____
   I think you _____

3 I _____
   I think you _____

4 I _____
   I think you _____

5 I _____
   I think you _____

6 I _____
   I think you _____

7 I _____
   I think you _____

8 I _____
   I think you _____

B   *I love / I like / I don't like ...ing*

1 I _____
   I think you _____

2 I _____
   I think you _____

3 I _____
   I think you _____

4 I _____
   I think you _____

5 I _____
   I think you _____

6 I _____
   I think you _____

7 I _____
   I think you _____

8 I _____
   I think you _____

New English File Teacher's Book Beginner
Photocopiable © Oxford University Press 2009

A

	CARLOS	GEMMA	LIZ
Where / go?	on the Trans-Siberian Express	on safari in Kenya	on the Inca Trail
Who / with?		her sister	
Where / stay?	on the train		in small hotels and campsites
When / start?		10th August	15th July
When / come back?	21st September		
What / see?	Mongolia and Siberia		Cuzco and Machu Picchu

B

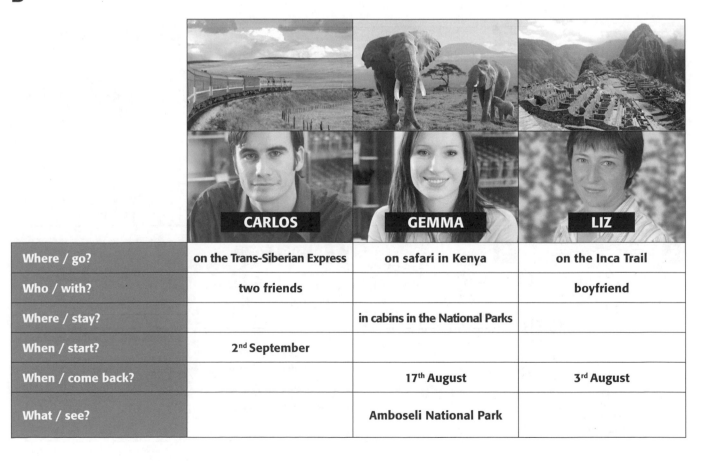

	CARLOS	GEMMA	LIZ
Where / go?	on the Trans-Siberian Express	on safari in Kenya	on the Inca Trail
Who / with?	two friends		boyfriend
Where / stay?		in cabins in the National Parks	
When / start?	2nd September		
When / come back?		17th August	3rd August
What / see?		Amboseli National Park	

New English File Teacher's Book Beginner
Photocopiable © Oxford University Press 2009

A

B

New English File Teacher's Book Beginner
Photocopiable © Oxford University Press 2009

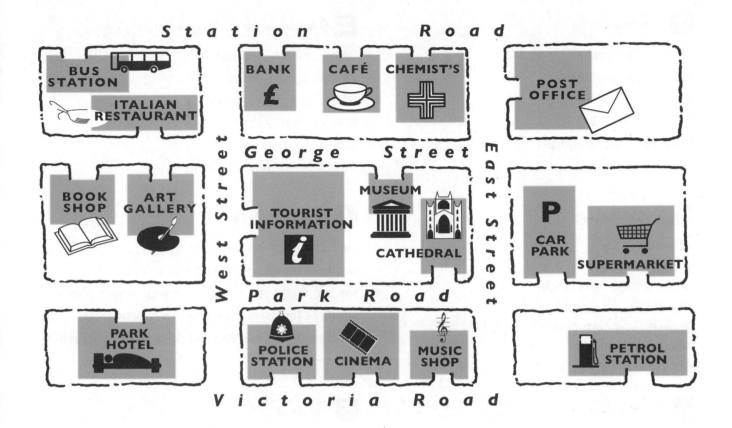

1. You are outside **the Italian restaurant** in George Street. Turn left and then turn right into West Street. Go straight on. Then turn left into Park Road. It's the big building on the left. Where are you? (**the cathedral**)

2. You are outside **the post office** in East Street. Turn left and go straight on. Turn right into Victoria Road. It's the second building on the right. Where are you? (**the cinema**)

3. You are outside **the bookshop** in George Street. Turn right and go straight on. Turn right into West Street. Go straight on and turn left into Victoria Road. It's the first building on the left. Where are you? (**the police station**)

4. You are outside **the museum** in George Street. Turn right and then turn right again into East Street. Turn right into Park Road and go straight on. It's the last building on the left. Where are you? (**the Park Hotel**)

5. You are outside **the petrol station** in Victoria Road. Turn right and go straight on. Turn right into West Street. Go to the end of the road and turn left. It's the last building on the left. Where are you? (**the bus station**)

6. You are outside **the supermarket** in Park Road. Turn right and go straight on. Turn left into East Street and turn left at the corner. It's on the left at the end of the road. Where are you? (**the petrol station**)

7. You are outside **the cinema** in Victoria Road. Turn left and then turn left again into East Street. Go straight on to the end of the road and turn left. It's the second building on the left. Where are you? (**the café**)

8. You are outside **the art gallery** in George Street. Turn right and go straight on. Turn left into East Street. Go to the end of the road and it's on the left on the corner. Where are you? (**the chemist's**)

9. You are outside **Tourist Information** in West Street. Turn left and go straight on. Turn left into Victoria Road. It's the third building on the left. Where are you? (**the music shop**)

New English File Teacher's Book Beginner
Photocopiable © Oxford University Press 2009

1 Personal details

What's your surname?

How do you spell it?

What's your address?

What do you do?

What's your email address?

What's your mobile number?

2 Think of someone in your family

What is his / her name?

What does he / she do?

Where does he / she live?

How old is he / she?

Is he / she married?

Does he / she have children?

3 Your typical day

What time do you get up?

What do you have for breakfast?

Where do you have lunch?

How do you go to work or class?

When do you have dinner?

What do you do after dinner?

What time do you go to bed?

4 What can you do?

say two things you can do in a park

say three things you can have in a coffee bar

say two things you can do with your mobile phone

say three things you can buy in a supermarket

say three things you can you do in your town on a
    Saturday night

5 Where you live

Do you live in a house or a flat?

Do you live near here?

What's your postcode?

How many bedrooms are there?

Is there a bus stop near you?

Are there any shops near you?

6 Past (*be*)

Where were you at this time yesterday?

Were you in bed last Sunday at 9.30 in the morning?

Were you alone last night?

Were you at home yesterday afternoon at 5.30?

Who were you with last Saturday night?

7 Simple past

What time did you get up this morning?

Did you go out last Friday night?

Where did you have dinner yesterday?

How did you come to class today?

What did you have for lunch yesterday?

Where did you go on holiday last summer?

8 What do you think of…?

_____ (an actor)

_____ (a singer or group)

_____ (an actress)

_____ (a TV personality)

_____ (a TV programme)

9 Future

What are you going to do after this class?

Are you going to go to bed early tonight?

What time are you going to get up tomorrow?

Where are you going to have lunch tomorrow?

What are you going to do next weekend?

Are you going to study English next year?

10 Time and dates

What time is it now?

What time does this class start?

What time do shops usually open in your country?

What's the date today?

When's your birthday?

When does this course finish?

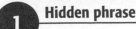

1 Hidden phrase

A vocabulary revision activity

SS work with a partner to solve clues which reveal a hidden phrase. This can be done as a team race. Copy one sheet per pair.

> **VOCABULARY**
> International words, numbers 1–20, countries, nationalities, classroom language, basic expressions

- Put SS in pairs and give them a sheet face down. Tell them they are going to complete a puzzle with vocabulary from File 1 as quickly as possible.

- Explain that if they get the clues across correct, they will form three words vertically in the shaded area.

- SS all start at the same time and the first pair to finish shouts 'stop'.

- If they are having difficulty, you could let them check with their books.

- Check answers, getting SS to spell the words to you and then writing them on the board.

> **1** twelve **2** board **3** Chinese **4** coat **5** Bye **6** Hurry
> **7** spell **8** name **9** breakfast **10** sorry **11** coffee
> **12** taxi **13** hotel **14** meet **15** Poland **16** Thank
> **17** fifteen **Hidden phrase:** Vocabulary File One

2 Word search

A vocabulary revision activity

SS work with a partner to find words from several categories in a grid. Copy one sheet per pair.

> **VOCABULARY**
> colours, family, adjectives, numbers, plural objects

- Put SS in pairs and give out the sheets. Focus on the categories (numbers, things, colours, etc.), and tell them they are going to look for five words in each of the categories.

- Focus on the example (FORTY) and show them where it is. Tell SS that words are either horizontal or vertical.

- Get SS to go through the grid, first horizontally and then vertically, circling or highlighting words, and then writing them in the categories. Set a time limit of 10–15 minutes.

- When the time is up, check answers category by category. Get SS to give you the grid reference to explain where the first letter of each word is, e.g. FORTY starts at 1/16.

	16	17	18	19	20	21	22	23	24	25	26	27	28	29	30
1	F	O	R	T	Y	T	P	H	O	T	O	S	M	R	P
2	D	J	F	B	Q	K	P	U	V	B	L	A	C	K	E
3	R	W	A	T	C	H	E	S	S	I	X	T	Y	E	L
4	T	D	S	W	X	Z	P	B	B	Q	M	O	T	Y	C
5	J	R	T	A	C	H	E	A	P	Z	I	R	L	S	H
6	N	Y	E	L	L	O	W	N	G	E	G	A	L	X	I
7	U	V	Y	O	Z	T	N	D	R	B	D	N	S	F	L
8	M	T	N	F	Q	Y	L	A	E	K	F	G	O	O	D
9	B	T	S	O	N	A	G	C	E	B	I	E	P	C	R
10	R	W	N	M	W	N	N	E	N	B	F	R	B	V	E
11	E	E	I	C	U	D	A	U	G	H	T	E	R	X	N
12	L	N	N	L	P	L	D	K	F	J	Y	Y	O	T	P
13	L	T	E	O	F	S	I	S	T	E	R	G	W	A	N
14	A	Y	T	N	O	R	X	Y	Q	A	I	O	N	L	H
15	S	N	Y	G	L	A	S	S	E	S	M	I	D	L	F

numbers	forty (1/16), sixty (3/24), twenty (9/17), ninety (10/18), fifty (8/26)
things	photos (1/22), watches (3/17), glasses (15/19), umbrellas (7/16), keys (2/29)
colours	black (2/25), yellow (6/17), green (6/24), orange (4/27), brown (10/28)
adjectives	cheap (5/20), good (8/27), fast (2/18), long (12/19), tall (12/29)
family	son (9/18), daughter (11/21), sister (13/21), husband (1/23), children (4/30)

3 Categories

A vocabulary revision race

SS work with a partner to group words into categories. Copy one sheet per pair.

> **VOCABULARY**
> jobs, places of work, food and drink, question words, common verbs, time, nationalities, countries, numbers 1–100

- Put SS in pairs and give out the sheets. Focus on the three columns, and highlight that the three example words (crossed out) all belong to the same group (days of the week).

- Now focus on word 1 in the first column (nurse). Elicit that it's a job, and ask SS to find another job in the second column (waiter), and then one in the third column (lawyer). Tell SS to write this group for number 1.

- Now tell SS to continue with word 2 in the first column (hospital), etc.

- Do this as a race so the first pair to finish shouts 'stop'.

- Check the words as a class. Finally, elicit what category each group of three words belongs to, e.g. days of the week, jobs, etc.

> **1** nurse, waiter, lawyer **2** hospital, factory, restaurant
> **3** meat, fish, vegetables **4** book, newspaper, magazine
> **5** water, beer, juice **6** breakfast, lunch, dinner **7** Where,
> What, How **8** listen, live, speak **9** half past one, twenty
> to two, quarter past four **10** English, Spanish, Russian
> **11** China, Turkey, France **12** thirty, seventy, ninety

4 Verb circles

A vocabulary revision activity

SS work with a partner to match nouns with the verbs they are used with. Copy one sheet per pair.

> **VOCABULARY**
> verb–noun collocations

- Put SS in pairs and give out the sheets. Explain that SS have to write the words or phrases at the top of the sheet into one of the circles according to the verb they are used with.

- Focus on the first word *work* and elicit that it goes in the circle with *go to*. SS then continue in pairs.

- Check answers. SS could then test each other with **A** (looking at the sheet) saying a word, e.g. *breakfast*, and **B** saying the verb phrase, e.g. *have breakfast*.

go	home, shopping, out
go to	work, university, bed
go to the	beach, cinema, gym
do	housework, exercise, sport
play	tennis, the guitar, computer games
have	a shower, breakfast, a coffee

5   What is *floppit*?

A vocabulary revision game

SS guess the meaning of an invented word *floppit* in various sentences. Copy one sheet per pair.

> **VOCABULARY**
> times and dates, common verbs, past forms, ordinal numbers

- Write *floppit* on the board and explain that it's not a real word, but an invented word which replaces a real word in this vocabulary game. Write the following sentences on the board, asking the SS each time to guess the word that *floppit* replaces:

  *She works in a restaurant. She's a **floppit**.* (waitress)

  *I wasn't at work yesterday. I was at **floppit**.* (home)

  *I **floppited** to the cinema last night.* (went)

- Put SS in pairs and give out the sheets. Set a time limit for SS to guess what *floppit* is in each sentence.

- Check answers, getting SS to spell the words to you and writing them on the board.

> **2** presents   **3** match   **4** date   **5** months   **6** arrive
> **7** pay   **8** stayed   **9** met   **10** change   **11** take   **12** eighth
> **13** made   **14** bought   **15** traffic   **16** find

6   Draw it

A vocabulary revision card game

SS take turns to draw an object for the group to guess. Copy and cut up one set of cards per group.

> **VOCABULARY**
> hotels, places

- Put SS in small groups of three or four, and give each group a set of cards face down or in an envelope.

- Demonstrate the activity by taking a card and drawing the word on the board. Tell SS to try to guess the word you are drawing. **Don't** say anything, but gesture if the SS are right or nearly right.

- Explain that they are going to do the same and **emphasize that the person doing the drawing mustn't speak.** The student who guesses the word keeps the card. The winner is the person with most cards.

- Set a time limit.

  Extra idea If you don't have time to cut up cards, put SS in pairs. Copy one sheet per pair and cut it down the middle. SS take turns to draw a word each from their sheet for their partner until he/she guesses the word.

7   Mime it

A miming game

SS take turns to mime words for their partner to guess. Copy one sheet per pair and cut into **A** and **B**.

> **VOCABULARY**
> activities, weather, directions, adjectives

- Mime a few words for SS to guess, e.g. *doing housework, studying,* etc. Don't speak, but let SS know by gesture if their guesses are almost right.

- Sit SS in pairs, **A** and **B**. Explain they have to mime the words and phrases in **Your words** to their partner. Their partner then writes them in **Student A's** or **B's words**, on the right. SS have the first letter to help them. **Remind them they mustn't speak when they are miming.**

- Monitor the activity. When SS have finished, check they have all spelled the words correctly.

> **Student A's words**
> **1** camping   **2** turn right   **3** cycling   **4** taking photos
> **5** running   **6** between   **7** reading   **8** hot
> **Student B's words**
> **a** cooking   **b** opposite   **c** straight on   **d** travelling
> **e** painting   **f** flying   **g** turn left   **h** cold

New English File Teacher's Book Beginner
Photocopiable © Oxford University Press 2009

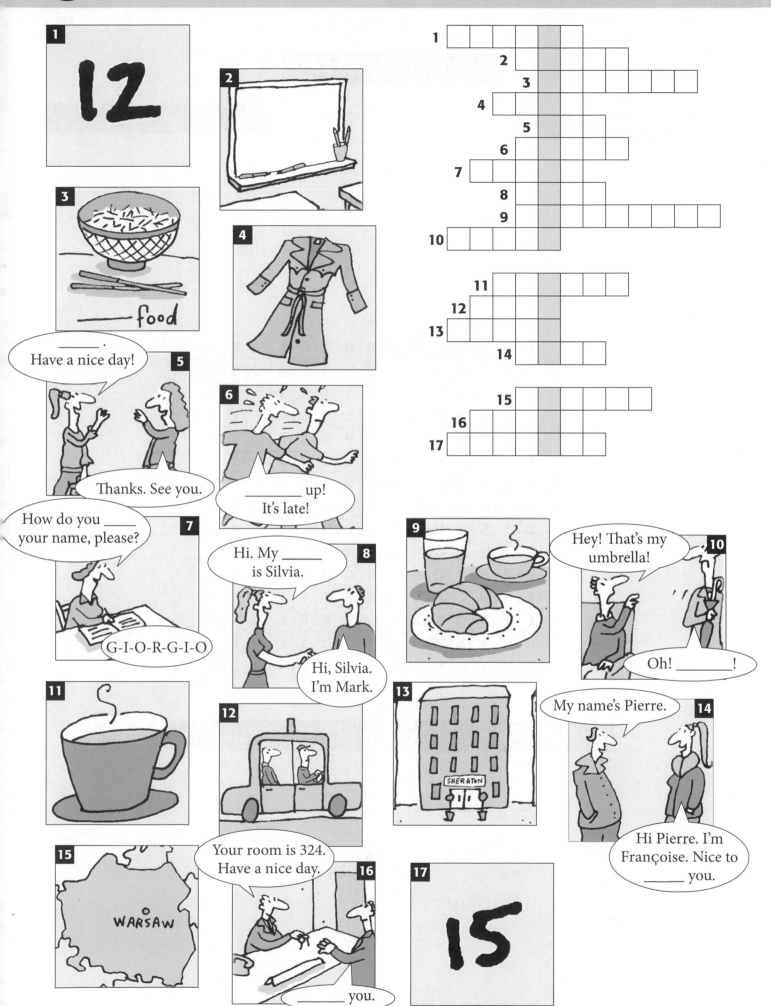

New English File Teacher's Book Beginner
Photocopiable © Oxford University Press 2009

numbers	
1	*forty*
2	
3	
4	
5	

things	
1	
2	
3	
4	
5	

colours	
1	
2	
3	
4	
5	

	16	17	18	19	20	21	22	23	24	25	26	27	28	29	30
1	F	O	R	T	Y	T	P	H	O	T	O	S	M	R	P
2	D	J	F	B	Q	K	P	U	V	B	L	A	C	K	E
3	R	W	A	T	C	H	E	S	S	I	X	T	Y	E	L
4	T	D	S	W	X	Z	P	B	B	Q	M	O	T	Y	C
5	J	R	T	A	C	H	E	A	P	Z	I	R	L	S	H
6	N	Y	E	L	L	O	W	N	G	E	G	A	L	X	I
7	U	V	Y	O	Z	T	N	D	R	B	D	N	S	F	L
8	M	T	N	F	Q	Y	L	A	E	K	F	G	O	O	D
9	B	T	S	O	N	A	G	C	E	B	I	E	P	C	R
10	R	W	N	M	W	N	N	E	N	B	F	R	B	V	E
11	E	E	I	C	U	D	A	U	G	H	T	E	R	X	N
12	L	N	N	L	P	L	D	K	F	J	Y	Y	O	T	P
13	L	T	E	O	F	S	I	S	T	E	R	G	W	A	N
14	A	Y	T	N	O	R	X	Y	Q	A	I	O	N	L	H
15	S	N	Y	G	L	A	S	S	E	S	M	I	D	L	F

adjectives	
1	
2	
3	
4	
5	

family	
1	
2	
3	
4	
5	

New English File Teacher's Book Beginner
Photocopiable © Oxford University Press 2009

	A	B	C
	~~Tuesday~~	What	speak
1	nurse	twenty to two	juice
2	hospital	Turkey	Russian
3	meat	live	magazine
4	book	seventy	restaurant
5	water	beer	quarter past four
6	breakfast	~~Friday~~	lawyer
7	Where	newspaper	vegetables
8	listen	Spanish	dinner
9	half past one	waiter	~~Wednesday~~
10	English	factory	ninety
11	China	fish	How
12	thirty	lunch	France

A	B	C
Tuesday	*Friday*	*Wednesday*

	A	B	C
1			
2			
3			
4			
5			
6			
7			
8			
9			
10			
11			
12			

Put the words in the circle with the verb they go with.

work

bed

cinema

gym

tennis

beach

shopping

sport

a shower

home

out

a coffee

housework

the guitar

university

breakfast

computer games

exercise

go
_____
_____
_____

go to
_____
_____
_____

go to the
_____
_____
_____

do
_____
_____
_____

play
_____
_____
_____

have
_____
_____
_____

New English File Teacher's Book Beginner
Photocopiable © Oxford University Press 2009

1 The day before today was *floppit*.   *y e s t e r d a y*

2 It was my birthday last week. I got a lot of *floppits*.   _ _ _ _ _ _ _ _

3 There was a very good football *floppit* on TV last night.   _ _ _ _ _

4 The *floppit* today is 7th June.   _ _ _ _

5 A year has twelve *floppit*s.   _ _ _ _ _ _

6 What time does your flight *floppit* in New York?   _ _ _ _ _ _

7 I'm sorry. You can't *floppit* by credit card in this shop.   _ _ _

8 Last summer we *floppited* in a small hotel in Paris.   _ _ _ _ _ _

9 Tom *floppited* his wife when they were Erasmus students in Norway.   _ _ _

10 I don't have any dollars. I want to *floppit* some euros.   _ _ _ _ _ _

11 We couldn't *floppit* photos because we didn't have a camera.   _ _ _ _

12 The *floppit* month of the year is August.   _ _ _ _ _ _

13 When Joanna was in Rome she *floppited* some wonderful friends.   _ _ _ _

14 He *floppited* a new computer in PC Centre last week.   _ _ _ _ _ _

15 I arrived late because the *floppit* was terrible.   _ _ _ _ _ _ _

16 I can't *floppit* my phone. Do you know where it is?   _ _ _ _

New English File Teacher's Book Beginner
Photocopiable © Oxford University Press 2009

a towel	a lift	a bedroom	a pillow
a lamp	a garden	a shower	the first floor
a remote control	a cupboard	a present	a seat
a petrol station	a chemist's	a car park	a river
next to	under	upstairs	a mirror
a boat	a laptop	the sea	a church

New English File Teacher's Book Beginner
Photocopiable © Oxford University Press 2009

A

a Mime (= explain without speaking) word **1** to Student **B**.

b Watch Student **B** mime word **a**. Try to guess the word and write it. Then continue to take turns.

Your words

1. camping
2. turn right
3. cycling
4. taking photos
5. running
6. between
7. reading
8. hot

Student B's words

a c _ _ _ _ _ _
b o _ _ _ _ _ _ _
c s _ _ _ _ _ _ _ _ _
d t _ _ _ _ _ _ _ _
e p _ _ _ _ _ _ _
f f _ _ _ _ _
g t _ _ _ l _ _ _
h c _ _ _

B

a Watch Student **A** mime word **1**. Try to guess the word and write it. Then continue to take turns.

b Mime (= explain without speaking) word **a** to Student **A**.

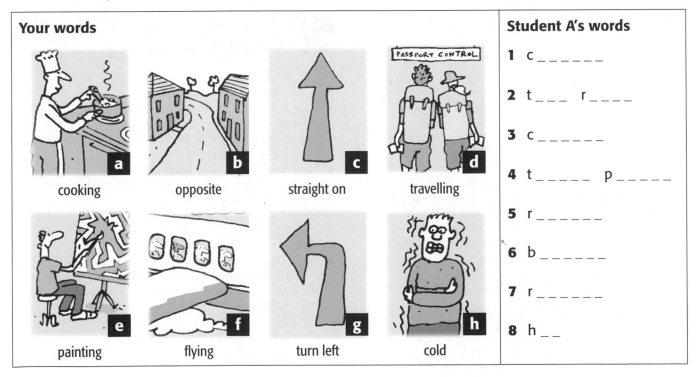

Your words

a. cooking
b. opposite
c. straight on
d. travelling
e. painting
f. flying
g. turn left
h. cold

Student A's words

1 c _ _ _ _ _ _
2 t _ _ _ r _ _ _ _
3 c _ _ _ _ _ _
4 t _ _ _ _ _ p _ _ _ _ _
5 r _ _ _ _ _ _
6 b _ _ _ _ _ _
7 r _ _ _ _ _ _
8 h _ _

D-I-S-C-O (1.50)   CD1 Track 51

PE   Listening for missing words

LANGUAGE
adjectives

- Give each student a sheet and focus on **a**. Tell SS to look at the four groups of adjectives.
- If you speak your SS' L1, you may want to translate the adjectives or SS can look them up in a dictionary.
- Focus on the lyrics, and the four groups of adjectives. Show SS that in each verse there is a missing word beginning with D, another with I, another with S, and another with C.
- Focus on **b** and on verse 1. Tell SS that they are going to listen to it, and they must write *1* next to the adjective that they hear for each letter. **They MUSTN'T write the words into the gaps yet.** Play verse 1. Allow SS to compare their answers, then play it again. Check answers then play it again as necessary.
- Repeat with the other verses and check answers.

D		S	
delightful	4	super sexy	2
delirious	1	sensational	4
desirable	2	superficial	1
disastrous	3	super special	3
I		**C**	
irresistible	2	crazy crazy	3
impossible	3	complicated	1
incredible	1	candy	4
incredible	4	cutie	2

- Focus on **c**. SS write the words in the gaps. Now play the whole song from beginning to end.
- If your SS like singing, play the song again for them to sing along, and finally focus on the **Song facts**.
- The complete lyrics of the song are on *p.29* of the Teacher's Book.

 You're beautiful (2.26)   CD1 Track 78

C   Listening for missing pronouns and possessive adjectives

LANGUAGE
personal pronouns and possessive adjectives

- Give each student a sheet and focus on **a**.
- Explain that these words are missing from the song. The words from the first circle go with the first verse, and the words from the second circle with the second verse.
- Play the first verse and get SS to put the words into the correct place. Play it again if necessary.
- Now play the chorus for SS to read and listen, and then verse 2 for SS to complete it. Check answers.

1 My	**2** My	**3** I	**4** She	**5** She	**6** I	**7** she	**8** my
9 we	**10** She	**11** my	**12** I	**13** I	**14** we		

- Focus on **b**. Go through the song line by line, helping SS to understand the meaning. Explain/translate the highlighted adjectives, or get SS to look them up in their dictionaries, and get SS to write them in their notebooks.

- Focus on the **Song facts** and go through them with SS.
- If your SS like singing, play the song again for them to sing along.
- The complete lyrics of the song are on *p.40* of the Teacher's Book.

 Friday I'm in love (3.38)   CD2 Track 37

PE   Matching rhyming words

LANGUAGE
rhyming words

- Give each student a sheet. Focus on **a** and go through the words in each circle, eliciting the pronunciation and meaning. Then get SS to match the rhyming pairs.
- Check answers.

head–bed   too–you   black–back   heart–start
wait–late

- Focus on **b**. Explain that they are going to listen and put the pairs of words into the song. Play the song once, pausing after each verse for SS to write in the missing words. Replay as necessary, and check answers.

1 too	**2** you	**3** heart	**4** start	**5** wait	**6** late
7 black	**8** back	**9** head	**10** bed		

- Focus on **c**. Go through the song, helping SS understand the meaning. Explain/translate the highlighted phrases, and get SS to write them in their notebooks.
- If your SS like singing, play the song again for them to sing along, and finally focus on the **Song facts**.
- The complete lyrics of the song are on *p.59* of the Teacher's Book.

 Money, money, money (4.29)   CD2 Track 67

PE   Predicting rhyming words

LANGUAGE
rhyming words

- Give each student a sheet and focus on **a**. Tell SS that the missing words all rhyme with the last word in the line before. Then play the first two lines for them to check, and elicit that the word is *pay*.
- Now play the first verse once. Then play it again, pausing after each missing word for SS to write. Do the same for the second verse and check answers.

1 pay	**2** me	**3** man	**4** ball	**5** mind	**6** me
7 Monaco	**8** same				

- Focus on **b**. Go through the song, helping SS understand the meaning, and referring to the **Glossary**. Explain/translate the highlighted words and phrases which are all to do with money, and get SS to write them in their notebooks.
- If your SS like singing, play the song again for them to sing along, and finally focus on the **Song facts**.
- The complete lyrics of the song are on *p.73* of the Teacher's Book.

5 B Perfect day 5.13 CD2 Track 81

Listening for extra words

LANGUAGE
mixed vocabulary

- Give each student a sheet and focus on **a**. Tell them that all the lines numbered 1–12 **have an extra word**, but the unnumbered lines are correct.
- Play the first verse once for SS to cross out the extra words. Replay as necessary.
- Repeat with the second verse, then check answers.

> **2** very **3** all **4** city **5** see **6** go **7** My **8** here
> **9** good **10** about **11** always **12** very

- Go through the song, helping SS to understand the meaning. Use the **Glossary**. Then focus on **b** and get SS to re-read the first verse and in pairs to write down the three places (the park, the zoo, the cinema). Write their answers on the board.
- If your SS like singing, play the song again for them to sing along, and finally focus on the **Song facts**.
- The complete lyrics of the song are on *p.82* of the Teacher's Book.

6 C I'm a believer 6.20 CD3 Track 37

Missing verbs

LANGUAGE
verbs in the past

- Give each student a sheet and focus on **a**. Elicit the past simple of *think* (thought) and tell them that this is the first missing word. Tell SS to continue in the same way, working in pairs to complete the song with past simple verbs.
- Focus on **b** and play the song once for SS to check answers.

> **1** thought **2** was **3** saw **4** thought **5** was **6** gave
> **7** got **8** wanted **9** got

- Focus on **c**. Go through the song, helping SS understand the meaning and using the **Glossary** to help. Explain/translate the highlighted words and phrases, and get SS to write them in their notebooks.
- If your SS like singing, play the song again for them to sing along, and finally focus on the **Song facts**.
- The complete lyrics of the song are on *p.102* of the Teacher's Book.

7 C Three little birds 7.14 CD3 Track 59

Matching halves of lines

LANGUAGE
mixed vocabulary

- Give each student a sheet and focus on **a**. Explain that the first halves of lines from the song are on the left, and the second halves on the right. Give SS a few moments to read sentence halves 1–9 and a–g.
- Focus on the example (1b). Highlight that SS will need to use two halves in a–g twice.
- Play the song for SS to match the lines. Pause and replay as necessary. Check answers.

> **1** b **2** e **3** b **4** e **5** d **6** g **7** f **8** a **9** c

- Go through the song, helping SS to understand the meaning and using the **Glossary** to help.
- Focus on **b**. Play the song again and ask them if they think it is happy or sad. Elicit that the singer pronounces *going to* (/ˈɡɒnə/), and that this is typical in songs and fast speech.
- If your SS like singing, play the song again for them to sing along, and finally focus on the **Song facts**.
- The complete lyrics of the song are on *p.115* of the Teacher's Book.

a Look at the song lyrics. Then look at the four missing words for each letter. Check the meaning in your dictionary, or ask your teacher.

D		I		S		C	
delightful	__	**i**rresistible	__	**s**uper sexy	__	**c**razy crazy	__
delirious	*1*	**i**mpossible	__	**s**ensational	__	**c**omplicated	__
desirable	__	**i**ncredible	__	**s**uperficial	__	**c**andy	__
disastrous	__	**i**ncredible	__	**s**uper special	__	**c**utie	__

b Now listen to Verse 1. Write 1 next to the missing words. Do the same for verses 2–4.

c Write the words in the song. Listen again and check.

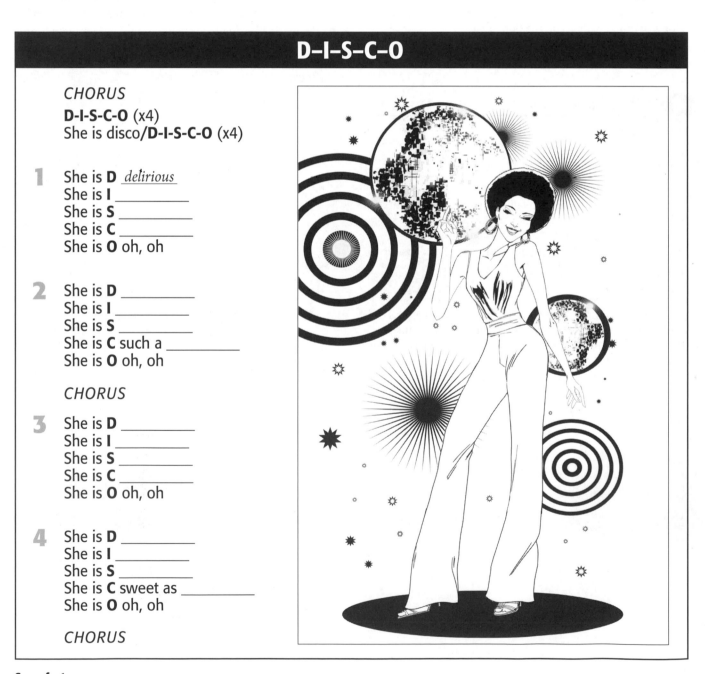

D–I–S–C–O

CHORUS
D-I-S-C-O (x4)
She is disco/**D-I-S-C-O** (x4)

1 She is **D** *delirious*
She is **I** _____
She is **S** _____
She is **C** _____
She is **O** oh, oh

2 She is **D** _____
She is **I** _____
She is **S** _____
She is **C** such a _____
She is **O** oh, oh

CHORUS

3 She is **D** _____
She is **I** _____
She is **S** _____
She is **C** _____
She is **O** oh, oh

4 She is **D** _____
She is **I** _____
She is **S** _____
She is **C** sweet as _____
She is **O** oh, oh

CHORUS

Song facts
D-I-S-C-O was an international hit for the French group Ottawan in 1981.

a Listen to the song and complete each verse with the words in the circle.

You're beautiful

1
¹____ life is brilliant (x2)
²____ love is pure
³____ saw an angel
Of that I'm sure
⁴____ smiled at me on the subway
⁵____ was with another man
But ⁶____ won't lose no sleep on that
'cause* I've got a plan

CHORUS
You're beautiful
You're beautiful
You're beautiful, it's true
I saw your face in a crowded place
But I don't know what to do
'cause I'll never be with you

2
Yes, ⁷____ caught ⁸____ eye
As ⁹____ walked on by
¹⁰____ could see from ¹¹____ face that ¹²____ was flying high
And ¹³____ don't think that I'll see her again
But ¹⁴____ shared a moment that will last till the end

CHORUS

La la la la la la la la la
You're beautiful
You're beautiful
You're beautiful, it's true
There was an angel with a smile on her face
When she thought that I should be with you
But it's time to face the truth
I will never be with you

* 'cause = because

Circle 1 words: My, I, She, My, I, She

Circle 2 words: She, we, my, my, I, she, we, I

b Go through the song with your teacher. Learn the highlighted adjectives.

Song facts

You're beautiful was an international hit for British singer James Blunt in 2005. The song is about his ex-girlfriend. He saw her with her new boyfriend on a London Underground station.

New English File Teacher's Book Beginner
Photocopiable © Oxford University Press 2009

a Match the words in groups A and B that have the same sound.

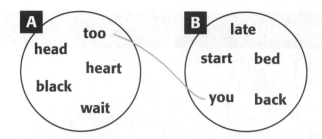

A
head too
heart
black
wait

B
late
start bed
you back

b Listen and complete the song with the pairs of rhyming words.

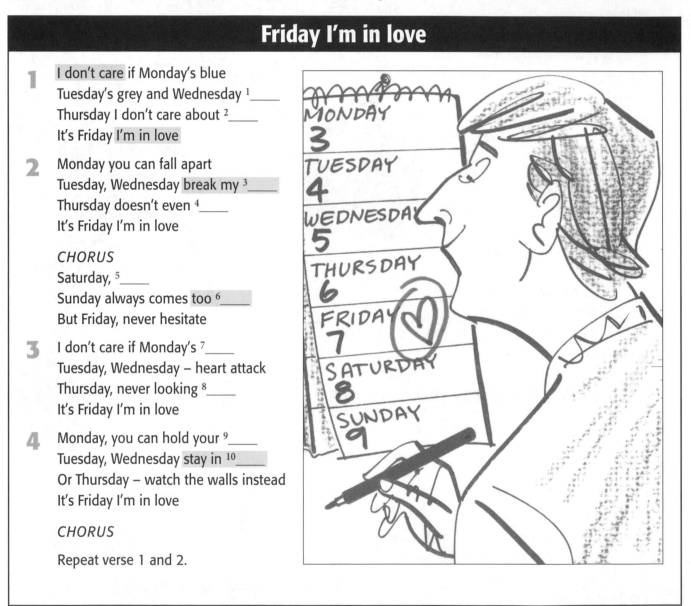

Friday I'm in love

1 I don't care if Monday's blue
Tuesday's grey and Wednesday [1]____
Thursday I don't care about [2]____
It's Friday I'm in love

2 Monday you can fall apart
Tuesday, Wednesday break my [3]____
Thursday doesn't even [4]____
It's Friday I'm in love

CHORUS
Saturday, [5]____
Sunday always comes too [6]____
But Friday, never hesitate

3 I don't care if Monday's [7]____
Tuesday, Wednesday – heart attack
Thursday, never looking [8]____
It's Friday I'm in love

4 Monday, you can hold your [9]____
Tuesday, Wednesday stay in [10]____
Or Thursday – watch the walls instead
It's Friday I'm in love

CHORUS

Repeat verse 1 and 2.

c Go through the song with your teacher. Learn the highlighted phrases.

Song facts

Friday I'm in love was an
international hit for the British
band The Cure in 1992.

a Listen and complete the missing words. They all rhyme with the word at the end of the previous line.

Money, money, money

I work all night, I work all day
To pay the bills I have to ¹ **p**_____
Ain't it sad?
And still there never seems to be
A single penny left for ² **m**_____
That's too bad
In my dreams I have a plan
If I got me a wealthy ³ **m**_____
I wouldn't have to work at all
I'd fool around and have a ⁴ **b**_____

CHORUS
Money, money, money
Must be funny
In the rich man's world
Money, money, money
Always sunny
In the rich man's world
Aha-ahaaa
All the things I could do
If I had a little money
It's a rich man's world (x2)

A man like that is hard to find
But I can't get him off my ⁵ **m**_____
Ain't it sad?
And if he happens to be free
I bet he wouldn't fancy ⁶ **m**_____
That's too bad
So I must leave, I'll have to go
To Las Vegas or ⁷ **M**_____
And win a fortune in a game
My life will never be the ⁸ **s**_____

CHORUS

Glossary
ain't it = Isn't it
wealthy = rich; with a lot of money
fool around = to do silly things
have a ball = to have a good time
I can't get him off my mind = I can't stop thinking
 about him
If he happens to be free = If he's not married
I bet = I'm sure

Song facts
Money, money, money was an international hit for the Swedish group
Abba in 1976. It is also in the popular film and show *Mamma Mia!*

b Go through the song with your teacher. Learn the highlighted words and phrases.

a Listen to the song. Cross out the extra words in the numbered lines.

Perfect day

Just a perfect day,
1 Drink ~~cold~~ sangria in the park
2 And then later when it gets very dark
3 We all go home
Just a perfect day
4 Feed animals in the city zoo
5 Then later see a movie too
6 And then go home
Oh it's such a perfect day
I'm glad I spent it with you
Oh such a perfect day
You just keep me hanging on
You just keep me hanging on

Just a perfect day
7 My problems all left alone
8 Weekenders here on our own
9 It's such good fun
Just a perfect day
10 You made me forget about myself
11 I always thought I was someone else
12 Someone very good
Oh it's such a perfect day
I'm glad that I spent it with you
Oh such a perfect day
You just keep me hanging on
You just keep me hanging on

Glossary
You just keep me hanging on = You help me stay alive
on our own = alone

Song facts
Perfect day was first recorded by Lou Reed in 1972. It was used in the
1996 film *Trainspotting*.

b Read the first verse of the song again. What three places did they
go to on their perfect day?

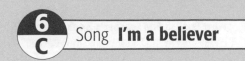

6 C Song **I'm a believer**

a Complete the song with the past forms of the verbs in brackets.

b Listen and check.

I'm a believer

I ^{1}_____ love was only true in fairy tales   **(think)**
Meant for someone else but not for me
Love ^{2}_____ out to get me   **(be)**
That's the way it seemed
Disappointment haunted all my dreams

CHORUS
Then I ^{3}_____ her face   **(see)**
Now I'm a believer
Not a trace
Of doubt in my mind
I'm in love
And I'm a believer
I couldn't leave her if I tried

I ^{4}_____ love ^{5}_____ more or less a givin' thing   **(think, be)**
Seems the more I ^{6}_____ , the less I ^{7}_____   **(give, get)**
What's the use in tryin'?
All you get is pain
When I ^{8}_____ sunshine I ^{9}_____ rain   **(want, get)**

CHORUS

What's the use in tryin'?, etc.

CHORUS

Glossary
fairy tales = traditional stories for children
meant for someone else = only for another person
out to get me = wanted to hurt me
Disappointment haunted all my dreams = I never got what I wanted
Not a trace of doubt in my mind = I'm 100% sure
a givin' thing = something you give (givin' = giving)
What's the use in tryin'? = Why try? (tryin' = trying)
All you get is pain = It hurts you

Song facts
I'm a believer was a hit for the American group the Monkees in 1966. The song was used in the 2001 film *Shrek*.

c Go through the song with your teacher. Learn the highlighted words and phrases.

New English File Teacher's Book Beginner
Photocopiable © Oxford University Press 2009

a Listen to the song and match the two parts of each line. Write a–g in the boxes. You need to use two of them twice.

Three little birds

1 Don't worry… [b]
2 'cause every little thing… [ ]

CHORUS

3 (Singing) Don't worry… [ ]
4 'cause every little thing… [ ]

5 Rise up… [ ]
6 Smiled with… [ ]
7 Three little birds… [ ]
8 Singing sweet songs… [ ]
9 Saying: This is… [ ]

a of melodies pure and true
b about a thing
c my message to you
d this morning
e is going to be all right
f pitch by my doorstep
g the rising sun

Glossary
melody = the music of a song
'cause = because
rise up = get up
pitch by = stop next to

Song facts
Three little birds is a song by the reggae group Bob Marley & the Wailers. It is one of Bob Marley's most popular songs.

b Listen again. Is the song happy or sad? How does the singer pronounce *going to* in the song?

187182